THE CONSTITUTIONAL FOUNDATIONS OF WORLD PEACE

SUNY Series in Global Conflict and Peace Education
Betty Reardon, editor

THE CONSTITUTIONAL FOUNDATIONS OF WORLD PEACE

Edited by

Richard A. Falk
Robert C. Johansen
Samuel S. Kim

STATE UNIVERSITY OF NEW YORK PRESS

Published by
State University of New York Press, Albany

Printed in the United States of America

For information, address State University of New York Press,
State University Plaza, Albany, N.Y., 12246

Production by Cathleen Collins
Marketing by Fran Keneston

Library of Congress Cataloging in Publication Data

The Constitutional foundations of world peace / edited by Richard A.
Falk, Robert C. Johansen, Samuel S. Kim.
p. cm. — (SUNY series, global conflict and peace education)
Includes bibliographical references and index.
ISBN 0-7914-1343-8. — ISBN 0-7914-1344-6 (pbk.)
1. International organization. 2. Constitutional law. I. Falk,
Richard A. II. Johansen, Robert C. III. Kim, Samuel S., 1935-
IV. Series.
JX1954.C486 1993
341.2—dc20 92-3839
CIP

10 9 8 7 6 5 4 3 2 1

for Saul H. Mendlovitz:
world order pioneer
warm and loyal friend
keeper of the Global Covenant

Contents

List of Contributors

Chadwick F. Alger, Mershon Center and Department of Political Science, The Ohio State University, Columbus, Ohio, United States

Mary Catherine Bateson, Clarence J. Robinson Professor of Anthropology and English, George Mason University, Fairfax, Virginia, United States

Elise Boulding, Professor Emerita Dartmouth College, Hanover, New Hampshire, United States

Richard A. Falk, Center of International Studies, Princeton University, Princeton, New Jersey, United States

Robert C. Johansen, Institute for International Peace Studies, University of Notre Dame, Notre Dame, Indiana, United States

Samuel S. Kim, Woodrow Wilson School of Public and International Affairs, Princeton University, Princeton, New Jersey, United States

Friedrich Kratochwil, Department of Political Science, University of Pennsylvania, Philadelphia, Pennsylvania, United States

Ali A. Mazrui, Institute of Global Cultural Studies, State University of New York at Binghamton, Binghamton, New York, United States

Patricia M. Mische, Global Education Associates, New York, New York, United States

James H. Mittelman, Department of Comparative and Regional Studies, School of International Services, The American University, Washington, D.C., United States

Toshiki Mogami, Division of Social Sciences, International Christian University, Tokyo, Japan

Radmila Nakarada, Institute for European Studies, Belgrade, Yugoslavia

Marc Nerfin, International Foundation for Development Alternatives, Nyon, Switzerland

Betty Reardon, Teachers College, Columbia University, New York, New York, United States

Lester Edwin J. Ruiz, Division of Social Sciences, International Christian University, Tokyo, Japan

D. L. Sheth, Centre for the Study of Developing Societies, New Delhi, India

R. B. J. Walker, Department of Political Science, University of Victoria, Victoria, British Columbia, Canada

Burns H. Weston, The Graduate Program in International and Comparative Law, University of Iowa, Iowa City, Iowa

Preface

During the latter half of the 20th century, the first half century of the global age, human society has outgrown most of its political institutions. The scope and severity of the problems of this age has brought the world political system to the point of crisis. There are few who would continue to defend the total inviolability of national sovereignty, and most recognize that international interdependence requires significant adjustment in the nation-state system. Yet there is little public discussion about the nature and consequences of those adjustments. Citizens have not been invited to participate in the discourse of global politics. Indeed, policy matters beyond national borders are handled in ways reminiscent of an age in which autocracy was accepted and legitimate. While leaders seek support of their "foreign" policies, the major decisions regarding a nation's positions and actions in the world at large are made at the highest executive levels with relatively little or no consultation with the citizenry, or its representatives. These decisions are often made in secret and sometimes involve deception of the electorate whose franchise does not extend to foreign policy and certainly not to "global governance." One purpose of this volume is to challenge and change this disenfranchisement.

The criteria and processes for global policy making that determine the present purposes and modes of world governance are at odds with the growing global consciousness, international citizen's movements and increasing demands for democracy in public affairs. In recent decades publics have used various means to articulate their concerns about world issues, and have had significant, if limited, influence. Now, however, the concern is with actual participation in policy making. Strikes and demonstrations no longer serve. It is time for serious consideration of how to restructure the international system toward both greater democracy and more effective and humane planetary management. The essays presented here comprise just such a serious consideration.

While neither the leadership nor general public have addressed the need for structural change, both need to educate themselves about the issues and the possibilities. Their need has not been unheeded. For more than a quarter of a century scholarly inquiry and policy research into global problems and alternative possibilities for their resolution have lead a number of researchers and activists to intensive, often unprecedented study of questions of global governance. Some of the most significant of these studies have been conducted by the World Order Models Project. Founded in 1967 by Saul Mendlovitz and the late Harry Hollins, both well known in the world order field. In 1990 the project was awarded the UNESCO Prize for Peace Education. Professor Mendlovitz's role in conceptualizing and guiding the inquiry is reflected in the essays in this collection, all authored by persons who have had some association with his work and that of the World Order Models Project. The collection has been edited by two project associates, Richard Falk and Samuel Kim so as to illustrate the methods and approaches which have informed world order research and made it a unique and productive field of peace research.

The considerations of global governance presented here comprise an anthology of issues, cautions and possibilities of interest to all concerned about the future of world politics. It is hoped that this volume will contribute to broad and serious discussion about the ways to achieve a humane and democratic system of global governance. It offers a global framework which enriches and illuminates the issues explored in other volumes of this series. It is in many ways the keystone volume, recommended as the basic work for all who seek to use the series as tools for reflecting on the learnings, social changes and policy reforms necessary to the achievement of a just world order.

Betty A. Reardon
Series Editor
July 1992

Acknowledgments

More than most, this undertaking has been the work of many. It started out as a celebration of the contributions to scholarship and promotional activity in the area of world order studies. We felt that Saul Mendlovitz had attained a stature and reached an age that made recognition of his achievements by friends and colleagues appropriate, if not overdue. It also provided a pretext for the likeminded to gather and reflect upon a common theme.

From the inception of our effort, it was the intention, in keeping with Saul's own serious engagement, to combine looking backward with going forward. We quickly hit upon the theme of "global constitutionalism" as a focus of inquiry for the academic participants, being both a topic at the core of Saul's own work, but also a world order perspective that has been relatively neglected in recent years. Despite the growing complexity of international relations, almost no sustained inquiry into the governance implications had been undertaken over the course of the last twenty-five years. It seemed to us as if the iron cage of realism had stymied the political imagination. This book represents a transnational joint venture into the seemingly forbidden terrain of governance on a global scale.

On the human side of this project, we were assisted and guided in the early stages by two of Saul's most intimate and persevering supporters, Harry Hollins, who has since died, and Ira Wallach. They helped us greatly with a one-day colloquium and dinner at the Harvard Club in New York City on May 24, 1989, which came as a surprise to Saul, and give us the chance to present him with a volume of the draft chapters that appear in revised form in this book. Saul's children and partner (Sybil Baldwin) were enthusiastic participants, and helpful with arrangements.

We would like to thank particularly the scholarly contributors to the volume, many of whose original essays were revised and reduced on length at the request of the publisher. Others, not represented in the volume, contributed in a variety of other ways, including the transmission of important messages.

In a more formal sense we wish to thank the Center of International Studies of Princeton University, especially its then director, Henry Bienen (now Dean of the Woodrow Wilson School of Public and International Affairs) for encouragement and support. Samuel Kim wishes, in addition, to express gratitude to the Peter B. Lewis Fund for continuing to support his research and writing. Robert Johansen thanks the John D. and Catherine T. MacArthur Foundation for support of research undergirding his contribution. We are especially thankful to June Garson, who works for Richard Falk, for her characteristically skillful, efficient, and gracious role in coordinating the whole undertaking, ranging from the Harvard Club dinner to assistance with the final preparation of the manuscript for publication.

From the outset, Lester Ruiz, director of the Transnational Academic Program of the World Order Models Project, has been our collaborator on this project, truly our leader in relation to editorial and publications arrangements.

Finally, we would thank Betty Reardon for taking the initiative to include this volume in the State University of New York Press series, *Global Conflict and Peace Education,* of which she is the General Editor. We felt that such a publishing arrangement was especially appropriate in light of Betty's long professional association with Saul and her own deep commitment to the thematic content of the volume.

Richard A. Falk
Robert C. Johansen
Samuel S. Kim

Part I

FRAMEWORK

1

Global Constitutionalism and World Order

RICHARD A. FALK, ROBERT C. JOHANSEN, AND SAMUEL S. KIM

LOOKING BACK

This collaborative volume seeks a retrospect/prospect appraisal of the changing relationship between global constitutionalism and an emerging world order in the post-Cold-War era. Throughout this collective inquiry it seems useful to recall Marx's famous observation about history-making, that we do not—and cannot—make our own history just as we please but only "under circumstances directly encountered, given, and transmitted from the past."[1]

We begin with reflections on Saul H. Mendlovitz, who, as the founder and director of the World Order Models Project (WOMP) over its entire life history of more than twenty-five years, has done much to shape the course of this world order journey out of the past. Indeed, without his inspiring and prodding leadership there would have been no WOMP in the first place nor would it have survived the turbulence of world politics and the diffuseness of our professional lives. The present volume was conceived and inspired by our desire to pay tribute to his seminal and lasting contributions in the development of world order studies as both a transnational academic enterprise and a critical social movement.

Contrary to many outside critics, the Models Project has never identified itself with the advocacy of world government or world federalism. At least until recently, most WOMP participants and writing have been skeptical, if not openly hostile, to the idea of global constitutionalism. It has concentrated instead on evolving a transnational framework of world order values, thinking, and action through the broadest possible participation of scholars and activists from the major cultures and ideologies of the world.[2]

And yet, more than anyone in his generation, Mendlovitz, through his intensity and perseverance, has kept alive the notion that a global constitutional order as an essential axiom is theoretically necessary and historically inevitable. His call has sometimes seemed a prophetic voice in the wilderness, constantly speaking out for a constitutional approach to world order, imploring us to think about the unattainable, and for some of us, the undesirable. "As I see it," he wrote in 1975 about the prospect of world government, "the questions we should be addressing to ourselves are: How it will come into being—by cataclysm, drift, more or less rational design—and whether it will be totalitarian, benignly elitist, or participatory (the probabilities being in that order)."[3]

Mendlovitz's particular vision of global constitutional government has been a mixture of historical, normative, and functional considerations, mutually complementary and reinforcing, but of descending relative significance. He has long been convinced that the drift of historical tendencies is toward an integrative order that overcomes the neo-Darwinian circumstances of the state system.

The Models Project, or at least Mendlovitz and his early Western collaborators, can be said to be rooted in the cosmopolitan tradition of world order thinking that goes back to the Stoics, emerging in the modern world by stages through Hugo Grotius, Immanuel Kant, and Woodrow Wilson. One discerning critic situates the WOMP approach in the Kantian tradition of optimism about human prospects, but altered to fit contemporary circumstances: (1) the greater sophistication of and emphasis upon macro-level research into alternative world order designs and methodologies; (2) the detailed explication of transition strategies; (3) the focus on the global interrelatedness of the present human problems—the global *problematique;* and (4) the broadening of world order values to be realized—not just the traditional value of peace but other values concerned with the economic, social, ecological, and political dimensions of a better world.[4]

Mendlovitz is not pollyannish about the human and political consequences of this prospect of a new global constitutional order. On the contrary, his best guess over the years has been that political elites of the present system are working away on their cold-hearted blueprints for centralized governance, while those who insist that justice become an indispensable element of such an integrated global governance are either off collecting moonbeams or tinkering with adjustments that add up to little more than nothing. The rest of those who ponder the future of world politics are mainly captive of some variant of "realism," which we consider both a concealed and distasteful utopia, unrealistically presupposing and unnecessarily affirming the durability of the system of states. Mendlovitz foresees political integration as the human future, but not in a form that is preprogrammed in its most critical properties. To shape such a common destiny beneficially depends on political engagement of a serious sort, especially the moral imperative to intervene militantly on behalf of the poor, the oppressed, the marginal. One characteristic of his version of global constitutionalism is an unwavering insistence that compassion is coequal and so closely linked with stability as to be integral with it.

A second aspect is normative, assessing world politics according to value, specifically those selected and relied upon by WOMP: peace, economic well-being, social justice and human rights, environmental quality, and participatory politics. The primary reason for scholarly involvement is to increase the possibility that the global drift toward integration will result in a more peaceful, sustainable, and just world. At the same time Mendlovitz has a practical side, believing that the desired shift in world order thinking can only occur if all sectors of international society perceive it to be beneficial in terms of their own security, while simultaneously enhancing common security. A variety of social forces throughout the world need to be mobilized if world order transition politics is to challenge effectively the less beneficent rival visions of an integrated world.

Mendlovitz's orientation is predominantly historical and normative, but it also remains sensitive to the functional realities of the present. By the latter is meant the usual litany of practical concerns: the global problems of complex interdependence, of the global commons, and of international social and economic life. Such concerns, taken on their own, are likely to produce over time an integrative type of world order, but in the form of a dystopia, that is, lacking a nucleus of world order values to serve as a normative lodestar. The dominant impulse of those pursuing system-maintaining world order is managerial, reactive, technocratic, and above all market-oriented. With only a nominal, ritualistic commitment to participatory democracy, they seek to handle from above, in the most efficient possible manner, the growing menace of political entropy and ecological decay. Their main motivation is to ensure species survival, while interfering as little as they can with overall economic growth and the dynamics of the market.

This interpretation of our situational reality has sustained Mendlovitz's normative commitment to a global constitutional approach to world order. If the emergent world order is to be integrative and benevolent, then it is essential to stimulate concerned scholars and social activists to form a broad, global united front, that develops plausible and, above all, preferable alternatives to the mindless implementation of a technocratic ethos. In this regard, Mendlovitz, early in his professional development, was attracted by the pioneering work of those who had earlier set forth various plausible scenarios of a new world order in traditional constitutional terms: the Chicago Committee to Frame a World Constitution[5] and, especially the Clark-Sohn collaboration, culminating in the three editions of *World Peace Through World Law.*[6] He continues to be drawn even now to sophisticated advocacy of constitutional thinking, provided it incorporates a democratizing perspective on the politics of persuasion, as well as to the operations of global governance itself.[7]

The tenacity with which these less-than-fashionable constitutional perspectives have been held by Mendlovitz over the years is itself impressive. Most of his WOMP colleagues have been reluctant to accept this view that the world will inevitably be integrated, nor have they found it either intellectually engaging or useful to work out the specifics of a constitutional arrangement on a global scale. On the contrary, many world orderists who have participated in the Models Project have been convinced that these institutional preoccupations misleadingly taint their intellectual and political credentials, stamping them as wooly-headed, starry-eyed utopians, or as globaloney savants whose intelligence is being siphoned off in the service of an ill-conceived project of legal engineering that, if it were ever to succeed, would produce one more "brave new world." The WOMP orientation, in contrast to Mendlovitz's particular world order emphasis, was in practice actually quite antithetical to the traditional idea of a global constitutional order sustained by a central government.[8] Some participants, especially from the Third World, even worried that WOMP was an unwitting partner of US imperial geopolitics, packaging its design for world governance in humanistic wrappers, thereby obscuring its true character—made in and on behalf of the United States.[9] In general, at odds with Mendlovitz's positive reconstructionist conceptions, most world orderists felt more drawn to critical and diagnostic perspectives (what's wrong) and, later on, to a bottom-up world order populism with a special focus on salient and attainable next steps associated with the primary impetus toward justice (e.g., anti-apartheid; Tibetan and Palestinian self-determination, human rights and democracy in Burma and South Korea).

In fact, the Mendlovitz orientation toward these matters has evolved and deepened over the last three decades of involvement in and dedication to world order thinking. In particular, he has incorporated and come to endorse strongly the democratizing and process-oriented emphases of the WOMP mainstream. He has encouraged diverse strands of thought from all parts of the world, provided only that they generally accept world order values as common ground and starting-point. In this regard, he has exhibited an extraordinary capacity to enlarge upon or even put aside his own preferred scheme for realizing world order values while doing a brilliant job of locating and soliciting the involvement of some of the most gifted and socially engaged scholars throughout the world.

Such scholars were not easy to find and, when found, were engaged in a wide range of pursuits that were often quite removed from any explicit dedication to world order values. Mendlovitz managed to convince them that it was worth joining WOMP and becoming passengers in the same particular planetary lifeboat where common concerns could be reconciled despite sharply varying orientations. Among the most prominent world order stalwarts, charmed and motivated by the leadership of Mendlovitz, were Yoshikazu Sakamoto, Rajni Kothari, Ali Mazrui, and Johan Galtung. Each, a strong individual with his own intellectual and normative agenda, but sharing, in varying styles, a position at the interface between liberalism and democratic socialism, and a temperament resistant to close institutional affiliation and ideological labels. They had developed vivid political identities through the force of their own arguments and by an immersion in political controversy and conflict within their own countries and regions. They never abandoned their distinctiveness, but were persuaded to add a world order dimension to their scholarly and political engagements. And it is out of the ferment generated by their interaction with one another that the development of world order thinking has evolved.

Once within the framework of world order thinking, strong tensions emerged over the character and purpose of the WOMP enterprise. For many recruits, world order thinking was valuable to the extent that it fostered a non-Marxist, non-liberal critique of imperialism, especially U.S. imperialism, as it functioned in the real world. But even in this role, some otherwise congenial scholars were offended, considering the world order framework as too idealistic in its tone and viewing U.S. funding and administration of the project as imposing an unavoidable Western and Northern slant on all the work undertaken. Mendlovitz, without abandoning his own quite different conception of world order (that is, as generating a collaborative, integrated, organizational alternative for world society to current arrangements based on state sovereignty), was able to persuade these divergent world order "radicals" to remain generally within the confines of the intellectual undertaking.

Of course, in this growth, the undertaking never possessed a single vision or focus. It was sometimes perceived in the West as a type of neo-Wilsonian revival of idealistic thinking that was marginalized during the Cold War by the ascendancy of several strains of "realist" and "neo-realist" international relations theory. These strains conceived of international society as a kind of anarchy and regarded "balance of power" and/or "regime" approaches to world order as the only valuable and viable ones. WOMP work has also been criticized by more conservative free-market advocates as a disguised variant of socialism notable for its hostility to the activities of a new breed of global nonstate actors (multinational corporations and international banks), and allegedly jeopardized its proclaimed long-range goals by taking divisive positions on controversial issues of the day. Sometimes this criticism was directed at what was alleged to be its Third World orientation, a perception associated with claims that WOMP launched unfair and strident attacks upon Western reliance on technology, with its related theory of "progress."

Those of us associated with Saul Mendlovitz—and they include every participant in the present volume—and with the unfolding character of world order thinking, were ourselves caught up with these tensions and diversities. The process has been, overall, a creative one, allowing mutual learning and over time enabling a more coherent understanding of world order thinking to emerge. Mendlovitz has presided over this process, generating through his efforts most of the resources needed for the work to go forward and arranging for its results to be disseminated by a stream of publications.[10]

LOOKING FORWARD

The development of the Models Project under the leadership of Saul Mendlovitz and the rapidly changing global situation make it timely to reconsider the relevance of global constitutionalism to the basic world order project of enhancing the prospects for a better world. Just as the world order thinking of the 1950s and 1960s committed the fallacy of premature optimism in relation to global constitutionalism, the world order thinking of the 1970s and 1980s can also be said to have committed the opposite fallacy of premature pessimism about the normative potential of a global constitutional order. At no time since the end of World War II has the notion of a new global constitutional order seemed more urgent, promising, and open-ended than in the aftermath of the Cold War, undoubtedly a period of fluidity and transition when it comes to world order arrangements. The generally triumphant record of popular calls for democratization within and across state boundaries in the past several years—in South Korea, the Philippines, China (suppressed), Taiwan, Thailand, Eastern Europe, the Soviet Union, Nepal, Burma (suppressed), Haiti (deposed), Mongolia, Chile, Zambia, South Africa and elsewhere—is indeed one of the most positive and encouraging social forces of our time, creating the foundations at a societal level of democratic global constitutionalism. At the very least, this new global setting is the point of departure for our collective inquiry into the relevance of global constitutionalism to the wider undertaking of achieving a just and peaceful world.

By "global constitutionalism" we mean something broader and wider than the nineteenth-century tendency to advocate a war/peace system as a political blueprint, and something less legalistic than a positivist or Austinian (only rules backed by effective sanctions qualify as "law") extension of effective law enforcement to a global scale. Global constitutionalism is here defined broadly and synergistically as a set of transnational norms, rules, procedures, and institutions designed to guide a transformative politics dedicated to the realization of world order values both within and between three systems of intersecting politics in an interdependent world. The first system, the states system, is comprised of territorial state actors and their supporting, and increasingly transnationalized, infrastructure of corporations, banks, military, and media. The second system consists of international governmental institutions, including the UN system. The third system is represented by nonstate groups and individuals acting through nongovernmental organizations (NGOs), citizen associations of various sorts, and critical social movements. Global constitutionalism is also envisioned as a process dedicated to deepening and widening democracy both within and across state boundaries, as well as insinuating democratic practices into all levels of political activity, including that associated with international institutions. The successful realization of democratic global constitutionalism, in contradistinction to traditional world federalism, does not necessarily entail any further centralization of world authority, and may indeed work in the opposite direction by affirming tendencies toward the emergence of a global civil society from below.

BRIDGING THE PATHWAYS TO A NEW WORLD ORDER

Of course, George Bush, during the crisis that preceded the Gulf War in early 1991, briefly inserted the imagery of a "new world order" into the political dialogue of this period. It seems evident that Bush meant by the phrase to imply merely a more cooperative approach to global geopolitics in the aftermath of the Cold War, not any more comprehensive restructuring of international relations in a system-transforming approach to a truly new world order. Leaving aside the question as to whether this use of "new world order" was mainly a tactical device to rally support for an anti-Iraq coalition under UN auspices, our sense of the phrase is quite different, directed primarily to the possibilities of comprehensive restructuring in accord with preferred world order values that are incorporated, by now, in the evolving international law of human and environmental rights, as well as espoused by the Models Project. This latter sense informs our encouragement of perspectives based on global constitutionalism.

Although WOMP participants have not been oblivious to the normative potential of global constitutionalism, they have rarely addressed it explicitly. In spite of diverse disciplinary backgrounds and varying methodological and conceptual inclinations, the contributors to this volume are persuaded that global constitutionalism is an idea whose time has come. It is also an idea that is starting to capture the breadth of the historical, cultural, and normative perspective now required to respond effectively and humanely to the challenge of system transition from the Cold War to a post-Cold-War era. Beyond that, global constitutionalism is proposed as a concept that links the possibilities of a transformative politics embedded within and across the three intersecting systems of political action.

Without being too rigidly bound by the requirements of any particular perspective and methodology, the authors of this volume address the following questions: What is the meaning of global constitutionalism in a world mired in countervailing trends of global integration and ethnonationalist fragmentation? Given this contest between centralizing and decentralizing pressures, what kinds of alternative global structures of power and authority are desirable and feasible? What is the relationship between state sovereignty and global constitutionalism under conditions of profound global, regional, transnational, and substate transformations? To what extent and in what specific ways can the antinomy between "being" and "becoming"[11]—between having and enjoying—be resolved in a new global constitutional order? As the history of civil rights in the United States has shown, it is one thing to have civil rights in the Constitution and quite another actually to enjoy them in everyday social and political life; constitutionalism at the societal level includes practices as well as texts. What role, then, can global constitutionalism play in the shaping and sharing of a more peaceful, just, and sustainable world?

What are the prospects of global constitutional processes for generating the texts and practices to realize desirable forms of global polity and governance?

In the essays that comprise this volume, contributors address these and related questions from various disciplinary perspectives, as well as from the vantage points of persisting governance by the states system, by augmenting international modes of governance, and by the cumulative effects of initiatives from below associated with citizens associations and transnational social forces.

NOTES

1. Karl Marx, *The 18th Brumaire of Louis Napoleon,* in Lewis Feuer, ed., *Basic Writings on Politics and Philosophy: Karl Marx and Friedrich Engels* (New York: Doubleday, 1959), p. 320.

2. See Richard A. Falk and Samuel S. Kim, *An Approach to World Order Studies and the World System* (New York: Institute for World Order, 1982).

3. Saul H. Mendlovitz, "Introduction," in Saul H. Mendlovitz, ed., *On the Creation of a Just World Order* (New York: Free Press, 1975), p. xvi.

4. See Ian Clark, *Reform and Resistance in the International Order* (New York: Cambridge University Press, 1980), pp. 35–39. For another line of macrohistorical inquiry into world order reform and how WOMP fits into various categories of world order thinking, see Louis René Beres, *People, States, and World Order* (Itasca, IL: Peacock, 1981).

5. Saul H. Mendlovitz, ed., *Legal and Political Problems of World Order* (New York: Fund for Education Concerning World Peace Through World Law, 1962), pp. 62–73.

6. Grenville Clark and Louis Sohn, *World Peace Through World Law* (Cambridge, MA: Harvard University Press, 1958; 2nd rev. ed., 1960; 3rd enlarged ed., 1966).

7. The ideas of Georgi Shakhnazarov and Silviu Brucan on "world governability" and "world authority," respectively, are attractive to Mendlovitz, but only if read in a setting informed by the embrace of democratizing approaches to change at the global level. For examples of Shakhnazarov and Brucan's thought, see Richard A. Falk, Samuel S. Kim, and Saul H. Mendlovitz, eds., *The United Nations and a Just World Order* (Boulder, CO: Westview Press, 1991), pp. 166–177, 546–549.

8. See, Mendlovitz's introductions to all individual volumes of the *Preferred Worlds for the 1990s* series. For a fuller bibliography on the corpus of world order publications as of the early 1980s, see Falk and Kim. For more recent works, see Saul H. Mendlovitz and R. B. J. Walker, eds., *Towards a Just World Peace: Perspectives from Social Movements* (London: Butterworths, 1987) and R. B. J. Walker and Saul H. Mendlovitz, eds., *Contending Sovereignties: Redefining Political Community* (Boulder, CO: Lynne Rienner Publishers, 1990).

9. This line of criticism is especially present in the work of Rajni Kothari, e.g., in his *Towards a Just World* (New York: Institute for World Order, 1980).

10. See note 8.

11. On the philosophical and practical significance of the difference between "being" and "becoming," see Chandler Morse, "Being Versus Becoming Modern: An Essay on Institutional Change and Economic Development," in Chandler Morse, et al., *Modernization by Design* (Ithaca, NY: Cornell University Press, 1969), pp. 238–382.

2

The Pathways of Global Constitutionalism

RICHARD A. FALK

A PROJECT OF GLOBAL CIVIL SOCIETY

It is only recently that the idea of world order has received careful intellectual appraisal. No longer is "world order" an idealistic countervision to the power dynamics of realist thought, with its stress on the sovereignty of the state and the normality of war as a social institution. The Gulf War blurred the distinction between geopolitics and utopian convictions. We could never be quite sure, especially in the months of crisis leading up to the war itself, whether George Bush was promising a new structure of international relations based on respect for international law and on centrality for the United Nations, or whether his use of the phrase "a new world order" was little more than a bid for public support and an invitation that governments join the North in one further war in and against the South.[1] This latter view of "new world order" assumes that international relations after the Cold War resemble what they were during the Cold War, minus the Soviet Union and the associated rivalry between capitalist and socialist outlooks. By late 1991 it is evident that "the new world order" was meant in this more superficial sense of maneuvering of post-Cold War coalition building within an abiding framework of sovereign states organized territorially.

In contrast to that thinking and behavior, this chapter is concerned with new world order in a more ambitious claim to foster structural change based on such values as peace, societal well-being, democratization, and human and ecological solidarity. Here, "global constitutionalism" seems relevant as a perspective. This outlook is based on both will (or desire) and interest (or necessity): a more institutionalized (although not necessarily more centralized) form of governance that avoids war in conflict situations and works towards a world in which the well-being of all is safeguarded by enforceable rights, and the environment is protected on behalf of future generations as well as those now alive.

But such normative foundations offer little more than a clearing in the forest. The pathways to realizing such a vision are numerous, yet remain little explored. My purpose is to identify several of these paths, and to assess their relation to the future of the vision.

Part of what makes global constitutionalism politically relevant at this time is the emergence in rudimentary form of the first global civil society in human history—that is, globally constituted attitudes, social connections, information networks, transnational collaboration, and citizens' associations—an ensemble of diverse cumulative forces and tendencies that has many innovative potentialities. It is this cumulative profile that is the backdrop—a democratizing project that extends beyond the borders of states and derives its political identity from its primary association with the human predicament at this historical juncture. This perspective is guided by the conviction that global constitutionalism deserves serious study by those dedicated to change for the better in the world. "Global constitutionalism," as used here, is itself a manifestation of global civil society in a nascent form. These societal roots are important, making the undertaking plausible as a political project at this time, and providing a specific normative grounding, ensuring that whatever emerges as global governance embodies world order values, and does not merely represent a gigantic technocratic fix designed to handle complex forms of interdependence that seem quite ominous if left on their own.

THE SCOPE OF GLOBAL CONSTITUTIONALISM

The extension of constitutionalist thinking to world order concerns focuses on the problem of governance. One familiar solution is the establishment of a world government with centralized institutions equipped with coercive machinery to ensure that its authority is respected, especially by sovereign states.

Yet, it is a mistake to reduce the perspective of global constitutionalism to governmental alternatives to the state system. Governance implies a cluster of various values, norms, procedures, regimes, institutions, and practices that enable coherent forms of order to be common or general features of international life. This coherence entails considerable centralized capabilities with respect to the following governmental functions for the world as a whole: legislative organs to establish binding standards of behavior; administrative capacity to interpret these standards; financial powers, including revenue sources, and taxing power; rules and procedures determining membership and participation in international institutions and the status of international actors, as well as modes to render all actors accountable; verification of compliance with behavioral constraints and enforcement mechanisms; disaster, relief, and refugee services; regimes for protecting and managing the global commons; regulation of collective violence and supranational police; frameworks for world economic life, including trade, monetary and financial spheres, and protection against agreed-upon categories of disruption (debt, price shifts, boycotts, credit lines); and finally, a "global constitution," or, possibly, some invisible "document" that establishes an organic law for the community of states, nations, and peoples which frames and constitutes the political world.

The concern of global constitutionalism is further restricted by a commitment to forms of world order desirable according to world order values.[2] By contrast, there could evolve a variety of global constitutional arrangements, under an array of sponsorships, which would seek to sustain or establish structures of dominance and privilege—for instance, global imperial, corporate, and even populist conceptions aligned with social forces not reconcilable with world order values.[3] Our concern with global constitutionalism implies a conception of justice and order guided and inspired by an acceptance of world order values, which are themselves always in the process of gestation and evolution, expressive of democratizing concerns but also protective of limits on political options.

United Nations

The obvious reaction to such an enumeration of the dimensions of governance on a global scale is to assert that the United Nations Organization and its various organs and agencies under the United Nations Charter already provide the promise of a weak form of global constitutionalism. It is probably correct to believe that the United Nations could provide a satisfactory approach to global constitutionalism if it were strengthened and substantially reconstituted.[4] But the United Nations actually generates only a nominal constitutional order with respect to critical governance functions, and in many respects transmits and reinforces the distortions of international life. The capacity of the main UN organs is severely constrained by various commitments in the Charter to uphold the sovereignty of states, by the veto accorded permanent members of the Security Council, and, perhaps, most of all, by the failure to endow the UN institutions with resources and capabilities to control deviant behavior or to coordinate and mandate cooperative undertakings. The UN system as now functioning has been integrated into the hierarchical world order of unequal states. Its usefulness rises and falls according to its changing support by major states; during the long period of the Cold War, the Organization reflected the tensions between the superpowers and their blocs. The United Nations never has had the sort of role or created the kind of expectations that one could identify with even a minimalist global constitutional order.

It is conceivable that, given the new challenges in international life, some dramatic changes in leadership and outlook in major states, and the exertion of pressure by public action, the UN could be transformed sufficiently in the future to provide the essential central guidance machinery for the first global constitutional order in history. Perhaps such a prospect remains the most likely path toward the more satisfactory forms of global governance. After all, the basic institutional framework is there in place, a somewhat limp balloon that can take substantive shape if inflated by the energies and resources of its membership.[5] Yet, unless membership rules are drastically revised, the UN would, even in a revitalized form, serve only as a continuing vehicle for the adjustment of the state system to a changing context.

Another way of regarding the situation is to insist that global constitutionalism doesn't necessarily presuppose any degree of centralization. States, even while remaining the principal actors, have at their disposal a variety of instruments, from multilateral treaties to various institutional arrangements at regional and global levels, to constitute by more informal initiatives an innovative global governance system. These could even be based on an invisible constitutional structure arising from widespread acknowledgment and respect for the rules and processes of international law. Such a perspective, associated with the political language of "a practical internationalism" (or similar phrasing) is, at its base, an attempt to reconcile a state-centered realism with the perceived needs for a greater degree of governance on a global scale. It bases its hopes upon gradualism and an evolutionary path to a more coherent future based on the self-interest of states as represented by their leaders.[6] The relatively rapid process by which international arrangements to eliminate the use of ozone-depleting chemicals were established can be regarded as one line of positive development, and the Law of the Seas Treaty framework as another.

Again, in our analysis, this type of approach to global constitutionalism is not convincing in theory or application. The inward-looking, top-down character of territorial states, their reluctance to give up discretion over financial and behavioral policy, especially when it comes to external challenges, their unevenness of experience and perception, as well as the growing complexity and interdependence of many facets of international life, make statism a poor basis on which to build a global constitutional order. If we consider the quality of political life from the perspective of world order values, or on the basis of the sustainability of the life-support systems, the record of statism is exceedingly poor. Here it is less a matter of marginality of capabilities and more a question of normative priorities and dominant behavioral practices. States, especially leading states, are organized around ideas of modernism and industrialism, and often tend to seek security for their own society through the war system. The patterns of interaction among states continue to account for some of the most serious dangers and disabilities in the world, including ecological overload, militarism, and inequitable and destructive distributions of resources. It seems mistaken, if not utopian in the most negative sense—that is, generating disillusionment—to expect over a few decades the magnitude of adjustment in states' outlook and behavior needed to establish a satisfactory global constitutional order.

Practical Internationalism

Such an assessment is not, however, meant to rule out states and the states system as having an impressive and constructive but relatively untested latent potential for promoting world order values.[7] States can be induced by pressures from within and development from without to support more helpful arrangements for an improved global constitutional order, including a stronger, more autonomous United Nations and a variety of enhanced arrangement for better realizing world order values.[8]

Post-Catastrophe Adjustment

A traumatic variant of practical internationalism is the insistence that it will take a catastrophic jolt to shake loose the political and social forces needed to construct a satisfactory global constitutional order. As with the other approaches, there is a partial insight here. Only after major wars have there been serious, deliberate efforts to create "constitutional" mechanisms to forestall further breakdown of international order (the Concert of Europe after the Napoleonic Wars, the League of Nations after World War I, the United Nations after World War II). Science fiction writers have long examined more robust variations on this theme: a unifying threat to survival from a real or fictitious enemy planet or a reconstruction of political life after nuclear war, with an organizing theme of human community and based on beliefs that are quite consistent with world order values. What this dependence on catastrophe conveys, above all, is the fixity of an existing international order better understood as anarchic than as having latent capabilities for fostering global governance.

But the "optimistic" view that catastrophe will bring out the best in terms of political potential has been tested only in very limited settings, and seems, in the end, dubious. For one thing, significant catastrophes arouse concern, but little behavioral or structural change. In this regard, the marginality of constitutional postwar experiments seems pale by comparison to the robustness of anarchic resilience.[9] Similarly, the breakdown of international economic or environmental life in the future is far more likely to induce forms of eco-fascism than eco-solidarity.[10] The self-absorbed and selfish way states behaved in the Great Depression of the 1930s is far more likely to prefigure their responses to catastrophic challenge than is any surge of altruistic and empathetic behavior. Domestically oriented statist political reflexes are likely to continue controlling an era of perceived global catastrophe.

Geopolitical Solutions

Considerable attention has recently been devoted by international relations specialists to the hypothesis of hegemonic stability. The influential assessments by Charles Kindleberger about the breakdown of international economic order in the 1930s stimulated others more concerned with international relations. Kindleberger's main contention was that such order can be reliably sustained only when stabilized by a single dominant state.[11] Variations on this theme, most creatively worked out by Robert Gilpin and Robert Keohane, including extension to war/peace settings, emphasize the desirable effects of coordination among a few ascendent states or a bipolar standoff with reasonably stable lines of demarcation.[12] Such geopolitical conceptions of governance, conceived mainly as the management of economic power and the neutralization of military power, is blatantly indifferent to value consequences (except in the tautological sense of perpetuating the status quo by a statecraft of prudence) and is vulnerable to shifting configurations of relative capabilities based on technological cycles and rhythms of rise and decline.[13] Of course, certain geopolitical options are preferable to others, as measured by world order values, and those that reduce risks of a complete breakdown through nuclear war or ecological collapse may deserve interim support. At the same time, there is little reason to believe that geopolitical approaches to governance can offer much more than holding patterns during a period of transition, and their implicit normative premise is based upon a demeaning view of human nature.

Social Movements

Finally, some thinkers have recently been pointing to social movements as bearers of world order values, including the bases for satisfactory forms of global governance.[14] Three main ideas inform this conviction:

1. Such movements (e.g. peace, environment, women) are generally motivated by a normative agenda compatible with a fuller realization of world order values, and are especially, reactive against the war-prone, exploitive, ecologically damaging aspects of modernization as characteristic of the state system.
2. These movements have arisen in response to the maladaptive rigidities of large, established bureaucratic structures and in opposition to entrenched interests that depend for success upon sustaining the status quo. Furthermore, these movements adopt time and space horizons that correspond more closely with their visions of what is desirable and necessary, and as a result are led to espouse almost unwittingly some fairly radical form of globalism.
3. These movements are acting out of a species identity that tends to regard the well-being of the planet and all of its peoples as an endangered global commons and seeks to preserve the beauty and resilience of the biosphere, as well as to bring dignity and equity into social and political relations by acting in transnational settings with dedication to a better future through mobilizing democratizing energies.

These social movements arising out of civil society in various domestic circumstances have only emerged as important actors in the political landscape in the last two decades. Much of popular environmental consciousness is a consequence of the alarming information assembled, analyzed, and provided by nongovernmental organizations and social movements. It is sometimes reinforced by dramatic actions intended to gain attention and arouse concern. In turn, political parties have been initiated (and others, reoriented), for example, the "Green" parties in sixteen European countries, with Green parliamentarians in eight of them, with representation as well in the European Parliament. The forming of parties has been divisive in Green circles, and the entry into party politics has so far had mixed results. Similarly, objective information about human rights, generated by citizens associations and voluntary organizations operating transnationally, has increased awareness of abuses, induced greater attentiveness by international institutions, and helped make more—although by no means all—governments accountable, at least in relation to some minimum standards in international law.

But, as yet, there is no serious evidence to make us believe that these social movements can do enough directly (or indirectly) to achieve a satisfactory global constitutional order. Their activities are circumscribed by statist domination over administrative capabilities and by military traditions and expectations; but the epic exploits of Solidarity in the early 1980s demonstrated that a spontaneous reformist movement can mobilize wide and deep enough popular support to challenge the orientation and priorities of even an ultra-authoritarian state, and over time, at least under certain conditions, induce dramatic concessions. Similarly, the Western European peace movements helped establish an anti-nuclear political climate in the early 1980s that some years later influenced the agenda of even a conservative West German government.[15] Yet as encouraging as these instances are—and there are many others drawn from diverse issues—the overwhelming reality of international political life remains once of state-guided global policy based on destructive security and economic practices and a calculus of interests pursued by governments at the state level which cannot be generally reconciled with world order values.

Furthermore, social movements have tended to be issue-oriented, avoiding the promotion of overall solutions and reluctant to regard governance as a fit object of advocacy or even reflection. As will be suggested in a later section of this article, this attitude of activists seems to be changing, but it is unlikely that these movements will, on their own, endorse the development of a satisfactory global constitutional order, or have the political capabilities to achieve drastic global reforms. Such movements are invaluable as exploratory and catalytic agents, but establishing a more desirable world order is likely to depend on a different transition scenario. These social movements can be regarded as preparatory and contributory, but not likely to be potent enough to fashion transformation on their own.

LOOKING AHEAD

Global constitutionalism has been evolving over the course of the century, but not consistently, nor in a manner that makes comparisons through time very meaningful. There were, of course, the two postwar constitutional impulses that led to the formation of the League of Nations and the United Nations. After World War I, those especially persuaded by Woodrow Wilson's vision of an alternative to the balance of power, conceived of the League as the genuine basis of a new system of world order premised upon collective procedures. Even aside from the refusal of the United States to participate, adhering instead to its traditional posture of interwar isolationism in relation to Europe, the League framework failed even on paper to significantly encroach upon the war-making prerogatives of sovereignty. It was naive to suppose that the League, as constituted, could have provided an alternative to the typical pattern of state-centered behavior. The League did not even claim autonomous capabilities for its organs. At most, it could and did facilitate discussion of an international crisis and could conceivably launch a war-avoiding or collective security initiative by some or all states. The League functioned in practice neither better nor worse than should have been expected. As soon as world peace was challenged by the expansionist policies of Germany, Japan, and Italy the inadequacies of the League became evident; the absence of the United States was, at most, an aggravating factor.

With the onset of World War II, this first gesture in the direction of global constitutionalism was interpreted in various ways around the world, especially by influential United States policymakers. There was a consensus that in the future the United States must stay involved in world political life even after the warfare ceased, and that the League must be reestablished in a more ambitious form. The second attempt to build a global constitutional presence was distinguished from the first by being renamed and relocated. The decision to make New York City the headquarters of the United Nations acknowledged both a shift in the locus of power away from Europe and the importance of obtaining U.S. participation from the outset. Yet the UN Charter, and the early practice of the Organization, made it clear that the international framework established in 1945 was basically an instrument designed for discussion and cooperation, dependent for action upon consensus, especially among the states victorious in World War II.

There was, of course, one further ingredient: the atomic bomb. This apocalyptic element in international life heightened, at first, the receptivity to more substantive moves of a global constitutional character. But this mood was short-lived, and in any event, never as strong as some have assumed by reciting the immediate rhetorical post-Hiroshima calls by powerful leaders for world government. There was definitely an American-led effort to internationalize control over all facets of atomic energy which took shape in the Baruch-Lilienthal proposals (and some Soviet counter-proposals).[16] Opinions continue to vary as to the sincerity and sustainability of these proposals. With the rapid deterioration of U.S.–Soviet relations, other factors came to dominate the political imagination of leading states and their representatives: the importance of military strength and firm alliance commitments, and the overriding need to learn the lesson of the 1930s, and avoid, at all costs, a repetition of appeasement.

The United Nations in its early years reflected this shift in the international situation from anti-fascist alliance to cold war. The Organization became an arena of ideological tension, with the unequal distribution of influence working in favor of the policies of the United States, at least at the level of propaganda. As well, the atomic bomb became an integral feature of U.S. security policy, treated by successive presidents as indispensable both for the containment of superior Soviet conventional forces and as the only affordable means by which the United States could project its power globally. Such a nuclearist dependency has been challenged by some prominent ex-officials (e.g., Robert McNamara, George Kennan, McGeorge Bundy), but there has never occurred a serious U.S. attempt to denuclearize world politics, and it is unlikely to happen even after the Cold War. The United Nations was not allowed to evolve beyond this role of coordinating and facilitating the activities of states, and providing a potential instrument for superpower diplomacy. UN prestige and importance have risen and fallen depending mainly on the conjuncture of leading state interests, although the temperament and abilities of the Secretary General can enhance or confine the UN role. The Gulf War of 1991 illustrates this conception of the UN stretched beyond its constitutional limits, as the Security Council by means of Resolution 678 mandated, in effect, unrestricted war against Iraq under the exclusive operational control of the U.S. government and its coalition partners.[17]

As we enter the last decade of the twentieth century, the reality of global constitutional practice remains a marginal factor in world politics:

- States retain full control over their military capabilities and by help from allies.
- States are generally not obliged to submit disputes with other states to a third-party procedure of peaceful settlement, and even if obliged to, the prospects of compliance are not high in the area of war and peace.[18]
- International treaties remain the principal instrument of cooperation on behalf of the global common good, containing generally weak procedures for dispute settlement, and even weaker provisions for implementation.
- International institutions command only a very small proportion of public resources, and lack any standing police or military forces; what they do possess can be deployed effectively only if major states agree.
- The peoples of the world remain overwhelmingly dependent on their domestic governments for protection against all forms of political violence and against abuses of human rights, for obtaining basic human needs, and for achieving some protection against health hazards and environmental decay.
- Nationalism continues to be the most potent mobilizing force in the world, whereas globalism has yet to generate either mass or elite enthusiasm.[19]

But despite the resilience and persistence of statism, there has emerged in the last several years a new conjuncture of forces and perceptions that creates an unprecedented opportunity for the growth of global constitutionalism in the years ahead. These developments combine practical and normative factors relating to the abatement of strategic conflict in the North amid a rising tide of global challenge and globalist opportunity. The flexible imagery of constitutionalism (and governance) provides one important political language of response by which to comprehend this generally new encouraging, and quite possibly short-lived, international situation, some dimensions of which can be set forth.

Geopolitical Setting

The Cold War seems over, although its residues persist in high defense budgets, large peacetime military and intelligence establishments, and mind-sets about enemies. Gone is the tense rivalry between superpowers adhering to antagonistic ideologies as well as the disposition to treat virtually all political conflict as dominated by bloc concerns, East and West, thereby disregarding local issues and acting as if only the strategic impact upon bloc strength was relevant in any conflict. Such an approach was especially detrimental when applied to Third World settings. After 1990, the Soviet Union relinquished its superpower status and then its very existence, moderate relations emerged in relations among industrial states, and the European alliances with the United States disappeared as political factors. This new atmosphere creates a greater opportunity for cooperative undertakings and makes constructive arrangements protective of the global public interest possible. The internal crises of the ex-Soviet Union has generated a new set of concerns about stability in the North that represents a total reversal of Cold-War preoccupations. Now the concern is that the successor states to the Soviet Union could cause wider international problems and that the West should avoid this result, if possible, by extending large amounts of capital to the governments of these states.

There is another more structural element present. Both superpowers have been overextended, but not in the same ways. Even before its disappearance, the Soviet Union had withdrawn from its overseas commitments because its leadership acknowledged the urgent need for drastic domestic reforms at home. The federal executive branch in the United States has been unwilling to acknowledge domestic priorities, and has not yet responded in effective ways to the challenges the country faces in the world market, not only from Japan, but from Europe and from the more dynamic economies in the Third World, especially the four East Asian tigers, possibly abetted in the next few years by a fifth, Thailand.

Without the organizing simplicity of the bipolar confrontation characteristic of the Cold War years, other threats and dangers became more apparent, as did other ways to obtain security than "deterrence," with its implicit balance of terror, expensive and unpredictable arms race, and its overall failure to appreciate nonmilitary aspects of security. If the 1990s sustain the momentum of the late 1980s, political and imaginative space will exist to consider and explore a range of conceptions of world order, including several that advocate the buildup of global constitutional forms.[20]

Global Commons

The evidence is growing that the scale and character of human activity is causing serious deterioration in the global commons that will eventuate in multiple catastrophes of planetary scope unless concerted action is taken to restore eco-stability: ozone depletion, the greenhouse effect, destruction of tropical forests, toxic waste disposal, ultra-hazardous technologies, air and ocean pollution. This is, at best, a formidable agenda. It is aggravated by the rapid increase in world population, especially in the South, by the desperate quest on the part of the very poor to satisfy basic human needs, and by the great difficulty of allocating relative shares of responsibility in a world of sovereign territorial states of vastly different capabilities and contributions in the aggregate situation. Even if we could agree on what needs to be done, it will be difficult to agree on who pays what, on restraints on preferred modes of behavior (e.g., reproductive freedom, reliance on automobiles for private transport) as well as on confidence-building measures to promote compliance.

Yet there are some hopeful developments. The seriousness of the problems is being acknowledged by the mainstream. We should not underestimate the significance for heightening awareness of *Time* magazine's decision to designate "a Planet in Jeopardy" as their "Man of the Year" in 1988, as well as their periodic follow up coverage, and of the emphasis elsewhere in the mainstream media. More important even than the prominence of *Time's* designation itself was the accompanying text, with its strong mobilizing message: Unless unprecedented levels of peacetime cooperation among states occur in the very near future, there is virtually no prospect of avoiding ecological collapse.[21]

What will become evident very soon is that heeding these calls in a serious, effective manner will require abridgment of traditional territorial sovereignty. Protecting the global commons, under existing conditions of planetary crowding and at current levels of industrialization, will depend on common standards of conduct institutionally enforced. Voluntary restraints are certainly not sufficient, nor are arrangements that depend upon each government's providing its own interpretation of rights and duties and its own model of enforcement.

The many tensions between the geographic scope of environmental harm and the political organization of the world based on territorially distinct states suggests a radical split in scenarios for the future: either a persistent statism inducing ecological decay and terrifying vulnerability for human societies and ecosystems, leading to ecological collapses; or the impressive expansion of supranational institutional means to protect the global commons. What makes this period less discouraging, is that the mandate for the latter type of adjustment is gaining a hearing, beginning to reshape political dialogue and societal expectations, and already creating green market opportunities for big business. Already in Western Europe it is impossible to be a successful mainstream politician without being a credible environmentalist! This shift has come about rapidly and with some dramatic, even comic, repercussions. Who could have imagined even a few years ago Margaret Thatcher, herself a paragon of statist attitudes, initiating as she did as Prime Minister, in 1989, an international conference that called for the complete phaseout of ozone-depleting chlorofluorocarbons?

A final observation on this dimension: As the inadequacies of statism become more evident, governments seek to respond within the existing international framework, exhibiting the resilience of the state system. The states system can be partially superseded through this resilience, that is, by governmental solutions that generate international standards for states' behaviors and the institutional means for their enforcement. The Law of the Sea Treaty, despite its nonratification by several key countries, represents an instance of a successfully negotiated set of complex international agreements, which if fully activated and made operational, would greatly increase the global constitutional presence in the world. One could imagine such a process of global constitutional expansion taking place across the entire range of environmental concerns, with the cumulative effect being so impressive that observers would begin to suggest that a new post-state system of world order had been brought into existence through the political initiative of statist leaders.[22]

Integrative Trends and Tendencies

There are a series of long-term trends and tendencies that bring the peoples of the world and their governments under the sway of both shared experience and a sense of their interdependence on many counts. The number of transactions across frontiers of all sorts are increasingly making international contact and dependence a more general feature of life at all levels of social organization.

Cities, for instance, have grown more aware of their own relationship to the world beyond the sovereign state, and the idea of "municipal foreign policy" has increasingly engaged local officials concerned about whether the central government pursues interests that promote the economic well-being and political values of their particular local community. One symbolic expression of world order concern in several parts of the world has been the proclamation of themselves as "nuclear-free zones" by municipal governments. Another has been the twinning of "sister cities" between countries that are antagonistic, even at war, at the state-to-state level. These connections are strengthened through group visits that include political discussion by delegations drawn from societal sectors (workers, teachers).

Another expression is the sense of shared access to world events by way of TV beamed by satellite, a reality made vivid by the dependence around the world on CNN for news coverage of the Gulf War. The World Cup soccer championship is now watched simultaneously around the world by more than one billion people. A shared planetary experience is generated, as well as the appreciation of both human sameness and cultural difference. Such dissemination of information and events is reinforced by the spread of common cultural forms—rock music and jazz, informal dress style, and the proliferating imagery of planetary oneness, now characteristic even in corporate logos. Such globalization is not necessarily beneficial, and depends for its effects on the values and beliefs embodied in popular culture.[23]

The development of many electronic means to process, store, and deploy information has eroded the significance of territorial boundaries, as well as generated incentives and capabilities to expand the scope of operations to the entire planet. All governments seek to exert control over the flow of information. Even democratic societies rely on secrecy to withhold information from their own citizenry. At the same time, access to sensitive information is now possible from so many angles that it is becoming more difficult for even authoritarian governments to restrict access to information.

Across a range of activities, governments are losing their capacity to uphold on their own traditional expectations of citizens—for example, insulation of the economy or defense against external attack. More significantly, perhaps, even health is difficult to deal with territorially, given the internationalization of several dimensions of environmental decay.[24] In effect, the state has grown stronger administratively and militarily, while its ability to manage territorial boundaries effectively has been declining. This process is altering our understanding of the character and benefits of sovereignty.

The overall consequence of integrative tendencies is to challenge the centrality of the state in international political life.[25] This challenge is accentuated by the three-sided neutralization of military power as a shaping force: the impossibility of defense in the nuclear age; the fear of escalation above the nuclear threshold; the great difficulty of projecting military power overseas through interventionist tactics. As a consequence, states and public opinion, for functional reasons of effectiveness and for psychological reasons of legitimacy, are more inclined to regard global institutional solutions as necessary, and even desirable.

The United Nations Reassessed

Closely related to the emerging developments discussed so far is an ongoing positive reassessment of the United Nations as providing the format and mechanisms most appropriate in many circumstances for complementing efforts by states to handle international challenges in each of the domains associated with world order values. In effect, a second surge of hope and expectations about the UN role in world affairs has been unfolding since 1987, although sidetracked and possibly halted, at least temporarily, by the appropriation of the UN symbolism on behalf of the coalition fighting the Gulf War against Iraq.

The earliest surge of hopes and expectations relating to the UN was a casualty initially of the Cold War, and then of the global activism of Third World countries from the mid-1960s to the mid-1970s. A process of disenchantment on all sides had become prevalent by 1980, with a view that the Organization had become an irritant, and was useful, if at all, as an ornamental presence. The early Reagan years were notable for withholding financial payments as part of the UN-thrashing by the U.S. government, the country within whose territory the Organization was located and which had always contributed the largest annual share of its budget.

But, helped by a competent Secretary General, the United Nations by 1988 again seemed like a proper focus for global reformers, at least until the Gulf War. With the waning of the Cold War, the UN became increasingly useful for the resolution of regional conflicts, as well as for fashioning action on the global agenda. With the geopolitical milieu so favorable, and the Soviet government reversing its posture from one of cynical reluctance to participate to that of enthusiastic booster, an array of opportunities was presented for institutional growth within the UN framework. In the 1990s, if this basic attitude can be revived, and if the momentum of concern with global challenges mounts, it is quite likely that the UN will be given roles and capabilities in a whole series of settings: peacekeeping, dispute settlement, administration of the global commons, more general environmental protection, and arms limitation and disarmament, as well as providing backing for an array of humanitarian undertakings.

The cumulative impact of such an augmented United Nations is difficult to foresee with any precision, especially as at this time when the recently concluded controversial use of the UN in the Gulf War is so predominant. And, of course, even without the Gulf War, any scenario of expansion and growth is unlikely to be linear: Reversals and disruptions in the years ahead are very probable. But on balance the structural movement of forces seems supportive of an enhanced UN over the course of the next decade or so. At some stage, if confidence grows and is reinforced by the rising costs of statism, a shift in political loyalty could occur, resulting in far stronger, nonmediated populist attachments to the United Nations, generating pressure for the restructuring of the United Nations along more democratic and supranational lines.[26] Such an unfolding could commence with a serious call to insert more constitutional accountability into future actions by the Security Council and by the formation of a third chamber of the United Nations in which representation was partly determined by direct popular elections and partly by granting status and membership to voluntary organizations active in the promotion of world order values.

More fanciful projections of UN reform might include the consolidation of the General Assembly and Security Council into a single chamber, the elevation of a Chamber of Peoples to the central organ of legislative authority, and the establishment of the new third chamber—The Chamber of World Order Values—constituted by representatives of transnational groups properly accredited.

The political reinforcement of these developments would be crucial. Above all, the play of social forces in major states would have to look beyond the state for protection of the basic concerns of civil society. Again the 1980s provide encouragement for this complementary connection between demands at the domestic level and the transfer of resources and authority to the various actors within the United Nations arena.[27]

There are many variations on these themes, but the basic conviction is that the United Nations, despite the controversies of the Gulf experience, has a major opportunity in the 1990s to play a constructive and enlarged role, and that if it does, a process of growth with critical implications for world order might unfold. The United Nations would then emerge as the centerpiece in the dynamic unfolding of global constitutionalism.

Europe 1992

From the perspective of world order values the planned move toward the predominantly economic integration of Western Europe is of uncertain and ambiguous consequences, and has generally been opposed by those elements in European society most in accord with the vision of an expanded global constitutionalism. These perceptions of its value effects, at least in the shortrun, are probably correct.

At the same time, from the perspective of structural reform at the global level, it is important to appreciate these symbolic and substantive consequences—the region that gave birth to the modern system is taking the initiative in modelling a political community in which state boundaries are of greatly reduced significance and regional operating space becomes the dominant economic and political motif. Such developments will have assured political and psychological spillover effects. If the European Community generally succeeds as a project—that is, improves Europe's position in the world market and provides a better life for a larger proportion of the populations of most participating countries—then the experience and precedent is almost certain to stimulate regional experiments of varying scope and emphasis elsewhere in the world. If, in addition, the European Community establishes a superior level of environmental protection, sustains itself as a zone of peace, and embodies a rising level of democratic governance and human rights, the experience could become charismatic in world history.

Of course, such a favorable projection is subject to numerous contingencies. It is also difficult to assess the various altering connections with statism on one side, globalism on the other. But regional forms of development contribute to global constitutionalism in two distinct ways: first, by building up the regional level of political identity and undertaking; secondly, by shifting the legitimacy and political balance away from reliance on the state as supreme international actor.

Transnational Social Movements

A remarkable feature of this period has been the formation of a large number of organizations and associations devoted to one or another aspect of world order values, and operating on a nongovernmental basis of funding and loyalty. These initiatives comprise a vast pluralist array, ranging across the entire agenda of global concerns, varying from country to country, region to region, cultural circumstance to cultural circumstance. To attach the word "movement" to this welter of activity is as much a hope as a fact. There is, however, a shared normative drift toward cooperative problem-solving, away from patterns of domination and wasteful use of resources, toward health and economic well-being, and an underpinning of affirmation for the preciousness of life and for human bonding with nature.

As might be expected, the slippage of confidence in modernity also engenders some destructive social reactions, including a variety of fundamentalist fixes and conspiracy scapegoats that locate blame in some specific center of evil.[28] The Cold War was itself as much a manifestation of the psychopathology of the nuclear age as it was a rational phase of geopolitics.[29] There is, at present, a strong set of antimodernist reactions that are postmodern in our normative sense.

At this stage, the diversity of tactics for, preoccupations about, goals in, and attitudes toward the future is, in part, an expression of an exploratory mood, responses to the inadequacies of modern beliefs in the invisible hand of industrialism. But they are not at all clear or agreed about what sort of postmodern possibilities are desirable and attainable. At this stage, there is no single path that commands overwhelming allegiance except at high levels of normative abstraction—the pursuit of ecological stability, the avoidance of nuclear war, the stabilization of the world economy, the affirmation of human dignity.

It is not evident whether these initiatives will come together as a coherent movement or series of movements, or whether they will maintain their specific distinctive substantive priorities, locus of action, and tactical methods for the foreseeable future. It is clear by now that some of these undertakings—Amnesty International, the Worldwatch Institute, Solidarity, Greenpeace—have had an extraordinary effect on behavior, perceptions, social expectations, and even official conduct. Others have contributed to underlying shifts in attitude that are difficult to assess by tangible impact—the women's movement, the Western European peace movement, the changing contours of environmentalism.[30]

These various initiatives have several of the characteristic features of global constitutionalism: a rejection of violence; a bypassing of the state; an endorsement of supranational approaches; a bias toward the substitution of human identity for national identity and the global public interest. As such, this transnationalist ferment helps to establish a political climate favorable for global constitutional expansion.

Global Catastrophe

The untenability of the state system, even as augmented by existing mechanisms of coordination, is exhibited most vividly, perhaps, by a series of catastrophic accidents with extra-territorial effects. Nuclear power and nuclear weaponry are emblematic of a broader class of problems. The accidents at Three Mile Island and Chernobyl suggest the possibility of release of harmful amounts of radioactivity into the global atmosphere leading to many thousands, possibly hundreds of thousands, of additional fatal cancers. Oil tanker breakups going back to the *Torrey Canyon* and forward to the *Exxon Valdez* suggest harm to the oceans as a whole. Reports of military accidents are more conjectural, but no less relevant—lost nuclear bombs, planes crashing with nuclear warheads, accidents involving nuclear submarines.

Even if these accidents do not have a global impact, their occurrence shakes public confidence in a territorially based world order system. The chemical accident at Bhopal bringing death or serious injury to many thousands of people in the immediate vicinity of the Union Carbide plant, raised questions about the vulnerability of Third World peoples to corporate conduct that is irresponsible, and about the reduced standards of corporations' local accountability to municipal and regional authorities as a result of bribery and corruption.

Ideas about global catastrophe from accidents of this sort are tied together with fear of "the bomb." The sense that species survival rests on the forbearance of a few world leaders acting secretly is not reassuring.

A healing image is of a world in which better means become available to reshape political forms so as to reduce the vulnerability of peoples to these types of harm. More concretely, such steps may be possible as the regulation of and restrictions upon ultra-hazardous activity by some agreed-upon standards and procedures; stricter means for imposing responsibility for the effects of such accidents to ensure that burdens are not concentrated on the victims; major technological emphasis on the design of less catastrophe-prone systems; major progress toward denuclearization of military security and energy policy.[31]

Global Bonding

There has evolved a gradual sense of shared global tastes, especially among the young, expressed in music, dress, preferred life styles. This global culture seems connected to the call for democratic rights of expression and other world order values. This tendency does not necessarily translate into an endorsement of global constitutionalist approaches, but it does seem to encourage the formation of less territorial types of political identity and affinity. Furthermore, the root commitment of this sense of a shared global reality is a feeling of the unity of the species and the planet. It seems reasonable to believe that this transnationalization of life styles, which has some negative characteristics (e.g., deprecating indigenous cultural forms; uncritically adopting the other elements of Westernization that go with its life style; deferring to the West, despite its materialist, consumerist, and often violently destructive ethos), creates a political climate that would be supportive of sovereignty-diminishing steps in the direction of a humane global constitutional order.

Millennial Hopes

The approach of the year 2000 is certain to orient reflective thinking toward bold solutions on the macro-level. As long as a political framework seems fundamentally sound and widely accepted, there is a tendency to restrict serious reformist efforts to micro-adjustments. As such, global constitutional conceptions have struck most serious interpreters of the political scene as naive, utopian, and diversionary, except possibly as long-range goals.

But, with the planet in jeopardy from so many challenges and with the state considerably demystified as a legitimate and competent guardian of territorial interest, there is less resistance to macro-level thinking. Global constitutional proposals are a form of such thinking that is avowedly responsive to the actual challenges being posed.[32] This responsiveness in the setting of a deepening millennial mood could provide the backdrop for serious advocacy, debate, and even political organizing around schemes and plans for global constitutional arrangements.

At the same time, it is as important as ever that drastic images of global reform be concerned with process as well as plan. The transition from here to there relates both to normative integrity (upholding values as means as well as ends) and to political viability (overcoming the sense of irrelevance that arises when a preferred future is not carefully and convincingly linked to a problematic present). All that millennial receptivity does is to allow these bolder conceptions of the future to be taken more seriously in various policy arenas and in public discourse.

CONCLUSION

More than at any other time since 1945, global constitutional perspectives seem relevant to our consideration of the future. We must learn from the dismissal of these perspectives in the past. It is important to attend carefully to political and economic obstacles. A mindless affirmation of global constitutional solutions and blueprints of global governance system will not persuade nor mobilize. What is needed is thought and action that relates present struggles to future aspirations. The evolving orientation and outlook of world order studies seem helpfully positioned, for reasons described in this essay to make some useful contributions to thought and action at this stage.

NOTES

1. The terminology of the North against the South is far from satisfactory. Iraq as an oil-rich state in the Middle East can be viewed also as part of an ongoing struggle between the West and the non-West, especially as played out in the region, or alternatively, as between the First World and Third World. This latter terminology implies a hierarchy among states that has been increasingly challenged by those representing "the Third World," who prefer such terms as "non-aligned" and "South." See e.g. the Report of the South Commission, *The Challenge to the South* (Oxford: Oxford University Press, 1990), esp. 1–24. See also the earlier Brandt Commission Report, *North-South: A Program for Survival* (Cambridge, MA: MIT Press, 1980).

2. One set of proposals based upon world order values was developed in the 1970s by the World Order Models Project. My own effort in this direction is contained in *A Study of Future Worlds* (New York: Free Press, 1975), 11–39.

3. Alternative world order frameworks are outlined and assessed in the global setting of the 1970s in Falk, "A New Paradigm for International Legal Studies," *Yale Law Journal*, Vol. 84, pp. 969–1021 (1975).

4. The influential, ambitious, carefully crafted Clark-Sohn proposals, are developed in Grenville Clark and Louis B. Sohn, *World Peace Through World Law*, 3rd rev. ed. (Cambridge, MA: Harvard University Press, 1966).

5. See Richard Smoke, *National Security and the Nuclear Dilemma: An Introduction to the American Experience* (Reading, MA: Addison-Wesley, 1984), 29–36, 45; John Lewis Gaddis, *The United States and the Origins of the Cold War, 1941–1947* (New York: Columbia University Press, 1972). Such interpretations confirm the Gaddis view that a realist orientation prevailed among architects of US foreign policy in the period after World War II, and not the Smoke view that idealism had its day in court, that the United Nations was tried, but failed.

6. For various formulations, foundational and contemporary, see David Mitrany, *A Working Peace System* (Chicago: Quadrangle, 1966); Ernst B. Haas, *Beyond the Nation-State: Functionalism and International Organization* (Stanford: Stanford University Press, 1964); Richard N. Gardner, "Practical Internationalism," in Graham Allison and Gregory F. Treverton, eds., *Rethinking America's Security* (New York: Norton, 1992), 267–78.

7. For a very systematic attempt to argue prescriptively for such a reorientation of United States foreign policy see Robert Johansen,

The National Interest and the Human Interest: An Analysis of U.S. Foreign Policy (Princeton: Princeton University Press, 1980). See also Falk, *A Global Approach to National Policy* (Cambridge: Harvard University Press, 1975); Mel Gurtov, *Global Politics and the Human Interest* (Boulder, CO: Lynne Rienner, 1988).

8. See various unpublished papers of Daniel Deudney on the theme of "planetary republicanism," especially "Toward Planetary Republicanism," April 1988.

9. See Wesley T. Wooley's discussion of initial post-Hiroshima calls by prominent leaders for restructuring international relations in *Alternatives to Anarchy: American Supranationalism Since World War II* (Bloomington, Indiana: Indiana University Press, 1988), 3–13.

10. Remarks on the reactionary political effects of failures to achieve timely ecological adjustments by the Danish physicist Neils Meyer at a conference under the auspices of The Great Peace Journey held in Stockholm on March 6, 1989.

11. For an extension of this line of analysis stressing the role of a leading state in providing hegemonic stability see Robert Gilpin, *War and Change in World Politics* (Cambridge: Cambridge University Press, 1981), esp. 9–105.

12. Gilpin, note 11, and Robert O. Keohane, *After Hegemony: Co-operation and Discord in the World Political Economy* (Princeton: Princeton University Press, 1984). The more extreme structural realist approaches to these issues can be found in the work of Kenneth Waltz, above all, and in an extreme form by John Mearsheimer, "Back to the Future: Instability in Europe After the Cold War," *International Security* 15:5–56 (1990).

13. See Raymond Aron's emphasis on the virtue of prudence in diplomacy as "the morality" appropriate to international relations. Aron, *Peace and War: A Theory of International Relations* (Garden City, New York: Doubleday, 1966), 580–85, 608–12.

14. Cf. R. B. J. Walker, *One World, Many Worlds: Struggles for a Just World Peace* (Boulder, Colo.: Lynne Rienner, 1988); Walker and Saul H. Mendlovitz, eds., *Contending Sovereignties: Redefining Political Community* (Boulder, Colo.: Lynne Rienner, 1990); Richard Falk, *Explorations at the Edge of Time: The Prospects for World Order* (Philadelphia: Temple University Press, 1992).

15. For instance, the dispute between the German Chancellor, Helmut Kohl, and the American President, George Bush, over the NATO position toward negotiating the elimination of all battlefield and short-range nuclear weapons. The German position reflected the impact and outlook of the European peace movement.

16. For overview, but with the partisan slant of an insider, see

McGeorge Bundy, *Danger and Survival: Choices About the Bomb in the First Fifty Years* (New York: Random House, 1988), 130–196.

17. For argument along this line see Falk, "Reflections on the Gulf War Experience: Force and War in the United Nations System," *Juridisk Tidskrift* 3:181–93 (1991–92).

18. The U.S. repudiation of the outcome of the World Court proceedings arising from Nicaragua's allegations in relation to the contra war was a major setback from the perspective of respect by leading states for the judicial settlement of major international disputes. For narration of the relevant events and evaluation from a hyper-realist perspective see Thomas M. Franck, *Judging the World Court* (New York: Priority Press, 1986), especially 27–76.

19. The range of nationalist movements is extremely varied in style and orientation, but relevant to political life in all regions of the world. The breakdown of multinational states in the aftermath of the Cold War—Yugoslavia, Soviet Union, Czechoslovakia—is a particularly notable feature of the present historical moment. For useful general commentary on the nationalist phenomenon see Ernest Gellner, *Nations and Nationalism* (Oxford: Basil Blackwell, 1983); E. J. Hobsbawn, *Nations and Nationalism Since 1780* (Cambridge, Eng.: Cambridge University Press, 1990).

20. Global constitutionalism as a focus does not imply a unidirectional political process that is associated with the buildup of central political institutions. The strengthening of regional institutions, of frameworks for economic and environmental cooperation, of UN reform, and of expanding roles for transnational social forces associated with global civil society are several dimensions of global constitutionalism.

21. Cf. *TIME*, Jan. 2, 1989; for broad perspective see Jessica Tuchman Mathews, "Redefining Security," *Foreign Affairs* 68:162–177 (1989); Gareth Porter and Janet Welsh Brown, *Global Environmental Politics* (Boulder, Colo.: Westview, 1991).

22. A discussion of the transition from feudalism to statism had this character of deferred acknowledgment and long interim of overlap. Analysis in relation to present world order challenge is found in Falk, *Revitalizing International Law* (Ames, Iowa: Iowa State University Press, 1989), 3–57.

23. For instance, a militarist and materialist popular culture, if globalized, ensures a violent and ecologically irresponsible destiny for the planet.

24. The transnational character of disease has been vividly expressed by the spread of AIDS. Territorial monitoring is of so little utility that it is not even attempted.

25. This dynamic has progressed most evidently in the setting of Western Europe, generating historic tensions between Eurocrats and Euro-skeptics in relation to the fate of the 1991 Maastricht Treaty. These tensions are complex at both elite and popular levels.

26. There are many means by which such developments could evolve: more participation by formal restructuring (as in proposals for a second chamber that is either popularly elected or constituted by representatives of certified NGOs); grassroots transnational mechanisms for monitoring the activities of UN organs by reference to the Charter, to the constraints of international law, to the goals of peace, equity, and human rights. Democratization at the global institutional level has two dimensions: *accountability* by those acting on the basis of a UN mandate; *participation* in the process of shaping the mandate.

27. During the 1980s, the beginning of a new transnational agenda of concerns began to gain prominence in many states, although in the early 1990s, due to the persistence of economic hardship, this agenda has been pushed back to the margins, at least temporarily. The unwillingness of any candidate to make a proactive approach to global environmental issues a priority during the 1992 presidential elections is indicative of this retreat, and the implication that the public only cares about short-run material issues (jobs, inflation, growth, taxes) and social questions (policy on abortion).

28. The modernist orientation carries with it a vision of continual progress by way of technological innovation, which includes a promise to the disadvantaged that their circumstances will improve in *this* world; when this promise is broken, the avoidance of despair makes it tempting to develop ideas of the evil other, and in fundamentalist Islamic thought, modernism itself is associated with evil.

29. For exploration here see Robert Jay Lifton, *The Broken Connection: On Death and the Continuity of Life* (New York: Basic Books, 1983); see also Spencer R. Weart, *Nuclear Fear: A History of Images* (Cambridge: Harvard University Press, 1988); Mary Kaldor, *The Imaginary War: Understanding the East-West Conflict* (Oxford: Basil Blackwell, 1990).

30. For one useful inquiry see Thomas R. Rochon, *Mobilizing for Peace: The antinuclear movement in Western Europe* (Princeton: Princeton University Press, 1988).

31. In the aftermath of the Cold War, denuclearizing efforts have been almost exclusively focused on various dimensions of nonproliferation, pointedly avoiding the challenge and opportunity to renounce the legitimacy of this weaponry unconditionally, and to proceed as far as feasible in the direction of total nuclear disarmament.

32. In this regard the emphasis on global governance by the Stockholm Initiative on Global Security and Governance is notable, as is the followup that includes a commission located in Geneva to concentrate on global governance. See *Common Responsibility in the 1990s* (The Stockholm Initiative) (Stockholm: Prime Minister's Office, 1992), 36–42.

3

Toward a New Code of International Conduct: War, Peacekeeping, and Global Constitutionalism

ROBERT C. JOHANSEN

ENHANCING WAR PREVENTION THROUGH SYSTEM CHANGE

Throughout the history of the modern state system, most political leaders have pursued the task of war prevention without taking on the broader and more fundamental task of changing the structure of the international system and its accompanying, war-legitimizing code of international conduct. In separating war prevention from system change, political leaders have produced only meager results: Wars recur, and the militarily competitive, anarchical international system continues, year after year, to prostitute national priorities and exact horrendous economic, political, and environmental costs, resulting in the unnecessary poverty and death of untold millions of people.[1]

An alternative approach, proposed here, is based on the understanding that war prevention and international system change are inseparable tasks. The preferred form of system change is to implement it in accordance with the growth of global constitutionalism based on the values of human dignity.[2] Global constitutionalism and war prevention are indeed a tangled embrace: We cannot make much progress in one domain without significant achievement in the other. To a limited extent, these interconnections were vaguely recognized by the various architects of the Hague Conferences of 1899 and 1907, the League of Nations Covenant, and the United Nations Charter.

Immediately following each of the two world wars in this century people vaguely sensed the need to change the international system in order to achieve a durable peace. The trauma of the wars had stripped away the complacency with which they normally accepted politics and diplomacy as usual. But, this recognition never became a day-to-day guide to policy. As time passed, leaders in practice ignored the momentary intellectual and moral recognition that the balance of military power possessed fatal flaws, which had to be corrected if war was to be prevented. Even advocates of arms control usually sought merely to reduce the numbers of particular weapons rather than reduce the role of military power in international relations more generally.

Peace has always been undependable within the international system established by the Treaty of Westphalia in 1648, because this system is based on a decentralized balance of military power. War prevention is only a side effect, not the primary purpose, of the balance-of-power system. States have maintained this system through the repeated use of military force. Yet, if we chose to depart from this system and transform it gradually into a legally constituted balance of *political* power, a more durable peace probably could be maintained within an evolving global constitutional order in which security no longer was based on military self-help. In moving toward that goal, genuine progress in global constitutionalism and war prevention would occur simultaneously.

To be politically effective, any effort to prevent war by advancing global constitutionalism based on the values of human dignity must necessarily give high priority to assuring the consent of the governed. This priority places a strategy of war prevention in an uncommon light, one which is politically more realistic, requiring such a strategy to include deliberate efforts to institutionalize governmental accountability to people. Yet in this age of complex interdependence, it is intellectually misleading and politically ineffective to focus, as we have in the past, primarily on a national government's accountability to the people who live within the confines of its national territory.

Under conditions of interdependence, regardless of how democratic a national government may appear to be internally, an increasing number of its decisions have undemocratic consequences: They affect people outside the borders of its domestic "democratic" political processes. The outsiders have not had opportunity to give or withhold their consent to decisions that affect them. Stated differently, many decisions that affect the people within one country are made by people in other countries; they live outside that country's domestic political process. Even an enormous political economy like that of the United States, for example, is deeply affected by decisions made in Tokyo or Brussels. To take another example, the security of future corn and wheat production in the United States is being potentially threatened by an increasingly arid climate in the grain belt due to irresponsible burning of fossil fuels by consumers not only in the United States but in many other countries as well.

Traditional thinking about democracy has been severely limited by national blinders that in practice encourage us to ignore the rights of people outside our own nation. Any decision to go to war is an extreme denial of democracy, because the lives of the targeted people are deliberately taken by a government that has not represented them in its decision to bomb, burn, and destroy them. The democratic accountability suggested by global constitutionalism and required by truly effective efforts at war prevention means that more responsible and principled governing authority must be developed not only "vertically" within domestic societies from the local to the national level, but also "horizontally" across national borders and "vertically" to encompass world society at the global level.[3] The people of Israel, for example, should be able to influence Iraqi decisions about acquiring missiles with poison warheads because they directly affect Israeli security. Similarly, Egyptians have a right to insist that Israel and Iraq possess no weapons of mass destruction. More broadly, the people of Poland, Germany, Finland, and Sweden, for example, should be able to influence the safety standards used for a nuclear reactor built in Chernobyl because its operations affect their lives.

Despite the need to promote system change if we are to take war prevention seriously, there never has been a sustained diplomatic program aimed at positive system change.[4] When President George Bush's rhetorical flourishes about "a new world order" are examined closely, for example, they show that in practice the Bush administration has merely sought global endorsement of U.S. military policy, not U.S. endorsement of and commitment to a global policy that would gradually demilitarize the code of international conduct. Bush's "new world order" does not promote positive system change associated with global constitutionalism.

Washington's policies are especially tragic because several new conditions arising in the 1980s have offered unprecedented, so far unutilized opportunities for security enhancement and the implementation of global constitutionalism. First, reforms in the former Soviet Union, the success of anti-authoritarian revolutions in Eastern Europe, and the end of the Cold War have provided a multitude of opportunities for establishing a more cooperative code of international conduct, for strengthening the UN's capacities for peacekeeping, and for progressively integrating the political economies of former adversaries—a powerful factor in developing Franco-German peace after almost a century of military hostility. Second, global environmental and economic stresses have underscored the need for more international governance, not merely on a bilateral basis but also through regional and global organizations endowed with sovereignty that could be shared with more traditional national governing authorities. Transnational environmental interconnections and the fact that the only lasting national security is common security[5] continue to change the nature of sovereignty, despite governments' refusal to grant formal permission for the factual changes in sovereignty that do occur. Third, "people power" has arisen to reshape politics in Iran, the Philippines, South Africa, South Korea, Burma, Poland, Hungary, the former German Democratic Republic, Czechoslovakia, Romania, Bulgaria, most republics of the former Soviet Union, China, Albania, and elsewhere. These movements have not always yielded certain success or even progress, but on balance their growth has weakened the hand of promilitary "anti-constitutionalists" in both their domestic and international domains. Fourth, the most relevant to the present discussion, a small but growing number of people from many countries are beginning to act on the knowledge that the utility of the national use of military force has fallen below the utility of multilateral peacekeeping for the purpose of maintaining peace and bringing justice in many contexts. The remainder of this essay analyzes ways to seize these unprecedented opportunities and enhance UN peacekeeping as an instrument for encouraging a new code of international conduct that would nurture system change.

UN PEACEKEEPING AND SYSTEM CHANGE

Strengthened United Nations peacemaking, monitoring, peacekeeping, and enforcement can, if utilized wisely, now provide a fertile link between war prevention and other dimensions of international system change. Efforts to institutionalize more effective peacekeeping within an evolving global constitutionalism could be the focal point for developing an overall strategy to achieve a warless world with more justice and environmental harmony. In any case, peacekeeping is of central importance in advancing a global constitutional order, just as a sheriff and posse comitatus in the "Wild West" brought progress when compared to irregular vigilantes or no law enforcement at all.

Of course progress is not inevitable. The failure of past efforts at achieving governance at the global level casts a long, dark, yet revealing shadow over the present opportunities. In order to take prudent advantage of these, it is useful to explore six proposals for enhancing security and advancing global constitutionalism more broadly. These are rooted in the understanding that, to be most effective, political strategies should simultaneously emphasize the need to increase the *governability* of world society, making it less war-prone, and the *governing ability* of world security institutions, making them more capable of enforcing norms against war. These emphases, if taken seriously in today's world politics, would transform the policies of the major military powers[6] and gradually demilitarize the code of international conduct.

At present, the chronic preparation for war and the distant yet ever-present expectation of war among states obstructs the growth of constitutionalism because preparations for war and the threat and use of force undermine the governability of world society. Even claims that force will be used only in self-defense impede the growth of constitutionalism, since such claims still legitimate every nation's preparations for war. Such claims by one country are widely perceived in other countries to be self-serving and nationally partisan, thereby prompting counter military preparations, also justified as "self-defense." A new code of conduct cannot be achieved as long as states insist that they have a right to brandish weapons of mass destruction and to ignore extra-national constraints on decisions to threaten or use military force. This has remained true even when the use of force has had UN endorsement, as occurred with the U.S.-led war against Iraq, because Washington pressed the Security Council to use force too quickly and on the basis of a double standard in upholding the Charter principle against aggression.[7] Any nationally partisan use of force justifies threats and use of force by other nations at other times.

Added to the ungovernability of world society is the lack of governing ability possessed by today's United Nations and regional international organizations. War prevention remains dangerously unreliable because the world's governments have not endowed world security institutions with sufficient constabulary and economic and political resources to promote just and peaceful change through nonviolent means, to enforce the Charter prohibition against military aggression, to encourage the demilitarization of world society, and to enforce demilitarization once it has occurred. The lack of effort to create stronger world security institutions inexcusably continues even during this relatively risk-free period in which the United States and other major powers have no serious threats to their security. As a result, national governments feel forced to continue relying on military force and on what are, from a planetary perspective, nationally partisan decisions about when to use it.

To replace the customary acceptance of the threat or use of force with a diplomatic program to delegitimize national military force and establish fair international political and legal processes of dispute settlement and enforcement constitutes today's most pressing political requirement and most promising moral opportunity for enhancing peoples' security everywhere on earth. This opportunity entails nothing less than the gradual replacement of the militarily competitive balance-of-power system with international norms and organizations based on a balance of legally constituted political power. Such an idea, of course, is not new.[8] The problem in the past has been to find practical ways for turning such an idea into reality. Toward this end, the proposals that follow are designed to be implemented without threatening any nation's legitimate security needs in the short run; yet they open the door to system change in the long run.

Before discussing the specific proposals, it is politically relevant to note that, in an increasing number of regional conflicts, UN peacemaking and peacekeeping can be more effective than the use of national military forces. This is not the place to examine the utility of war, yet there is ample evidence that the usefulness, if not the use, of war is declining, while the utility of multilateral peacekeeping is increasing.[9] Even the Gulf War against Saddam Hussein in 1990–1991, greeted with almost universal triumphalism in the United States, had enormous costs and meager benefits compared to what probably could have been achieved through negotiations and by allowing more time for economic sanctions to work.

Although certainly no panacea, UN peacekeeping, which should be sharply distinguished from the U.S.-led Gulf military operation endorsed by the UN Security Council, often can be more successful than unilateral and bloc-related efforts to dampen military conflicts, because nationally-led military actions lack legitimacy, do not enjoy worldwide support, and often cannot resist excessive violence to attain nationally partisan goals. UN peacekeeping forces have worked best when they are widely perceived to be impartial, eschew violence, receive broad international support, and implement norms laid down by the world community.

UN peacekeeping almost certainly will have an important future as the best instrument available for handling many of the security problems likely to arise in the foreseeable future. These future security needs include: to discourage clandestine movement of arms and armed forces across borders in regional conflicts (the initial reason professed for United States concern about Nicaragua in the 1980s); to discourage wars like the one between Iraq and Iran and to avoid their escalation if they occur; to curtail arms transfers; to discourage proliferation of nuclear, chemical, and biological weapons and missile delivery systems; to monitor and enforce armistices, peace agreements, and arms treaties; to provide sanctuary for displaced persons and refugees; to dampen inter-ethnic violence; to prevent outer space from becoming another source of military threat; and to deter outright annexation such as Iraq's of Kuwait in 1990. Meeting these security needs requires agencies with widely accepted legitimacy, such as the United Nations can provide, in order to contain conflict; to provide good offices for negotiated settlements; to monitor borders, cease-fires, and troop withdrawals; to oversee referenda or elections in strife-torn regions; to protect unarmed, victimized people; to protect neutral shipping; and to enforce economic sanctions.

SPECIFIC MEASURES

To become a more effective antidote to war and an agent of global constitutionalism, the United Nations, its member governments, and the world's publics could implement measures in six areas. First, the UN Security Council and the UN system more broadly would benefit from reorienting their priorities in order to engage in anticipatory peacekeeping and *preventive conflict resolution,* rather than to be satisfied with reacting to crises after they threaten to erupt into violence. Now that the Cold War is over, the Security Council could become an effective world crisis monitoring center. Toward this end, the Council could equip itself and the UN Secretary General with more official fact-finding missions and skilled roving ambassadors to gather information and make recommendations for dampening conflicts. The Council would gain needed visibility, motivation, and credibility if the foreign ministers of all the Council's members met periodically, perhaps two or three times a year, at the UN to discuss threatening crises and their resolution. The Council could also establish standing regional conflict resolution committees. Had one been active in the Middle East in 1990, it might well have provided the diplomatic leadership necessary to have deterred an Iraqi attack on Kuwait.

To enable swift response to crises, the Security Council could give the Secretary General blanket authority in advance to dispatch unarmed UN observation forces in preset corridors along tense international borders anywhere in the world. Later, the Secretary General might be authorized to send similar forces to any place on earth where the Secretary General determined that their presence would contribute to peace. With this peacemaking apparatus in place, the Council could press more vigorously and successfully for the negotiated resolution of outstanding political problems, such as the Israeli–Palestinian issue, wherever they exist.

Second, the UN needs *strengthened capacities in peacekeeping.* The Gulf crisis demonstrated that the UN is handicapped in relying on ad hoc forces because the Secretary General cannot immediately dispatch UN forces to a war zone. Secretary General Javier Perez de Cuellar asked in vain for authority to organize a standby peacekeeping operation in the fall of 1990.[10] If UN forces could have been available even earlier and could have moved to the Kuwaiti border during June or July of 1990, they might have deterred Iraq from an invasion. Moreover, if one goal in making world society more governable is to dampen the growth of national armed forces, then governments must be able to rely on a UN force ready to help in time of need.

To give a substantial boost to its capacities for war prevention, the United Nations needs a permanent peacekeeping force of its own. It could be individually recruited by the United Nations from volunteers from all countries. It probably should include some naval or coast guard capability to help enforce economic sanctions. A permanent force could be immediately available; it would be less subject to charges of bias than ad hoc personnel now drawn from the national armed forces of UN members; it could be more effectively trained, organized, and commanded, equipped with specialized units, and judiciously employed to carry out the unusually delicate tasks of peacekeeping, which seldom resemble conventional military action. Its availability and a growing reputation for successful operations would reduce the temptation for military powers to intervene and to nurture client state relationships. A permanent UN force could also give genuine meaning to the idea of UN-protected countries, thereby reducing conditions that give rise to client state relationships, cutting demand in the international arms trade, and removing one rationale for maintaining foreign military bases.

A permanent force might raise total U.N. peacekeeping costs, including all present operations, to as much as $20 billion annually. The total costs could be divided among all nations of the world in proportion to each country's percentage of total world military expenditures.[11] Costa Rica, with no military armed force, would pay nothing, whereas the United States and Russia, which together have accounted for 60 percent of world military spending, would together pay approximately $12 billion. Countries like Germany and Japan, which for historical reasons have avoided military forces commensurate with their economic power, might fulfill their worldwide security responsibilities by voluntarily contributing substantial money to a UN peacekeeping fund rather than by enlarging their defense forces or feeling obligated to deploy existing ones outside their own territories.

A permanent, individually recruited UN force could perform an educational role in the global classroom of international politics that is as important as the added security that UN forces might immediately provide in any particular conflict. The creation of such a force would nurture the idea that world security institutions can indeed impartially enforce norms endorsed by the world community on behalf of that community. Worldviews could be gradually changed as people saw a UN force, made up of young people, from the United States, Russia, and all other nations, delivering security services in a highly professional manner while willingly undergoing personal risk for the sake of peace. The proposed UN force could help stimulate the transition to a warless world because it would remind nations of the difference between police enforcement and military action.[12] Armies try to achieve victory; police seek tranquility. Police try to enforce law on individuals, whereas armies impose their will on entire societies. Although UN peacekeepers sometimes carry arms, these soldiers have no enemies. Their function is more akin to police enforcement than to combat.

Third, to support both peacemaking and peacekeeping, the UN needs a permanent *monitoring and research* agency. It could employ UN aircraft, satellites, and other advanced surveillance techniques to guard against clandestine movement of military forces, tests of missiles or nuclear weapons, and violations of economic sanctions during enforcement actions. It might deter preparations for covert operations or military attack, especially if their success depended on clandestine operations or surprise.[13]

Fourth, the United Nations needs more sophisticated *instruments of enforcement.* If the Security Council developed preplanned enforcement measures and committed itself to carry them out, it could have an important deterring effect on those who may consider such military aggression as Hussein conducted against Iran for almost a decade and against Kuwait in 1990. Preplanned enforcement measures could ensure that future enforcement strategies reflected the concerns of the world community, not of only one or two dominant powers, and could be designed to make economic sanctions as effective as possible in order to minimize loss of life and possibly avoid any need for war during their enforcement.

Fifth, to be a more effective peacemaker and agent of global constitutionalism, the UN needs to ensure that it remains *faithful to the spirit of the Charter.* Its processes must be genuinely multilateral, its substantive decisions must be principled, and its policies must minimize violence:

- Future deterrence of aggression would be aided by adhering in good faith to even-handed multilateral processes, rather than allowing one dominant member to exert unwarranted control over UN decisions, as happened when the United States pressed the Council to gain early endorsement of the U.S.-led bombing of and war against Iraq in 1991. Decisions about enforcement also must be more fairly balanced to apply equally to all nations. Preplanned enforcement measures would encourage countries like the United States to end its present double standard on the nonaggression principle: stringent for its adversaries and lenient for itself and its friends.
- In order to achieve more balanced discussion of political issues, more equitable representation of the world's population on the Security Council, and more protection against the danger that a single nation can dominate the Council, the UN should give favorable consideration to the proposal, in which Brazil and Japan have shown interest, for adding five more permanent members to the Council, but without veto power.
- The UN experience in the Gulf War of 1991 demonstrated that the UN must do much more to restrain itself from blessing unnecessarily bloody wars when carrying out its responsibility to enforce the nonaggression principle. The Council was understandably enthusiastic about being able for the first time to achieve the multilateral unity needed to act as the Charter intended. But it largely overlooked its second, equally solemn obligation to avoid violence insofar as possible in enforcement. It should not authorize military action without limiting how and where it may be used. To be prepared for future enforcement, the Military Staff Committee should be activated to discuss constraints on types of weapons and targets. In addition, it should explore how to employ high technology more creatively to make enforcement effective without killing large numbers of people.

Sixth, it is time for scholars and officials to discuss ways of *holding public authorities individually responsible* for actions that violate the universally endorsed ban on all breaches of the peace. This standard was spelled out and applied in the Nuremburg and Tokyo War Crimes Tribunals that adjudicated crimes against the peace after World War II. It is sensible to focus more attention on individual responsibility because of the growing power of international public opinion and because one of the most effective deterrents to war could be officials' knowledge that the world community will hold them personally accountable for planning or carrying out acts of aggression.

Of course it is unrealistic to assume that the United Nations might suddenly be empowered to apprehend a head of government who has engaged in aggression. It would also be foolishly self-defeating for the United Nations to begin or to prolong a costly war for the purpose of removing a convicted war criminal from office. But it is important for the UN and the world community to reaffirm the norms against aggression, whenever they are violated, by conducting judicial proceedings against alleged war criminals, in absentia if necessary, and to do all in its power to discredit officials and soldiers convicted of crimes against the peace. Such actions would strengthen the norms against aggression and could aid indigenous efforts to oust guilty politicians from office.[14]

The Iraqi aggression against Kuwait and the U.S.-led war against Saddam Hussein illustrate these points. Because the United States and the world community were never clear about what would happen to Hussein if he invaded Kuwait, he was far more likely to commit aggression than if he had known from the outset that the world would not only oppose his aggression but also authoritatively call into question his right to rule. Indeed, by acquiescing in Hussein's earlier aggression against Iran, by giving him billions of dollars to conduct that eight-year war, by selling Iraq advanced arms and technology for making nuclear weapons, missiles, and poison gas, and by engaging in many other acts of complicity with his crimes, the world community made his aggression in 1990 more likely.

The justification for attempting to delegitimize a ruler like Hussein could be based on the grounds that the Security Council is charged with the responsibility for maintaining peace and security. The Charter gives the Council extremely broad powers to do whatever it deems necessary to combat aggression and achieve lasting peace. Hussein allegedly violated the widely recognized norm that government officials who plan and carry out aggressive war are guilty of crimes against the peace. Hussein's aggression established a prima facie case that he is a war criminal. A similar case exists against many other soldiers and civilians who helped plan and execute that assault on Kuwait. It is difficult, of course, to imagine how Saddam Hussein might have been brought before an international criminal court, rather than merely face charges in absentia. But the picture looks different for trying some Iraqi commanders who were captured during the war against Iraq's occupation of Kuwait. Significantly, the claim of some

Nazi officials on trial, that they were merely following orders imposed by an authoritarian government, was denied at that time as an adequate legal defense.

Because of the UN's extraordinary responsibilities for maintaining world peace, the Council might determine that any government officials who allegedly violated the peace would be subject to judicial proceedings in an international criminal court to determine whether they had committed war crimes. If guilty, economic sanctions imposed to reverse aggression might then also be maintained to press war criminals out of office. Where a government has engaged in aggression, the UN could claim the right to replace the government that committed the aggression with an alternative committed to the nonaggression principle, as a universal rule that no one on earth is entitled to break. Dictators could be put on notice that, if they became aggressive, the United Nations would employ economic and diplomatic sanctions not only to reverse their aggression but to replace them with more legitimate office holders. Even lengthy sanctions could be sustained on the grounds that war criminals constitute a threat to the peace until they resign or are forced from office by a combination of external pressure and indigenous protest.

Sanctions to hold unscrupulous leaders personally accountable to an international standard might also help mobilize some victimized segments of the indigenous population, through strikes and noncooperation, on behalf of UN enforcement—an important ingredient in helping enforcement succeed without major war. Insofar as UN economic sanctions might encourage a restive population or some military personnel to split from their militarily aggressive government in order to avoid their own personal punishable complicity in war crimes, efforts to hold the accused government accountable also would move world society toward enforcing rules against aggression on guilty individuals, rather than on entire societies. To focus responsibility for breaking international law on the individuals most responsible for the misdeeds, rather than on those who only happen to live in the aggressive country, is an emphasis likely to strengthen further the deterrent against future aggression.

PROSPECTS FOR UN PEACEKEEPING AND GLOBAL CONSTITUTIONALISM

These six areas of innovation demonstrate an enormous potential for enhancing the utility of UN peacekeeping and for generating an influential international learning process that could help people adopt more compassionate world views and more realistic security policies aimed at demilitarizing the code of international conduct. It is time to use such ideas in developing a serious international political program for the abolition of war.

New leadership in the former Soviet Union and new security assessments in Europe, Asia, Africa, and North and South America make this a time of unusual opportunity. If the United States is willing, a breakthrough far more fundamental than the end of the Cold War could occur. Although heavily burdened with internal problems, influential reformers in the former Soviet Union have spoken out for an interstate version of perestroika, a genuine restructuring of international relations. Moscow has asked the United States and other great powers to strengthen international institutions and to revamp the code of international conduct in order to equip these institutions for managing the pressing global problems that no nations can handle alone. Georgi Shakhnazarov, one of Gorbachev's special assistants, wrote in *Pravda* that Soviet policy sought to increase the "governability of the world."[15] Speaking at the UN General Assembly, Deputy Foreign Minister Vladimir Petrovsky said Moscow's aim was to establish "through the United Nations a comprehensive international strategy for establishing the primacy of the rule of law in relations between states."[16]

To demonstrate their seriousness, Soviet officials in the late 1980s designed numerous proposals, from establishing a UN naval force, for the protection of neutral shipping, to revitalizing the UN Military Staff Committee and enhancing the Security Council's capacities for peacekeeping, to creating an organization to govern space and keep it demilitarized. The philosophy behind Soviet proposals, according to Petrovsky, was "based on the need to ensure the primacy of law in the policy and practice of states."[17] Tragically, Washington did not respond with even mild interest to most of the more than two dozen Soviet proposals, even though progress in demilitarizing the global system is in the long-term interest of the United States. U.S. leadership continues to fail the U.S. public, though a remarkable 85 percent of the public in 1991 wanted the United Nations, rather than the United States, to take the lead in handling future conflicts, and an even larger number believes that the United Nations should "play a much bigger peacekeeping and diplomatic role than it did before the Gulf War." More than two years before the Gulf War threatened and the Warsaw Pact was formally dismantled, 71 percent of the U.S. public already favored the creation of a standing UN peacekeeping force.[18]

Equally important, Third World countries are using multilateral diplomacy in historically unprecedented ways. Even revolutionary governments, like the Sandinistas, have employed the World Court to try to halt violence against their country, and there is growing support throughout the Third World for using the UN's good offices and regional and global judicial institutions for dispute settlement if the major powers will participate on an equitable basis. Indeed, new Soviet thinking, an environmentally and economically conscious Europe, and the willingness of Third World countries to employ UN election monitors and peacekeeping forces have offered more opportunity to institutionalize peace and advance global constitutionalism than has ever existed in history—even more than accompanied the creation of the United Nations.

To avoid squandering this opportunity requires unifying a critical mass of people around the theme of domesticating the international system, demilitarizing it, democratizing it, governing it. If enough people insist, it is possible to transform the balance of military power into a balance of legally constituted political power, equilibrated through world political institutions. If we are to keep the present opportunity alive, scholars and diplomats need to prepare a variety of concrete proposals, not unlike the six presented here, to take advantage of the underutilized potential for multilateral peacemaking and peacekeeping, proposals that will generate educational and diplomatic programs of political strength and moral power, proposals that will empower more and more people to take practical steps toward global constitutionalism and the abolition of war. These can be based in part on a conscious effort to give our personal political affiliation to a world polity that does not yet find adequate representation in world security institutions, but exists in our hearts and minds.[19] This affiliation, informed by a positive vision of global constitutionalism, can provide the foundation for personal acts and political programs that will bring a more peaceful, just, and environmentally harmonious world polity into being.

NOTES

1. I would like to thank Saul Mendlovitz for his inspiration over many years, and, tireless leadership and support for working on the themes contained in this chapter.

2. For elaboration of the meaning of "global constitutionalism," see Chapter 1 above. For discussion of the values of human dignity, see Robert C. Johansen, *The National Interest and the Human Interest: An Analysis of U.S. Foreign Policy* (Princeton, NJ: Princeton University Press, 1980), pp. 3–37.

3. For elaboration of these arguments, see Robert C. Johansen, "Real Security Is Democratic Security," *Alternatives* 16 (Spring 1991):

209–242; and David Held, "Democracy and Globalization," *Alternatives* 16 (Spring 1991): 201–208.

4. By "positive system change" I mean global constitutionalism based on the values of human dignity. At the time of the Second World War, Adolf Hitler's vision of a Third Reich and Japanese proposals for a Greater East Asian Co-Prosperity Sphere illustrated obviously negative forms of system change.

5. See the Palme Commission on Disarmament and Security Issues, *Common Security in the Twenty-First Century* (Stockholm: The Palme Commission, 1989), and Independent Commission on Disarmament and Security Issues, *Common Security: A Blueprint for Survival* (New York: Simon and Schuster, 1982).

6. A number of the internationalist policies for strengthening the peacemaking and peacekeeping roles of the UN and the World Court, advanced by Mikhail Gorbachev and Eduard Shevardnadze's Soviet policy in the later 1980s, have already taken these emphases into account.

7. For analysis of these points, see Robert C. Johansen, "The U.N. After the Gulf War: Lessons for Collective Security," *World Policy* 8 (Summer 1991): 561–574.

8. Recommendations in harmony with this idea were discussed, for example, in 1795 by Immanuel Kant in *Perpetual Peace and Other Essays*, Ted Humphrey (Indianapolis: Hackett Publishing Company, 1983) and more recently by Grenville Clark and Louis B. Sohn, *World Peace Through World Law*, 3rd enlarged ed (Cambridge, MA: Harvard University Press, 1966). Of more immediate relevance to global constitutionalism are Johan Galtung, *The True Worlds* (New York: Free Press, 1980), Richard Falk, *A Study of Future Worlds* (New York: Free Press, 1975), and Saul H. Mendlovitz, *On the Creation of a Just World Order* (New York: Free Press, 1975).

9. This issue is discussed in Robert C. Johansen, "U.N. Peacekeeping: The Changing Utility of Military Force," *Third World Quarterly* 12 (April 1990): 53–70. The declining utility of national military power is well illustrated by the superpowers' tragic experience in Vietnam and Afghanistan. In each case, the superpower could not have achieved less through nonmilitary diplomacy than it achieved through military might.

10. "U.N. Chief Urges Standby Peace-Keeping Unit," *Washington Post*, September 19, 1990, p. 18.

11. Disputes over the percentage of world military expenditures that particular governments appropriate each year might be handled by asking any government that claimed its spending differed from the UN estimate to submit detailed information in accordance with the standardized reporting procedures for military spending that the UN

has already established. More than a dozen nations have submitted budgetary figures in accordance with the UN's standardized reporting instrument. Department for Disarmament Affairs, *The United Nations Disarmament Yearbook* 14 (New York: United Nations, 1990): 341–48; United Nations Department for Disarmament Affairs, *The United Nations and Disarmament: 1945–1985* (New York: United Nations, 1985), pp. 150–54.

12. For an early discussion of the prospects for using international police enforcement as an instrument of world order transformation, see Robert C. Johansen and Saul H. Mendlovitz, "The Role of Enforcement of Law in the Establishment of New International Order: A Proposal for a Transnational Police Force," *Alternatives* 6 (1980): 307–338.

13. For discussion of the politics of establishing a global monitoring agency and other UN reforms, see Robert C. Johansen, "The Reagan Administration and the U.N.: The Costs of Unilateralism," *World Policy Journal* 3 (Fall 1986): 601–641.

14. It is of course dangerous to contemplate an action so threatening to the existing world order as to remove a ruling head of government from power unless it is absolutely clear that such an action would be legitimate only after following due process in trying an alleged war criminal in an impartial international judicial tribunal. Enforcement of the outcome of a trial could then be carried out by the UN on behalf of the world community. In accordance with traditional international law, it is imperative that no country or bloc of national governments attempt to change the government of another country through the use of force. U.S. efforts to remove Hussein from office through aerial bombardment clearly fall in the latter prohibited category because there has been no trial of Hussein, nor has there been worldwide endorsement of the U.S. effort to remove Hussein from office, in contrast to the UN-endorsed action to remove Iraqi troops from Kuwait.

15. Georgi Shakhnazarov, "Governability of the World," *International Affairs* (Moscow), 1988, no. 3, p. 22. See also *Pravda*, January 15, 1988, p. 3.

16. Paul Lewis, "Soviets Urge Stronger Role for World Court," *New York Times*, October 8, 1989, p. 4.

17. Lewis, p. 4.

18. "The New World Order—What the Peace Should Be," *Americans Talk Issues*, Survey No. 15 (March 19–24, 1991); pp. 16–19; *Americans Talk Security*, Survey No. 6 (May 1988); 72.

19. See Richard Falk, "Manifesting World Order," *TFF Newsletter* (Lund), Nos. 7–8 (November 1988); 8–15.

4

In Search of Global Constitutionalism

SAMUEL S. KIM

INTRODUCTION

For the first time since the end of World War II it is common to hear, and even faddish to say, at least in the United States, that the moment for a "new world order" is now here. That the destructive pattern of superpower bipolarity and rivalry has collapsed cannot be gainsaid. What remains unclear and indeterminate—and hence challenging—is the shape and content of the emerging world order. Will we merely shift from the Cold War to another form of deadly international conflict and confrontation? Or will we relapse into a "new" hegemonic world order via Pax Americana II? Alternatively, can we capture the widening horizon of the opportunities that lie before us in this moment of Grotian system transformation, as we think globally but act locally in the creation of a solid foundation for a more just, democratic, and peaceful world order?[1]

These are hard questions with no easy answers. The post-Cold-War world seems increasingly like a turbulent multicentric one pausing at a crossroads where competing trends—globalism, statism, ethnonationalism—are pulling and pushing the quest for a new world order in divergent directions. The rapidly changing global scene lends itself to conflicting prognostications about the shape of international life to come. More than ever before in modern history, statism is being contested from all directions. During much of the postwar era, statism, as enshrined in the old Westphalian principle of state sovereignty and as ambiguously codified in the UN Charter, has been challenged from above by global integration and without by interstate aggression. In the post-Cold War era statism is becoming increasingly threatened from below and within by the sudden rise and rapid proliferation of forces of ethnonationalist fragmentation in many multinational states. The fact that only a small fraction of "potential nations" has made a successful transition to "nation-states" as "member states" of the United Nations poses a challenge to their identity in the quest for a new world order.

Given this contest between centrifugal and centripetal forces, what kinds of alternative global structures of power and authority—and human identities—are desirable and feasible in the shaping of a just world? What are the prospects of global constitutional processes for bringing about new forms of humane global polity and governance? In what sense and to what extent can we say that now is the time for reclaiming global constitutionalism for an emerging world order?

The purpose of this essay is to explore the limits and possibilities of global constitutionalism in a changing world order. After a brief introduction to traditional world order thinking, as exemplified in the Clark-Sohn world federalist model, it proceeds to delve into the adequacy of its underlying assumptions. We then examine critically the development of postwar global lawmaking as a real-world laboratory and point of departure for suggesting an alternative formulation of global constitutionalism.

TRADITIONAL GLOBAL CONSTITUTIONALISM REVISITED

Through the centuries, the idea of constitutionalism has persisted in Western political thought—that a viable world order required nothing less than the replacement of "anarchical" international society with some species of world government. The many medieval and classical approaches to world order—as in the writings of Pierre Dubois (1307), Erasmus (1517), Duc de Sully (1595), Emeric Crucé (1623), William Penn (1693), the Abbé de Saint-Pierre (1716), Jeremy Bentham (1789), and Immanuel Kant (1795)—expressed various strands of reform through a panoply of proposed constitutional and institutional changes. However, these constitutional proposals for world order were only theoretical abstractions devoid of much practical impact on statecraft.

In the twentieth century, constitutionalism has been projected onto the global scene. The League Covenant and the UN Charter are both embodiments of global constitutionalism. Yet the outbreak of World War II, the imperfection of the Charter-based international order, the advent of nuclear weapons, the onset of the Cold War, and the growing interconnectedness of international political and economic life all served to revive more intensive consideration of the possibilities of global constitutionalism. F. H. Hinsley's sweeping indictment of all twentieth-century world order projects as totally atavistic—that all modern peace proposals are nothing but copies or elaborations of some seventeenth-century programs as the seventeenth-century programs were copies of still earlier schemes[2]—seems to ignore two important emergent differences in the institutional context and the normative wellspring of postwar global constitutionalism. Practically all the proposals for world constitutionalism in the postwar era have taken the UN Charter and its institutional arrangements as a point of departure. This is not surprising, since the UN as the premier world body is an open system in continuous interaction with the flow of global megatrends, its politics instantly reflecting and effecting momentum towards one or other of the competing approaches to world order. Unfortunately, however, most of these world constitutional approaches have emanated from the citadel of the global hegemon, the United States, their leading proponents North Americans (e.g., Clarence K. Streit, Nicholas Murray Butler, Maynard Hutchins, Grenville Clark, Emery Reves, Louis Sohn).

Of all the twentieth-century proposals for world constitutionalism, however, *World Peace Through World Law*, by Grenville Clark and Louis Sohn remains the most comprehensive, detailed, rigorous model of world constitutionalism. Conceived and written by two prominent North American international lawyers, and published in three editions in 1958, 1960, and 1966, the Clark-Sohn model was perhaps the most significant example of world order thinking, at least for the 1960s, and its influence was evident in the inaugural phase of world order studies.[3] That even some realist scholars devoted so much attention to refuting the Clark-Sohn model may be taken as a disguised tribute to its serious and concerned scholarship.[4]

Indeed, unlike most other approaches to world order, the Clark-Sohn world constitution model provides a high degree of precision and specificity on new principles, procedures, and institutions (e.g., an elaborate membership plan and weighted voting system, a comprehensive but phased disarmament plan, "United Nations Peace Force," and "World Equity Tribunal") needed to transform the UN into a putatively effective, albeit limited, world government. The fundamental premise of the model is claimed to be identical with the pronouncement of President Eisenhower on October 31, 1956: "There can be no peace without law."[5] Focusing upon a thoroughgoing revision of the UN Charter, article by article, with the addition of various Annexes, the Clark-Sohn model (in the first and second editions) envisioned a species of world government conceived of as creating a system of enforceable world law resting upon general and complete disarmament in the limited field of war prevention. In the third enlarged edition, Clark and Sohn presented two alternative plans for a world organization empowered not only to enforce world law against international violence but also to promote world economic and social development. The first plan is a continuation of the Charter revision approach. The alternative plan envisioned "a new world security and development organization which would supplement the existing peace-keeping machinery of the United Nations, and which, together with the United Nations, would have the necessary minimum powers to prevent war."[6] Under either plan, the model seeks to transfer some functions, capabilities and resources from national governments to a restructured set of global institutions.

However, the Clark-Sohn model embraced a number of dubious underlying assumptions. The fundamental premise is based on the Hobbesian either/or dichotomy of world governmental authority versus world anarchy—either there is world peace based on a world authority (and world law) or there is world anarchy and "war of all against all": A world without central government is a nasty world of no normative restraints on endless warfare. This assumption—curiously enough shared by both Realpolitik realists and Idealpolitik legalists, even though their prescriptive remedies are a world apart—overstates the degree of anarchy in world politics, because of their highly formalistic and misleading notion of "anarchy" as the absence of government, and understates the extent to which contemporary world politics is institutionalized and "regime-governed" in many issue areas.

World law is assigned a mission impossible based on a highly exaggerated notion of "law power." It emerges as the necessary and sufficient condition for world peace: World law is the creator, not the creature, of world authority. Indeed, world law is projected as a self-sufficient autonomous force upon which world peace depends, but which itself depends upon nothing else. The model embraces the Austinian positivist-hierarchical notion of law as the enforceable system of sovereign commands over subjects. Implicit in the model, ironically, is both the realist and the Marxist conceptions of "power," including "law power," as social control and domination (more will be said about this later). However, the absence of a government does not ipso facto negate the influence of norms and laws, nor does the presence of a government ipso facto guarantee law and order in any society. To merely establish governmental authority in the absence of a unifying global consensus or the social conditions and norms required to elicit compliance is not the way to cope with the world order challenge of our time. Even in a domestic polity with central authority, the state does not and cannot mobilize its enforcement power to back up every law. For the most part, legal rules are followed not because of the state's police power but because of customary social habits, norms, and self-interest. The "anarchical" international society today without a central government seems remarkably more stable and orderly than a great many domestic societies with central governments in the Third World.

Furthermore, the Clark-Sohn model seems to have accepted the nineteenth-century textual notion of constitutionalism as a formal written document, applied to a global system. There is also a curious internal contradiction, as the model proceeds from the premise of the insufficiency of the existing international legal order (treaties, customs, and self-restraints) for a viable international order. Yet the remedy proposed is more law—world law. An alternative to the state system emerges not as an alternative to, but as an amplification of, the state system to a global scale, a world state. If international law—and intergovernmental response—is insufficient to sustain international order, there is no reason to believe that world law by itself can do the trick for the more elusive challenge of creating and sustaining a new world order.

The logic of this "world peace through world law" approach stands on shaky historical grounds. If we equate the periods of war with the absence of world law in the modern history of international relations, how can we account for the periods of peace? Like all monocausal theories of war, this model too proceeds from the premise of a single-cause explanation of war—the absence of world government—and prescribes a legalistic quick fix. The proposition that war can be eliminated by legal fiat, and that a world without war can be brought about through world law, finds no empirical support in peace research. As a complex and recurring social phenomenon, war can be eliminated only through a protracted process of transforming the most fundamental values, beliefs, attitudes, and myths that prop up the war system.[7]

Moreover, there are no recent successful cases of international federalism, with the possible exception of Eurofederalism. The federalist approach of directly confronting the attributes of state sovereignty, and replacing them with supranational procedures and institutions of decision making and conflict resolution has not worked, or perhaps more accurately has not given a chance to work. In early postwar Europe, the continental federalists were the original force behind the establishment of the Council of Europe (CE) in 1949. Yet the governments quickly joined this nongovernmental federalist drive, beating the nongovernmental federalists at their own game. The CE was endowed with a measure of supranationalism in form but not in substance. With the failure of two frontal attempts to bring about a federal Europe—a revitalized Council of Europe in 1949–1951 and the European Political Community in 1952–1954—European federalism ground to a temporary halt. After several decades of jagged development, the European Community, not the CE, is once again moving toward greater economic integration unencumbered by any formal federal constitution. Whether this economic integration will transform itself into a federalist union seems dependent upon resolving the question of national identity.

The Clark-Sohn model is a world order prognostication by exclusion, failing as it does to suggest a way of unifying theory and practice, as if law or lawmaking and politics constitute two separate and independent domains of social process. It ignores the sociologically grounded realization that social conflicts and conflict resolution are inevitably political. Instead, it appeals to the enlightened self-interest of the powers that be to take the initiative towards a normative world peace through an enforceable world law. The fact that this legalistic approach to world order originated from the United States during the post-1945 heyday of American hegemony in world politics, and the fact that the Truman, Eisenhower, and Kennedy Administrations each were committed in varying degrees to world law as a matter of principle (or as a matter of world order rhetoric), has only strengthened the perception in the Third World that world federalism of this kind is no more than a globalizing ideology emanating from a "law and order" superpower, designed to institutionalize Pax Americana under the legitimizing rubric of "world law."

As the most comprehensive and thoroughgoing constitution modelling, the Clark-Sohn proposals have the virtue of precision and specificity. But such clarity has been obtained through the fallacy of prematurely optimistic prognostication. Taking "a hopeful view" in the 1960 second edition, senior coauthor Grenville Clark (who singlely authored the "Introduction" to this *World Peace Through World Law* book) ventured "a reasoned prediction" that a new world system of enforceable world law accompanied by total and universal disarmament would have come into force by 1969–1971.[8] In the third and final edition, Clark admitted that his 1960 prediction "was too optimistic," but proceeded to say that he still retained "a reasonably optimistic view as to the prospects and, as of 1966, [I] believed that such a plan will have been formulated by some important government or group of governments by 1980 and that within five years thereafter (by, say,

1985) such a plan will have been ratified by all or nearly all the nations, including all the major Powers."[9]

The influence of the Clark-Sohn model was confined to academic debate on world order in the 1960s. It never found its way into any U.S. foreign policy debates or UN-sponsored global lawmaking. Thus it offers a sobering lesson for the world order modelling movement—that normative forecasting generates its own self-serving tendency to overstate the feasibilities of system transformation. Indeed, the story of utopias is full of shattered blueprints and hastily updated time tables for the coming of a brave new world.

GLOBAL LAWMAKING OR GLOBAL POLITICS?

The absence of a world government has not deterred norm-creating and lawmaking activities in the United Nations. Paradoxically, it is the absence of a global Leviathan coupled with the accelerated pace of the globalization of human life that produced more international agreements during the first forty years since World War II than during the previous four millennia.[10] Common interest in shaping a stable and predictable external environment, in sharing certain vital information about the changing rules of international transactions, and in coping with transnational "traffic" problems provide the bases for the UN's normative politics. With international society still divided by competing ideologies, cultures, and interests, UN lawmaking serves, to a degree, as a socialization agent for developing a common normative language for clarifying and regulating increasingly complex and interconnected international political and economic life.

With the entry of so many new actors, issues, demands, and aspirations into the United Nations system, the postwar lawmaking process has gradually shifted to political forums with universal membership, where participants can transform both the criteria and content of contemporary international law in collective response to changing global realities. This process relies more heavily upon informal means of norm making and standard setting through multilateral diplomacy and global bargaining, rather than the more formalistic legal procedures of treaty making or following the slower process of developing customary international law through state practice, acceptance, and acquiescence. As a result, the distinction between global politics and global lawmaking is substantially blurred, if not completely erased. Still, the distinction between global politics and global lawmaking is useful for analytical purposes, to examine the relationship between laws (the visible tip of the iceberg) and norms (the submerged iceberg itself). Put differently, the promise/performance disjuncture in various world order issue areas can be delineated by examining the nexus between "law-in-book" and "law-in-action."

It should come as no surprise that United Nations lawmaking with respect to international violence has until recently been urgent but problematic. By any standard, the United Nations's record in this domain, although fluctuating, has been generally disappointing. There are double lags here. What is ("law-in-book") lags far behind what ought to be ("law-in-aspiration"), while state behavior ("law-in-action") falls far short of formal obligations ("law-in-book"). The promise/performance gap was widening in the 1970s and most of the 1980s. At the highest level of general principles, the twentieth century witnessed a great leap forward on restraining and renouncing the use of interstate force, from the Covenant to the Pact of Paris (the Kellogg-Briand Pact) to the UN Charter to the Nuremberg Principles. And there has been no shortage of endless self-righteous lip service to these grandiose principles in the foreign policy rhetoric of state actors.

Yet rhetoric/reality disjuncture has reached the point where the Charter principle that "all Members shall refrain in their international relations from the threat or use of force" (Article 2 (4)) has been honored more in the breach than in observance, as made evident in some 139 international wars and armed conflicts during the first four decades of the UN's existence. Legalistically speaking, the problem here is a familiar one. Every set of declaratory principles, including the Charter, embodies mutually competing, often contradictory, principles. The Charter principle of non-threat and non-use of force is balanced and qualified by the principle of the inherent right of individual or collective self-defense (Article 51). During the Brezhnev and Reagan and Bush years, the Soviet Union and the United States both stretched the latter principle to such an extent as to deprive the former principle of normative utility. Indeed, the principle of individual and collective self-defense has become a fig leaf justifying virtually any use of force in the Third World.

By and large, contemporary international law in the domain of high politics is abstract and amorphous. Lacking specificity, these general principles can be more readily stretched as a flexible propaganda instrument than as a context-specific normative restraint. At the more functional level, the domain of "low politics," and the international law of reciprocity, compliance is greater because of the clarity and specificity of the legal rules, as well as its not being a zero-sum game.

Despite the steady torrent of UN lawmaking, the difficulty of achieving global consensus on specific legal rules is made loud and clear in the UN Special Committee on Enhancing the Effectiveness of the Principle of Non-Use of Force in International Relations by its intersystemic disagreements on a global treaty on the non-use of force. Ironically, the Special Committee was set up in 1977 by the General Assembly, acting on a Soviet proposal to include in its agenda an item entitled "Conclusion of a World Treaty on the Non-Use of Force in International Relations." What the Soviet Union proposed, its troops invading Afghanistan disposed.

The globalization of the war system and the predominance of the *para bellum* deterrence doctrine stand in the way of progressive development and codification of the international law of peace. Contemporary international law cannot be said to be predominantly pacifist. The development of the international law of war—the so-called international humanitarian law of war—continues to outpace that of the international law of peace. The recrudescence of the "just war" doctrine, the dominant tradition of Catholic thinking on war and peace since Christianity became the official religion of Rome during the reign of Emperor Constantine, far from energizing the development of the international law of peace, has provided a doctrinal alibi for all major global actors—revolutionary warfare for the Third World, the Brezhnev Doctrine until recently, for the Soviet Union and the Reagan Doctrine for the United States. Even the U.S. Catholic bishops' heroic attempt to break new ground in the official Catholic teaching on war and peace in the nuclearized world collapsed owing to their theological fidelity to the just war doctrine. The fact of aggression, oppression, and injustice in today's world, the bishops asserted in their 1983 Pastoral Letter on War and Peace, "serves to *legitimate the resort to [nuclear] weapons and armed force in defense of justice.*"[11]

The phenomenal growth of "soft law" on peace stands out in contrast with the paucity of specific prescriptive rules crystallized into multilateral treaties. In four decades of lawmaking, not a single multilateral treaty on the non-use of force has yet been concluded under the auspices of the United Nations. Since 1947 the International Law Commission (ILC) has been instructed by the General Assembly to formulate the principles of international law recognized in the Charter and Judgment of the Nuremberg Tribunal in the form of a draft "Code of Offenses against the Peace and Security of Mankind." Forty years later the ILC still could not produce consensus on several of the more crucial issues, such as the *ratione materiae* (Which crimes would be the code cover?), the *ratione personae* (Will the code apply to individuals or states or both?), or the means of enforcing it.

Of course, soft law on the non-use of force, adopted in the form of consensual declaratory resolutions, abounds. After seven years of work by the Special Committee on the Question of Defining Aggression, the

General Assembly adopted by consensus Resolution 3314 (XXIX) on December 14, 1974, in which it, inter alia, approved the Committee's Definition of Aggression and called upon all states to refrain from all acts of aggression and other use of force contrary to the UN Charter. The Definition was designed as an authoritative guide for the Security Council in identifying acts of aggression. Yet a wide divergence of opinion and skeptical views among the permanent members of the Security Council, necessarily papered over by the so-called "consensual" resolution on the nature, scope, and applicability of "aggression," call into question the normative potency of the Definition.

The political fact of international politics has remained and continues to remain today, albeit in a lesser degree, that soft law of this kind commands only a pro forma endorsement of convenience, and only as long as it does not interfere with national interest unilaterally determined. The principal determinants deterring states from resort to force, in its varying combinations and permutations, still remain more military, political, ideological, and economic than legal. To date, the Definition seems to have exerted no discernible impact upon state behavior or upon the crisis management performance of the Security Council. Even such relatively clear-cut cases of aggression as the Iraqi attack on Iran in 1980, the South African incursions into Angola, the Israeli surprise attack on the Tamuz nuclear reactor complex in Iraq in 1981 and invasion of Lebanon in 1982 (and, alas, almost habitual bombing of southern Lebanon) have passed as nonlegal events, as if the Definition did not really matter. Saddam Hussein paid a heavy price (or has he really?) by learning too much from this established Cold-War pattern of state behavior and by applying it too readily in a post-Cold-War setting.

The UN's performance in the field of arms control and disarmament (ACD), in both absolute and comparative terms (e.g., the superpower ACD performance), is no less disappointing. The 1982 session of the General Assembly passed a record number of fifty-seven disarmament resolutions, as if to paper over the fact that its Second Special Session on Disarmament, held in mid-1982, was a complete failure. The rising curves for the number of UN disarmament resolutions and for world military expenditures and arms sales have converged in recent years. Clearly, the nuclear issue, for the nuclear haves, is too important a business to be left to the collective management of the United Nations—whether through its special session or through the Conference on Disarmament—where the nuclear have-nots enjoy an overwhelming majority. As for the nuclear have-nots, they have no place to go but to the United Nations to exert disarmament and denuclearizing pressures through hortatory resolutions on the weapons systems they do not possess.

It is somewhat ironic, but certainly not surprising, that the two superpowers took such an active role in both the General Assembly and the Geneva-based Eighteen-Nation Committee on Disarmament in the negotiations (1965–1968) leading to the establishment of the Non-Proliferation Treaty (NPT) regime—indeed a monument to the self-serving superpower arithmetic image of a nuclear world order. In fact, the final treaty was based on a revised joint American-Soviet draft treaty submitted to the General Assembly on March 14, 1968. The operational norms and procedures of the NPT regime discriminate between nuclear haves and nuclear have-nots, based on the logic of nuclear illogic—that nuclear weapons are good or safe in the hands of the great powers but bad or unsafe in the hands of the small powers. This illogic was initially papered over by a simple bargain. The nuclear have-nots promised no horizontal proliferation by not going nuclear in return for a promise from the nuclear powers to curb vertical proliferation (Article 6). Almost all of the signatory nonnuclear weapon states have kept their half of the bargain, but the nuclear powers have not. Given the discrepancy between its reciprocal structure and its one-sided implementation, the long-term viability of the NPT is problematic. Unless linked to a larger quest for normative transformation, structural equity, and demilitarization and denuclearization, nuclear nonproliferation is a mirage. On the issue of global arms trade—the Big Five of the Security Council account for over eighty-nine percent of global arms sale—the UN has yet to take the first step, of establishing a registry of global arms sales.

The UN's performance on the resolution of international conflicts and disputes has fallen far short of the Charter promise of a collective security system. The Security Council has failed not because of the absence of law or constitutional mandate but because of failure in superpower politics. Putting it bluntly, politics, not law, is the primary determinant of the success or failure of the Security Council. The adoption of the Definition of Aggression in 1974 was accompanied by a precipitous decline in the UN peacekeeping performance in the following years (1974–1986). The revival and expansion of UN peacekeeping since 1987 have come about despite the continued deadlock over establishing new rules and procedures by the Special Committee on Peacekeeping Operations.

In short, there is little relationship, if any, between "law-in-book" and "law-in-action" as far as UN peacekeeping is concerned. Where there is a political will and consensus among the Big Five, there is always a "legal" way through or around the Charter; indeed, this is the meaning of the Uniting for Peace Resolution (1950) as well as of an informal "Chapter VI½" amendment.

Recognition of the inability of the Security Council to fulfill its intended constitutional role in implementing a collective security system, coupled with a widely shared belief that the UN had to exercise a minimal demonstration of authority for maintaining international peace and security if it were not to repeat the fate of its League of Nations predecessor, brought about a politically more feasible, militarily more modest, legally more ambiguous alternative to the Charter-based collective security system, what came to be known as "peacekeeping." Falling in the gray zone between the pacific conflict settlement provisions of Chapter VI and the enforcement provisions of Chapter VII—hence dubbed the "Chapter VI½" innovation—peacekeeping was conceived of to bridge the growing gap between what should be done in theory and what could be done in practice. And this innovation—an informal constitutional change—has come about without any formal revision or amendment of the Charter.

The track record of UN peacekeeping has been a mixed and changing one, with successes beginning to drop in the 1970s, with a still sharper drop during the first half of the 1980s. Much of the decline after 1970 can be explained by the growing indifference to multilateralism by the permanent members, in particular the United States. Yet the Third World has also become a major culprit (and loser) in the 1970s and beyond. Even in such an easy case as the 1982 Falklands-Malvinas conflict and the resulting British–Argentine War, the Third World showed a manifest inability or unwillingness, or both, to transfer the dispute from the Security Council, where any further action was foreclosed by the British and American veto, to the General Assembly via the Uniting for Peace Resolution. Here again the failure can only be explained in political, not legal, terms.

Changes both within and outside the UN in 1987–1988 facilitated a shift from the Cold War to a new era of multilateral cooperation. Perhaps more than any other single global actor, the Soviet Union under Mikhail Gorbachev and his "new thinking" in foreign policy were responsible for bringing about a global season of peace and for ushering in a new era of great-power consensus on UN peacekeeping operations. Gorbachev embarrassed and even shamed Reagan by reversing traditional Soviet hostility to the UN as a global peacekeeper. Even before the awarding of the 1988 Nobel Peace Prize to the UN peacekeeping forces, the Soviet Union had already put forward several proposals for insuring "comprehensive security in military, political, economic, ecological, humanitarian, and other fields" and to give the United Nations an enhanced role "in the maintenance of global peace and in the solution of global problems." This new Soviet conception of a comprehensive global security system includes the proposal for a UN naval peacekeeping force as well as the proposition that the member states routinely earmark some of their armed forces for UN peacekeeping operations, thus establishing a standing UN peacekeeping force of its own.

The Gorbachev Revolution is part of the sudden rise in global learning in certain parts of the world. Superpower Détente III (1987–1991) has reflected and effected this shift from the high costs of unilateralism to the cost-effective benefits of multilateralism in order to gain more breathing space for putting domestic houses in order. The eight-year-long Iraq–Iran War is a reminder that there are no easy winners in modern war, especially in inter-Third-World wars. It has become easier to avoid losing a war than to win it, even if one side is militarily superior. War has become easier to terminate through the United Nations than through continuous fighting or until exhaustion. Security Council Resolution 598 (July 1987) is a turning point for the revival and expansion of UN peacekeeping, for it embodied for the first time in UN history the unanimity of the Big Five on such a topic (the five permanent members themselves actually submitted an unprecedented joint draft resolution), leading to the establishment and deployment of a United Nations Iran-Iraq Military Observer Group (UNIIMOG) a year later to monitor the UN-imposed cease-fire. The conclusion of the Geneva Accords in April 1988 and the establishment of the United Nations Good Offices Mission for Afghanistan and Pakistan (UNGOMAP) represent the first instance of the superpowers becoming co-guarantors of an agreement negotiated under the auspices of the UN Secretary General. Historically, a Cold-War conflict such as this was beyond the political reach of UN peacekeeping. Yet UNGOMAP was established prior to the official demise of the Cold War and the collapse of the socialist world in late 1989.

It is worth noting that the Security Council departed from the consent principle in UNIIMOG as well as in the Comprehensive Political Settlement Agreement for Cambodia sponsored by the Big Five in 1990, by imposing its own peacekeeping and peacemaking solution upon the belligerent parties without their prior consent. Of course, there is nothing in the Charter that prohibits the Security Council from deploying its own peacekeeping forces or from imposing its own peacemaking solution without the consent of all the parties.

Clearly, the Security Council makes, interprets, and executes its own "law" as it sees fit. It has seldom used its constitutional mandate to seek any advisory opinion from the World Court. There is very little in the Charter that specifically authorizes the Security Council to cope with the incidence of internal (state-making) armed conflicts. In practice, however, the Charter prohibition not to intervene "in matters which are essentially within the domestic jurisdiction of any state" (Article 2 (7)) has seldom stood in the way of UN involvement in those situations capable of mobilizing a great-power political agreement. Paradoxically, the ad hoc and elastic nature of UN peacekeeping, the main target for a variety of institutional reform proposals, has actually become the main source for a complex network of cooperation evolving among the Security Council, the Secretary General, the General Assembly, and the belligerents in regional and local conflicts. It has also become the main source of UN involvement in state-making conflicts. The nature and scope of UN peacekeeping expanded considerably in recent years to encompass an increasing variety of roles and functions, such as the disarmament of insurgents (Nicaragua and Cambodia), the provision of humanitarian and welfare assistance (Cyprus, southern Lebanon, and the Kurdish region of Iraq), and even the monitoring and supervision of elections (Namibia, Haiti, and also in Angola, Cambodia, and Western Sahara).

Until Resolution 678 of November 29, 1990, authorized member states "to use all necessary means," the Security Council seemed to be readying itself to play a role in the shaping of a new world order by progressively blurring the distinction between peacekeeping and peacemaking, with Chapter VII provisions for peace-enforcment falling by the wayside. However, this resolution is a textbook case of hegemonic manipulation of the Security Council, deviating from all UN peacekeeping operations from 1956 to the present. The ultimate irony is that the much-heralded "new world order" got mistranslated into an almost transparent UN fig leaf for an essentially U.S. war. By giving the United States a military blank check, the Security Council abnegated its own constitutional responsibilities and accountability, with no authority to do so, and in so doing facilitated a too hasty retreat from the outer reach of its power to use nonviolent sanctions. America's coercive carrot-and-stick diplomacy succeeded in producing a 12:2:1 majority vote in the Security Council, but this victory commands at best dubious and precarious legitimacy.[12] The resolution can at best enjoy border-line legality, since a stricter interpretation of the Charter requirement for "the concurring votes of the permanent members" (Article 27 (3)) raises serious legal difficulty. Moscow's "absence" during the initial phase of the Korean War, and Beijing's "nonparticipation in the vote" from 1971 to 1980, provides a misleading and shaky precedent for interpreting China's "abstention" as constituting a concurring vote in this particular case. In this first critical experiment in making new ground rules for the new world order in the Security

Council, the real loser may well be UN-sponsored nonviolent sanctions (which were prematurely preempted for an American war) and UN peacekeeping and peacemaking (which were prematurely relinquished by the resurgence of American hegemony).

Although great advances and innovations during the past four and a half decades have been made in UN norm-generating and lawmaking activities in various domains of world order problems, especially in the areas of global human rights and environment, there is a danger in uncritically accepting quantitative change as evidence of system-transforming change. Because of its seriously anachronistic problem of global representation, UN lawmaking focuses on statist values and interests, leaving little space for global human values and interests. The voices of "we, the peoples of the United Nations," in whose name and behalf the UN Charter was promulgated, remain largely unrepresented, unheard, and unlegislated. The basic challenge ahead for a post-Cold-War world order lies in seeking not so much an alternative world organization or government as a better tie between UN norm-creating and lawmaking activities and the voices of the unheard and the unrepresented, by opening up more space for and linkage with the nonstate social actors and movements struggling at the periphery of the present international system.

EXPANDING THE BOUNDS OF GLOBAL CONSTITUTIONALISM

Ironically, all the significant theories of world constitutionalism, including the Clark-Sohn model, have been postulated either implicitly or explicitly on the realist conception of "power" as the ability to control and maintain order. As Berenice A. Carroll argues sharply, a failure of peace research too lies precisely in its uncritical acceptance of the prevailing conception of power as social control; this is a pathway to the cult of violence disguised as "power" and a means of maintaining an international system of violence and injustice; peace research should shift away from its preoccupation with persons, groups, and institutions conceived as powerful toward an alternative conceptualization of power as social competence.[13]

Clearly, what is required is an alternative conceptualization of "power"—the power of the powerless—in contradistinction to the realist notion of power and violence (and power and hegemonic order) as mutually complementary. Drawing upon Carroll's feminist conception of "power as competence," we define power as "shared social competence" to collectively solve global problems, and to shape world order values and produce desired world order effects. The resort to force as an expression of power or as a way of maintaining social order, as manifest in the "body-count mentality" of the U.S. military in Vietnam in the 1960s, President Bush's rush to war in January 1991, and the law-and-order mentality of Deng Xiaoping and his cohorts in post-Tiananmen China, is really an expression of powerlessness, of peacemaking incompetence. The reconceptualization of power as social competence endows the powerless with an emancipatory opening. Embodied here is the rejection of the "enemy-of-my-enemy" logic of Realpolitik and the acceptance of the functionalist notion that the enemies of humankind are those pathological social forces threatening human survival, human needs, human rights, and human habitat.

In this reconceptualization of power as a positive, sharing, problem-solving competence, information is and becomes power, knowledge is and becomes power, and law too is and becomes power, opening up more functional and empowering ways of thinking and acting in the pursuit of a global human security system. The power of the UN lies not in military and economic resources, which the world body is congenitally ill-endowed to mobilize in any way except as an expression of superpower hegemony, but in the power of legitimacy. Legitimacy makes or unmakes any government in its domestic society. Likewise, legitimacy facilitates the exercise of UN authority; it is the oil that lubricates global normative politics—this is what the so-called "UN politics of collective legitimation and delegitimation" is all about. Legitimacy is the outer reach of Third World normative power. It is as well, the outer reach that the power of the powerless outside the UN. Above all, legitimacy is both the beginning and the end of the power of nonviolence, as it strikes at the heart of power elites by withdrawing the consent, obedience, and cooperation of the people. One dedicated, determined man, Rafael Lemkin, indeed exercised this power of legitimacy to its ultimate by becoming the main architect of a lasting monument to the Holocaust, the UN-sponsored Genocide Convention. Amnesty International under the leadership of Sean MacBride was largely instrumental in the adoption of the Anti-Torture Declaration and its codification into the Anti-Torture Convention. The UN Environmental Programme, with only a $34 million annual budget, equivalent to what the Pentagon spends every sixty minutes, is more competent and problem-solving than the U.S. war system in the exercise of the power of legitimacy via its crucial role in the development of global environmental norms and laws (e.g., the Vienna Convention and the Montreal Protocol on ozone protection of 1985–1987 and the draft Convention on Climate Change).

The conception of power as shared competence may serve as a defensive counter-Sisyphean mechanism to prevent us from falling back on calling only for changes that conform to the interests of the powers that be. Of course, social empowerment depends on the extent to which information, knowledge, and law are shared widely among social actors at all levels of human organization. It is no secret that secrecy is the lethal weapon of oppression in a totalitarian society; this also breeds a disregard for people's security and well-being even in such a democratic society as the United States, as manifest in the explosion in recent years of ecological time bombs at several ageing nuclear weapons plants. Information sharing and knowledge expansion as an integral part of shared social competence is a way of democratizing world order transition politics.

To translate shared social competence as a concept into new forms of ongoing social and political practice in an interdependent world requires democratic global constitutionalism. One of the few patterns that holds up in the modern history of international relations is that democracies generally do not fight against each other.[14] This means that the prospect of world peace is keyed to the widening zone of the democratic policies, as in the long peace in Western Europe. Another pattern that is less widely recognized but becoming increasingly obvious is that the viability of democracy within each polity has to be rethought in the context of the increasing globalization of international economic and political life. One lesson of the Cold War is that, in fighting fire with fire, democracies become less democratic and more authoritarian. Global constitutionalism would have to proceed from the Second Image Revised and Reversed thesis—global democratic forces too become the cause instead of just the consequence of domestic democracy.

The challenge is to seek a systemic framework that leads to the search for new understanding of the dynamics of democratic politics and that also shows the way to redirect our energies into new forms of political action. A framework for world order politics of this kind may be conceived of as consisting of three systems of intersecting politics. The first system, the states system, is comprised of territorial state actors and their supporting infrastructure of corporations, banks, military, and media. The second system consists of international intergovernmental organizations, including the United Nations. The third system is represented by nongovernmental citizens thinking globally but acting locally through the nongovernmental organizations (NGOs) and critical social movements.[15]

The emergence of the states system is a complicated historical phenomenon, to be sure, but we should not accept it as a natural or even immutable irreversible one. The spread of the state system to every corner of the world is relatively recent, with its largest expansion coming in the first two decolonizing decades of the post-war period. The same period has witnessed the more dramatic growth of international organizations, both intergovernmental and nongovernmental. The revolutionary changes of the postwar era have failed to transform the Westphalian states system. What has really happened is not so much the demise of the state as the progressive delegitimation of the states system. The general historical trend of recent years has been moving in the direction of rising authority/legitimacy crises in most states. This is the case because, on the one hand, most states are promising more and more with more and more laws yet delivering less and less, while, on the other, people everywhere are becoming more literate, urban, mobile, demanding, and politicized, with a rising threshold of intolerance for human deprivation and political oppression. In post-Tiananmen China, for example, oppression and legislation have been moving upward in tandem, while legitimation has been moving downward at almost equal speed.

At the core of this deepening legitimacy crisis is the widening promise/performance gap, as more and more states pursue security in a manner that seems to guarantee only insecurity. In the nuclear and ecological age, security is still defined in prenuclear terms, as if there were no connection between the security of the nation and the security of humankind and between elites' security and people's security. At the same time, many of the more significant, if less visible, sources of structural transformation can be found in both worldwide economic and technological transformations and subnational social movements. It is this confluence of changes at the second and third system levels, coupled with the deepening legitimacy crisis of the first system, that creates new possibilities for democratic global constitutionalism.

It is not possible to predict whether democratic global constitutional undertakings can be initiated in time to avert cataclysmic nuclear holocaust or ecological system collapse. The momentous but unexpectedly peaceful recent transformation of the bipolarized international "insecurity" systems sharply contradicts conventional realist wisdom that a world order transformation is possible only through a systemic global war, and as such is a hopeful sign for the nonviolent revolutionary quest for a new world order. One thing is sure, however: Our future is never predetermined; it is always the creation of the present and the present is always involved in the creation of our vision of the future. Of course, mere imaging of a preferred future without struggle amounts to no more than an armchair exercise in wishful thinking. The transition to a peaceful, humane, and just future world requires a series of concrete purposive measures designed to alter the present course of world politics. What is required is not a single approach through only one of the three systems but a synergist intersystemic approach linking up all the progressive forces of all three system levels in our common journey to a more peaceful and lawful future.

A democratic constitutional approach to world order has a positive role to play during the period of system transition, but only if it is grounded in the understanding that law by itself cannot work as a magic wand and only if it is responsive to, and linked with, the wider process of political change under way in the global community. At this juncture of the world historical process, there still exists a large gap "between the international law horizons of realistic feasibility and the world-order horizons of human necessity."[16] This gap can be bridged not so much by having more law or legal engineering as by positively interpreting and committing contemporary international law in the service of realizing world order values. World order populism without world order legalism lacks a normative lodestar, while world order legalism without world order populism lacks a democratic base and mobilizing energy. While acknowledging that law is part of politics and even indispensable in the value-clarifying and policymaking processes, we have to recognize, as well, that it has in the past generally worked better as an instrument of oppressive authoritarian "law and order" governments than as a normative restraint on their abuse of power.

The prospects for improving a democratic global constitutional approach depend on how social actors attempt to come to terms with the broad dynamics of change in an interdependent world, dynamics that pose both great systemic perils and new systemic opportunities for transition politics. In the realist first-system approach that pivots around international life at the level of the state alone, the connections between large-scale global processes and local social movements remain largely obscured. This is not to say that the state remains an island in the sea of change. All states are now caught up, in varying degrees, in the globalizing processes of economic, technological, social, cultural, and political transformation. The dilemma here is that we still live in a world in which people's security is monopolized by the state, yet many of the most important forces that affect people's security are beyond state control. Common security and people's security thus remain essential but elusive. Basically, there are two challenges: the challenge of connecting and mobilizing the progressive sectors of the first-, second-, and third-system actors vertically and horizontally; and the challenge of seeking a normative baseline consensus for uniting diverse social actors—and their feelings, thoughts, and actions—in the common journey towards a common human security system.

Most approaches to world order have been overly preoccupied with a dialectical framework of challenge and response at only one systemic level. If it is utopian to attempt to build a world system of enforceable world law on top of the second interstate system, which is after all a supplement to, not a substitute for, the states system, it seems almost as utopian to seek the nongovernmental, third-system approach to world order transformation by leaving the states system as the primary political reality of our times.

The synergistic intersystemic approach is premised upon the creative interplay of new understandings and new opportunities occurring in the first, second, and third systems. The appraisal of the state's role in world politics, especially in relation to world order values, is an open and controversial one, attracting diverse perceptions and analyses. As the dominant reality of contemporary international life the state has come to be identified with all destructive—and, at times, creative—potentials and tendencies of the international system. Even on the much touted role of the state as a positive vehicle of nationalism and nation building to ward off external pressures, the real story is more complicated and paradoxical. In most multinational states—according to one estimate, there are some two hundred states, but at least eight hundred movements of effective nationalism, and seven thousand potential nationalisms, if ethnicity is taken as the criterion[17]—states necessarily become an instrument of control for dominant nationalisms by oppressing subordinate nationalities within their borders.

Yet, challenged by the increasing complexity and vulnerability of modernity, the deepening legitimacy crisis and rising populist pressures from below, some states are capable of responding with creative normative initiatives. In the context of UN politics, many of the normative initiatives for the progressive development of international law have originated from the states of the Third World. To cite only a few notable examples: the 1963 initiative of Bolivia, Brazil, Chile, Ecuador, and Mexico for a nuclear-free zone in Latin America; China's pronouncement and popularization of the nuclear no-first-use principle in 1964; Malta's proposal for treating the oceans as a "common heritage of mankind" oceans in 1967; Mexico's leadership in formulating the Charter of Economic Rights and Duties of States in 1972; Algeria's initiative in January 1974 calling for the Sixth Special Session of the General Assembly to inaugurate the NIEO process; and Nicaragua's lawsuit against the United States in the World Court in 1984. In the process, in both of participants and subject matter, the frontiers of contemporary international law have been expanded to the point that it is possible now to speak of global law and global lawmaking.

Undoubtedly, the most significant and surprising statist normative initiative for a world constitutional order originated from the least expected source—the socialist citadel of superstatism, the Soviet

Union under the leadership of Mikhail Gorbachev. The Soviet proposal for "a comprehensive system of international security," first expounded in Gorbachev's unusual newspaper article, "Realities and Guarantees for a Secure World," in the September 17, 1987, issues of *Pravda* and *Izvestia,* and subsequently refined and elaborated in various official documents and the scholarly literature from 1987 to 1989,[18] is significant both in terms of its normative content and the new opening it offers to second- and third-system actors. It is surprising because it represents a remarkable breakaway from the entrenched and seemingly irreversible Soviet attitudes and policy toward international law and organization, underscoring in the process a role reversal of the two superpowers in the normative domain of world politics.

By and large, the Soviet Union in the pre-Gorbachev years acted out its siege mentality in UN politics, seeing itself as a beleaguered state in a permanent minority position, and reacting to any idea of supranational authority as both utopian and dangerous. Any revision of the Charter, in particular any change in the principle of unanimity, "would have a self-defeating effect and would destroy the entire structure of international law."[19] Viewed against this backdrop, Gorbachev's comprehensive system of international security—and the idea of expanding the sphere of "world governability" advanced by Georgi Shakhnazarov,[20] a close advisor to Gorbachev—is all the more surprising because it came at a time of precipitous Soviet status decline in world affairs.

At the core of the Soviet "new thinking" is a new concept of "security." The traditional concept of national and universal security based primarily on military means of defense is now pronounced to be obsolete. The idea of national security in an interdependent world is a mirage. Security needs to be defined instead in a multidimensional way, embracing the military, political, economic, humanitarian (including human rights), and ecological threats. Indeed, the concept of an interdependent world in the nuclear and ecological age provides the master key to resolve the antinomy between state sovereignty and universal sovereignty. As Foreign Minister Eduard Shevardnadze put it in his 1988 UN Speech,

> What we are speaking of now is voluntarily delegating a portion of national rights in the interests of all and, paradoxically enough, in order to strengthen national security while at the same time strengthening universal security. The interrelationship of events in an interdependent world increasingly compels us to delegate some national prerogatives to an international organization. In fact, this is already happening.[21]

The idea of the voluntary transfer of certain sovereign rights, via the United Nations and international law, to the world community as the way of enhancing national security and common global security can only be characterized as "revolutionary." As if to render credible such claims and to dramatize the role reversal of the two superpowers in the Security Council, the Soviet use of the veto in the Security Council, since 1985, has completely vanished, while the United States veto continued unabated, (until May 1990) at an average annual rate of six.

Equally revolutionary is the Chernobylization of foreign policy thinking—the notion that national security and national secrecy have now come into conflict. By establishing new, previously inconceivable, rules of transparency, the world is now moving toward creating "a common sovereign right—the right to survive.[22] The removal of secrecy, as shown in the recent exchange of Soviet and American inspectors for on-site inspections of each other's military facilities, is said to have become an important factor enhancing the sense of security. Verification, the longstanding Soviet bête noire and American joker in past arms control and disarmament negotiations, is now said to be no longer a mere preference but a definite imperative of our time. In this glasnost spirit, the Soviet Union proposed the establishment of an international monitoring and verification agency and an international register of conventional arms sales and supplies, all within the framework of the United Nations. In an ecological age, humans' so-called "peaceful constructive activity" without global control is turning into "a global aggression against the very foundations of life on earth."[23] Based on such ecological thinking, the Soviet Union endorsed the growing worldwide Green peace movement as well as the Brundtland Commission Report, *Our Common Future.* Also proposed has been a discussion on how to turn the United Nations Environmental Programme into a council capable of making effective decisions to ensure ecological security.

International law is the flip side of the comprehensive system of international security. "The Soviet Union is convinced," according to an official document submitted to the UN Secretary General, "that the comprehensive system of security is at the same time a system of universal law and order that ensures the primacy of international law in politics."[24] From states of law to a world of law—this is now claimed to be the logic of the inexorable global trend. For the enhancement of "universal security," resting upon politico-military, economic, humanitarian, and environmental guarantees, legal guarantees are viewed as of paramount importance. This is now a point of departure for a long-term development of international law. The nine-year Soviet involvement in Afghanistan had violated Soviet law and international norms of behavior, we are told, just as the Krasnoyarsk radar station was an open violation of the Anti-Ballistic Missile Treaty with the United States.[25] Notice, in contrast, the determination and high-tech military readiness with which George Bush disposed of the Vietnam syndrome—finally, it seems, a Vietnam-qua-Iraq could be bombed back into the Stone Age (e.g., 80 percent of Iraq's power grid is out of service) with catastrophic epidemiological and environmental crises threatening the entire region.

In the Soviet new thinking, the World Court was also to be revitalized to make more extensive use of its potential in solving outstanding international legal issues. To this end, the mandatory jurisdiction of the Court had to be recognized by all member states on mutually agreed terms. The UN General Assembly and Security Council could also contribute to the revitalization of this principal judicial organ of the United Nations by making greater use of the Court's advisory opinion. In February 1989, Moscow accepted without reservation the compulsory jurisdiction of the World Court with respect to six international human rights conventions, as well as recognizing the right of Soviet citizens to appeal to international organizations in human rights cases.

In essence the Soviet proposals amounted to a second-system reformist approach to world order. Almost every aspect of the comprehensive system of international security was keyed to giving the United Nations expanded authority in the management of common national-global problems in the military, political, economic, ecological, and human rights fields without going through the seemingly impossible Charter amendment process. Indeed, there was a craving for strengthening the UN as the most cost-effective way of making the world safe for Soviet internal economic development. Taken together the Soviet proposals constituted a call for a new global constitutional order.

The linkage between the Soviet proposals and the third, nongovernmental system remains yet to be fully tested. Still, Gorbachev by way of the comprehensive common security system seemed to be opting out of the arms race and the international system of the Cold War. If Gorbachev served as "the true midwife of German unity," as Foreign Minister Hans Dietrich Gensher publicly pronounced,[26] he has also gone further than any other statesmen in issuing an open and credible invitation to end the Cold War on the Korean peninsula paving the way for entry of the two Koreas into the United Nations. In the process he has deprived national security managers in the West of their "image-of-the-enemy" alibi, while at the same time opening up new space for third-system actors' movements for dealignment, democracy, and demilitarization.

Today, normative challenges and initiatives for a new world order mainly originate from social actors and movements in the third system who bear the brunt of the oppressive reality of the first system. They express our best hopes, if not always best ways, for world order transformation. Despite the transformational potential of these third-system actors, their actual achievements to date are rather meager. The challenge of vertical and horizontal connections has remained elusive. The slogan of peace activists—thinking globally, acting locally—has largely remained just a slogan, as Chadwick Alger and Saul Mendlovitz's study of grassroots movements confirms, for localists and globalists have worked in isolation from each other, diminishing the potential impact of linkage between the two. The problem, or what Alger and Mendlovitz aptly call "the local/global problematique," is also made manifest in varying approaches to transformation (i.e., ideological, spiritual, community-organizing, life style, and interpersonal).[27]

There is also the problem of horizontal issue linkage, as most social movements work as single-issue movements in the domain of their special concern. Given the limited material resources at their command, perhaps this is the best way to proceed. To date, the Green peace movement represents a rare example of horizontal and vertical linkages with substantial impact on the first system. We have a lot to learn from the Greens, whose empowerment grows out of the power of nonviolence, not out of the barrel of guns. Nonviolence is and becomes both the end and the means of peace politics.

The impact of most social movements on the second system varies from issue to issue, with the greatest influence from the UN's norm-making and standard-setting activities in the human rights and environmental fields but with virtually no influence in the economic field. Tellingly enough, the modest achievements of the United Nations in the arms control and disarmament field came about largely through the normative initiative and pressure of nonstate peace activists. The proliferation of nuclear-free zones is suggestive of the manner in which diverse social actors are carrying out the local solutions to global problems. This kind of populist social activism is another way of saying and showing that the slogan of peace activists—thinking globally and acting locally—requires nothing less than local responsibility to act globally. UN lawmaking provides an indispensable institutional nexus for catalyzing the local-global linkage politics and then canalizing people power into global lawmaking.[28]

The essential and inescapable point emerging from the preceding analysis is the need to redefine global constitutionalism as an organic part of the world democratizing process rather than as a set of fixed and enforceable rules of world politics. Even in domestic society, law is never separate from politics but always a necessary part of it, giving normative coherence and structure to the value-clarifying and policy-making process. In world politics, as in domestic politics, then, there is need for a teleological conception of lawmaking as an authoritative allocation of values as well as an affirmative instrument of goal pursuit, one that links law and politics as organic parts of the collective, cumulative process of world community building. Such a dialectical approach sees world politics and world law as the two sides of the same process, rejecting both the traditional positivist conception of international law, as the codified and consented body of state wills, and the more talismanic conception of world law, as exemplified in the Clark-Sohn world constitutional model. As well, a democratic global constitutional approach is skeptical of any grandiose schemes or legal-institutional blueprints as the master key to the promised land. Law is only one among several problem-solving and value-shaping instruments that can facilitate the pursuit of a more peaceful and just world order.

NOTES

1. Research for this paper was supported by the Peter B. Lewis Fund of Princeton University's Center of International Studies. I would also like to thank Richard A. Falk and Robert C. Johansen for their most helpful comments and suggestions on an earlier version of this paper.

2. F. H. Hinsley, *Power and the Pursuit of Peace* (New York: Cambridge University Press, 1967), p. 3.

3. Grenville Clark and Louis B. Sohn, *World Peace Through World Law* (Cambridge, MA: Harvard University Press, 1958; 2nd rev. ed., 1960; 3rd enlarged ed., 1966). All references in the present essay are based on the third enlarged edition. For the pioneering series of world order studies, see Saul H. Mendlovitz, ed., *Legal and Political Problems of World Order* (New York: Fund for Education Concerning World Peace Through World Law, 1962); Richard A. Falk and Saul H. Mendlovitz, eds., *Toward a Theory of War Prevention*, vol. 1; *International Law*, vol. 2; *The United Nations*, vol. 3; and *Disarmament and Economic Development*, vol. 4 (New York: World Law Fund, 1966).

4. Inis L. Claude, Jr., *Power and International Relations* (New York: Random House, 1962), chs. 6–7.

5. Quoted in Clark and Sohn, 3rd ed., p. xv.

6. Clark and Sohn, 3rd ed. p. xiii (emphasis in original).

7. For a more detailed treatment of this line of reasoning and analysis, see Richard A. Falk and Samuel S. Kim, eds., *The War System: An Interdisciplinary Approach* (Boulder, CO: Westview Press, 1980).

8. This second-edition Introduction is reproduced in the third edition. See Clark and Sohn, 3rd ed., pp. xv-liv, especially at p. xliii.

9. Clark and Sohn, 3rd ed., p. liv.

10. Benjamin B. Ferencz, *A Common Sense Guide to World Peace* (New York: Oceana Publications, 1985), Part 1, pp. 1-42.

11. National Conference of Catholic Bishops of the United States, *The Challenge of Peace: God's Promise and Our Response* (Washington, DC: United States Catholic Conference, 1983), p. 25 (emphasis added). For a critical analysis, see Samuel S. Kim, "The U.S. Catholic Bishops and the Nuclear Crisis," *Journal of Peace Research* 22, no. 4 (1985): 321-333.

12. For a careful but persuasive normative analysis along these lines see Burns H. Weston, "Security Council Resolution 678 and Persian Gulf Decision-Making: Precarious Legitimacy," *American Journal of International Law* 85, no. 3 (July 1991): 516-535.

13. Berenice A. Carroll, "Peace Research: The Cult of Power," *Journal of Conflict Resolution* 16, no. 4 (December 1972): 585-616.

14. Michael Doyle, "Liberalism and World Politics," *American Political Science Review* 80, no. 4 (December 1986): 1151-1169.

15. See Richard A. Falk, Samuel S. Kim, and Saul H. Mendlovitz, eds., *Toward a Just World Order* (Boulder, CO: Westview Press, 1982), pp. 1-10.

16. Richard A. Falk, *Revitalizing International Law* (Ames: Iowa State University Press, 1989), p. 62.

17. Ernest Gellner, *Nation and Nationalism* (Ithaca, NY: Cornell University Press, 1983), pp. 44-45.

18. See Richard A. Falk, Samuel S. Kim, and Saul H. Mendlovitz, eds., *The United Nations and a Just World Order* (Boulder, CO: Westview Press, 1991), pp. 166-177, 188-197, 542-545; Foreign Minister E. A. Shevardnadze's UN Speech of September 28, 1988, in Foreign Broadcast Information Service, Daily Report, Soviet Union, September 28, 1988, pp. 2-9; Georgi Shaknazarov, " 'Questions of Theory': The World Community Is Amenable to Government," *Pravda*, January 15, 1988, reprinted in *Alternatives* 14 (1989): 245-251.

19. See UN Doc. A/C.6/31/SR. 47 (1976), p. 9.

20. Shaknazarov, p. 250.

21. Shevardnadze, p. 4.

22. Shevardnadze, p. 4.

23. Shevardnadze, p. 7.

24. UN Doc. A/43/629, Annex (September 22, 1988), p. 6.

25. *The New York Times,* October 24, 1989, pp. A1, A14.

26. Quoted in *The New York Times,* September 13, 1990, p. A6.

27. Chadwick F. Alger and Saul H. Mendlovitz, "Grass-Roots Initiatives: The Challenge of Linkages," in Saul H. Mendlovitz and R. B. J. Walker, eds., *Toward a Just World Peace: Perspectives from Social Movements* (London: Butterworths, 1987), pp. 333-362.

28. Elise Boulding, "Peace Learning," in Raimo Vayrynen, ed., *The Quest for Peace* (Beverly Hills, CA: Sage, 1987), p. 327.

5

The Constitutional Element in International Political Economy

JAMES H. MITTELMAN

World order studies began as a critique of the nation-state system, a program to eliminate war and global inequality, a type of international reformism dedicated to the ideals of social justice. Positing that national sovereignty spawned most of the major global problems facing humankind, the architects of world order studies emphasized constitutional structure and legal models. They provided a conception of constitutionalism centering on the need for supranational institutions and legal process at the global level. More recently, this focus has broadened to account for transnational movements and values, inspiring a large number of scholarly works that offer a forward perspective of a peaceful and egalitarian world.

This essay is an acknowledgment of the world order movement's distinctive intellectual role in fusing the themes of constitutionalism and global transformation. My purpose here is to assess the contribution and limitations of world order studies as well as to suggest ways to link this line of inquiry to international political economy.

THE ANALYSIS OF GLOBAL PROBLEMS

Before delving into world order studies, it is important to be explicit about criteria of evaluation. Specifically, a discourse over the ultimate test of theory entails three competing claims. First, empiricism takes the world of experienced occurrences to be the object of scientific inquiry, and treats any appeal to underlying causes as unscientific metaphysics. Building on the positivist distinction between facts and values, empiricists hold that theories are verifiable in experience, and therefore refer to the flux of observable events. On this view of science, the definitive test of theory is its power of prediction, which is subject to falsification by the demonstration of contrary data.[1]

An alternative claim is contained in Marxist analysis of the class structure and politics of capitalism. In rejecting the empiricist notion that prediction is the ultimate test of theory, Marxists argue that reliance on brute facts to rebut concepts is not the way to prove or disprove theory. Empirical evidence itself does not suffice as a mode of resolution, since questions must first be posed at the theoretical level where concepts are established. For Marxists, theory is a means of action, and proof lies in historical practice. In other words, theory explains origins and delineates constraints emerging from historical structures. It probes limits imposed by contradictions and explores possibilities in the realm of strategy.

A third claim is advanced by a variety of non-Marxist theorists whose chief concern is the creation of a just society. John Rawls is clearly one of the leading contemporary thinkers in this tradition. Although it would take us too far afield to try to capture the richness and complexity of his work, Rawls's premise is that society is a "cooperative venture for mutual advantage." Justice is defined in terms of two principles grounded in the structure of society. First, each person is to have an equal right to the most extensive liberty compatible with similar liberty for others. Second, social and economic inequalities are to be arranged so that (a) they are to the greatest benefit of the least advantaged and (b) are attached to offices and positions open to all. Most important, for Rawls, what is in everyone's advantage means that the worst off person is better off than that person would be under any other arrangement. How does one determine the standards for making such a judgment and ascertain whether a society is acting in the interest of distributive justice? Ultimately, normative theorists like Rawls appeal to reflective intuitions about justice.[2]

Quite clearly, there is no common measure for gauging the utility of rival theories. The yardsticks most often employed—prediction, historical practice, and reflective intuitions—are widely divergent. One might argue in favor of eclecticism and, on this basis, regard the discrepancy among standards of evaluation as nonproblematic. But is it sensible to push this argument to the point of asserting that since theory must constantly develop, one should embrace a multitude of theories and, thus, a multiplicity of criteria of evaluation? I think not. New theoretical knowledge emerges in distinct contexts and grows out of the anomalies of existing theories. By anomalies, I mean inconsistencies and the gap between the expectations of theorists and unfolding events.[3]

To illustrate briefly, an international relations literature oriented in the mid- to late 1940s toward reducing state power in favor of regional and eventually global cooperation reflected optimistic expectations about the possibilities for economic harmony rooted in the post-World-War-II world order. But with the breakdown of the Bretton Woods system and mounting economic discord, theorists adopted a somewhat more sober view of the prospects for global harmony and sought to resurrect the study of political economy. Indicators of changing emphasis in a generation of scholarly literature are the shift from Ernst Haas's integration theory and David Mitrany's functionalism, on the one hand, to Robert Keohane's regime analysis and notion of hegemonic stability, George Modelski's long cycles, and Robert Gilpin's structural realism, on the other.[4]

Paralleling this shift in mainstream scholarship, Marxism encountered changing conditions and unexpected phenomena. The architects of socialism envisaged that the aftermath of working class revolutions would be marked by the easing of class distinctions, the diminution of the state, and internationalism among societies subscribing to Marxist principles. In fact, self-serving bureaucratic classes emerged, the state apparatus ossified, and societies that professed to be socialist went to war with each other.[5]

There developed a variety of new approaches to explain such unanticipated phenomena. Charles Bettelheim argues that although the Soviet Union claimed to uphold the banner of socialism, its pattern of development should properly be understood as state capitalism.[6] As regards Eastern Europe, Rudolf Bahro similarly shows that "actually existing socialism" strayed from a Marxist course.[7] Taking a global approach, Immanuel Wallerstein and his colleagues contend that there is a single world economy, and it is capitalist, such world systems theorists also maintain that socialism cannot emerge within the interstices of capitalism. Revolutions may help countries change their niche in the international division of labor, but socialism will be born only when the organism of capitalism is moribund. The destruction of capitalism involves the creation of a new order: a socialist world government.[8]

When an existing theory fails to account for changing conditions, it is open to challenge from either within or outside its own set of premises. Critics can accept the bedrock values and goals of a theoretical tradition, or they may identify questions and issues produced by a different paradigm. It is the responsibility of the critic to be exacting and honest about the moral preferences upon which a particular line of reasoning rests. One should be forthright in acknowledging underlying assumptions, for the social sciences do not admit of immaculate perception.

In this respect, world order inquiry is exemplary, even if one disagrees with the priorities set by its advocates or the prospects for achieving them. The standard that world order authors adopt is neither predictive nor a dialectical conception of historical practice. Rather, world order studies rest on explicit commitment to a set of values intuitively derived: peace, economic well-being, social justice, ecological stability, and positive self-identity. Meant to provide a basis for inquiry and action, these values are advanced not merely within a national setting, but primarily in a global context.

WORLD ORDER VALUES

Informed by both this value framework and diagnostic research on planetary dangers, world order scholars design models of envisaged futures. These models are not straight-line projections of current trends and patterns. Rather, authors are encouraged to be inventive and to propose transitional strategies linking preferred futures to the values posited at the outset. The modelling process thus entails testing hypotheses and developing scenarios for social transformation.

The contributions of this approach are several.[9] To begin with theory, world order studies take us beyond the limits of positivism, the fact–value distinction deeply ingrained in the conventions of social science, by making a compelling case for normative social research. The identification of explicit values undergirds an integrated view of the human condition. But besides warning against the dangers of legalism and formalism, world order authors advance a broad sociological approach to problems that defy national solutions and are global in scope: war, poverty, social injustice, environmental decay, and alienation. Furthermore, the authors are iconoclasts who early had the courage of their convictions to break with state-centered models. Contributors to the "Preferred Worlds for the 1990s" series proposed alternative systems compatible with a just world order.[10] So, too, have Saul Mendlovitz and Rajni Kothari in co-editing *Alternatives,* a journal launched in 1974 to promote a future world order. Although its internal critics have cautioned that world order thinking can serve as an ideology of Western domination and a genre of cultural imperialism,[11] Mendlovitz and his colleagues have sought to promote transnational and cross-cultural research.[12]

On the other hand, what are the shortcomings of world order studies? One criticism centers on their decision to use a broad, eclectic theoretical framework. For Mendlovitz, this decision "is based on the conviction that amongst existing theories of political process and law, no single theory is capable of dealing with the range of problems we shall be discussing."[13] Some analysts defend this position by cautioning against the genetic fallacy—attempting to rebut an argument by reference to its sources, rather than to the strengths and weaknesses of the argument itself. In this view, there is nothing wrong with building a novel argument out of several disparate theoretical sources to formulate a coherent position. Punching home this point, one observer notes: "Pure theoretical archetypes, operating in airtight containers are not the fount of all knowledge."[14]

True, insistence on theoretical purity is a weak argument. But eclecticism, like other approaches, can be judged on its logical consistency. At issue is whether theories, in their underlying assumptions and modes of analysis, are incommensurable. For example, class and elite analysis: The Marxist concept of class springs from production and posits continuous conflict among social forces in a capitalist era. Elite analysis emerged in the work of Mosca and Pareto as an explicit alternative to class analysis. Dialectical and nondialectical conceptions are juxtaposed. In the Marxist case, the bourgeoisie is locked in opposition to the popular classes. In the other, the major historical actors are one or a combination of elites—the military, intellectuals, political officials, etc.—while the masses are passive; contradictions do not drive history; and conflicts are reconcilable. Any synthesis of these two approaches invites logical inconsistencies. The point is not to counsel intolerance, but to encourage rigorous analysis and sharp distinctions.

One such distinction is apparent from outside the parameters of a world order framework. From a political economy vantage point, the emphasis of world order analysis on building constitutional models or preferred futures is too abstract, too remote from historical analysis. Modelling runs the risk of becoming a mechanistic exercise without grounding in concrete historical conditions. As noted, concepts and theories must be understood in light of their changing context. Historical inquiry produces explanation through the use of case studies, the identification of contingent relationships, and critical analysis of competing interpretations. Historical context is integral to comparative judgment, for such reasoning helps to develop standards for the validity of lessons and parallels, as well as the values of and risks in generalization.[15]

This is not to say that world order thinking is ahistorical. Indeed, Mendlovitz contends that "three major historical processes, or, if you will, revolutions, have propelled humankind towards global community, and now towards global governance." These are "the ideological revolution of egalitarianism, the technological and scientific revolution, and the closely allied industrial-cybernetic revolution.[16] But what is crucial is causality. To claim that most global problems "are generally aggravated if not directly caused by the imperatives of national sovereignty"[17] is to argue by assertion. War, poverty, social injustice, environmental decay, and alienation all existed before the 1648 Treaty of Westphalia legitimated and regularized the nation-state system. Before 1648 there was no dearth of conquest, slavery, feudal bondage, looting, depletion of natural resources, murder and expulsions of collectivities.

Moreover, in the modern era following colonialism, national sovereignty is but a thin veneer covering permeable political systems and porous economies. Even so, nationalism is thriving. Its stirrings arise from an ideology that benefits only a small segment of society. The deeper issue is: What are the enabling conditions for the promulgation and widespread adoption of this ideology?

This takes us to power. Even if politics is the decisive center of power, world order studies have been remiss in not actually entering the abode of production. World order theorists do not tell us how to conceptualize the labor process and its relationship to the state system.[18] Such criticism clearly emanates from outside a world order approach, and pushes world order studies toward a political economy framework.

CHALLENGES AND NEW DIRECTIONS

In recent decades, analysts have reconstituted a political economy approach because we are witness to and actors in a period of structural change. Structural analysis is in vogue, but what is meant by structure? And which structures are key to the future of world order?

Perhaps the most important refinements in thinking about structural analysis are contained in the work of Anthony Giddens. In his usage, structures are enduring properties with institutional features. These properties constitute rules and resources that may be transformational. They provide the limits of and possibilities for the exercise of power. To cite Giddens' apt phrase, structures get at the "circuit switches" of system reproduction and transformation.[19] Structures both enable and constrain historical actors, whereas agency denotes the events perpetrated by actors in a context in which they could have acted differently.[20] Put in this way, one can move beyond the structure–agency debate. The concepts of structure and agency may be seen as complementary. To think of human agency as structured does not diminish its importance.[21] Furthermore, it is wrong to convert an analysis of structures into structuralism. This form of inquiry banishes history, leaving the state without actors.[22]

Let us now turn to three levels of structure: ideology, politics, and economics. From the standpoint of world order, the corresponding areas that merit further attention are nationalism, democratization, and the reform movement in collectivist societies. Obviously, there are other challenges and directions that could be discussed, but I will limit my comments to these aspects.

Nationalism

The salience of ideology derives from the institutional order of modern capitalism. This is not a type of order like any other, but the first form of societal organization to encompass the entire globe. It has been built upon the formation of nation-states and the internationalization of capital. The development and reproduction of this system is closely associated with the expansion of consensus. If consensus does not work, the system resorts to coercion. More typically, however, the system draws legitimacy from a mix of consensus and coercion, consensus being the dominant element.[23]

Properly understood, nationalism is an ideological mechanism for advancing the interests of dominant strata and securing consent within domestic society. Internationalism universalizes the values of the nation-state system and thereby maintains the relations of structured domination. The correlation between nationalism and internationalism is a dynamic interchange linked to concrete economic and social conditions. This shifting balance is neatly illustrated by recent debates in the United States over foreign economic policy, especially the call for protectionism, and educational policy. For the sake of brevity, I will merely touch on the economic context and then discuss the upsurge of nationalist ideology in the sphere of higher education.

During the 1970s alone, approximately 32 million jobs were lost in the United States.[24] At the same time, millions of jobs, mainly in the service sector, were created, too. Job turnover, unemployment, and economic disruption were all intense. Threatened by economic change, confronted by a global economy not under the control of their own government, those susceptible to such forces have lashed out. But against what? The global economy is a difficult target. The panoply of targets selected by the marginalized, fundamentalists and other groups on the far right includes world government and global education.[25]

During the Reagan years, there was a systemic reordering of national priorities and policies, nationalism unmistakably taking precedence over internationalism. There were major foreign policy shifts during the two terms of the Reagan Administration: more unilateralism, less global cooperation, reduced commitment to the key institutions and norms of the international system, such as the United Nations. There is no doubt that the Reagan years marked major changes in U.S. foreign policy attitudes and practice.[26] Indeed, a study by Eugene Wittkopf documents the fact that internationalism was supported by fewer Americans in the early 1980s than at any other time in the post-war period.[27] While these trends do not strictly demonstrate right-wing assaults on internationalist thinking, they provide a fertile environment for the resurgence of nationalism and, in some cases, intolerance of competing viewpoints.

Struggles over curriculum have arisen in this climate. Two books that appeared on best-seller lists, E. D. Hirsch's *Cultural Literacy* and Allan Bloom's *The Closing of the American Mind*,[28] are framed in a global perspective and embrace a world view that merits careful scrutiny. Numerous reviewers of different persuasions have failed to dig out their ideological underpinnings.

The problem with American education, as Hirsch and Bloom see it, is that students do not know enough and cannot think well enough to function in modern society. For these observers, the blame lies with popular culture, elementary and secondary schools, misguided teachers who offer vocational and trendy subjects, and an incoherent curriculum. Their real culprit, however, is moral relativism: the belief that one opinion is as good as another, one fact as salient as the next, and none transcendent above its cultural or historical context.

A mastery of national culture, Hirsch argues, is essential to the ability to communicate. While cautioning that nationalism may become excessive, Hirsch claims that multicultural education should not be the main focus in schools. While multicultural study imparts tolerance and perspective, it should not interfere with the teaching of "American literate culture."[29] Although his style is generally less combative than Bloom's, Hirsch nonetheless advances a provocative thesis: The absolute standard for education is core information about national—not local or world—culture, itemized in a 64-page list compiled by the author and two of his colleagues at the University of Virginia.

For Bloom, "a smattering of facts learned about other nations or cultures" and relativism, or "openness" to different ways of life have eclipsed the real purpose of higher education: the quest for a good life. The crisis of liberal education consists of our incapacity to recognize the lack of "a unified view of nature and man's place in it," the view when great minds debated on the highest level. The number of students who know about and love Western Europe has dwindled, replaced by students focusing on Third World countries and their development needs. "This is not learning from others but condescension and a disguised form of a new imperialism. It is the Peace Corps mentality. . . . "[30]

Nowhere do the anti-relativists take insensitivity to, or ignorance about, other cultures to be a problem. Nowhere do the anti-relativists consider ethnocentrism to be a shortcoming. Rather, Bloomians claim the moral relativist argument to be the extreme of absolute tolerance of all beliefs. Presumably, these beliefs include genocide, anti-Semitism, and racism—a position few relativists would defend. Anti-relativists such as Bloom fail to grasp that it is an incapacity to take the place of the other, a pervasive provincialism, that is at the root of an inability to make moral judgments. It is not moral relativism, as the champions of national culture and insularity would have it, but a parochial form of moral ideology that precipitates indifference.[31]

Democratization

Very broadly, the ideological mechanisms of the capitalist state serve as a structural constraint on democratic participation. While democracy allows for the expansion of political and social rights, the capitalist state separates production and politics, and maintains a class bias in public policy. Democratic rights—freedom of speech, suffrage, assembly, etc.—are a necessary but by no means sufficient condition for remedying the ills of capitalist life.[32]

In its search for remedies the former Soviet Union did not fare well. For Moscow, economic growth was problematic. What is more, the Chernobyl tragedy showed the inadequacies of the Soviet system of management. In the mid-1980s, the war in Afghanistan persisted without resolution. So, too, the situation in Eastern Europe—with unrest among Polish workers, ethnic tensions in Yugoslavia, experiments with the market in Hungary—remained unquiet. Democracy offered a possible way out. The Soviet press gained a measure of freedom and began to exert pressure on a bloated bureaucracy. There followed the freeing of political prisoners and the return to prominence of the 1960s intelligentsia. With the ascendancy of the Gorbachev reform coalition, the Central Committee advanced democratization as a major element of perestroika,[33] but failed to satisfy societal demands.

Meanwhile, a vigorous debate over the meaning and institutional forms of democracy has emerged in Latin America. Adopting Maria Helena Moreira Alves' categories, it may be useful to outline four schools of thought on democratization.[34] In brief, liberal definitions of representative democracy center on public influence on government through such institutions as political parties, regular elections, and alternation of parties in power. But the difficulty in attempting to graft this Western model onto the Third World is that the internationalization of capital is highly uneven. Large segments of society are excluded from economic benefits. This unevenness provides a fertile climate for political instability and lessens the chances for the institutionalization of democracy.

In countries such as Brazil, Argentina, and Chile, "guided democracy" has allowed for the slow institutionalization of political participation and has slightly broadened the base of authoritarian regimes.[35] Nonetheless, the implantation of a "controlled and gradual process of democracy" has meant neither an end to the mechanisms of repression nor a transformation of social relations. Rather, the concept of "authoritarian democracy" may be understood as a way to give the state a facelift while safeguarding the privileges of the few.

Many members of the Catholic Church in Latin America have staked out a reformist position on democratization. Mindful of liberation theology, they hold that it is not sufficient to institutionalize a system of representative democracy. Through vote buying, clientelism, and influence peddling, liberal democracies tend to reproduce patterns of domination. To stop those with economic power from shaping policy decisions, the proponents of communitarian democracy call for alternative mechanisms to increase the influence of the marginalized sectors of the population. The proposals do not embody revolutionary change but rather reforms initiated by community-based organizations: neighborhood associations, women's movements, and popular councils in municipalities. These organizations have in fact been formed with varying degrees of success in Brazil, Nicaragua, and Chile.[36]

In Central America, there is a distinct discourse over what constitutes a democratic government in the context of mass poverty. For groups seeking radical change, the accent is on participant democracy. A truly democratic state is understood as a means to eliminate the marginalization of the poorest sectors of society and to build institutional mechanisms that provide access to power for subaltern classes. From this perspective, democracy cannot be achieved without social equality.[37]

So, too, in Africa. Of what good to a peasant producer are constitutional guarantees of the political rights of an individual if he or she cannot read or write? What good are these constitutional guarantees to a peasant uncertain whether scratching the earth will ensure bare subsistence? At issue is sheer survival. Constitutional guarantees of freedom of expression, assembly, suffrage, and other rights are disembodied abstractions, mere formalism, if democracy is not accompanied by social equality and economic development.[38]

In Africa's first three decades of independence, developmentalism meant that the state would attend to the production and distribution of goods if the masses turned a blind eye to democracy and pledged their political support to the ruling order. Now with Africa in the throes of a protracted economic crisis, this social contract is no longer in force. The issue of democracy is on the agenda, a cause that motivates a variety of popular movements in Africa.[39]

For South Asia, Rajni Kothari notes the effects of the ecological and cultural crisis wrought by "modernization."[40] Apparently, the state proved incapable of providing the kind of development consistent with the needs and aspirations of the people. Hence, feminists and minority groups are trying to limit the power of the state and initiate democratic reorganization. These groups seek to achieve human and civil rights, broadly construed. As von Freyhold rightly observes, despite all the differences between regions and countries, "capitalism is creating a global predicament which provokes similar answers."[41]

Reform

Achieving democracy entails structural reform. Whereas revolution means a rapid restructuring of social relations in which a dominant class is replaced by subaltern classes, reform is a gradual change of institutions and the roles they play. A revolution is a rupture with the past. However, the objective of reform is to maintain the essential features of the existing order. Mao sought to transform the pre-1949 social order, but Deng Xiaoping is committed to maintaining the hegemony of the Communist Party and the state's control of the macro-economy. To this end, Deng and his associates have engineered structural reforms: large-scale and long-term changes, perhaps of several decades' duration. Those structural reforms have engendered distinctive problems and a series of predicaments.

One is the tension between the establishment of pace-setting regions versus a commitment to an egalitarian ethic. The State Council of China has decided that some provinces will be national pace-setters for reform and thus serve as locomotives to power the economic growth of the country. It is deemed necessary to make regional advances so that economic structures will form a "staircase pattern." Thus, the coastal region of Guangdong has large areas of mountainous and contiguous territory that evince slow economic growth. Yet also in Guangdong Province, Shenzhen is reputedly China's fastest-growing city and the largest of China's four special economic zones, designated environments driven by overseas capital and participation in the international division of labor. Cheap labor is a crucial factor of production in Shenzhen's expanding import and export trade.

The cost of this pattern of growth is uneven development among and within regions, accompanied by heightened disparities in income distribution. Regionalism has created inefficiencies: a reluctance to integrate provincial markets and cooperate in building economic infrastructure. Then, too, there is the matter of whether the rationale for lifting controls on the market to let loose the creative energies of the regions is reminiscent of a "trickle-down" approach. Research on other countries suggests that a trickle-down strategy does not filter wealth to the direct producers.[42] Severe regional imbalances run the risk of polarizing society beyond politically tolerable limits.

Another dilemma centers on sectoral priorities. What political difference does it make if one begins with agricultural reform, as did China from 1979 to 1984, and then gives priority to urban areas? Closely related, should one introduce economic reforms and postpone political reforms? Or should one emphasize the political dimension at the outset before turning to the economic aspect of reform, as in Gorbachev's Soviet Union?[43]

A third dilemma concerns what types of openings to the outside world are appropriate. Should China direct its international efforts primarily toward integration in the regional division of labor? Given the dynamism of the Pacific Basin's "little tigers," should China seek to align itself with the economically open and outward-looking countries in Asia? Or is there danger in borrowing from models built on dissimilar foundations (land scarcity, lack of resources, etc.)? Is there also a problem in adopting incompatible technologies?

There is no easy way out of these dilemmas, for the model of central planning is in general crisis. While its failings have spawned market reforms, experience in the West also reflects failures of the market. Some problems cannot be solved by the market. Structural reform in planning offers the possibility of success if democracy in economic processes and in political institutions are intertwined. To work, economic self-determination and political democracy must coalesce.[44]

Economic reformism, as well as the vitality of nationalist ideologies and the move toward political democracy, all indicate that the nation-state is still the dominant social unit in the world arena. World order scholars call for international reform, but as their framework highlights, it is only national reform that is the order of the day. The push for conservative educational reform in the United States, the former Soviet Union's emphasis on perestroika, and China's opening to the market all have been based on or directed at national-level choice. Although these programs have transnational dimensions, the persistence of a world order anchored in the nation-state system is patent.

What counteracts this pattern is the increasing integration of the global economy. The changing international division of labor constrains national choice. In recent years, the major changes in the international division of labor include the migration of industrial activities, especially component manufacture and assembly, from industrialized to Third World countries. This relocation has been facilitated by technological innovation providing for greater specialization in the production process. The new arrangement is linked to conversion to export-oriented industrialization that offsets high production costs in older sites. A more mobile, flexible form of capitalist production creates a different labor force—itself mobile, in some cases cheaper, and often without entitlement to social welfare or basic services.[45]

The main point is that production in the late twentieth century is an increasingly global rather than national process. The emergent international division of labor generates systemic pressures on the nation-state system. Even if the nation-state remains the major focus of identity, the international division of labor sets narrower limits on the possibility of local response.

CONCLUSION

World order studies emphasize that theory has a normative purpose: to maintain or transform social conditions. Under no circumstances is theory a passive reflection of social conditions. Since what constitutes society is always changing, it would be wrong, however, to rest a case for global transformation on an intuitive, undertheorized concept of constitutionalism.

It is not my intent to underestimate the significance of constitutional arrangements. On the contrary, the social relevance of constitutions derives from the allocation of economic rewards and political power. Moreover, constitutions are means to maintain or create the conditions for social harmony, thereby providing an aura of legitimacy. Constitutionalism may stand at the center of theory insofar as it is understood as embodying the rules and resources, the limits to and promise of, the transformation of world order.

If our studies are to have bearing on the future of world order, our sights must be raised to confront the interconnections among nationalist ideology, the challenge of democratization, and economic reform movements. The great unresolved issue of the modern era is the contradiction between an embedded nation-state system and the anarchy of capitalist production. Tugging world order in opposite directions is the dialectic of nationalism and the internationalization of national economies. These are the principal forces that will shape the future world order.

NOTES

1. Jeffrey C. Isaac, *Power and Marxist Theory: A Realist View* (Ithaca, NY: Cornell University Press, 1987), pp. 9, 20.

2. John Rawls, *A Theory of Justice* (Cambridge, MA: Harvard University Press, 1971), pp. 4, 302-303; and Alan Ryan, "John Rawls," in Quentin Skinner, ed., *The Return of Grand Theory in the Human Sciences* (Cambridge: Cambridge University Press, 1985), pp. 101-119. On a Rawlsian component in international relations, see Charles R. Beitz, *Political Theory and International Relations* (Princeton, NJ: Princeton University Press, 1979), pp. 125-176; and Peter Manicas, "Liberal Theories of Justice" (mimeo, University of Hawaii, n.d.).

3. Thomas J. Biersteker, "Historical Discontinuities and Theory Development in International Political Economy" (unpublished paper, May 1984), pp. 2-3; and Thomas Kuhn, *The Structure of Scientific Revolutions* (Chicago: University of Chicago Press, 1970.

4. Ernst B. Haas, *Beyond the Nation-State: Functionalism and International Organization* (Stanford, CA: Stanford University Press, 1964); David Mitrany, *A Working Peace System* (Chicago: Quadrangle Books, 1966); Robert 0. Keohane, *After Hegemony: Cooperation and Discord in the World Political Economy* (Princeton, NJ: Princeton University Press, 1984); George Modelski, "The Long Cycle of Global Politics and the Nation State," *Comparative Studies in Society and History* 20; (April 1978): 214-238; Robert Gilpin, *The Political Economy of International Relations* (Princeton, NJ: Princeton University Press, 1987).

5. Paul M. Sweezy, *Post-Revolutionary Society* (New York: Monthly Review Press, 1980), pp. 134-138.

6. Charles Bettelheim, *Class Struggles in the USSR I: First Period, 1917–1923* (New York: Monthly Review Press, 1976).

7. Rudolf Bahro, *The Alternative in Eastern Europe,* tr. David Fernbach (London: Verso, 1981).

8. Immanuel Wallerstein, *The Capitalist World-Economy* (Cambridge: Cambridge University Press, 1979), esp. p. 34; and Christopher

K. Chase Dunn, ed., *Socialist States in the World-System* (Beverly Hills: Sage, 1982).

9. This evaluation of world order studies builds on James H. Mittelman, "World Order Studies and International Political Economy," *Alternatives* 11, no. 3 (Winter 1983/84): 325-349.

10. On preferred worlds for the 1990s, the capstone work is Saul H. Mendlovitz, ed., *On the Creation of a Just World Order: Preferred Worlds for the 1990s* (New York: Free Press, 1975).

11. Fouad Ajami, "World Order: The Question of Ideology," *Alternatives* 6, no. 3 (Winter 1980/81): 473-485; Rajni Kothari, *Towards a Just World,* WOMP Working Paper No. 11 (New York: Institute for World Order, 1980), p. 23.

12. Richard A. Falk and Saul H. Mendlovitz, eds., *The Strategy of World Order,* 4 vols. (New York: World Law Fund, 1966); Richard A. Falk and Saul H. Mendlovitz, eds., *Regional Politics and World Order* (San Francisco: Freeman, 1973); Richard A. Falk, Samuel S. Kim, and Saul H. Mendlovitz, eds., *Toward a Just World Order* (Boulder, CO: Westview Press, 1982); and Saul H. Mendlovitz and R. B. J. Walker, eds., *Toward a Just World Peace: Perspectives from Social Movements* (London: Buttersworth, 1987).

13. Saul H. Mendlovitz, ed., *Readings and a Discussion Guide for a Seminar on Legal and Political Problems of World Order* (New York: Fund for Education Conerning World Peace through Wold Law, 1962), p. viii. The eclecticism expressed here is characteristic of world order studies.

14. James A. Caporaso, "The International Division of Labor: A Theoretical Overview," in James A. Caporaso, ed., *A Changing International Division of Labor* (Boulder, CO: Lynne Rienner, 1987), p. 40.

15. Michael Fry, *History and International Studies* (Washington, DC: American Historical Association, 1987), pp. 10, 12.

16. Mendlovitz, *Creation of a Just World Order,* "Introduction," p. xvi.

17. Mendlovitz, *Creation of a Just World Order,* "Introduction," p. viii.

18. For a seminal attempt to relate the labor process to the state, see Michael Burawoy, *The Politics of Production: Factory Regimes Under Capitalism and Socialism* (London: Verso, 1985).

19. Anthony Giddens, *The Constitution of Society: Outline of the Theory of Structuration* (Berkeley and Los Angeles: University of California Press, 1984), pp. 23-24.

20. Giddens, p. 9.

21. Isaac, pp. 33-38.

22. An example of structuralism is Barry Hindess and Paul Q. Hirst, *Pre-Capitalist Modes of Production* (London: Routledge & Kegan Paul, 1975).

23. Consensual ideology constitutes the core of Gramsci's concept of hegemony. See Antonio Gramsci, *Selections from the Prison Notebooks,* trans. and ed. Quintin Hoare and Geoffrey Nowell Smith (London: Lawrence and Wishart, 1971); and Robert W. Cox, *Production, Power, and World Order: Social Forces in the Making of History* (New York: Columbia University Press, 1987).

24. Barry Bluestone and Bennett Harrison, *The Deindustralization of America* (New York: Basic Books, 1982), p.26.

25. See James A. Caporaso and James H. Mittelman, "The Assault on Global Education," *PS: Political Science & Politics* 21, no. 1 (Winter 1988): 36-44. Some of the passages below draw on this article.

26. The decline of internationalism is discussed more fully by Thomas L. Hughes, "The Twilight of Internationalism." *Foreign Policy,* no. 61 (Winter 1985/86): 25-48; and Morris H. Morley, ed., *Crisis and Confrontation: Ronald Reagan's Foreign Policy* (Totowa, NJ: Rowman and Littlefield, 1988).

27. Eugene R. Wittkopf, "On the Foreign Policy Beliefs of the American People: A Critique and Some Evidence," *International Studies Quarterly* 30, no. 4 (December 1986): 434.

28. E. D. Hirsch, Jr., *Cultural Literacy: What Every American Needs to Know* (Boston: Houghton Mifflin, 1987). Allan Bloom, *The Closing of the American Mind: How Higher Education Has Failed Democracy and Impoverished the Souls of Today's Students* (New York: Simon and Schuster, 1987).

29. Hirsch, p. 18.

30. Bloom, p. 34, 346-347.

31. I have elaborated on these themes in "Opening the American Mind: International Political Science," *PS: Political Science & Politics* 22, no. 1 (Winter 1989): 40-44.

32. Isaac, pp. 176-77, 228.

33. Boris Kagarlitsky, "Perestroika: The Dialectic of Change," *New Left Review,* no. 169 (May-June 1988): 63-83.

34. Maria Helena Moreira Alves, "Democratization Versus Social Equality in Latin America: Notes for Discussion," paper presented to the Conference on Comparative Politics: Research Perspectives for the Next 20 Years, City University of New York Graduate School, September 7-9, 1988.

35. See Guillermo O'Donnell, *Bureaucratic Authoritarianism: Argentina in Comparative Perspective, 1966–1973* (Berkeley and Los Angeles: University of California Press, 1988); and Guillermo O'Don-

nell and Philippe C. Schmitter, eds., *Transitions from Authoritarian Rule: Tentative Conclusions about Uncertain Democracies* (Baltimore: Johns Hopkins University Press, 1986).

36. Alves, pp. 13-16.

37. Alves, pp. 17-22.

38. Claude Ake, "The African Context of Human Rights," *Africa Today* 34, nos. 1/2 (November 1987): 5-12.

39. Issa Shivji, "Reawakening of Politics in Africa," lecture, University of California, Institute of International Relations, Berkeley, September 19, 1984, cited by Michaela von Freyhold, "Labour Movements or Popular Movements in Africa," *Review of African Political Economy*, no. 39 (September 1987): 30-31.

40. Rajni Kothari, "Peace and Human Rights," *END Journal*, April-May 1985, cited by von Freyhold, p. 31.

41. Von Freyhold, p. 31.

42. James H. Mittelman, *Out from Underdevelopment: Prospects for the Third World* (London: Macmillan, New York: St. Martin's Press, 1988), especially pp. 89-108.

43. These and related questions are raised by Michael Oksenberg, "Reflections on the Process of Great Political Reform," paper presented to the Conference on Comparative Politics: Research Perspectives for the Next 20 Years, City University of New York Graduate School, September 7-9, 1988, especially p. 23.

44. For a more complete account of these dilemmas, see James H. Mittelman, "The Dilemmas of Reform in Post-Revolutionary Societies," *International Studies Notes* 15, no. 2 (Spring 1990): 65-70; also, Robert W. Cox, "Economic Reform and the Social Structure of Accumulation in Socialist Countries," paper presented to the World Congress of the International Political Science Association, Washington, D.C., August 28–September 1, 1988.

45. Folker Fröbel, Jurgen Heinrichs, and Otto Kreye, *The New International Division of Labor* (Cambridge: Cambridge University Press, 1980); and Caporaso, *Changing International Division of Labor.*

6

Ecological Security in an Interdependent World

PATRICIA M. MISCHE

THE GREAT WALL

Between the fifth and third centuries B.C., a series of walls were built in northern China by several of the seven warring kingdoms that then made up China. The goal: to establish and protect their separate sovereignties and to ensure their security against nomadic invaders. Despite these walls, in 221 B.C. the armies of Qin Shi Huang were able to conquer the other six kingdoms, making Qin the first historical emperor of a united China. To consolidate his power and assert imperial sovereignty, Qin ordered that those portions of the walls dividing the kingdoms be demolished, and those running along the northern frontier be connected and extended in a new Great Wall more than six thousand kilometers long. Over three hundred thousand men were commandeered for the ten-year project and forced to work under great hardship; many died in the process.

Qin's ultimate purpose was immortality through a dynastic reign that would continue in perpetuity. But his new dynasty was short-lived: Only fifteen years later it was replaced by the Han dynasty. And today, not many outside China know the name of the man who ordered the Great Wall.

Over the centuries, the Wall fell into disrepair, a victim of the forces of nature. A number of rulers ordered it reconstructed or extended, but inevitably nature reclaimed it. Today, although its remaining portions are maintained as a legacy of human achievement (it is one of the few human-made structures visible from space), the Great

Wall has no real significance, other than as a symbol, for the security and sovereignty of China. In fact, it is a testimony to the long-term failure and folly of the human quest for territorial sovereignty.

The Wall is dwarfed by the mountain reaches on which it stands like a thin, nervous line. Life and power lie in the mountains, which support a myriad of plant and animal species. Microorganisms turn stone to soil; insects, rodents, and goats traverse the wall's ruins, nibbling plants that grow through the cracks, oblivious to humans' grand designs. Trees on the slopes provide wood for fuel and homes; their roots hold soil and water against erosion and drought. Rain and melting snow flow in rivulets down the slopes, then converge in gushing rivers on their course toward lowland rice paddies and wheat fields that feed much of China's population of one billion people. China's security, now and in the future, depends ultimately on the integral functioning of these dynamic and interactive earth processes.

It also depends on economic health. Thus each year the wall is overrun by thousands of foreign tourists, bringing foreign currency and foreign ways. Their presence is tolerated, even sought, because Chinese leaders know that a favorable balance of payments may be a stronger foundation for security in an era of global economic competition than is military power or sovereign walls. The Great Wall's strategic benefit for China today is not that keeps people out, but that it brings them in.

Long ago, cannons, and more recently tanks, planes, and missiles, rendered obsolete such walled defenses around castles and countries alike. But even though the walls and castles have become tourist attractions, the wall as a metaphor for sovereignty has kept its hold on the human imagination. The minds of most national leaders are fixated on building ever bigger and better walls. So in the face of Hitler's buildup, France based it security on a Maginot Line along its borders, only to suffer when the Line was quickly outflanked by German troops. So today some harbor fantasies of a great Maginot Line in the sky called the Strategic Defense Initiative, which is supposed to block enemy missiles and protect our sovereignty. Never mind that even if it could be made to work, the Great Wall in the Sky could easily be outflanked, overwhelmed, undermined, or underflown, becoming one of the more spectacular and costly failures in the human quest for walled sovereignty.[2]

Today there is no walling out the rest of the world. In an age of technologies for surveillance and of global economic and ecological interdependencies, Great Walls, whether on the ground or in the skies, are faulty metaphors for conceptualizing, as well as faulty strategies for protecting, sovereignty. Our national boundaries are more like the skin on our bodies: permeable membranes through which life flows between our own existence and that of the rest of the world. We share common vulnerabilities and possibilities, ever affected by each other's activities and by the life of the biosphere in which we subsist; our respective sovereignties need to be understood in this interactive and dynamic context. It is no longer possible to wall each other out, or in.

This assertion has to do not only with spatial relations across national boundaries, but also temporal relations: our interactions across time with those yet to come, who will be affected by our decisions. All living creatures have a strong instinct to ensure their own and their species' continuity. The Emperor Qin envisioned his life continuing not only through his progeny, but also through his achievements, i.e., the outcomes of his choices, actions, and policies in the present. But he was deluded in thinking a wall could ensure this. Today a grand failing among humans is not that we are too much preoccupied by our continuity, but that we think about it too narrowly, within individual, territorial, or temporal parameters that are too limited. Unlike those tribal peoples who made decisions based on their effects on the seventh generation hence, we think only of the moment, or, at most, in terms of five-year plans. We have constructed mental walls between one generation and the next, between ourselves and our grandchildren, as if our choices, actions, and policies had no bearing on their lives. We also give too little thought to our utter dependence, and that of our great-grandchildren, on the ongoing integrity of the Earth and its nonhuman as well as human species.

THE PRIMACY OF ECOLOGICAL SECURITY

Security is commonly defined as "freedom from danger; safety." Within the framework of the prevailing state-centered system, national security is thought of in military terms, as the capacity of one state to thwart armed invasion by another. More recently it has also come to mean the capacity to compete economically in the global marketplace for access to markets and scarce resources, and for a favorable balance of trade and payments. Ecological security has seldom been included, much less been a priority, in the matrix of national security.

Yet the real "present danger" has little to do with superpower polarities on an East/West axis, or even rich/poor polarities on a North/South axis. It has more to do with polarities between human activities and the life-sustaining capacities of the Earth—polarities that threaten the ecological security of East, West, North, and South alike.

We are at a new point in human history and in the planet's development, when it has become critical to reconsider our security priorities in light of new threats to life from human assaults on the Earth.

We can begin such a reconceptualization of security by asking: What are the principal threats to survival today?

For early human societies, the answer was the powerful forces of nature: volcanos, earthquakes, storms, droughts, floods. Over time, humans learned to protect themselves from many of these, through precautions, modifications in habits and habitats, and new inventions.

Gradually the locus of threats shifted to the social sphere in interhuman relations. Enmity, fear, and xenophobia were institutionalized over time, given ideological and political content (e.g., "Better dead than red"), and built up until they constituted mega-threats, which were met by mega-weapons and supported by mega-myths so pervasive that life itself was no longer a primary value and the world hung on the verge of Armageddon. But these threats, and their resolution, are a product of human volition; humans created them and humans can turn them off.

Today a new class of risks is emerging. Although they have to do with nature, this time the danger arises not from what nature can do to humans, but the impact of human activities on nature, with their consequent effects on the human. This time, while humans created the problems, they may not be able to turn off their consequences.

Human assaults on the planet today are of a new kind and scale. Symptoms include depletion of the stratospheric ozone layer, essential to protect people and crops from solar ultraviolet radiation; carbon dioxide buildup, threatening a global greenhouse effect and worldwide climatic changes; acid rain; increasing levels of chemical, radioactive, and other toxic pollutants in water, air, and soils, contributing to a rise in cancers and other environmentally induced diseases, health problems, and genetic damage; the loss of topsoil and increasing desertification, contributing to hunger and starvation for millions; chemical and biological, as well as nuclear weapons; and the massive destruction of forests, further compounding the carbon dioxide threat. The life of the Earth is also threatened by the loss of millions of plant and animal species due to overindustrialization, deforestation, pollution, selective breeding, and monocropping. These life forms are part of us and our cultures; their loss will impoverish both the Earth and the human.

Unlike threats in the social sphere, these cannot be defined ideologically, nor can they be resolved through conventional competition for power. A more powerful arsenal or state is no advantage. And, once threats to Earth's ecosystems go beyond a certain point, with interactive and compounding dynamic effects, they may take on a life of their own, accelerating out of human control toward an uncertain conclusion, possibly including major changes in Earth's life-supporting capacities.[3] Whereas the Earth may adapt and take care of itself in some fashion,[4] humans may not be able to withstand or adapt fast enough to these changes in the Earth's life-system.

In this event, the cause of human death will not be the forces of nature but a failure of human vision. The epitaph of the species, imprinted in fossilized bones, might then read: "Here lies Homo sapiens, 'the wise human,' who failed to learn that the Earth is a total, living system, and human security a function of, and inseparable from, the life of the Earth."

SOVEREIGNTY AND THE EARTH

When we try to approach a resolution of today's ecological crises, we soon run into a central dilemma: *The Earth does not recognize sovereignty as we now know it.* Existing concepts of state sovereignty are incongruent, even antithetical, to the prerequisites for global ecological security.

Sovereignty has been defined popularly as "a theory of politics that deals with an ultimate overseer or authority."[5] But the legitimate locus of sovereignty has been perceived differently in different societies and periods. These variations are affected by how each given society has answered a central question: Who can legitimately make or change the rules or laws? Who is the ultimate arbiter in maintaining order? Many thinkers, including Aristotle, Bodin, Hobbes, and Rouseau, have offered philosophical answers. The locus of *internal* sovereignty (individual–state relations) has variously been the monarchy, the people (popular sovereignty), the constitution, the law, Parliament, parliamentary and judicial institutions, or shifting pluralist groups. As for *external* sovereignty (inter-state relations), each state has generally upheld its right to be the final arbiter of decisions and rules affecting its affairs and territory.

The modern ideology of state sovereignty was developed over the last four hundred years parallel with the decline of feudalism and rise of capitalism and the nation-state system. A rising middle class worked to break the power of the aristocracy by asserting popular or constitutional sovereignty. At the time, many people still believed the world was flat, while the emerging scientific paradigm held the universe to be like a great machine with many separate parts. In the social extensions of this scientific paradigm, societies and states were viewed as closed systems that could exist and function apart from the others, sufficient unto themselves.

At a time when peoples and states lacked travel and communications technologies to interact more than occasionally, and when prevailing economic systems made such interaction unnecessary, societies could and did function as entities unto themselves. Where sovereignty was not threatened, there was not much need to define or defend it. But as new technologies emerged and economic and military interpenetration increased, the myth of absolute state sovereignty arose, at least in part as a defense against more threatening forms of interpenetration and external domination.

Today, although the myth of state sovereignty has proven persistent and resilient, it is beginning to be challenged, especially in the face of several new realities: (1) increasing global-scale interdependencies in economic, monetary, technological, political, military, cultural, interpersonal, societal, and ecological spheres (i.e., new transboundary systems and dynamics symptomatic of an emerging global civilization); (2) the increasing capacity of humans to alter Earth's life-sustaining processes (i.e., new dynamics in human–Earth relations); (3) the increasing capacity of present generations to jeopardize future life (i.e., new dynamics in intergenerational relations); and (4) new scientific paradigms and knowledge about the way the Earth functions.

With regard to the latter, scientists are shattering atomistic and mechanistic worldviews with empirical evidence of a world comprised of multiple, complex, open, living, interacting systems. While our tribal ancestors and spiritual visionaries through the ages had an intuitive sense of powerful forces and laws governing their survival, an age of rationalism relegated these views to the realm of superstition. The new empirical evidence, supported by mathematical formulas and computer models, cannot be so easily dismissed.

A reexamination of sovereignty and security must be undertaken within the framework of these new understandings. If the Earth were flat it might be possible to prevent ecological threats from penetrating one's sovereign territory by putting up walls. But the Earth is not flat; it is round. It curves back on itself. It rotates and revolves. Moreover, it is not a static, determined system following a Newtonian model of mechanical equilibrium; nor is it comprised of separately acting, replaceable parts. It is a living, interactive system comprised of interactive subsystems, interactive species, and complex, dynamic, interactive processes.

None of the earth's various bioregions are totally self-sustaining or sovereign.[6] There is only one air system and one water system, upon which the entire planet and its human and nonhuman subsystems depend. Toxic materials released in one region are carried across entire continents by air or water; the chlorofluorocarbons (CFCs) released in one country deplete the ozone layer upon which all depend, regardless of elimination of CFC use elsewhere; excess burning of fossil fuels in one country contributes to a global greenhouse effect threatening all countries. Claims of national sovereignty or immunity are useless against these threats.

Like air and water, birds and animals cross political boundaries. Fish respect no exclusive economic zones or sovereign fishing rights. Pollutants dumped in the oceans find their way, concentrated in fish and shellfish, back to our dinner plates. The destruction of the Amazon rainforest threatens not only Amazonian communities, but all creatures on Earth. In the sovereignty of the Earth, to touch one part is to touch the whole.

What is being said here is underscored by most ecological threats. Unlike the prevailing concept of the absolute sovereignty of more than one hundred seventy independently acting nation-states, and in direct conflict with it, *the sovereignty of the Earth is indivisible.* What then does national sovereignty mean relative to ecological security? Who owns the rainforests? Who owns the ozone? Who can speak for Earth?

No modern philosophy of sovereignty provides an adequate answer to such questions. Each has a fundamental flaw: the locus of sovereignty—be it high priest, king, parliament, or people—is perceived to be limited solely to humans, and to lie within strict group and territorial confines. This homocentric and territorial locus excludes the deeper sources of power and authority in the cosmic laws that govern the workings of the universe, the Earth, and its biosphere. Humans are only beginning to understand these laws, which they did not make, upon which all human survival depends, and to which all human sovereignties must owe allegiance.

SOVEREIGNTY AS AN INTERACTIVE PROCESS

Any new vision of sovereignty for our times must have a larger frame of reference than the human alone; and it must be thought of not in fixed or territorial terms, such as a walled state, but rather as a dynamic, interactive process involving a system of relationships and of energy and information flow between different spheres of sovereignty. Even among humans, sovereignty can dwell in more than one place at the same time: in a family, in people at local or national civic levels, in the state, in a global authority. The given situation or agreed-on principles or laws may determine who is the final arbiter; but this determination usually emerges out of a system of human relationships and interactions. In relations between the human and nonhuman worlds, at least four systems of planetary activity affect the dynamic of sovereignty: (1) the biosphere, (2) the technosphere, (3) the sociosphere, and (4) the noosphere.

The first three have been described by many authors. The "biosphere" refers to the "sphere of life" or the space where life exists or may exist. It is the system of nature, comprised of the atmosphere, lithosphere, and hydrosphere, or the air, minerals and waters of the Earth, all of which support living organisms and, indeed, are parts of Earth's life system. This system has evolved over more than four billion years, through atmospheric, geological, and biological processes that long preceded the appearance of humans. Eventually a system emerged that made possible and now supports the life of humans; in turn, it is increasingly affected by human activities.

The "technosphere" is the system of structures made by humans and set in the space of the biosphere, such as villages and cities, factories, roads, vehicles, gas and oil pipelines, communication networks, power plants, dams, irrigation and drainage structures, farmlands, and parks. Although under human control, these components are also under the influence of the biosphere.[7] Every day humans produce new kinds of materials not found in nature, which may have unintended consequences in the biosphere.

The "sociosphere" is comprised of the prevailing political, economic, and cultural institutions humans have developed to manage their relations with each other and with the other two systems.[8]

In addition to these three, some thinkers, including French paleontologist Pierre Teilhard de Chardin (1881–1955) and Russian scientist Vladimir Vernadsky (1963–1945), have asserted the existence of a fourth sphere, which they called by and Vernadsky Teilhard the "noosphere." This is the new sphere of mind and spirit, of consciousness and reflective thought, that envelopes the biosphere. Put another way, the noosphere is "the biosphere as altered consciously or unconsciously by human activities."[9] In the view of both Vernadsky and Teilhard, this sphere is not only a portion of space, it is also an epoch that has emerged out of Earth's evolutionary processes, and, through humans, is now transforming the Earth.[10]

Most Western philosophers who considered the question of sovereignty did so exclusively within the realm of the sociosphere. They did not consider at all the interaction of human and nonhuman worlds within the larger biosphere, or sovereignty as a dynamic involving the interrelationships of all four spheres. And even within the context of the sociosphere, they did not foresee that multiple and diverse national, economic, and cultural sociospheres would become increasingly interdependent within an emerging global sociosphere; nor did they consider the impact of present policies on the health of future generations in a multitemporal sociosphere.

We are now at a critical juncture in history and in inter-human and human–earth relations. We are moving rapidly into a global civilization, and into a period in which humans, with their new knowledge and technologies, have increasing power to intervene in the biosphere and affect the next stages of planetary evolution, including the health of future generations. But we have not yet developed the commensurate mental or moral tools, or an adequate philosophy or ethic, much less an adequate global polity and policies, to guide our new interrelations in a way that will ensure human survival and well-being. There has been a tragic lag in human development, which we are now challenged to overcome.

In this new historical context, sovereignty needs to be reconceptualized within a total-systems context as a dynamic process involving multispatial, multitemporal, multispecies, and multisystems interactions. It is dysfunctional to wall ourselves in or out in separate space or time zones, or even separate species zones; and it is dysfunctional to consider sovereignty as a static state. Sovereignty needs to be viewed in a fluid, relational, dynamic context, with multiple spheres of activity, authority, control, and laws affecting any given situation. Such a reconceptualization will be critical to the healthy functioning of any coming global civilization and of the planet itself.

NOT IN MY BACK YARD

I am not recommending here the total abandonment of the principle of national sovereignty. Paradoxically, global ecological security may require the strengthening and protection of national sovereignty on the one hand, and on the other, some pooling of sovereignties in the global community or sociosphere, for the sake of the ecological security of all. Without pooling some sovereignty in strengthened global systems and international law, individual countries cannot protect themselves against ecological threats from outside their borders. Even threats from within a country may be so entangled in global economic, political, or military dynamics that the situation cannot be resolved without global cooperation.

The situation of many poorer countries exemplifies the paradox. Poverty is a cause as well as an effect of environmental degradation in many developing countries. As the Brundtland Report on Environment and Development states, "It is mass poverty which drives millions of people to overexploit thin soils, overgraze fragile grasslands, and cut down yet more of the rapidly disappearing tropical forests, these great lungs vital for the global climate and thereby for food production."[11] Therefore, in seeking effective environmental solutions, economic imbalances must also be addressed. What is needed is sustainable development that simultaneously supports economic growth, a more just and equitable distribution within and among nations, political reforms, and fair access to necessary knowledge and resources—without compromising the ecosystem and with it the ability of future generations to meet their needs.

This is a tall order for any society, even in the best of circumstances—but it becomes virtually impossible for poorer countries confronted with debilitating foreign debt, rising interest rates, interrupted international commercial and financial flows, and adverse terms of trade. Such all-too-common circumstances have led many countries to overuse their resource base, export precious natural resources, and ignore environmental degradation for the sake of short-term economic survival.[12] Because the economic forces involved cannot be controlled locally or even nationally, many poorer countries cannot extricate themselves from this predicament unilaterally; a concerted, multilevel, cooperative approach to problem solving at the global level is required.

But even while many developing countries call for more cooperative and equitable international systems, they have also been pressing for greater national sovereignty. This apparent contradiction is not a failure of logic, but a pragmatic recognition that some global forces raise havoc with their development goals. In light of the continuing colonial and neo-colonial legacy, in which their resources are plundered, their labor exploited, their cultures eroded, and their environmental health degraded, the attraction of national sovereignty is understandable. In light of some of the ecological threats they face, it is even more understandable. For example, many developing countries have become victims of "toxic terrorism," their lands and waters used as garbage dumps for the toxic wastes of the richer, more industrialized countries. Big profits are involved. While companies have had to pay from $250 to $2,500 a ton for toxic waste disposal in the United States and Europe, where they are also required to follow strict disposal guidelines, deals have been made in Africa for only $3 to $100 a ton, no environmental impact questions asked.[13] The profits go to middlemen who contract to dispose of the waste at a higher price than they pay to Third World recipients.

Latent racism, in the new form of "ecological apartheid," may also be involved. Those exporting toxic wastes would often be loathe to dump it in their own neighborhoods, affecting their own children, but have fewer scruples about putting African, Asian, or Latin American children at risk. So too, minority and poorer people within the richer countries, such as slum dwellers and Native Americans in the United

States, are especially vulnerable to having their lands used as toxic dump sites.

The resulting NIMBY (Not In My Back Yard) response by peoples of Africa, Asia, and the Pacific, therefore, has a legitimate place in a world ecological strategy. In fact, it may be negligent not to raise sovereign flags against ecological threats from outside one's borders. Such assertions of national and regional sovereignty—and insistence that those who produce the garbage must be responsible for it—may be at least a start toward protecting present and future populations from the effects of toxic dumping.

However, while important, the sovereign NIMBY approach by itself is not adequate to resolve all or even most threats to ecological security. It is not a relevant strategy for dealing with the ozone depletion or global greenhouse threats, which require comprehensive global solutions. And in some cases local and national environmental efforts, lacking the protection of global systems, have triggered harsh reprisals from powerful economic and political interests.

In an increasingly interdependent world, all are vulnerable to the actions of a few. The great irony is that, in spite of the common view that sovereignty is a prized possession of which an approaching global civilization threatens to rob us, we have already lost it; yet, in its name, we have failed to develop global institutions capable of protecting the very security and sovereignty we desire.

EXISTING INTERNATIONAL AGREEMENTS

If we turn our attention to international agreements already related to the environment, we find two distinct and seemingly paradoxical trends: on the one hand, increasing numbers of international agreements; on the other, increasing environmental degradation.

Since 1921, there have been over one hundred forty international multilateral treaties and other binding agreements related to the environment. In addition, there are many nonbinding resolutions and declarations, such as the 1972 Stockholm Declaration and the 1982 World Charter for Nature. All but two of these multilateral treaties were adopted in the last fifty years, and over half in the latter third of this period. At first glance this trend suggests a growing readiness to transcend state sovereignty and develop cooperative efforts to deal with transboundary environmental problems. How then can we account for the fact that, in the same period, environmental degradation seems to be getting worse?

A number of factors need to be considered. First of all: Is environmental degradation really getting worse, or does it only seem worse because we are now more aware of it, with more precise ways to measure and predict it? Certainly, since the 1960s, public consciousness regarding risks to the Earth has grown considerably. Innumerable books,and other publications have contributed to this, as have the increasing numbers of environmental conferences and organizations. The 1972 UN Conference on the Environment in Stockholm put environmental issues on the global agenda for the first time in a concerted way, exponentially increasing public understanding of ecological dangers, establishing agreement on some principles of environmental protection, and bringing forth the United Nations Environmental Programme. And space-age technologies have given us all a new, shared image of our one Earth, as well as new instruments to detect and monitor ecological problems. Still, this is not an adequate answer to our paradox. These same technologies provide evidence that some problems, such as depletion of the ozone layer, really are getting worse and may continue to do so unless we restrict certain pollutants.

A second possibility, of course, is that many of the treaties are too recent to have had much effect. For example, the 1987 Montreal Protocol on Substances That Deplete the Ozone Layer only came into force in 1989; the 1989 Basel Convention on the Control of Transboundary Movements of Hazardous Waste and Their Disposal is not yet in force. For some ecological problems, including ozone depletion, a long lead-time is required before a human remedy will have a measurable effect.

But the fact is that the Montreal Protocol was considered inadequate by experts even before it entered into force, because it only requires gradually reducing CFC production to 50 percent of 1986 levels by the end of the century, and makes exceptions for developing countries with lower CFC outputs. Some scientists predict that, under these allowable levels, ozone-depleting chemicals in the atmosphere will not decrease, but actually double in 50 years.[14] This is why another intergovernmental meeting was convened in London in March 1989, at which 12 European countries decided to totally eliminate their production and use of these chemicals by 2000.

Similarly, the Basel convention on toxic waste was considered by many experts to be too little, too late even before the ink dried. Existing levels of toxic waste, some of it dumped on unknown sites around the world in unlabeled, erodible containers, will affect untold numbers of people far into the future. And the Basel agreement does not halt future commerce in poison; it only takes a cautious step toward regulating it by requiring exporters to get importing countries' permission. Even that requirement is full of loopholes; toxic waste expert James

Puckett called it a virtual "international stamp of approval" on continued toxic dumping.[15]

All this underscores a third possibility: Despite their increasing numbers, existing international treaties are simply not adequate in the face of the gravity of our situation. Indeed, most existing treaties are seriously limited. Many focus primarily on economic or military goals and are only secondarily or peripherally related to ecological security. Most were undertaken piecemeal and/or are limited to selected pollutants, regions, or species, with little or no coordination between them. They were reactive rather than anticipatory: while a treaty might cover one substance currently deemed a public health threat, hundreds of new substances, equally or even more dangerous, could be produced tomorrow. Or toxic substances prohibited from use in one region could be dumped on the markets of another. Many of the treaties dealing with pollution are limited to controlling or regulating, but not prohibiting, dangerous substances, or else they are full of loopholes, or have been ratified by only a few countries, not necessarily those most responsible for the problem. Those states not wanting to be obligated by treaty requirements simply avoid ratification, or work to water down or eliminate clauses they do not want to be bound by.

Even when ratified by significant numbers of countries, most treaties are very weak in compliance or enforcement measures, or omit them entirely. Cautious steps are taken toward cooperating in research for purposes of making recommendations, or undertaking education or the exchange of information, but when it comes to real environmental protection, the treaties stop short.

Finally, much of existing international environmental law further defines and reinforces state sovereignty, even while the very nature of ecological security requires pooling or transcending it. Evidently the treaty process does not go deep enough. While the rapid increase in international environmental agreements represents growing public concern over ecological security, the process of intergovernmental treaty making has been undertaken within the constraints of outmoded concepts of sovereignty and security. So those one hundred forty or more treaties that attempted to deal with transboundary environmental problems were negotiated without the states first undertaking the global mind change that is a prerequisite to resolving these issues.

THE TREND TOWARD GLOBAL GOVERNANCE

On the other hand, some of these international treaties do represent the beginning of states' cooperating regionally and globally to harmonize their national laws relative to transboundary issues and interests.

And a few treaties are first steps toward limiting or reconceptualizing sovereignty on behalf of the global common good.

In this regard, several treaties deserve special attention: the 1959 Antarctica Treaty, which in effect made Antarctica a global commons; the 1967 Outer Space Treaty, which declared that outer space was "not subject to national appropriation by claims of sovereignty, by means of occupation, or by any other means"; the Law of the Sea Treaty, adopted in 1982 but not yet in force, which features explicit mention of "global commons" and "common heritage"; and a cluster of treaties related to weather and climate.

Although the Antarctic, Outer Space, and Law of the Sea treaties were not aimed primarily at ecological protection, and were limited to specific regions or spheres of the planet, they established some precedents in designating certain regions as global commons, and in attempting, even if not always successfully, to limit or transcend sovereignty there. We must remember, of course, that when these treaties were adopted, few countries were yet at a point where they could economically exploit the remote regions of Antarctica, outer space, or the deep-sea beds; perhaps this accounts for the relatively low initial resistance to foregoing claims on these areas.

Furthermore, many governments recognized that it was in their national self-interest to demarcate these regions as global commons, to prevent their being seized by more powerful states. This indicates that self-interest can be a force not only for resisting global systems of governance, but also in moving toward them.

In any case, this trend toward recognition of some global commons is not an isolated phenomenon. The past few decades have in fact seen an increasingly strong tendency toward the development of global-level public policy in all areas of human concern. A 1979 study by Robert Manley confirmed that global-level policies have proliferated since 1945; in addition to the environment, the study covered forty-seven other areas, ranging from economic, educational, health, scientific, social, and communications issues to common-use areas. In all these fields, although national sovereignty remains a considerable force, global-level policies and systems exist in various stages of development. They may evolve grudgingly and with little coordination, but the push toward global systems of governance is unmistakable.

This trend is fueled by the growing awareness that nation-states are too big to solve some problems, just right for others, and too small to solve global-scale crises. National leaders are relatively powerless to resolve global problems through national policies alone. Some measure of global cooperation and policy and systems development is essential. Yet global governance as used here is not synonymous with centralized world government; such governance exists in highly decentralized as well as centralized social systems. And it involves a complex combination of psychological, cultural, economic, and other dynamics of adhesion—not only, or even primarily, legal or governmental agreements. The increasing communication and interaction of people around the world in almost every facet of their lives—from the arts, athletics, business, education, health, science, and tourism, to international social movements for peace, human rights, and ecological protection—often result in bonding and solidarities, or at least perceived common interests, that weaken public consensus on absolute national sovereignty and strengthen global cooperation, identity, and adhesion.

What, then, is the relevance of existing environmental agreements to the pooling of sovereignty and to progress toward global ecological governance? It is a crude law of life that what already exists is possible. Some reconceptualization of sovereignty is already occurring. While large gaps exist, within the space of a few decades there has been progress, spurred not only from above, but from below as thousands of grassroots and nongovernmental organizations worldwide have pressed their governments to take action, or have themselves worked together across national lines to advance global ecological health.

Nevertheless, as we have seen, existing measures are not adequate to cope with the severe threats to ecological security we face today. What then would constitute a more adequate response?

TOWARD A MORE EFFECTIVE GLOBAL SYSTEM

A global system of ecological security must be at least as strong as the existing and anticipated strains placed on it. It must include many interacting forces, of which the following will be discussed briefly: (1) a strong and effective global polity; and (2) a global culture of ecological responsibility. The former is important; the latter indispensable.

A Strong and Effective Global Polity

Multiple spheres of human choices and activities—in both public and private sectors, and at local, national, and international levels—have an impact on ecological security. Thus the question is not whether we need governance in all these spheres, but rather now much in each sphere? How much should be left to the private sphere and how much authority or sovereignty pooled in the public sphere to resolve ecological problems? How much at local, national and global levels?

Subsidiarity. In trying to balance these spheres, my preference is that we be guided by the principle of subsidiarity. Simply stated: Whatever can be managed at the local level, should be. Only when a problem exceeds the competence of a particular locality should it be taken up by a larger social structure. Thus, referring to a problem as "global" does not necessarily mean that all its aspects can or should be resolved globally. Many dimensions of ecological security can be handled locally or bioregionally. Local peoples often have intimate knowledge and experience of local terrains and ecosystems, as well as a sense of roots and continuity with a given place, which nurtures a commitment to its ecological health and future.

However, many environmental problems, particularly transboundary ones, cannot be resolved through local polities alone. In this case, national, regional, and global systems are needed. The point is to have effective polities and policies in place at all levels where decisions and action may be required. And while local and national polities are relatively well developed (although environmental law may also need to be strengthened at these levels) there is still a long way to go in the development of an effective global polity for ecological security.

Strengthened International Environmental Law. Existing international environmental agreements have been piecemeal, uncoordinated, and often too little, too late. A more comprehensive and effective system of international laws and structures is needed. Some normative foundations for such a system have been established, albeit mostly in the form of such nonbinding declarations and resolutions as the 1972 Stockholm Declaration, the World Conservation Strategy, the 1982 Nairobi Declaration, and the 1982 World Charter for Nature. They need to be further developed, refined, and given enforcement capabilities.

An Ecological Security Council. In addition to strengthened international law, a stronger global authority is needed to deal with issues of ecological security. The existing United National Environment Programme (UNEP) has little real authority other than the power of its research and information, its educational programs and materials, and its ability to convene meetings and draft resolutions. While it has made important contributions in shaping global ecological awareness and policy development, its efforts are constantly challenged in the name of national sovereignty.

Some have suggested reconstituting the UN Trusteeship Council, which has now virtually completed its Charter mandate, as an Ecological Security Council, with authority comparable to the existing Security Council. Others think this too politically difficult, because it would require revision of the UN Charter; building such a Council from scratch might be easier. Another approach would be to strengthen UNEP by raising it from Programme to Council status.

However it comes into being, the mandate of such an authority should be to safeguard global ecological security. Its functions should include: (1) the prevention of global ecological crises, by way of early-warning systems, data collection and global policy development; (2) quick and effective response to global ecological crises; and (3) dealing with grievance and compliance questions relevant to international environmental law. In the latter case a special Commission might arbitrate disputes or refer them to the World Court. This implies also the development of an international criminal code relative to ecological crimes.

Admittedly, questions of compliance have been the weakest aspect of international law and global-systems development up to now. In the case of ecological crimes, enforcement becomes especially complex, because so many actors are in the private sector. Should the Nuremberg principle, which held that individuals can be held accountable for war crimes, be applied to crimes against ecological security? In the face of critical issues of future human survival can we afford to evade such questions?

Other International Organizations and Systems. It will be difficult, if not impossible, to advance very far toward ecological security without simultaneously cooperating to solve problems of foreign debt, massive poverty, monetary and trade imbalances, and other economic pressures on the world's poorer countries; or, for that matter, to end the exploitation of poorer countries by the richer. Stronger, most just and effective global economic systems need to be developed as an integral aspect of global ecological security.

In addition, international organizations currently dealing with world health, food, agriculture, the oceans, outer space, human rights, arms control and disarmament, all deal to some extent with aspects of global ecological security. It is now essential that their roles be defined and coordinated more effectively; this could be done through linkages with an Ecological Security Council.

A Global Culture of Ecological Responsibility

Ultimately, without the development of a global culture of ecological responsibility, it is unlikely that any international law can be fully developed, enforced, or effective. After all, although today more than sixty-one thousand international treaties cover almost every conceivable area of concern,[16] they often do not work because they do not get ordinary people involved. An effective system of ecological security requires the development of a powerful cultural force to tell the political forces what to do, and to hold them accountable. Cultural norms, public opinion, and group sanctions can sometimes be more demanding and win more adherence than the constitutions, laws, statutes, and treaties established by governments.

To speak of a *global* cultural force does not mean to lose cultural diversity; a global ecological ethos and ethic can be developed within the existing contexts of a diversity of living cultures and traditions. The United Nations Environment Programme recognized this when it enlisted the major world religions in an Environmental Sabbath program. The goal of the Environmental Sabbath is to help people grow in ecological consciousness and responsibility through the wellsprings of their own faith traditions, worship services, and religious education programs.

For ecological security both the law of governments and the law in the hearts and minds of people are necessary; they are interactive and can be mutually reinforcing. International environmental law is necessary to deal with belligerants whose irresponsible actions jeopardize the global common good. But in the final analysis, to be effective, international law must build on the law in the minds and hearts of people.

Sovereignty as Shared Responsibility. Today, concern for the future of humans and the Earth is growing in the minds and hearts of many people around the planet. In the absence of governmental leadership capable of coping with global-scale crises, various people's movements have begun to assert their own leadership and to collaborate across national borders on behalf of their common future. In the process an invisible global polity has begun to form that pays less and less attention to philosophies and declarations of state sovereignty. This polity is implicitly redefining sovereignty as a shared responsibility for the fate of humans and the Earth.

One indicator of this is the proliferation of international nongovernmental organizations, of which there are today more than eighteen thousand, the majority created in the latter half of this century. (By comparison, there are only about two thousand intergovernmental organizations.)[18] Many are pressing for a stronger voice in the United Nations, arguing that nation-states are not the only legitimate actors in shaping global policy. Many are working for a world community based on greater peace, justice, and ecological balance. They monitor and respond to a wide variety of global concerns, including human rights, hunger, health, peace and disarmament, economic development, and many issues related to global ecological security. Among the latter are efforts to save remaining rainforests, seed stock otherwise lost to monocropping, and endangered species, to develop and share ecologically sound technologies and energy alternatives, and to promote aquafarming, soil conservation, and land trusts. Members often come from many countries, religious beliefs, and political persuasions; their commitment to the future of the planet motivates them to rise above these differences in cooperative action.

Citizen Diplomacy and Citizens' Treaties. In the 1980s this invisible global polity began to assume more visible leadership, especially on behalf of world peace. Tired of Cold War hostilities, and seeing that all the petitions to governments had not brought an end to the arms race, peace groups decided to stop waiting for governments; instead they undertook their own "Track II" diplomacy, or people-to-people initiatives. Seeing where the people wanted to go, governments soon followed suit and stepped up disarmament efforts.

Similar cross-national citizen initiatives are now underway on behalf of ecological security. Among these people-to-people initiatives is a series of citizen treaties. The first of these, negotiated and drafted in 1988 and 1989, was the Earth Covenant: A Citizens Treaty for Common Ecological Security. More than a million people in eighty countries have signed the Earth Covenant, agreeing to live their lives by its principles of ecological security and sustainable development. Drafted with the input of people from all around the world, from rich and poor countries, North and South, East and West, the Earth Covenant represents a new, more mature stage in democratic evolution. It is an agreement of the people and by the people on behalf of their common future and the future of the Earth. It has been translated into many languages, and co-sponsored by many international nongovernmental organizations. It has also been endorsed and published by the United Nations Environment Programme, and is an example of people leading governments.

CHANGING OUR MINDS

The most important step in creating a model of an ecologically secure world—the step which must precede all others if they are to be meaningful and effective—is to change our mind-sets. We need to change the way we think about the Earth and human-Earth relations.

A fundamental mistake in the so-called "environmental" movement may be the use of the term "environment," which implies humans at the core of the world and "nature" at the periphery—a mere backdrop for the unfolding human drama. Use of the term distances and separates humans from the Earth. To the extent that language may be destiny—that it shapes our images of self and world, and our relationships in that world—the image of ourselves as separated from the Earth may lead us to accede to myths of human conquest and dominance over the Earth, and to a psychology of destruction, not only of our planet, but of each other and ourselves as well.

Human destruction of the Earth begins in the mind, when we first objectify it—see it as object rather than subject of creative life processes—and we gradually devalue, deny, or succumb to collective amnesia concerning our integral relationship and participation in those processes.

Psycho-historically, the distancing of ourselves from Earth processes may have been a step in collective individuation, involving the emergence and assertion in human consciousness of an identity distinct from the Earth. Much as adolescents seek to break away from their parents to assert their autonomy and discover their own distinct identity, so humans may have moved from a state of preconscious oneness with the Earth, in the early stages of human emergence from Earth processes, to a later state of conscious or semi-conscious separation, as the search for a distinct, specifically human identity took hold in the human imagination.

This may have been a major factor in the formulation of a dualistic worldview, in which the world of nature and the human world were seen as distinct and separate. This assertion of human independence from the Earth ultimately led to an assertion of dominance over the Earth, to reinforce the concept of human autonomy against the powerful and penetrating forces of nature. Thus, following the myth of separation came the myth of conquest, in which opposing forces, humans and nature, battled each other for supremacy in the human mind.

In most Eastern mythologies, opposites are accommodated as integral to each other's identity and existence. In the West, the myth of conquest required that dualities could only be reconciled by the destruction or subordination of one by the other. There was no room for tolerance or accommodation of otherness. Many of the ancient mythologies, such as the Babylonian epic of Marduk, depict a battle between a great mother goddess, creator of the universe and Earth, and her great-great-great-great-great-great-great grandson, who asserts his independence and, after centuries of battle, is finally powerful enough to kill her and become sole ruler of the universe.

The polarization of masculine/feminine imagery in these accounts—and the killing of the feminine—should not be overlooked. It represents a significant aspect of the psychology of destruction, integrally related to ecological destruction and the maintenance of the war system as well as the devaluing of women. In Western creation mythology, the male creator who emerged with the sublimation of the mother-Earth image is separate from and controlling the Earth. This image both mirrors and legitimizes the new human identity as separate from and dominant over the Earth, giving it an aura of divine causality and finality.

Another expression of Western distancing from nature came in the form of rationalism, when humans were defined as specifically human to the degree that their activities were distinct from and "superior" to those in nature. Thus Hegel, Kant, and other philosophers suggested that childbirth, suckling, and child care—all associated with women—were found instinctive in nature and were thus inferior activities, while rational thought was assumed to be unique to humans and therefore superior. In this school of thought, a person was human to the degree that he dissociated himself from nature; women, alas, could not escape their biology.[19]

Not only was this an assault on women and on intuitive forms of knowing; it also paved the way in the modern psyche for a massive assault on nature. Human reason subsequently found all manner of rationalizations for such assaults, including human "progress" and "national security."

THE CHALLENGE TO CREATIVITY

The myth of the hero as conqueror is deep and pervasive. It will not disappear by our merely bewailing or attacking it, which only gives it more energy and attraction. It needs to be replaced by a new, deeper myth of the hero, one in which heroic stature and power is not achieved at the expense of the "other," be it nature or other humans, but rather through mutual empowerment—what psychologist Rollo May defines as integrative power, or power with the other.[20] This would include a sense of empowerment in and with nature, as well as through integral relationships with other human beings.

If the first phase in the human psycho-historical journey is one of pre-conscious oneness with the Earth, followed by a second phase of human individuation, which has continued from the development of agriculture and the rise of traditional civilizations to our day, the third phase, which we are now approaching, may be one of synthesis, interdependence, a conscious and more mature unity. The challenge of adolescence is to move toward creative participation in the community, learning to function responsibly in an interdependent world. In human development as a continuation of planetary development, the human is now challenged to move into its adult phase, assuming a more conscious responsibility for the next stages in planetary evolution.

In asserting human separateness, the human has made it possible for the Earth to stand apart from and reflect on its own processes. Indeed, this period, guided by the myth of heroic power and separateness, has been accompanied by tremendous scientific and empirical inquiry into the Earth's functioning. The separation of the two opposing principles, "humans" and "nature," has in fact made possible their synthesis or reunification. The new powers we have developed through science and technology now demand that we be more closely attuned to Earth processes, that we be wiser and morally more mature than any previous generation, since our capacity for destructiveness is infinitely greater.

And so is the challenge to our creativity. We, who are products of the Earth's tremendous creativity, are now ourselves challenged to enormous creativity in helping the Earth survive in its functioning, creative integrity. The challenge we face is to call forth our creative vision, a creative transformation of existing paradigms and systems that feed the psychology of destruction, and the creative resolution of our present antagonisms.

Above all, we need to create in our minds and in our language, and thence in our behavior and policies, a sense of the inherent and operative intelligence and creativity in the Earth's functioning, an awareness and appreciation of the full range of the interacting, self-sustaining, and ever-renewing processes of nature.

Gaia, the name of the Earth goddess in early Greek myth, has been resurrected in some circles as a metaphor for the living Earth (a planet that is alive, as distinct from a planet that has life on it);[21] for many, the photo of the Earth from outer space has become an icon. We need to take this process further and reawaken in ourselves a sense of our unity—indeed, our identity—with the Earth. We need a transformation in worldviews, by which we come to see that the Earth is like a single cell in the universe; that the humans are not outside or over the cell, but are a part of it; and that we will live or die as this single cell lives or dies.[22] Without such a fundamental change of mind, it is likely that any emerging global civilization will simply extend existing paradigms and problematics to new global levels of danger.

Ecology is a new cultural force. It necessitates the development of a massive growth of consciousness by humans about the impact of our choices and activities on the fate of the Earth. In building the new global culture of ecological responsibility, the following values must be generated, taught, and institutionalized:

1. *reverence for all life*—valuing the other, including all other life forms;
2. *awareness of universal harm*—anticipating the effect of our activities and products on the total system;
3. *intergenerational equity*—an appreciation of future generations and their dependency on our choices;[23]
4. *respect for diversity*—understanding that evolution has proceeded on a path of increasing differentiation and complexity, with implications for interhuman relations: True security can never be based on domination or elimination of differences. We need to respect and value the many cultures in our global sociosphere. It also has implications for human–Earth relations: True ecological security requires that we cherish the diversity in nature and learn the art of coexistence with other life forms as well as other humans;
5. *communion*—affirmation of the ways in which, despite all our diversity, we share in one life and are mutually interdependent. Each reality of the universe is in communion with every other reality within the unity of the entire world order.

Most of all, we must learn to live on the Earth with consciousness and intentionality, and not just surrender to custom or fate. The future is increasingly a matter of human choice and human freedom. We need to will our way of life and take responsibility for creating a future in which life can continue in its incredible variety and beauty.

NOTES

1. Patricia M. Mische is co-founder of Global Education Associates, co-author of *Toward a Human World Order* and author of *Star Wars and the State of Our Souls.* This article is adapted from a longer research paper presented in Moscow, October 1988, at the

international conference on "The Coming Global Civilization: What Kind of Sovereignty?", co-sponsored by the World Order Models Project and the Soviet Political Science Association.

2. Patricia Mische, *Star Wars and the State of Our Souls* (New York: Harper & Row/Winston, 1985).

3. Noel Brown, Director of the New York liaison office of the United Nations Environment Programme, in an interview by Patricia M. Mische, December 20, 1988.

4. J. E. Lovelock, *Gaia: A New Look at Life on Earth.* (New York: Oxford University Press, 1979).

5. *Encyclopedia Britannica,* 15th ed., vol. 17 (1982), s.v. "sovereignty."

6. Thomas Berry, "Bioregions: The Context for Reinhabiting the Earth," *Breakthrough* 6, no. 3/4 (1985): 6–9.

7. M. Kassas, "The Three Systems and Mankind," *IPRA Newsletter* (International Peace Research Association, Rio de Janeiro) 17, no. 1 (January 1989): 18–25.

8. Kassas.

9. *Webster's New Collegiate Dictionary,* (1977), s.v. "noosphere."

10. See Pierre Teilhard de Chardin, *The Phenomenon of Man* (New York: Harper & Row, 1959); for Vernadsky's view, see Nikita Moisseyev, *Man, Nature and the Future of Civilization* (Moscow: Novosti, 1987).

11. Gro Harlem Brundtland and the World Commission on Environment and Development, statement to the UN General Assembly 42nd session, October 19, 1987.

12. Brundtland.

13. See for example, Polly Diven, "Our Newest Hazardous Export," *Christian Science Monitor,* October 27, 1988; "The Global Poison Trade," *Newsweek,* November 7, 1988; Daniella Pletka, "Developing Nations as Dump Sites," *Insight,* August 15, 1988; Third World Network, "Report on Toxic Waste Dumping in Third-World Countries" (Penang, Malaysia; August 1988).

14. See e.g., Cynthia Pollock Shea, *Protecting Life on Earth: Steps to Save the Ozone Layer* (Washington, DC: Worldwatch Institute, 1988); Philip Shabecoff, "Arctic Expedition Finds Chemical Threat to Ozone," *New York Times,* February 18, 1989.

15. Reported by Steven Greenhouse, "U.N. Conference Supports Curbs on Exporting of Hazardous Waste," *New York Times* March 23, 1989.

16. Elise Boulding. *Building a Global Civic Culture: Education for an Interdependent World* (New York: Teachers College Press, Columbia University, 1988).

17. *Environmental Sabbath,* a kit prepared under the sponsorship of the United Nations Environment Programme, New York Liaison Office, 1988.

18. Elise Boulding, "The Rise of INGOs: New Leadership for a Planet in Transition," *Breakthrough* 9, nos. 1/3 (1988): 14–17.

19. Carol McMillan provides an interesting analysis of this school of thought, and how modern feminists have responded in her book *Women, Reason, and Nature* (Princeton, NJ: Princeton University Press, 1982).

20. Rollo May, *Power and Innocence* (New York: Norton, 1972).

21. See for example, Lovelock; Norman Myers, ed., *Gaia: An Atlas of Planet Management* (New York: Doubleday, 1988); Elisabet Sahtouris, *Gaia: The Human Journey from Chaos to Cosmos* (New York: Pocket Books, 1989).

22. Thomas Berry, "The Ecological Age," *The Whole Earth Papers* (Global Education Associates) No. 12 (1979): 4–11.

23. Edith Brown Weiss, "Climate Change, Intergenerational Equity, and International Law," *Breakthrough* 10:4 (Summer/Fall, 1989), pp. 25–27.

Part II

INSTITUTIONALIZATION

7

Grafting the Past onto the Future of the United Nations System

TOSHIKI MOGAMI

THE UN SYSTEM AS A QUIET REVOLUTION

The drastic change in the composition of the UN membership since 1960 is discussed in any standard text on international organization. It is accompanied by various kinds of diagnoses or commentaries: a sociological one, which draws attention to the increased heterogeneity of the organization; a historical one, which underlines the universalization of the nation-state system; a political one, which signals the formation of various majorities in the General Assembly.[1]

More important than these viewpoints is that this numerical increase of the newly independent states could be interpreted as bringing about a systemic "revolution."[2] Revolution in the international system could have two meanings: One is total replacement of the state system by an alternative system, such as world government; the other is parallel establishment of an alternative system grounded on a different logic from the state system's. It is this latter interpretation that applies to the UN system.[3]

The essence of this "revolution" is that inside the UN there now exists a system in which the actual power relations of states is no longer be duplicated.[4] The system outside the UN, the Westphalian nation-state system, is one which, although based on the sovereign equality of states, acquiesces in de facto inequity among states. It is a world of individual states' liability, and no state is held responsible for neglecting other states' or their peoples' misery, nor for keeping the world under its hegemonic control. It is a stage for "global apartheid," if not a "jungle" in the Hobbesian sense.

By contrast, the new system to a considerable degree robs naked power of its meaning. After 1960, the impact of the one-state-one-vote principle and of decision making by majority vote was suddenly revealed with the influx of the newly independent states into the system. Catalyzed by their "great awakening," these states were pushed to assert themselves, so that this institutional setting became more than a procedural matter. Instead, it now provided those "weaker" Third World states with the power to make their voices heard.

It could be termed "revolutionary" because this mechanism turned the logic of power upside down. The less powerful outside the organization have now become more powerful inside the organization: an inversion in the locus of hegemony. Of course, such power is a contextual one that can be actualized only in the institutional setting already described. Consequently, the new "hegemony" should properly be called "in-organization hegemony."

To say that a revolutionary process has set in does not necessarily mean that the UN has started nudging the world in the direction of a more just, viable, and stable order; nor can we say that the adoption of epoch-making resolutions such as the one envisaging a New International Economic Order (NIEO) is evidence of a new order. It is sometimes to the contrary, at least in regard to ordered stability, since all this is a fundamental challenge to the legitimacy of the status quo, as is the case with any revolution, and an antithesis to the logic of the nation-state system.

The basic fact is that now the voices of the oppressed can become the primary organizational ideology,[5] and that this has been made possible precisely by the existence of the UN system with its antithetical mode of decision making. Their demands and aspirations pour into the organization and gain legitimacy quite naturally, for the problems that these people confront are of an existential nature, ranging from the menace of nuclear annihilation to extreme impoverishment and hunger, famine, and environmental destruction. As such, those with these problems cannot help but rush into any available forum once the oppressed or dispossessed are given a chance to express themselves. The rise of the Third World only made these problems conspicuous, and their exacerbation made it more imperative for those states to rely on the UN system, since it was almost the only instrument available to them.

Seen in this way, it would be erroneous to equate their acquisition of in-organization hegemony with the simple change of players in a struggle for power. First, no seizure of international power outside the organization has taken place synchronously with the materialization of this hegemony. Second and more to the point, the Third World's irresistible drive toward primacy inside the UN could be taken as an attempt to convert their particular interests, as opposed to those of the developed states, into more general human concerns. And the more existential the problems are, the more plausible such a pretension becomes.

Being contextual, the in-organization hegemony is materially circumvented, for the Third World does not have the power to change the reality laid out in the plans elaborated in the declarations or the codes of conduct (e.g., for multinational enterprises). The alternative system valid in the UN is not imaginary but real, yet gaining a majority in this system does not always beget effectiveness in the outside international world.

In this connection, it would not be appropriate to accuse the Third World of "nomomania"—"the abusive practice of forcing normative-oriented and ineffective declarations."[6] Tactically injudicious as it may be in some cases, norm-creation was the outer limit of the "power" of the Third World. Furthermore, in a world rife with existential problems and lacking rules with which to solve them, the demands for new norms in any case will continue to arise.

It should also be pointed out that no "ineffective declarations" can be "forced". Declarations that are actually "forced" are by definition "effective." Declarations that some feel "forced" on them are, rather, "unacceptable" to them. This point seems essential, as it is this sense of unacceptability that kindles counter-revolution.

REVOLUTION AND THE ISSUE OF POLITICIZATION

Perhaps few framers of the UN Charter anticipated that they were building into it a revolutionary mechanism, for they were simply following the "democratic" principle of the sovereign equality of states. And herein lies the paradox of the "revolution": that it is firmly based on the nation-state system, at least in outward form, rather than transcending it. This principle thus rendered the system more acceptable even to the powerful, as an extension of the existing system. As such, the onset of the revolution was a quiet one.

However, as this hidden revolutionary mechanism[7] becomes salient, with the cumulation of challenging declarations and codes of conduct, the discrepancy between the two opposing systems widens. That is, the outcome of the "revolution," in particular control of the organizational ideology by the solidarity of the weak, becomes unacceptable to the adherents of the pre-revolutionary system (which still exists) where "might makes right." This was the case especially with those possessing hegemony outside the organization, who experience a deep sense of frustration. Thus, a counter-revolution sets in.

As is well known, it was the United States that took the lead in attacking the UN system. The most drastic of these charges was obviously its withdrawal from the International Labor Organization (ILO) in 1977 and from the United Nations Educational, Scientific and Cultural Organization (UNESCO) in 1984. As the focus of U.S. censure seems to have been, among other things, the "politicization" of the Specialized Agencies, it is particularly important to consider this concept itself as well as the charges made about it.

"Politicization" is a disparaging, reproachful concept. It connotes that acts referred to as "politicized" should be mitigated and/or redressed. For instance, the indices of the "politicization syndrome" formulated by Victor-Yves Ghebali are the following six "dysfunctions".[8]

(1) dysfunction at the level of constitutional ideologies (continuous erosion of liberal basic principles in the constitutional documents, such as NIEO, which calls for governmental intervention);
(2) dysfunction at the level of membership (ritualistic condemnation, close to summary justice, of certain member states like Israel);
(3) dysfunction at the level of debate (the introduction of extraneous and controversial issues into General Assembly debates, such as Zionism, apartheid, colonialism);
(4) dysfunction at the decision-making level (outright confrontation and "nomomania");
(5) dysfunction at the program level (injection into the organization's working programs of projects extraneous or peripheral to constitutional mandates, such as disarmament issues diverted by Soviet propaganda objectives or calls for direct assistance to national liberation movements);
(6) dysfunction at the level of management and administration (the imbalance between the financial contribution and the benefits received from the organization, lack of transparency in administration, etc.).

Some comments must be made on this admittedly useful list. First, can all the points be justifiably grouped together under the rubric "dysfunction"? For example, is the affirmation of "constitutional ideologies" like NIEO to be regarded as dysfunctions in the organization? If so, then, it follows that only a constitutional ideology that upholds "liberal principles" will be held to represent the UN's functioning properly. To choose one principle as superior to others is one thing; to call an organization "dysfunctional" for its choice of an organizational ideology disagreeable to some, quite another. To take another example, it is also arguable whether the "outright confrontation" in decision making is to be judged evidence of organizational dysfunction. It is basically a matter of political style or prudence, although it may lead to a stalemate in the activities of the organization. What seems more important for a deeper analysis of the present confusion in the UN system is the reason for the apparently desperate posture of the powerful states under attack in the UN.

The index of extraneous issues may be more pertinent, given the mandate of an organization as the cornerstone for evaluating the propriety of its activities. Anybody would find it bizarre if the Universal Postal Union (UPU) spent most of its debates on biogenetics. But even this index encounters its own limitation with organizations like UNESCO, for example, whose mandate is quite extensive (See Article I of its Constitution). The criterion of limited mandate is not always applicable.

Second, a distinction should be made between objective causes of "politicization" and subjective perceptions of it. There are definitely several aspects of the operation of the organizations under attack which are unpleasant to some of its members, be they disarmament, peace, apartheid, or development; some of the issues may be considered extraneous to the activities of the organization. There may remain some member states which feel a vague resentment even toward those activities not clearly extraneous. For them, the term "politicization" now becomes a semiotic symbol subsuming all the ill-favored facets of the organizational activities, whether dysfunctional or not, whether extraneous or not. Used in such a context, "politicization" mainly refers to some member states' subjective perception.

Then where do we find the objective cause or the inner dynamics of "politicization"? To begin with, it was a natural consequence of the in-organization hegemony won by the Third World. There is nothing new in this. Recall the United States' efforts, during the Cold War, to mobilize UNESCO for campaigning against Communism,[9] or to prevent China from gaining or recovering its representation in the UN.

What is new is that, as Mohammed Bedjaoui once put it, "In the opinion of the developing countries, [it is] international organizations, and especially the United Nations, [that] provide an ideal context for the transformation of the international economic order and the development of all the peoples."[10] Here we see a departure from the idyllic pre-1960s view of international organizations, whereby they were mandated to promote the common interests of member states. The mandate and functions probably remain the same (which is another reason why we have to be about "dysfunctions"), but now the meaning of "common interests" is much less clear-cut than before. They are to be more than an aggregate or common denominator of separate national interests. Here, the urgency of the myriad of existential problems would justify, at least from the standpoint of the oppressed and dispossessed, identifying their particular interest with the common interests of all. Moreover, the problems are not only urgent but structural, so that few of them can be effectively tackled in an independent way. Instead, a more overarching structural reform is necessary. Such a rectification can only be pushed through multilaterally—hence an aggressive utilitization of international organizations.

Third, a distinction should also be made between "dysfunctions" that suggest unilateral restraint by the Third World, on the one hand, and those involving reciprocal compromise, on the other. The former has to do with political style or prudence. Excessive confrontation, repetitive condemnatory resolutions, which may turn out to be counterproductive, are better downplayed, however legitimate their claims may be. Otherwise, adversaries may simply walk out. At the same time, the "dysfunctions" that would require mutual compromise are, in fact, those that will beg major concessions by the "haves." The "have-nots" do not have much to exchange except more restraint in political style.

In summary, politicization of the UN system, particularly the Specialized Agencies, seems to have been inevitable. It is not so much a question of temporary "dysfunctions" as a historical product. The Third World may be to blame in some respects, yet its demands are legitimate enough, to say the least. And finally, the period of "politicization" was for the Third World a mixture of exaltation and frustration—the exaltation of having a voice on the international scene, and the frustration of not seeing their needs and demands fully met, as in the case of NIEO.

COUNTER-REVOLUTION

Although the objective, deep-seated causes and subjective perceptions of politicization should not be equally weighted, the latter nonetheless contributes to the reading of the historic meaning of "politicization."

To repeat, "politicization" is not a static, universally agreed "syndrome", but itself a political phenomenon involving accuser and accused. And it is the accusing side whose subjective perceptions tarnish it, turning it into a semiotic symbol of the abominable.

The criticisms against politicization came mainly, if not exclusively, from the United States, under the Reagan Administration, among others. It can be regarded as counter-revolutionary, whether good or bad, on the following grounds. First, politicization was the main offspring of the institutional revolution embodied in the UN system. Second, the criticism connoted a doctrinal revulsion, which led the United States to challenge even the core of the revolutionary mechanism, namely, the one-state-one-vote principle. Third, the backlash apparently represented the American (at least the Reagan Administration's) intention to regain "leadership" in the world.

It is a commonplace that revolution begets counter-revolution. But the uniqueness of the present revolution/counter-revolution nexus is that, instead of being a struggle for power within the same single system, it is the result of the concurrent existence of two systems governed by fundamentally different principles. The U.S. might have been able to simply forget about the internal changes in the UN, since the two systems are not on an immediately zero-sum basis. A gain in one does not automatically guarantee a gain in the other. However, the increasing legitimacy of a organizational ideology it does not favor is an irritant for a superpower with hegemony outside the organization. The superpower feels keenly the discordance between its clout outside and inside the UN system.

It is not necessary to list the U.S. assaults on the UN organizations, except that they include its withdrawal from the ILO and UNESCO, its withholding of contributions from them and the UN, the Kassebaum and Gramm-Rudmann Amendments of 1985, estrangements from other organizations such as the other two of the "Big Four" Specialized Agencies (the Food and Agriculture Organization and the World Health Organization). Of these, the withdrawal from UNESCO and the Kassebaum Amendment will be highlighted below, which should be sufficient to extract the essence of the matter.

The focus of the U.S. withdrawal from UNESCO was its alleged politicization by the inclusion in its organizational program of the peace and disarmament issue, its persistent condemnation of Israel, the row over the New World Information and Communication Order (NWICO), and so on.[11] But even these criticisms could be considered either unfounded or exaggerated. For example, as to the emphasis on peace and disarmament, a staff report to the Committee on Foreign Affairs of the U.S. House of Representatives indicated that only a negligible portion of UNESCO's budget was being allocated to this.[12] Besides, by the time the United States decided to withdraw, the two other bones of contention, Israel and NWICO, had nearly subsided.

Such perfunctoriness led Representative Jim Leach to complain, quite persuasively, that the withdrawal was "an unjustified response to an exaggerated problem."[13] It also suggests that the notion of "politicization" is often a highly subjective, therefore relative, perception. Take, for example, the earlier U.S. efforts to use the UN system for propagation of the Cold War, or the storm of McCarthyism introduced into the UN by the United States.[14] The United States did not repudiate them as politicized acts. No "politicization" arises when the hegemonies inside and outside the organization coincide. By the same token, the vociferous reaction of the Eastern bloc to changes more in line with U.S. policy after its return to the ILO attests to the relativity of the problem.

Thus, in many cases the charge of "politicization" boils down to the frustration of those member states whose views are not accepted in the organization. Quite simply, the more powerful, prouder, and less adaptive to changes outside the organization they are, the deeper is their frustration. Significantly, when the Reagan Administration listed the U.S. objectives in international organizations, the first of these was "to reassert American leadership in multilateral affairs."[15]

As mentioned earlier, frustration was felt by the instigators of politicization, as well: frustration at not winning effective solutions for the difficulties they had. Seen from this angle, politicization can be characterized as a collision of two contrary frustrations. Accordingly, its real source would be the very structure of a world full of problems and contradictions.

The counter-revolution continues on another front, that is, the outright attack on the UN itself. With the Kassebaum Amendment of 1985, the counter-revolution seems to have entered a new phase, for this contained a straightforward demand that a weighted voting system be employed in deciding financial matters. Touching upon the core of the revolutionary mechanism, this would betray a more serious counter-revolution.

A focal point in this phase is democracy in international organizations. Similar arguments had appeared during the UNESCO crisis. On the one hand, the United States harbored grievances against UNESCO for being undemocratic: It was an organization ruled by the "tyranny of the majority," whereas the essence of democracy was to respect the minority.[16] On the other hand, quite a few criticized the U.S. withdrawal exactly on the ground of democracy: To these critics democracy means "to live with other arguments, other perspectives, other ways of understanding social relations," and, therefore, "the assumption 'if the majority is against me I leave' is essentially antidemocratic."[17]

Now, with the Kassebaum Amendment's open demand for weighted voting, albeit in a limited way, one more dimension was added to the consideration of democracy in international organizations. Here again a similar demand had been made to UNESCO during its turmoil. In his letter dated July 13, 1984, to Director General M'Bow, Assistant Under-Secretary of State Gregory Newell proposed a new budgetary process, whereby the decision on the organization's budget would require the concurring votes of those member states whose financial contribution added up to at least fifty-one per cent of the entire contribution.[18]

It is doubtful whether the State Department was serious about the demand, since there remained less than half a year before the U.S. notification of withdrawal was to go into effect. In contrast, the Kassebaum Amendment looked more serious, in that it was an official enactment by the Congress, accompanied by a penalty (reducing the U.S. contribution by 20 per cent—from 25 to 20 per cent of the total—if the UN failed to respond to the U.S. demand). The penalty was actually carried out in the end.

This is no longer a struggle for democracy, but a revolt against it. Although there is room for argument as to whether the one-state/one-vote formula is the most democratic, it can still be said that, to quote Marc Nerfin, "in a democratic system, financial contributions and decision-making power are separate matters."[19] And it would be unconvincing to justify the demand on the ground of "no taxation without representation," because, among other things, there are poor states whose representation can be secured only through taxation of the more privileged: no representation without taxation, rather than vice versa—an instance of the revolutionary logic of the UN system.

This last comment may sound exaggerated, but the point is that even if valid, "no taxation without representation" cannot denote "more contribution, more representation." Its overtone is "less contribution, less representation" and thus less voice. But one thing is certain: The benefit principle ("the beneficiaries should pay") is neither applicable nor workable if and when the main theme is the development of the less privileged.

Whether reasonable or not, the Kassebaum Amendment seems to have been the culmination of the counter-revolutionary process. And in proportion to the bitterness of the conflict between two principles, the impression grows of the UN system's being more the source of international disorder than of order.

On the other hand, it should be borne in mind that there can be such a thing as disorder to achieve an alternative order. A search for an alternative order is often a search for an alternative principle, e.g., one that replaces hegemony with equity, which naturally tends to incur harsh reactions. Not incidentally, the axes of "politicization" are those problems that call for eventual solutions. Smashing the UN system is no answer to this, as the problems themselves will not disappear. Insofar as the disorder is undergirt by such an orientation toward alternatives, it can remain close to what Rajni Kothari calls "creative anarchy."[20] The vital question is, therefore, whether the UN system can survive the present crisis so that it can retain this momentum, although, of course, in a less conflictful manner.

A LULL IN THE STORM: REFORM PLANS

The UN system is certainly in distress and needs to be bailed out. It also needs to be improved in a variety of respects. But which of these two does it need more?

The tragedy of the UN system is that the chaos resulting from the revolution/counter-revolution entanglement, on the one hand, and chronic managerial problems, on the other, have both come at once. This engenders, even on the part of those who support the UN, a misunderstanding that improving it is the same as bailing it out. To be sure, the two tasks overlap to a certain extent. But the vital question is, "improvement on what philosophy and in which direction?"

Pondering drastic bail-out can be different from pondering improvement. The former is predicated on the assumption that the UN system is fundamentally worthwhile, its principles and activities forward-looking and wholesome, despite its short-term failures. The assumption of those wishing to improve the UN is either that the system has not fulfilled its mission adequately, to the point of becoming a useless entity, or that it has deviated from its "normal" course, or even that its very existence is counterproductive or even sinful.

Three major tracks for refurbishing the UN can be discerned in light of the these points, namely, (a) the Nerfinian track, (b) the Bertrandian track, and (c) the Group of 18 (G18) track.

The Nerfinian route is extracted from the proposals made by Marc Nerfin.[21] The highlight of his proposal is that the UN should be comprised of three "chambers": a Chamber of Princes to represent the governments of states, a Merchant Chamber that will represent the economic powers, transnational, multinational, national, and local; and a Citizen Chamber. Putting aside for the moment the commonly voiced criticism that it is merely utopian, we can delineate the characteristics of his proposal as follows:

First, the scope of the crisis perceived in this track is wider than "the crisis of the UN" per se. Nerfin enumerates ten crises (e.g., the security crisis, the development cooperation crisis), which he sums up as humankind's "mutation crisis."[22] It is less a crisis within the UN than a crisis surrounding the UN.

Second, the track is essentially affirmative about the past achievements and the revolutionary philosophy of the UN. According to Nerfin, it is "the only instrument of the human species" "to smooth the transition from the old order(s) to the new, more humane, order(s) which survival requires." This leads him to define the "UN crisis" as "largely a Northern expression of a felt challenge to the old order and a reflection of the North's unwillingness that change is necessary."[23]

Third, as a result, the reform plan of this track is not a simple streamlining of the methods and procedures of the UN organs (whose shortcomings he does not deny). It is rather a call for extending and strengthening the current orientation of the UN. Nerfin says that the primary role of an improved UN is to be "open to *new realities*, notably the multifaceted emergence of the Third World" and "open to *new aspirations*, notably the people's expressed need for liberation from the threat of the nuclear omnicide, from hunger and other forms of maldevelopment."[24]

Thus this track is meant to bail the UN out of the ongoing crisis in order to equip it better to solve the crisis that humankind is going through. However utopian the idea of a Three-Chamber UN may sound, the significance of the concept behind it has to be admitted.

The Bertrandian track is the product of the Bertrand Report of 1985 and a few other essays by Maurice Bertrand,[25] whose main point is that an "Economic UN," i.e., a new UN that concentrates on international economic cooperation, should be established.

In contrast to the Nerfinian route, it starts with an extremely low evaluation of the UN. The Report abounds in criticisms directed against the unproductiveness, lack of coordination, excessive overlapping, fragmentation, etc., of UN activities. Also in a sharp contrast to the Nerfinian track, it does not admit the value of the UN's role in setting standards and creation of norms, which Bertrand refers to as "mere talk."[26]

Unlike Nerfin, who envisages reform by extrapolating the present philosophy of the UN, Bertrand prefers to break with the present, which for him is nothing but conceptual vagueness, and reaches the conclusion that an unworkable, direct search for peace should be replaced with an indirect mode, namely, functionalism. It is noteworthy that to Nerfin the concept or philosophy of the UN since its "revolution" is clear, whereas it is not for Bertrand. Furthermore, creating a new order centers around the notion of "development" for Nerfin, while for Bertrand the main concern is with a broader notion of "peace," which then necessitates international cooperation in the economic field.

Bertrand's concept of a new order raises at least two questions, especially in connection with its functionalistic basis. First, peace between which actors (the superpowers, developed countries, less developed countries, etc.)? Functionalism as a mode presupposes at least a minimal homogeneity among the participants. The success of the European Community and the failure of the East African Community are evidence of this. If Bertrand is thinking of applying this strategy to, say, the relationship between the superpowers, it may work (although it does not preclude the need for a direct approach to peace). But it seems questionable whether the method can work in narrowing the gap between the rich and poor—in other words, development, which requires more than simple cooperation.

Secondly, bearing in mind Bertrand's emphasis on development, specifically his call for the creation of "regional development agencies,"[27] is this intended to institute a two-track UN, one that handles functional cooperation among the rich alone (or among the poor alone), and another that specializes in development? If so, how does it fit the overall design for global order in an Economic UN? Moreover, in view of Bertrand's forsaking of the managerial role of the UN and emphasis on its role as an negotiating forum, the question arises whether the member states are only expected to engage in negotiations, even as regards development? In fact, such negotiations have been tried for decades, to little avail.

To sum up, despite its penetrating critique of the UN malaise and an admirably consistent adherence to the philosophy of its reform, the Bertrandian track seems to suffer a certain ambiguity and incongruity. And even if these shortcomings are overcome, it is likely that this track will still leave the same impression. In comparison with the Nerfinian route, this proposal is equally grandiose but less utopian. Although less utopian, it does not appear more feasible. This paradox probably stems from the difference in their recognition of what we have called "revolution" and its deep causes.

This does not mean that the Nerfinian track is superior to the Bertrandian one as a strategy. The former is only too grandiose to be translated into practice immediately. The point, however, is that any idea for reform will have to be grafted onto the challenge of the aspirations from below as well as onto the deep-seated change that embodies that challenge. The Nerfinian track, although undoubtedly utopian, is a logical response to the world revolutionized by the UN system. It has been a revolution aspiring to more democracy, more equity, and more humaneness, onto which the Nerfinian track tries to graft the reform. The aspirations being almost irreversible, bailing out the UN is coextensive with bailing out the world; hence the logic of grafting and the fallacy of severance.

In the real world, however, a track totally different from grafting and slightly different from severance has begun to be pursued, as follows:

The G18 track originates from the Report of the Group of High-Level Intergovernmental Experts to Review the Efficiency of the Administrative and Financial Functioning of the UN (Group of 18) of August 1986, and is supplemented by General Assembly Resolution 41/213 of December 1986. As the contents of these documents, presumably well-known by now, are largely technical and administrative, we will not detail them here, but instead will only recapitulate a few interpretations of them.

The Report of the G18 is an answer to the UN's administrative and financial crisis. It contains seventy-one recommendations, including reducing the number of conferences and meetings, reduction of regular budget posts by fifteen per cent within three years, an increase in the ratio of staff employed on a permanent basis. These recommendations on the whole are concrete and sound, but the Group could not reach agreement on perhaps the most crucial and delicate issue: the planning and budgeting process of the UN.

The matter was carried over to the General Assembly, which, in Resolution 41/213, gave its solution. The resolution, among other things, gave the Committee for Programme and Coordination (CPC) a primary role in budgeting and programming, a role that has been assumed by an expert organ, the Advisory Committee on Administrative and Budgetary Questions. There is little doubt that the switch from experts to governmental representatives (although this oversimplifies the change) was meant to accord more weight to the voices of the disaffected states, the United States in particular.

Moreover, the resolution reaffirmed that decisions in the CPC would be made by consensus, tantamount to allowing each member state veto power on draft budgets that displease it. Being a de facto substitute for the Kassebaum Amendment, the new mechanism was greeted by the Reagan Administration with rejoicing.[28]

Counter-revolution is no longer a marginal exercise, but has secured its own legitimate foothold. What looked at a glance like a simple technical reform is turning out to be a vehicle of counter-revolution.

Admittedly, the counter-revolution at this stage is less vociferous than before, when the weapons of withdrawal or withholding of payments were being used. But since the new state of affairs keeps touching upon the quintessence of the revolution, it should still be viewed in the revolution/counter-revolution context. As if to reverse the quiet commencement of the revolution, a counter-revolution has crept into the UN system.

The new situation could also be seen as the attainment, however temporary, of an equilibrium between the revolutionary and counter-revolutionary forces. From the viewpoint that disorder in the UN system is likely to result in worldwide disorder, such a lull in the storm has been necessary. A persistent concern, however, is whether this halt in the UN's internal disorder will bring the kind of world order that the inner logic of the revolution has sought.

The present lull has been brought about partly by the moderation, or the tendency toward "realism," of the Third World countries.[29] It signifies a kind of "revolution fatigue" on their part; and, as long as the fatigue is from the sterility of confrontation for confrontation's sake and, of excessive rhetoric on issues (although this depends on how one defines the term "rhetoric"), it may be a welcome sign. But one has to see to it that this realism does not prove to be a simple atavism, a return to the old principle of might makes right.

CONCLUSION: TOWARD THE SECOND PHASE OF THE REVOLUTION

The so-called crisis of the UN has largely been a misplaced problem. The most legitimate subject of the crisis, if any, should have been how to make the UN a true agent for a just and viable world order at this juncture of history. However, that concern has been diverted to how to stop disorder within the UN, and only in terms of financial and administrative dysfunctions.

Administrative reforms such as the curtailment of unnecessary expenses, staff, conferences, and documents are obviously needed. On the other hand, it has to be recognized that reform like that proposed by G18, albeit necessary, is fundamentally a damage-limiting one born in the midst of confusion. More constructive and forward-looking reform plans, aimed at truly strengthening the UN, are yet to come. They could include financial autonomy, staff recruitment not necessarily based on the principle of geographic representation but on individual caliber, and so on. What is ultimately necessary, however, is an agreement as to what kind of UN the member states want. Seen in this light, a meaningful damage limitation, if any, would be to set up inside the UN or some Specialized Agencies machinery for selecting the agenda items, like the Drafting and Negotiating Committee of UNESCO. By helping the member states to eschew adopting an overly contentious agenda, it may attenuate excessive confrontation among them and ameliorate the atmosphere for defining what the UN is expected to do for human betterment. Needless to say, caution should be taken against any machinery that deprives the weaker and poorer states of the opportunity to express their needs and aspirations.

The description above by and large accords with our earlier prognosis that it is necessary to graft any reform of the UN onto the legacy of the revolution. The grafting continues the revolution as a qualitative change in the rules of the nation-state game and in its consequences.

The revolution was inevitable to a certain extent, the backdrop of the crisis being two historic forces each vying for the legitimacy of the kind of world order it conceives of, namely, a hegemonic one versus a non- or post-hegemonic one. The revolution, set in motion by the UN voting mechanism, was inevitable, not exclusively because of the mechanism itself, but also because of the enormity of global problems arising out of the nation-state system. So was the politicization also inevitable. Needless to say, futile confrontation for confrontation's sake will surely have to be eschewed.

At present, the counter-revolution seems to be gaining the upper hand, but the revolution is not dead yet. The mechanism that sustains it still exists, and, more important, a sense of the illegitimacy of hegemonic rule and of economic exploitation is deeply anchored in the minds of many people. The historic trend toward human equality being irreversible, the prescription for continuing the revolution should not be understood as merely taking sides politically with the Third World. The real choice is whether we can be clearsighted enough to take sides with the historical trend toward justice. In this sense it could be said that the UN system revolution is unfinished, not aborted.

The first phase of the revolution was mainly protest. The next phase has to be devoted to the actual redress of the protested grievances. At that stage, it will be more important to know exactly "what kind of UN people need" than "what kind of UN the member states want." Such a perspective will render it more pertinent to explore the as-yet-far-fetched Nerfinian idea of establishing a Citizens' Chamber. Until then, epiphenomenal aspects like institutional shortcomings will remain the focal point, but even in this transitional process, it should not be forgotten that the ultimate aim is to make the UN system suitable for solving the global malaise. In order to solve these world problems, the UN system will have to transform itself from a purely intergovernmental organization, and be responsive to the needs and aspirations of the global citizenry.

Postscript

This essay was written well before the Gulf War, in which decision making in the Security Council was not hindered by veto. What effects the War will have on the management of the U.N. remains to be seen, but the author believes that the main thesis of this essay remains basically valid.

NOTES

1. An abridged and slightly revised version of the author's "The U.N. System as an Unfinished Revolution," *Alternatives* 15, no. 2 (Spring 1990).

2. Toshiki Mogami, *The UNESCO Crisis and World Order: International Organizations as a Non-violent Revolution* (Tokyo: Token Publishing, 1987; in Japanese), esp. ch. 3 and Conclusion.

3. Throughout this essay, the term "United Nations" refers almost exclusively to its General Assembly, or sometimes the Assembly-type organs of the other organizations within the UN system. A qualitatively different picture will have to be drawn if the convergence of the wills of the permanent members of the Security Council becomes more stable, enabling it to direct the Organization's course of action.

4. This description seems to be coterminous with what Roberts and Kingsburry call "republican dethronement." See Adam Roberts and Benedict Kingsburry, "The UN's Roles in a Divided World", in their *United Nations, Divided World* (Oxford: Clarendon Press: 1988), p. 25.

5. Although the United Nations has never been a world government, it has nonetheless effected a certain kind of governance through the articulation of prevailing organizational ideologies, which differ from one era to another. See Toshiki Mogami, "The Turbulence of the U.N. System and the Mutation Process of International Governance," in Y. Higuchi et al., eds., *Constitutionalism for Peace and International Cooperation* (Tokyo: Keiso Publishing, 1990, in Japanese), pp. 3–25.

6. Victor-Yves Ghebali, "The Politicization of UN Specialized Agencies: The UNESCO Syndrome," in David Pitt and Thomas G.

Weiss, eds., *The Nature of United Nations Bureaucracies* (London: Croom Helm, 1986), p. 122.

7. Pierre de Senarclens aptly characterizes this by saying that the UN Charter was a "document subversif de l'ordre établi," in *La crise des Nations Unies* (Paris: Presses Universitaires de France, 1988), p. 41.

8. Ghebali, pp. 120–123.

9. Joseph A. Mehan, "UNESCO and the U.S.: Action and Reaction," *Journal of Communication,* Autumn 1981, p. 160.

10. Mohammed Bedjaoui, "A Third World View of International Organization: Action Towards a New International Economic Order," in Georges Abi-Saab, ed., *The Concept of International Organization* (Paris: UNESCO, 1981), p. 206.

11. Gregory J. Newell, "Perspectives on the U.S. Withdrawal from UNESCO", *Department of State Bulletin* 85, no. 2094 (1985): 53–56. See also U.S. State Department, "U.S./UNESCO Policy Review" of February 29, 1984, reproduced in Committee on Foreign Affairs, U.S. House of Representatives, *U.S. Withdrawal from UNESCO: Report of a Staff Study Mission February 10–23, 1984, to the Committee on Foreign Affairs, U.S. House of Representatives* (Washington DC: U.S. Govt. Printing Office, 1984), Annex 6.

12. Committee on Foreign Affairs, p. 28.

13. In Committee on Foreign Affairs, U.S. House of Representatives, *Recent Developments in UNESCO and Their Implications for U.S. Policy: Hearings before the Subcommittee on Human Rights and International Organizations and on International Operations of the Committee on Foreign Affairs, House of Representatives* (Washington, DC: U.S. Govt. Printing Office, 1985), p. 98.

14. See Julian Behrstock, *The Eighth Case: Troubled Times at the United Nations* (Lanham, MD: University Presses of America, 1987).

15. U.S. State Dept., p. 90.

16. U.S. State Dept., pp. 158–160.

17. Fernando Reyes Matta, quoted in "World Forum: The U.S. Decision to Withdraw from UNESCO," *Journal of Communication,* Autumn 1984, pp. 117, 119.

18. Committee on Foreign Affairs, *Recent Developments . . . ,* p. 171.

19. Marc Nerfin, "The United States Sanctions Against UNESCO and the Three Vetoes: Is a Democratic United Nations System Possible?" *Development Dialogue,* 1976, no. 2, p. 88.

20. Rajni Kothari, "World Politics and World Order: The Issue of Autonomy," in Saul H. Mendlovitz, ed., *On the Creation of a Just World Order* (New York: Free Press, 1975), p. 57.

21. Marc Nerfin, "The Future of the United Nations System: Some Questions on the Occasion of an Anniversary," *Development Dialogue,* 1985, no. 1, pp. 5–29.

22. Nerfin, "Future of the United Nations,".

23. Nerfin, "Future of the United Nations,".

24. Nerfin, "Future of the United Nations," (emphasis in the original).

25. Maurice Bertrand, *Some Reflections on Reform of the United Nations* (Bertrand Report) (Geneva: Joint Inspection Unit, JIU/REP/85/9, 1985); *Refaire l'ONU: Un programme pour la paix* (Geneva: Editions Zoé, 1986).

26. Bertrand Report, para.

27. Bertrand Report, paras. 160–165.

28. U.N. Association of the U.S.A., *Issues Before the 43rd General Assembly of the United Nations* (Lexington, MA: Lexington Books, 1989), p. 163.

29. Some of the Third World states were reportedly content with Resolution 41/213. See Yves Beigbeder, "La crise financière d l'ONU et le Group des 18: Perspectives de réforme?" *Annuaire français de droit international,* 1986, p. 438.

8

United Nations: Prince and Citizen?

MARC NERFIN

AN UNPRECEDENTED OPPORTUNITY

In the long march towards a just world peace along its intricate institutional paths, the present moment might well be unique.[1] At the very least, circumstances offer opportunities that have never existed before.[2]

These times seem to be those of unprecedented awareness, at least as far as one of the two superpowers is concerned, of the global nature of humankind's *problematique,* of the need for a new approach to security and of the role in that of the United Nations—an awareness that accompanies the rediscovery of "universal human values," such as the precedence of the whole over the parts, of global security over the security of a single country or camp, of the global environment over specific environments, of common interests over parochial ideologies, of society over classes, of the human species over states, nations, and countries.

As a result, in the military/political sphere, a number of regional conflicts are being settled, and more might be defused by the time this appears; disarmament has started; the realization is growing that war can no longer be the continuation of politics through other means. More fundamentally, there is an explicit rejection of the "image of the enemy" and related stereotypes. After all, the Constitution of the UN Educational, Scientific and Cultural Organization (UNESCO) was not that idealistic when it proclaimed that "Wars begin in the minds of men. It is in the minds of men that the defence of peace must be constructed. . . . "

In the ecological sphere—20 years after the Stockholm Conference—the depletion of the ozone layer, the greenhouse effect, acid rain, deforestation, desertification, the dumping of toxic wastes, especially in the Third World, the Faustian nature of the nuclear energy bargain, especially clear after Chernobyl, are at long last taken seriously, even sometimes dealt with; and more is in the offing—outer space, Antarctica, indeed the whole concept of the global commons. There is also some acceptance—40 years after the proclamation of the Universal Declaration of Human Rights and 12 years after the entry into force of the International Covenants on Economic, Social and Cultural Rights and on Civil and Political Rights—that human rights, at least some of them, but not yet peoples' rights, are a global responsibility. Then, against such a background, and most important from the point of view of constitutionalism and world order, there are significant openings in the global institutional field.

Mikhail S. Gorbachev's article, "The Reality and Guarantees of a Secure World" (*Pravda,* September 17, 1987),[3] the USSR aide-mémoire, "Towards Comprehensive Security Through the Enhancement of the Role of the United Nations (September 22, 1988),[4] Foreign Minister Eduard Shevardnadze's speech to the 43rd Session of the General Assembly (September 27, 1988)[5] and Chairman Gorbachev's address at the same session (December 7, 1988)[6] provide a wealth of suggestions, ideas, hints in virtually every field of UN activity.

The approach is bold: "Enhance resolutely the authority and role of the United Nations,"[7] "our House of Peace" and "Make it stronger not only as a unique international forum but also as an equally unique centre for ensuring universal and regional security, and the security of each country,"[8] "UN specialized agencies should become regulators of international processes."[9]

More specifically, and quoting Gorbachev almost at random: there is "need for making the status of important political documents passed at the UN by consensus more binding, morally and politically, on the basis of consensus, . . . [for] monitoring the implementation of General Assembly resolutions . . . [and for] a greater role of the Secretary General."[10] "The deep involvement of the UN in the resolution of major international problems has spotlighted the acute need for new mechanisms of verification and control . . . within the framework of the UN."[11] He calls for "the establishment of a reserve of military observers and armed forces of the United Nations."[12]

There is something for almost every UN agency in this initiatives fireworks: the Security Council (which should study the establishment of "*UN observation posts in explosive areas of the world*"),[13] the Economic and Social Council (ECOSOC), the UN Conference on Trade and Development (UNCTAD), UNESCO, the World Health Organization (WHO), the International Atomic Energy Agency (IAEA), and the Geneva Conference on Disarmament, which should "become a forum that would internationalize the efforts on transition to a nuclear-free, non-violent world"; a World Space Organization should be set up.[14]

A special importance is attached to environment seen as the second "window" of opportunity for global security. Foreign Minister Shevardnadze regretted "the absence of any global control" over the technosphere and suggested the channeling of funds released by the abolition of military programs "towards instituting an international regime of environmental security."[15] "The principle of governments' annual reports about their conservationist activity and about ecological accidents, both those that occurred and those that were prevented on the territory of their countries"[16] should be established. The UN Conference on Environment and Development (1992) should be held "at the summit level";[17] "we are working to have this forum produce results that would be commensurate with the scope of the problem. . . . Let us also think about setting up within the framework of the UN a center for emergency environmental assistance [which] would promptly send international groups of experts to areas with badly deteriorating environment";[18] "the Soviet Union proposes a discussion on how to turn UN Environmental Programme into an environmental council capable of taking effective decisions to ensure ecological security."[19]

"Our ideal is a world community of States which are based on the rule of law and which subordinate their foreign policy activities to law" said Chairman Gorbachev;[20] the aide-mémoire stresses "the affirmation of the primacy of international law in inter-State relations," and there is a call for the "elaboration of a major long-term program for the development of international law."[21] With respect to the International Court of Justice, its "mandatory jurisdiction should be recognized by all on mutually agreed upon conditions," the first steps in this direction to be taken by the permanent members of the Security Council.[22]

Perhaps the culmination is to be found in Sheverdnadze's speech when he spoke of "voluntarily delegating a portion of national rights in the interest of all. . . . The interrelationship of events in an interdependent world increasingly compels us to delegate some national prerogatives to an international organization."[23]

Staggering as this is, it remains within the realm of governments. But the civil society is not absent from the new thinking. Shevardnadze alluded to "the growing world-wide 'green peace' movement," Gorbachev to "broad-based and frequently turbulent popular movements. . . . the idea of democratizing the entire world order has become a powerful socio-economic force,"[24] as well as to "nongovernmental commissions and groups which would analyze the causes, circumstances, and methods for resolving various concrete conflict situations."[25] The aide-mémoire suggests for study, in the context of peace-keeping operations, "the use by the Security Council of special missions, which would include representatives of the public as well as officials."[26]

On the role of civil society in the strengthening of the UN, Mikhail Gorbachev made two specific points, to which we shall revert later, but deserving to be quoted in full here:

> We should have set up long ago a World Consultative Council under UN auspices uniting the world's intellectual elite. Prominent scientists, political and public figures, representatives of international public organizations, cultural workers, people in literature and the arts, including Nobel Prize laureates and [of] other international prizes of world-wide significance, [and] eminent representatives of churches could seriously enrich the spiritual and ethical potential of contemporary world politics.[27]

> Scientists, cultural figures, representatives of mass movements and various churches and activists of people's diplomacy are ready to shoulder the burden of universal responsibility. In this regard, I believe that the idea of convening, on a regular basis, under the auspices of the United Nations, an assembly of public organizations deserves attention.[28]

What is important is not the originality of these ideas, which for the most part had already been formulated, one way or the other, elsewhere,[29] but that they were put forward, at this stage, by the leaders of one of the two superpowers. They must be studied. Unfortunately, no one in the UN appeared either alert to the institutional opportunity, even less looking at their implications and examining how to set in motion the transition towards a more representative and therefore stronger world organization.

Leaving aside here ideas belonging to the space of the Prince—but the framework had to be set—we shall concentrate on the two ideas belonging uniquely to the Citizen's space, a space wide open to imagination, innovation, and experimentation. The challenge of giving a role to civil society in global affairs is to be taken up. The remainder of this chapter attempts to explore further its feasibility.

PRINCE, MERCHANT, AND CITIZEN

The powers that be, governmental or economic, have proven unable by themselves to ensure genuine security—that is, a just world peace, including its human, social, and ecological dimensions—nor another development.[30] They are more part of the problem than of the solution.

Looking at the core of human agencies, however, it can be seen that, contrasting with governmental power—the Prince—and economic power—the Merchant—there is an immediate and autonomous power, sometimes patent, always latent: people's power. Among the people—or "civil society"—some develop an awareness of this and act with others in an effort to improve the human condition. This is the Citizen. These citizens' associations—or third system[31]—do not seek either governmental or economic power. In making patent what is latent, the Citizen is an expression of the autonomous power of the people.[32]

In the Preamble of the United Nations Charter, the apparent contradiction between the high-sounding "We the peoples . . . " and the governmental monopoly of power in the UN is increasingly criticized. In fact, U Thant, in his opening message to the 1970 World Youth Assembly, said that, "While the Charter speaks in the name of peoples rather than Governments, mankind as such still has no direct voice in the United Nations."[33] This kind of soul-searching seems to have disappeared, at least at that level, until 1985, when Javier Perez de Cuellar wrote, in his annual *Report on the Work of the Organization,*[34] "In thinking of the future of the Organization, one is struck by the fact that the United Nations is almost unique among political institutions in having little direct contact with its basic constituency, 'the peoples of the United Nations'." There was no followup in either case. And there seems to be no indication, to judge from Sir Brian Urquhart's two major books[35] to suggest that other Secretary Generals may have been struck by this fault.

The preamble of the Charter is of course purely rhetorical. Even before it ends, it falls back on "our respective Governments," and the state remains, for the full length of the Charter, the only protagonist worthy of the name. These limitations are largely attributable to the original sin of the UN—to have been begotten, brought into being, and grown up as an organization of governments alone.

Civil society and Citizen, confronted with the results of the performance of the Prince and the abuses of the Merchant, are reemerging. For, as François Rigaux, president of the International People's Tribunal, points out, in debunking the,

> myth of the identification of state and law, . . . a number of interests which are essential for humankind are poorly taken care of by the state, sometimes because they are too small—hence the success of local organizations. . . . Then there are the big problems of humankind: peace, nuclear weapons, . . . ecological disasters . . . [for which] the state is not a better manager either. This is the locus of NGOs' activities: to better manage the "small" and . . . to express, as far as big problems are concerned, the essential demands of peoples.[36]

The challenge is to find ways to make this growing voice heard in the only universal forum available—the United Nations.

MEMORIES OF INFANCY

The people in whose name the Charter was promulgated never had anything to say in the UN, since they were deemed to be represented by "their" governments. When the Charter was adopted, war had given legitimacy to the founding governments, but no one in 1945 at San Francisco seems to have asked whether, for instance, the British government represented the people of India, or the French those of Algeria. Colonial empires were still the dominant North–South mode. Still, within the center, it was felt that something was not reducible to governments, something which was expressed through the concept of "nongovernmental organizations" (NGOs).

The Charter did provide (Article 71) for the Economic and Social Council (ECOSOC) to consult with international NGOs (then all Western) and "where appropriate" with national ones—but "after consultation with the Member of the UN concerned." "Consultation" was explicitly differentiated from "participation without vote," reserved to states not members of ECOSOC and to specialized agencies. The necessary arrangements were spelled out in ECOSOC Resolution 288 (X) of February 27, 1950, later superseded by Resolution 1296 (XLIV) of May 23, 1960, a monument to bureaucracy still in force.

Neither the Charter nor the resolutions defined what an NGO was and, as a result, the present list of those benefitting from "consultative relations," in spite of being classified in three categories (I, II, and Roster), is a hodgepodge of genuine citizen's associations (e.g., Amnesty International) and commercial outfits (e.g., the International Container Bureau). Whatever the future of these arrangements, a clarification would distinguish between Merchant and Citizen organizations.

Certain agencies, notably International Telecommunications Union, UNESCO, and International Labor Organization, are more open to nongovernmental actors. Their experience illustrates what is or could be possible, and provide perhaps the foundations of further development.

In ITU, described as "a potpourri of bureaucrats and industrialists," "the participation of private operating agencies in the activities of the international consultative committees [e.g., the International Frequency Registration Board] is widespread" and "representatives of scientific or industrial organizations may also participate," their "most important resources [being] the strength of their companies and organizations and their own personal qualifications."[37] But this relates more to links with the merchant than with the citizen, and thus falls outside the present discussion.

UNESCO has an interesting—and somewhat depressing—story. In 1944, Edward Phelan, ILO acting Director (in Montreal) and Wilfred Jenks, a future ILO Director General (1970–1973) who was then its legal adviser, convinced the committee drafting the Constitution of the new organization that "plenary votes should be cast by individuals rather than by countries"; the ILO tripartite representation system suggested a way "to allow participation by educators and others." But governments had the upper hand, in this and other more far-reaching proposals. Some participants "favored delegation seats reserved for nongovernmental representatives. Others wanted nothing more than their governments' consultation with the national cooperating body, which body itself might assume the form of a public authority." The compromise was that Executive Board members, as "persons competent in the arts, the humanities, the sciences, education and the diffusion of ideas, and qualified by their experience" were to serve in their personal capacity, "*on behalf of the Conference as a whole* [underlining mine, MN] and not as representatives of their respective Governments."[38] This remained so until 1954, when, on the basis of a 1952 U.S. proposal prompted by the Korean conflict, the UNESCO Constitution was amended so that each Board member, since then, has represented "the Government of the State of which he is a national."

The National Commissions (referred to above as the "national cooperating body") could have been an interesting innovation. Constitutionally "regarded as intermediaries between governments, peoples, and the organization," they exist in virtually every country, but "often commissions have simply provided resonance in their group constituencies for their governments' declarations." Yet NGOs seem to have a greater role in UNESCO than anywhere else: "UNESCO-accredited NGOs are noteworthy for their close symbiotic relationship with the organization, their variety, and their number. No other specialized agency maintains so many formal NGO ties."[39]

ILO offers a third model, which has survived the seventy years of the agency's existence. In spite of its limitations, it has the most advanced makeup of any organization in the UN system, and could well inspire others. The ILO General Conference, reads the Constitution, "shall be composed of four representatives of each of the Members, of whom two shall be Government delegates, and the two others shall be delegates representing respectively the employers and the workpeople of each of the members" (Article 3). Further, "Every delegate shall be entitled to vote individually on all matters which are taken into consideration by the Conference" (Article 4). However, "the Members [governments] undertake to nominate non-Government delegates and advisers chosen in agreement with the industrial organizations, if such organizations exist, which are most representative of employers or workpeople, as the case may be, in their respective countries" (Article 3, al. 5).

The dynamics of the ILO organization is such that it often gives the advantage, in practice, to nongovernment delegates, a situation further strengthened by the introduction, in 1979, of the possibility of secret ballot on any question not requiring a two-thirds majority. Incidentally, in 1948, the USSR recommended to ECOSOC amendments in the ILO Constitution with a view to increasing the weight of the nongovernment component.[40] The problem is, of course, the autonomy—or lack of it—in their respective countries, of the "workpeople" organizations, and, in view of the size of the "most representative" ones, their bureaucratization.

Finally, from a different angle, an experiment, which does not seem to have constituted a precedent so far, deserves mention as a "major departure from the traditional relationship between the UN and non-governmental organizations." In 1979, at a meeting on infant and young child feeding which took place "at the centre of WHO/UNICEF decision-making process," various groups of participants were involved on an equal footing: representatives of governments, scientists, health workers, executives of infant food manufacturing firms, representatives of the UN system, and constituent-based associations from both South and North. The composition of that meeting helped make it a "qualitative leap forward in the approach to infant feeding."[41]

IT IS DESIRE THAT CREATES LIFE

The UN is not only history, nor precedents: it is also an aspiration. From that point of view, the many schemes put forward since 1945, even if at best limited to advocacy, deserve consideration. Taken as a whole, they offer a powerful vision of a UN to be.

The late Max Habicht has written that he personally had in his possession twelve texts of World Constitutions or principles to this effect, and he lists them.[42] Guy Marchand, Secretary General of the Peoples' Congress, has for his part drawn up a list of some eight institutional or individual proposals for global citizens assemblies.[43] Without including all of these, but on the other hand incorporating some recent individual suggestions, a rough typology, arranged in an approximately increasing order of feasibility, would look more or less as follows:

World Assemblies Outside the UN

(a) The *Peoples Congress*, launched in 1966 by the "Appeal of the Thirteen" (including Lord Boyd Orr, Josue de Castro, Danilo Dolci, Alfred Kastler, Linus Pauling, Lord Bertrand Russell) has organized since 1969 symbolic "transnational world elections" by groups of about ten thousand people. The hope is that the Congress will become more and more representative and "prefigure a World Assembly democratically elected."[44]

(b) The *World Citizen Assembly*, established in 1975, convenes periodically an Assembly for people and groups concerned about the state of the earth and committed to building a world community.[45]

(c) The *World Constitution and Parliament Association* (WCPA) proposes a World Parliament with one chamber elected by the people and a World Executive responsible to the Parliament. A World Constituent Assembly (Innsbruck, Austria, 1977) adopted a Constitution for the Federation of Earth and until it is ratified by at least 25 countries, the WCPA helps to organize sessions of a Provisional World Parliament (three sessions have taken place, in 1982, 1985, and 1987). The first two sessions, held respectively in England and India, have passed eight bills to "outlaw nuclear weapons," for a "World Economic Development Organization," for ownership by the people of Earth all oceans and seabeds beyond 20 kilometers offshore, etc.[46]

In the UN Framework

(a) In the post-1945 period, the most comprehensive proposal remains that of Grenville Clark and Louis Sohn.[47] They envisage the transformation of the UN General Assembly into a popularly elected body of

744 members, the voting power of the states being in proportion to their populations. The Security Council, elected by the General Assembly, would be the executive branch of the world government.[48]

Unlike this one, other legislative models are of the bicameral type. Most retain the present General Assembly, with or without modifications, as the States' Chamber and propose to add a People's Chamber elected through direct universal suffrage. Others favor a "second Chamber" of intermediary bodies (e.g., international NGOs).

(b) The *World Association for World Federation*—Movement for a Just World Order Through a Strengthened United Nations—(WAWF), founded in 1947, now forms the World Federalist Movement with the Parliamentarians Global Action (PGA) and Youth for Development and Cooperation (YDC). Its London Manifesto (1950), proposes the revision of the UN Charter so as to transform the UN from a confederation of sovereign states into a federation of states which limits its members' sovereignty; a bicameral system is envisaged with a States' Chamber and a Peoples' Chamber.[49]

(c) Johan Galtung, examining the role of "nonterritorial" actors, envisages a double bicameral system. In addition to the territorial actors' representation, with a house for the States, "roughly corresponding to the General Assembly of today," and a House of Representatives, directly elected, there could be also two houses for the nonterritorial actors, one for International Governmental Organizations (IGOs) of which there are 378, and one for International Peoples Organizations (IPOs), which numbered 4,676 in 1986.[50]

(d) Maurice F. Strong, noting the "anomalous situation of the UN, in which it differs from all the other levels of governance," since "it has neither a direct access to its constituency or taxing power," suggests a bicameral system in which peoples' directly elected representatives sit in one chamber and representatives of governments in the other. UN finances would be covered through a system of taxation, primarily on international economic activities such as trade and financial flows and on the use of the International Commons."[51]

(e) The United Kingdom Medical Association for Prevention of War (MAPW) and the UK Association of World Federalists presented separate proposals for a UN Second Assembly to the 1982 UN General Assembly Special Session on Disarmament. An International Network for a UN Second Assembly (INFUSA) was established in 1983 by Jeffrey Segall on behalf of MAPW. In 1987, it brought together 25 international organizations (including WAWF) and 58 national ones, of which 31 were from the United Kingdom, 10, from the United States and 4 from the Third World. Since 1985, INFUSA has launched an annual Appeal to the UN General Assembly to consider the proposal for a UN Second Assembly. The proposal is quite elaborate: The proposed

Assembly would be a subsidiary organ of the General Assembly under Article 22 of the Charter; it would be composed of "nongovernmental persons" but "each Member state would have the right to decide on its own method of choosing the representatives from its country." The Second Assembly would be a "deliberative" organ assisting the General Assembly by expressing views and making recommendations.[52]

MISSION IMPOSSIBLE?

Two points could be made to suggest that nothing is entirely unfeasible in "this time . . . filled with extraordinary events" as Eduard Shevardnadze sees it.[53] First, one may wonder whether the "new thinking," and the opportunity that accompanies it, are not an indication that the untouchability of the UN Charter is perhaps a concept of the past. Would it not be worth trying to update it?

Second, as Johan Galtung put it when discussing the elections to the global House of Representatives, "they could be and should be direct, just as [are] the elections to the European Parliament today. If Western Europe can do so, the whole world should be able [to]."[54]

In fact, the European Parliament experience offers several precedents, the European Community being more than an intergovernmental organization, but less than a federation. First, like the UN, the European Community was originally conceived without a Parliament: "The first Schuman Plan of 9 May 1950 contained no reference to any parliamentary body."[55] However, the concept was included in the Treaty of Paris (1952), which provided (Article 21) that members would either be nominated or elected by universal suffrage, the decision being left to the state Members, so "there could have been a Parliament partly elected and partly nominated." This did not happen. Even if the Treaty of Rome (1958) provided for "elections by direct universal suffrage in accordance with a uniform procedure in all member states" (Article 138(3)), discussions remained inconclusive for many years, largely due to French opposition (Gaullist and Communist). Thus members were originally chosen by and from their own parliaments. The first direct elections were held only in 1979, each country using its own electoral system; the third elections took place in 1989 (the Parliament members are elected for five years).

Second, the composition of the European Parliament reflects the concern of countries like Belgium, Germany, and Italy for "infrastate," local realities. Yet since "party politics" dominate the national parliaments, virtually all national parties are represented in the European Parliament; they form eight groups, embryos perhaps of Europe-wide parties.

Third, the European Parliament "came into being without a specific role. It was a symbol"—but it "has shown itself to be a flexible and adaptable institution. . . . Seen in a historical perspective, its achievements . . . are considerable."[56] Its members managed to use extensively the limited powers they have been given, utilizing imaginatively its modest "supervisory and advisory powers," which now include an effective veto power over Commission proposals.

Fourth, the European construction provides, in addition to the Parliament, for a Council of Ministers, endowed with final decision-making power, could be compared to the UN General Assembly, although at a higher level of participation, and of course with many fewer members, meeting frequently at the summit or sectorial level. The Commission, as the executive organ of the Community, responsible only to the Parliament, could, *mutatis mutandis,* be seen—in contrast to the present Secretary General and Secretariat of the UN—as the equivalent of Clark and Sohn's new Security Council.

WHAT NOW?

There is no either/or choice between the status quo and the Federation of the Earth. One way or the other, a transition will have to be negotiated. The desired future having been sketched out, the challenge is to map out the paths and stages which, slowly or quickly, depending on circumstances and ingenuity, may get us closer to it. The cardinal rule is that no proposal, however incremental, contradict the final aim. This is a win-win game: Not only do the means justify the end, but they are also ends in themselves.

What follows is but a rudimentary attempt at identifying some signposts for the journey.

(1) One suggestion, more illustrative or even emblematic than propositional, perhaps simply maieutical, has been for a tricameral system at the UN. Published as a contribution to the celebration of the 40th anniversary of the United Nations, it was concerned with "the next 40 years." A Prince Chamber would represent the governments of the states (more or less the present General Assembly, however adjusted), a Merchant Chamber would represent the economic powers, be they transnational, multinational, national or local, and belonging to the private, public, or social sectors, and a Citizen Chamber would represent the people and their associations. No details were provided (it was partly a call to "imaginative and innovative institution designers") but it emphasized that the exercise should not only be directed at, but carried out with, the social actors themselves.[57]

Most problems of representation, election, etc., obviously remain wide open in this proposal, including that, equally untackled in other proposals, of the relation between people at large (represented through the electoral, parliamentary model), their associations, and the "elites." Nevertheless, electoral democracy could stem from the preliminary intermediary bodies, and in fact will not function properly, i.e., ensure effective participation, without them. Indeed, the whole problem of democracy, which remains unsolved within the nation-state framework, might be tackled afresh on the global level, which could offer hints to the nation-states themselves. It certainly will be less difficult, politically speaking, to organize the representation of the nongovernmental organizations than that of the civil society as a whole, and, at this stage, there may be no other choice. This implies that criteria need to be worked out to ascertain an acceptable level of representativeness.

(2) Further along this perhaps elitist, not to say aristocratic, "revisionist" route, one might wonder if, at least in exceptional circumstances, the civil society does not recognize itself in, and is not expressed by, certain individuals better than by organizations emanating from itself, however well-intentioned. Present circumstances might well dictate this in that there is a need to dramatize the role of civil society in world affairs, and the media are more prone to cover "names" than institutions. To take one example, one may speculate whether the people of Africa at the General Assembly Special Session on Africa (1986) would not have been more effectively represented by a panel of African writers, singers, movie makers, and scientists than by NGOs.

This is to say, in fact, that Chairman Gorbachev's suggestion for a World Consultative Council might well be the first practical step towards giving a voice to people in global affairs. Other governments (and even "experts") may not like it: Such an idea, "while discussed with great interest" at a UN Institute for Training and Research roundtable on the "Future Role of the UN in an Interdependent World" held at Moscow in September 1988 with the participation of some one hundred personalities, yet met with "no agreement in favour."[58] This underlines the difficulty that holders of conventional power have in accommodating to any new thinking. Still, as an even more reformist intermediate step, nothing prevents the Secretary General from convening regularly such a group, which might develop further.

(3) Three other immediate steps could be envisaged:

(a) Discussing the future of UNESCO in his last interview as Director General of UNESCO, Amadou Mahtar M'Bow specifically mentioned "the restitution of the Executive Board . . . [as] the sole representatives of the universal intelligentsia, whereas the organ, since the decision taken in 1954 at the request of, among others, the Americans, and when the Soviet joined, progressively became an increasingly political projection of the states. One should correct this drift. Others, I hope, will succeed in that."[59] It might have helped his successor—who reportedly pronounced himself in favour of such a restitution—if the journalist had asked, or Mr. M'Bow answered, the question of whether he himself had tried, and said who or what prevented him from succeeding. Such a change might be a significant new departure for UNESCO, help in its revitalization, and set a precedent for other UN agencies.

(b) In his book, *Refaire l'ONU* (Remake the UN)[60] Maurice Bertrand has a section on "Peoples' representation"—a concern absent in his earlier and more official report on the reform of the UN. Finding it difficult to imagine that peoples' representation could be arranged through NGOs, he considers that "one of the most interesting avenues in this respect could be the representation of professions in the governing bodies of UN sectorial agencies, alongside with governments." But corporatism has narrow limits. ILO alleviates them, in a sense, by accommodating on an equal footing both employers and employees. Teachers may be represented in UNESCO, doctors (and the pharmaceutical industry?) in WHO, industrialists in UN Industrial Development Organization. What about students, patients, or consumers? Maybe the UN could start by opening FAO to peasants.

(c) Some enlightened governments may reserve two of the five seats, in their five-person delegations to the General Assembly, to opposition parties and to a spokesperson for the civil society at large. A few do it occasionally, at least with parliamentarians. The practice could first be extended progressively, and when wider acceptance is gained, common criteria for appointment could be defined, and eventually, when the time comes for the Charter to be amended, adopt the ILO system of vote by individual rather than by countries.

(4) Still, basically, what is at the root of the discussion, is, with the need to recognize people as the subjects of global affairs, the autonomy of the civil society. The Citizen need not wait for the Prince to grant it rights; it should, rather, assume them. In this respect, within the realm of UN, from the Stockholm Conference on the Environment in 1972 to the Nairobi Conference on (and for, and by) Women in 1985, the NGO system has shown remarkable imagination. Clearly, these and other people's forums were parallel to, not part of, official gatherings. But influence and achievement exist also beyond the formal decision-making mechanisms, and they often affect the latter significantly.

At Stockholm, due to the political circumstances (Third World governments' reticence, absence of the USSR and other East European countries, the Western base of most citizens' groups), the people's forum had to be deliberately kept separate from the intergovernmental conference. Yet, writes the Conference's Secretary General, "there is no question that the positive results of the Stockholm Conference on the Human Environment were very largely a product of the concerted efforts of nongovernmental organizations and citizens groups."[61] It was perhaps the success it was because, and not in spite of, its forced autonomy.

Nairobi, only thirteen years later, was a different world. People (in that case, women's) presence was universal, and paramount. It is not too much to say it was the most significant event of the year: it was in fact the most impressive participation of people in the whole history of the UN. Forum 85, in which there were some fifteen thousand women from all over the world, was the first conference where governmental delegates could feel what the situation really was for everyone.

On the basis of such precedents, and perhaps also that of the 1970 World Youth Assembly, in spite of its institutional shortcomings, having been convened by the General Assembly,[62] one might perhaps think of a World Citizen Assembly to be organized, under UN auspices, by a global organization. Another suggestion emerged in 1988 during the General Assembly Special Session on Disarmament: some INFUSA members (see earlier section above) decided that it should promote, in cooperation with others, a "major open international conference under the theme 'Towards a more democratic UN system'."[63] In October 1989, a group of citizens' associations decided to promote a series of international conferences to discuss proposals for democratizing the UN system. The first such conference, called CAMDUN (Conference for a More Democratic UN) took place in New York in October 1990. In any case, there are many practical problems, but such undertakings may usefully test the potential of direct Citizen's participation in world affairs, and explore the feasibility of Chairman Gorbachev's suggestion in this respect (see first section, above).

(5) More immediately still, and without excluding previous suggestions, the Citizen can exercise its birthright by making the intergovernmental UN accountable to "We the peoples." This could be done through the preparation and wide dissemination, every year before the convening of the General Assembly of a *Citizen's Report on the State of the United Nations,* as a counterpoint to the annual Secretary General's *Report on the Work of the Organization.* Similar social audits could be prepared on all aspects of the UN system agenda, with an emphasis on the most global problems[64]

This, like the holding of Citizen's forums parallel to major UN meetings, does not depend on any intergovernmental or bureaucratic decision or even approval. Gandhi provided the lead: "The moment the slave resolves that he will no longer be a slave, his fetters fall. He frees himself and shows the way to others." Autonomy is also self-reliance. Perhaps this is just a matter of redirecting some of the enormous energies that citizens' groups are currently investing in sometimes less relevant exercises, including institution designing. The networks—the emerging mode of citizen's self-organization—are there. What is needed is vision, initiative, leadership.

For the first time since 1945, it appears possible to "save succeeding generations [starting with those presently living] from the scourge of war" and the threat of nuclear annihilation; to save the environment which is the support of our life; to eliminate the chasm between those benefitting from the prodigious productive capacity of techniques and those excluded by it.

Possible, not certain. Only imagination and action will enable us to see, beyond what is, what is feasible. Only human action will make the possible happen. The task is to ensure continuation of life, the survival of the human species and a life worth being lived for every one of its members. Not to colonize the future, but to leave it its chances, and multiply them. No proposal, no strategy is too ambitious for that. None is too modest either, provided it helps to carry out the task.

NOTES

1. This paper was written well before the Gulf War and, as it is going to press, the combination of the Bush Administration's arrogance and the UN Secretary General's resignation to it gives an air of unreality to what follows. Yet the crisis suggests strongly the need for a re-foundation of the UN, this time not by the victors, as in 1918 or 1945, but by the victims, "we the peoples."

2. Thomas M. Franck writes that "the current, unprecedently realistic Soviet attitude has created an exceptional opportunity that could give the United Nations a new lease on life," in "Soviet Initiatives: U.S. Responses—New Opportunities for Reviving the United Nations System," *The American Journal of International Law* 83 (1989); 531–543.

3. Mikhail S. Gorbachev, "Reality and Guarantees for a Secure World," *Pravda,* September 17, 1987, translated in the USSR Mission to the UN *Press Bulletin* (Geneva), no. 169 (1433).

4. UN Doc. A/43/629 (September 22, 1988).

5. *Press Bulletin,* no. 182 (1682).

6. Address by Mikhail S. Gorbachev at the 43rd session of the UN General Assembly, December 7, 1987, as distributed in English by the New York USSR Mission to the UN.

7. Gorbachev, "Reality and Guarantees."
8. *Press Bulletin,* no. 182.
9. Gorbachev, "Reality and Guarantees."
10. UN Doc. A/43/629.
11. *Press Bulletin,* no. 182.
12. UN Doc. A/43/629.
13. UN Doc. A/43/629.
14. Gorbachev, "Reality and Guarantees."
15. *Press Bulletin,* no. 182.
16. Gorbachev, "Reality and Guarantees."
17. *Press Bulletin,* no. 182.
18. Address by Gorbachev.
19. *Press Bulletin,* no. 182. p. 195.
20. Address by Gorbachev.
21. UN Doc. A/43/629.
22. Gorbachev, "Reality and Guarantees."
23. *Press Bulletin,* no. 182.
24. Address by Gorbachev.
25. Gorbachev, "Reality and Guarantees."
26. UN Doc. A/43/629.
27. Gorbachev, "Reality and Guarantees."
28. Address by Gorbachev.
29. Maurice F. Strong, Memorandum of January 24, 1989.
30. The 1975 Dag Hammarskjold Report on Development and International Cooperation, *What Now—Another Development* (Uppsala: Dag Hammarskjold Foundation, 1975).
31. Words are never innocent: The phrase "nongovernmental organizations" is politically unacceptable because it implies that government is the center of society, and people its periphery. To respect people's autonomy also requires some semantic cleaning up. This is why we use here, whenever possible, "citizen's groups," "associations," "third system," "the Citizen" rather than "NGOs."
32. Marc Nerfin, "A New UN Development Strategy for the 80s and Beyond: The Role of the Third System," in A. J. Dolman and J. van Ettinger, eds., *Partners in Tomorrow, Strategies for a New International Order,* (New York: Dutton, 1978), pp. 71–82; "Pouvoirs," *IFDA Dossier,* no. 33 (January-February 1983) pp. 2, 44; "Neither Prince nor Merchant: Citizen—an introduction to the third system," *IFDA Dossier,* no. 56 (November-December 1986).
33. UN Doc. 56/WYA/P/10 (July 30, 1970).
34. UN Doc. A/40/1 (September 4, 1985).
35. Brian Urquhart, *Hammarskjold* (New York: Knopf, 1972) and *A Life in Peace and War* (New York: Harper and Row, 1987).

36. François Rigaux, *International Transnational Associations Transnationales,* 1987, no. 3, pp. 157–160.

37. Robert W. Cox and Harold K. Jacobson, *The Anatomy of Influence, Decision Making in International Organization* (New Haven, CT: Yale University Press, 1974), pp. 59–101.

38. James P. Sewell, *UNESCO and World Politics* (Princeton, NJ: Princeton University Press, 1975), pp. 66–67.

39. Cox and Jacobson, p. 155.

40. Victor-Yves Chebali, *L'Organisation internationale du travail* (Geneva: Georg, 1987).

41. Thierry Lemaresquier, "Beyond Infant Feeding: The Case for Another Relationship Between NGOs and the UN System," *Development Dialogue,* 1980, No. 1, pp. 120–126.

42. Max Habicht, "Le droit de l'homme et la paix," *International Transnational Associations,* 1980, no. 2.

43. Guy Marchand, Memorandum of December 6, 1987.

44. Guy Marchand, "Le mondialisme, force politique," *International Transnational Associations,* 1980, no. 2; pp. 88–89 and Louis Perillier and Jean-Jacques L. Tur, *Le mondialisme* (Paris: PUF, 1977).

45. *Yearbook of International Organizations 1988/89* (Munich: K. G. Saur, 1988).

46. Philip Isely, Memorandum of April 1987.

47. Grenville Clark and Louis B. Sohn, *World Peace Through World Law* (Cambridge, MA: Harvard University Press, 3rd enlarged ed., 1966).

48. Paul Taylor and A. J. R. Gordon, eds., *International Organization, A Conceptual Approach* (London: Frances Pinter, 1978).

49. Note Shevardnadze and Gorbachev's proposals. *Press Bulletin,* no. 182 and Address by Gorbachev.

50. Johan Galtung, "International Organizations and World Decision-Making," *International Transnational Associations, Transnationales* 1986, no. 4, pp. 220–224.

51. Maurice F. Strong, "Some Thoughts on the Future of the UN," remarks at a meeting of the New York Chapter, Society for International Development, November 29, 1984.

52. Jeffrey Segall, communication of December 5, 1987; cf. *IFDA Dossier,* no. 64 (March-April 1988).

53. UN Doc. A/43/629.

54. note 50.

55. John Fitzmaurice, *The European Parliament* (Farnborough, Hants.: Saxon House, 1978), p. 51.

56. Fitzmaurice, pp. 2–3.

57. Marc Nerfin, "United Nations: The Next 40 years," *IFDA Dossier,* no 45 (January–February 1985), pp. 2, 32.

58. Michael Doo Kingue, *The Future Role of the UN in an Interdependent World, Report of the Chairman* (New York: UNITAR, 1988), p. 11.

59. Quoted in *Le Monde,* October 21, 1987.

60. Maurice Bertrand, *Refaire l'ONU* (Geneva: Zoé, 1986) and *Contribution et une reflexion sur la reforme des Nations Unies* (Geneva: United Nations, 1985) (Doc. JIU/REP/85/9).

61. See note 51 (new) supra.

62. Louis Simon, "The International Youth Conference as a Mechanism for Involving Youth in UN Policies and Programmes" and "The World Youth Assembly—Background and Performance," in Berhanykun Andemicael and Anthony J. Murdoch, eds., *International Youth Organizations and the UN* (New York: UNITAR, 1973), pp. 38–50, 69–81.

63. *World Federalist News* 8, no. 3 (January 1989).

64. Marc Nerfin, "A Citizens' Report on the State of the UN," *IFDA Dossier,* no. 64 (March/April 1988), pp. 2, 40.

9

IGOs, the UN, and International NGOs: The Evolving Ecology of the International System

ELISE BOULDING

Let us think of the international order as an ecosystem consisting of ten thousand societies living inside 180 nation states. Add to this ecosystem two thousand intergovernmental organizations (IGOs) and the associated treaty systems binding the 160 nation states. Add a United Nations system with its operating organs, associated agencies, and programs, maintaining fifty worldwide information systems. Then add to that eighteen thousand transnational bodies (NGOs) with substantial or exclusive participation by citizens, i.e., people's associations covering the whole range of human interests: business, industry, the sciences, the arts, religion, education, culture, sports, social welfare, international relations, economic and social development.

The ten thousand societies, some settled, some nomadic, many with a long history of migration, have been around for centuries. Their existence is firmly mapped in the minds of their constituent ethnic groups, but they will not be found in standard world atlases. The nation-state successors to the ancient empires and feudal domains, although recent political inventions, by contrast so completely fill in the atlases that they appear to *be* the sole international order. The intergovernmental, United Nations and nongovernmental networks that have accompanied the rise of nation-states, however, will not be found in any atlas. This means that they, like the ten thousand societies, are poorly mapped in the modern mind.

Because we think of the world in terms of nation-states, we have a faulty understanding of the contemporary social ecosystem of the planet. There are social as well as physical energy flows in that ecosystem, flows which may be thought of as what Odum (1988) calls "emergy." Saul Mendlowitz's world order values[1] represent one dimension of these energy flows. The energy flows within the total ecosystem and the values that drive them far exceed the energy flows within the nation-state system. They provide resources for system transformation from an international order based on the threat of power and military capabilities of states to an international order based on transnational and intergovernmental peacemaking and problem-solving capabilities. The ratio of diplomatic to military capability in the international system as a whole may be considered an indicator of progress in the transformation from the old to the new order. While military capability is in the hands of states, diplomatic capability has to be understood both at the state level and in terms of UN and international nongovernmental organizations' (NGO) additions to that capability. In what follows we will use military expenditures as a measure of military capability, and treaty making as a measure of diplomatic capability, at the national level. UN and NGO structures will be considered as transnational resources that interface with national capabilities to increase diplomatic capability.

"Diplomacy" is here taken to refer not only to formal negotiation between states, and the treaties and regimes that govern their interaction, but to all problem-solving transnational interactions taking place bilaterally and multilaterally among states and peoples, including the interactions initiated by the UN system and nongovernmental organizations. In actual practice, of course, diplomacy can be used to increase as well as decrease threat levels. The focus here will be on that type of diplomacy directed toward tension reduction and the peaceful settlement of disputes. First, some features of the diplomatic-military balance in the nation-state system itself will be considered, and the diplomatic capabilities added to that system by the United Nations, before looking at the international NGO component of diplomacy.

THE DIPLOMATIC/MILITARY BALANCE IN THE NATION-STATE SYSTEM

The military security system of the nation-state consists of (1) weaponry, personnel, training, procurement, deployment, and C_3 (command, communication, and control) systems; (2) research and development; (3) military alliance systems; and (4) overseas bases. The nonmilitary security system consists of a government's foreign office, its diplomatic corps, espionage systems, and treaties. The world's military security system, absorbing between five percent and six percent of the world Gross National Product (GNP), and by some estimates up to fifty percent of the world's research and development capacity, has been amply documented elsewhere and will not be reviewed here. Instead, we will use ranking in military expenditures as a rough indicator of military capability, and treaties as a rough indicator of diplomatic capability.

Diplomatic Capability

According to the World Treaty Index[2] there are roughly 61,736 bilateral and multilateral treaties currently in force. While a few of these represent military alliances, the vast bulk of the treaties are problem-solving agreements about boundaries, common markets, scarce resources, the global commons (space, the seas, the Arctic and Antarctic), transboundary pollution, and other regional problems. Regional treaty making goes on within Organization of American States (OAS); Organization of African Unity (OAU); Association of Southeast Asian Nations (ASEAN); the Arab League, the European Economic Community (EEC); and similar groups. It also goes on within more specialized bodies: the Contadora countries, the African-Caribbean-Pacific Group (ACP), the South Asian Regional Cooperation (SARC); the Gulf Cooperation Council (GCC); the Organization of Arab Petroleum Exporting Countries (OAPEC) and also OPEC; the Cartagena Consensus (11 Latin American debtor countries); the South Pacific Forum; and many more.

The treaty process can be considered a major aspect of the diplomatic capability of the international system. Treaty making is by definition a consensual process in which the interests of all parties must be considered. Of the two types of treaties—multilateral and bilateral—the multilateral requires the greatest skill, since the interests of a large number of parties must be considered.

The world treaty system as a whole moved away from multilateralism after 1945, with the Nordic countries and the United Kingdom an exception to the trend. Nevertheless, for most countries, between forty percent and eighty percent of the treaties are multilateral. The superpowers have had the fewest multilateral treaties; twelve percent for the United States, ten percent for the Soviet Union, trailed only by Mongolia with four percent. The trend away from multilateralism toward bilateralism and bipolarity, which the behavior of the superpowers represents, is to some degree mitigated by the efforts of the nonaligned countries to stay on diplomatic terms with both powers. A total of 41 out of 130 countries, almost one-third, have maintained major diplomatic relationships with both superpowers.[3]

While multilateralism is unpopular among the major powers, the need for coordination in a situation of actual interdependency has produced the alternative concept of "regime"—rules and procedures that define the limits of acceptable behavior on various issues. The emphasis is on a decentralized self-regulation based on mutual self-interest. It minimizes the need for a more active problem-solving interaction among states, and assumes the very set of common values which it also denies; but it may be thought of as a transition phenomenon during a period of rethinking international institutions.

The consensual structures that result in the treaties and regimes mentioned above consist in part of older alliance structures that produced first the League of Nations and then the United Nations. The 51 states signing the UN Charter in 1945, however, represent less than one-third of the present members of the UN. Most of the new members, and a few of the old, are now active among the roughly one hundred twenty Nonaligned Movement states (NAM). This movement is particularly important at present because it represents another set of consensual structures and has provided a strong surge toward multilateralism during the retreat to bilateralism by many of the founding states of the UN. The frequency of diplomatic encounters within the NAM does not of course guarantee a high quality of interaction. It has been pointed out that the proliferation of such meetings is draining the resources of the Third World. Nevertheless there are substantive issues Third World countries are slowly working through.

In the evolution of the UN, the Western tradition of majority vote and the Third World tradition of consensus have clashed. Consensus as used in the UN and in the NAM does not mean unanimity, but the willingness to go along, not to raise objections.

We can put no figures on the contribution to GNP per capita of expenditures for the world diplomatic system. The foreign service of any country is, in any event, very small compared to its armed services. For most countries it can be counted in the hundreds, although with support staff this goes higher. The NAM working groups all operate on shoestring budgets. As a continuously operating set of communication and information systems spanning all continents, however, this world diplomatic capability has an importance outweighing its size. In order to get a quick overview of the diplomatic capabilities of countries at different levels of military spending, we will look at some country profiles.

PROFILES OF DIPLOMATIC/MILITARY EFFORT IN COUNTRIES WITH DIFFERENT LEVELS OF MILITARY EXPENDITURES

We shall divide the world's countries into the top twenty and the bottom twenty states in terms of military expenditures per capita, indicating the number of treaties, memberships in intergovernmental bodies, and INGO national sections for each country, as well as coding the level of GNP per capita for that country based on World Bank data (1983). (See Tables 9.1 and 9.2)

The High Military Spenders

Most of the biggest military spenders per capita are in the Middle East, along with Israel (grouped with Europe for politico-cultural reasons) and the United States. The remainder are northern European countries. There are striking differences between the Middle East and other high spender countries in terms of number of treaties, intergovernmental associations and international NGOs. The Middle Eastern countries are small, for the most part rich, and not well represented in the IGO-NGO networks so characteristic of Europe and North America. The diplomatic activities of the Arab League, the Group of 77, and the Nonaligned Movement unfortunately do not show up in the measures we are using for diplomatic efforts (something that should be corrected in future analyses).

Iran, Iraq, and the United Arab Emirates appear to be the most active diplomatically in the Western sense, and represent a classic case of guns *and* butter. For historic reasons, Middle Eastern states' diplomatic activity generally stays within the region. Intra-Muslim politico-religious conflict is so intense at present, that it absorbs much diplomatic effort. North–South conflict has a different character, and receives relatively less attention from the Muslim states. The very fact that Israel is not on the maps of any other Middle Eastern country is evidence of the deep gulf between Europe and the Middle East. On the whole, there has been relatively little effort to cross the North–South gulf with diplomacy.

With the exception of the issue of Israel, European countries have been primarily focused on the conflict between East and West Europe. All the West European high military spenders have high treaty involvement and high NGO involvement, reflecting the fact that much of the existing international order was designed in and for Western Europe. The Soviet Union's role, in spite of Russia's role in initiating

Table 9.1 ***Governmental and Nongovernmental Diplomacy Profiles for the 20 Countries Top-Ranking in Military Expenditures, by Region***

Country	*Rank in Military Expenditures[a] Per Capita*	*Treaties[b]*	*IGOs[c]*	*International NGOs[c]*	*Rank in Population Size[d]*	*Rating on GNP Per Capita[e]*
North Africa, Middle East, and Southeast Asia						
Saudi Arabia	1	91	42	230	65	H
Qatar	2	4	28	60	152	HH
United Arab Emirates	3	487	36	103	147	HH
Oman	4	NA	NA	NA	NA	M
Brunei	6	NA	NA	NA	NA	NA
Kuwait	7	46	39	233	130	HH
Bahrein	9	NA	NA	NA	NA	NA
Libya	10	97	43	201	113	MH
Iraq	12	235	51	308	57	M
Iran	20	387	40	456	23	M
Northern Europe, North America, and Israel						
Israel	5	524	36	1032	100	M
United States	8	4,355	62	1,505	4	H
U.S.S.R.	11	1,869	90	642	3	MH
United Kingdom	13	2,850	77	1,930	11	MH
France	14	2,413	87	2,132	14	MH
Sweden	15	1,333	84	1,660	62	H
Norway	16	1,269	78	1,458	87	H
Federal Republic of Germany	17	1,522	84	2,032	9	MH

Table 9.1 *Continued*

Belgium	18	1,422	74	1,963	53	MH
Netherlands	19	1,498	77	1,908	43	MH

a. From Ruth Leger Sivard, *World Military and Social Expenditures* (Washington DC: World Priorities, 1985), pp. 38–42. Figures based on 1982 data.

b. From Peter H. Rohn, World Treaty Index, 2nd ed., 5 vols. (Oxford: ABC-Clio Press, 1984). Figures based on 1974 data.

c. Union of International Associations, *Yeabook of International Organizations*, 1984/85, 2 vols. (London: K. G. Sauer). Figures based on 1982 data.

d. From World Bank, *The World Bank Atlas* (Washington DC: International Bank for Reconstruction and Development/World Bank, 1985.

e. Ratings based on data in *The World Bank Atlas*, 1985. Rating code:

HH: $18,000 +	MH: $7,500–12,000	ML: $500–1,100
H: $12,000–18,000	M: $1,100–7,500	L: $200–500
		LL: under $200

NA = not available.

Table 9.2 ***Governmental and Nongovernmental Diplomacy Profiles for the 20 Countries Lowest-Ranking in Military Expenditures, by Region***

Country	*Rank in Military Expenditures[a] Per Capita*	*Number of Treaties[b]*	*IGOs[c]*	*International NGOs[c]*	*Rank in Population Size[d]*	*Rating on GNP Per Capita[e]*
Africa						
Cameroon	111	126	50	252	71	ML
Senegal	111	110	51	358	91	L
Madagascar	113	76	32	255	67	L
Togo	114	62	40	203	114	L
Central Afr. Rep.	116	81	38	94	117	L
Upper Volta	118	61	45	149	74	LL
Ruanda	120	41	29	119	94	L
Mali	120	106	41	134	79	LL
Malawi	124	74	55	124	83	L
Uganda	125	88	42	248	56	L
Mauritius	125	33	34	232	127	M
Chad	125	63	36	91	92	LL
Zaire	125	85	42	297	31	LL
Niger	125	101	47	119	88	L
Sierra Leone	125	92	40	227	106	L
Ghana	131	187	51	429	59	L
Asia						
India	114	663	57	1,001	2	L
Burma	118	61	17	137	24	LL
Nepal	131	80	20	149	—	LL

Table 9.2 *Continued*

Caribbean						
Haiti	120	242	37	205	82	L

a. From Ruth Leger Sivard, *World Military and Social Expenditures* (Washington DC: World Priorities, 1985), pp. 38–42. Figures based on 1982 data.
b. From Peter H. Rohn, World Treaty Index, 2nd ed., 5 vols. (Oxford: ABC-Clio Press, 1984). Figures based on 1974 data.
c. Union of International Associations, *Yeabook of International Organizations,* 1984/85, 2 vols. (London: K. G. Sauer). Figures based on 1982 data.
d. From World Bank, *The World Bank Atlas* (Washington DC: International Bank for Reconstruction and Development/World Bank, 1985.
e. Ratings based on data in *The World Bank Atlas,* 1985. Rating code:

HH: $18,000 +	MH: $7,500–12,000	ML: $500–1,100
H: $12,000–18,000	M: $1,100–7,500	L: $200–500
		LL: under $200

NA = not available.

the Hague Peace conferences at the beginning of this century, has been a more limited one. Nevertheless, the Soviet Union has the highest level of participation in intergovernmental organizations, and its number of treaties is substantial: again, a case of both guns and butter. Although Sweden, Norway, Belgium, and the Netherlands are thought of primarily as peaceable countries, they are in fact high military spenders per capita. The substantial diplomatic capabilities that exist in Europe have not prevented these countries from also helping to fuel the arms race.

While the big military spenders are divided between two very different sets of conflicts, yet the weapons systems flow freely across the gulf that diplomacy scarcely crosses. The sheer quantity of weapons involved in both sets of conflicts may well swamp existing diplomatic capabilities.

The Low Military Spenders

The low military spenders are, unsurprisingly, the poor nations of Africa and Asia, but not the poorest, nor the weakest politically. Only six of the twenty lowest nations fall in the LL category—under U.S. $200 GNP per capita (Table 9.2). India stands out: The second largest nation in the world by population, with GNP per capita well under U.S. $500, it has treaty involvements and international NGO participation that compare with the most diplomatically active of the middle spenders of Europe. It has been a major leader in the Nonaligned Movement from its beginning. In Africa, Ghana, Cameroon, and Senegal stand out as having treaty and international NGO involvements that compare with their richer middle-spending colleagues of North Africa. There appear to be some significant policy choices at work here. All three countries house international IGO, NGO, and UN secretariats, and have provided regional as well as international leadership in working for disarmament and development.

This exercise of looking at high and low military spenders can be misleading, since it leaves out many countries that play highly visible roles in the international arena. By focusing on military spending rank alone, however, in relation to GNP level, the relationship between military and diplomatic involvements become clearer. It is not surprising that high military spenders are generally rich, and also make above-average investments in diplomacy; nor that the lowest spenders are much poorer. What is interesting among these poorer nations, however, is that some of them have opted for an above-average level of diplomatic activity.

Because we have been dealing largely with rankings, the feeling for the relative imbalance of military and diplomatic investments can easily be lost. Until diplomatic investments can be quantified in terms of budgets, personnel and, outputs, we can only try to imagine what a certain number of treaties and people's associations mean over against particular specified military defense systems. Many diplomatic investments involve increased intergovernmental linkages via the UN and nongovernmental organizations.

PEACE-BUILDING CAPABILITIES IN THE UNITED NATIONS SYSTEM

But since the world diplomatic system in fact does not rest on nation-states alone but is buttressed by the UN and international NGO systems, let us look at each in turn.

The UN system consists of six major operating organs, 15 associated agencies, two universities, well over twenty research institutes, divisions, and special programs, and five regional commissions. These bodies operate 50 worldwide information systems, 160 UN centers (one in each member state), and innumerable regional and local offices to administer the programs with which they are charged.

This extraordinary array of problem-solving capabilities has developed in an ad hoc fashion as new needs have arisen. However, ad hoc growth creates bureaucratic inefficiencies, including substantial program duplication. Technical problems, furthermore, cannot be separated from political ones, so the UN machinery has many shortcomings. The redesign of the UN has been a major topic since its 40th anniversary. At the same time, the UN represents a major resource available to governments for nonmilitary conflict resolution. Yet until very recently, there was serious underrecognition of the UN as a conflict resolution resource. Failures have been publicized, successes ignored.[4]

A brief review of the specific conflict resolution capabilities of the UN might begin with the Good Offices Missions of the Secretary General,[5] which involves a quiet diplomacy conducted by personal representatives of the Secretary General in the early stages of a conflict; when successful, these situations never reach the public eye. This capability is now being expanded by the establishment of a new Office for Research and Collection of Information to enhance the early-warning capability of the Secretary General's office. The Department of Disarmament Affairs supervises the training of Disarmament Fellows selected each year from the foreign ministries of member states, publishes detailed documentation on disarmament-development linkages, provides a variety of services to member states on disarmament questions, and collaborates with the Liaison Committee of Disarmament-Concerned International NGOs.

The Security Council's unnoticed successes can best be appreciated by reading Davidson Nicol's *Paths to Peace* (1981),[6] which documents the working of consensus in the face of deep ideological differences. Charged with handling all the world's most intractable disputes, the Security Council sends out special missions to trouble spots on request; sometimes it succeeds in facilitating dispute resolution. In peacekeeping, the six-plus observer missions and seven peacekeeping forces the Security Council has sent out since 1948 have been an important part of postwar conflict management.[7] After years of working unnoticed, the UN peacekeeping forces have suddenly surged into public awareness with their newly important role in several major Second and Third World peace settlements now in process.

The Hague International Court of Justice, predating both the United Nations and the League of Nations, continues to hand down decisions on cases brought to it, as it has done since it was first established in 1899. Sometimes its jurisdiction is acknowledged, sometimes not, but the historical record shows a steady growth in the body of law developed by the court's decisions.[8]

The UN Institute for Training and Research was established to carry out research on the structures and procedures of the UN, and to provide training for UN personnel, including training in peacemaking.[9] The Geneva UN Institute for Disarmament Research, one of the newer UN institutes, collects arms control and disarmament data from member states, carries out studies of arms control and accidental war, and helps train UN Disarmament Fellows.

UNESCO's peace-related programs, located in its Social Science Division, focus primarily on peace research and education. It publishes a periodically updated international directory of peace research institutes, supports the NGO quarterly International Peace Research Newsletter and a Peace Research Yearbook, gives the annual UNESCO International Prize in Peace Education, and holds periodic "meetings of experts" on arms control research and peace development. Indirectly, UNESCO's work on informatics and free information flows[10] and on the linkage between traditional and modern cultures celebrated in the current World Decade for Cultural Development are important to peace building, as are its bibliographic publications in the natural, social, and cultural sciences.

The Tokyo-based UN University, mandated to deal with pressing global problems, has a program in regional and global security studies involving scholars working both in regional and global research teams. The Costa Rica-based University of Peace, mandated by the UN but not functionally linked to it, is developing a research and training program aimed specifically at expanding the supply of qualified peacemakers.

All other UN agencies, institutes, and programs, insofar as they deal with problems that cause conflicts between states (and they all do) are in effect increasing the diplomatic and problem-solving capacity of the world community. The regular budget of the UN grew from US $19,390,000 in 1946 to a 1984–1985 biannual budget of US $1.6 billion.[11] Compared to the world military budget (in 1988 somewhere between US $900 and $1,000 billion a year), this is not very much. The major budget cutback now going on in the UN represents a substantial, if temporary, reduction in world diplomatic capability.

PEACE-BUILDING CAPABILITIES OF THE NONGOVERNMENTAL SYSTEM

International nongovernmental or people's organizations (NGOs) are strictly a twentieth-century phenomenon. These transnational associations are based on people's interests and agendas in every field of human endeavor—everything from physics to basketball. They may have national sections in as few as three or as many as 140 countries. In 1909 there were 176 international NGOs. Today there are approximately eight thousand completely autonomous international NGOs and another ten thousand specialized bodies that have substantial or exclusive participation by private citizens, to a total of eighteen thousand reported in the 1986 Yearbook of International Organizations. With a ratio of eighteen thousand international NGOs to 2,000 IGOs, we can see that the institutionalization of people's associations represents a major shift in the nature of the international system. Yet international NGOs have been largely ignored by mainstream international relations scholars.[12] While international NGOs continue to be somewhat Eurocentric,—the phenomenon having originated in Europe,—they are increasingly numerous in the Third World, and represent a highly diverse set of problem-solving networks for the planet.

At their best, international NGOs represent the accumulated know-how of the international community in every field of human endeavor. Working within their own fields of competence, they bring expertise that neither governments nor the UN itself can command to solve specific international problems. International NGOs differ from governmental bodies in having longer time perspectives, a more complete historical memory, and an incipient planetary identity. Without suspending familial, national, and regional attachments, they work on behalf of world interests. Because they have accumulated face-to-face experience in dealing with colleagues in countries whose governments have had minimal contact with each other, particularly across the East–West divide, they have played a crucial role in creating a social climate and background level of understanding that, for example, facilitated recent official diplomacy between the United States and the Soviet Union and between the Warsaw and NATO Pact countries generally. NGOs have similarly paved the way for current U.S. involvement in Middle East diplomacy regarding the status of Palestine.

With increasing recognition that peace, development, and environmental conservation are all linked, environmental and development international NGOs are now coming into prominence with their reports on the state of the planet and recommendations for planet-conserving policies.

The International NGO Scientific Community

The international NGO scientific community has been particularly important in dealing with the threat of nuclear war and of war in general. The Pugwash Conferences on Science and World Affairs, started in the late 1940s, were the first opportunity for physical scientists to begin systematic work on problems of arms control and disarmament. They have continued to command the respect of governments over the years. The International Peace Research Association, bringing a social science approach to war/peace problems, was founded in 1965. More recently, the International Physicians for the Prevention of Nuclear War and the SCOPE group of the International Council of Scientific Unions have worked on problems specific to nuclear war and its prevention. The International Lawyers Alliance has concentrated on the legal aspects of war prevention. In addition there are a host of professional and civic international NGOs that now have special programs on the threat of nuclear war. Behind these stand the older international peace organizations, some of which go back over a hundred years (the International Peace Bureau of Geneva, for example). The professional and specialist international NGOs have contributed to the development of peace-building treaties, such as the 1959 Treaty of Antarctica, the 1967 Outer Space Treaty, the 1967 Treaty of Tlatelolco, the 1971 Seabed Treaty, and the 1985 Treaty of Raratonga. The civic and more general-interest NGOs contribute to the climate of opinion in which peace-building treaties become possible. There is a gradual process by which each generation's peace movements go from grassroots activity to the development of transnational networks to institutionalized existence as NGOs, with independent international headquarters and sometimes UN recognition. This has been happening in the past decade to the anti-nuclear movement, with an increasing close linking of groups on all continents.

International NGO Peace Action Networks

There are also a variety of citizens' peace strategies. These range from women's encampments at military installations and the blockading of military shipments, through international citizens' peace brigades stationing themselves between hostile parties (India, Lebanon, North Ireland, Central America—see the reports of Peace Brigades International) and the creation of civilian-based defense training units, to the declaration of towns, nations, and regions as nuclear-free zones, and the establishment of sister-city relations, all supplementing citizen efforts to change national security policies.

Church organizations are also international NGOs, and have been galvanized by the threat of nuclear war to a level of reflection and public activity on behalf of tension-reducing and peace-building national policies in many countries far beyond what had been seen in recent history. Twentieth-century women's movements have also provided significant leadership to peace movements right through this century, both at the theoretical level of analyzing the war-prone and historically pervasive social institution of patriarchy,[13] and at the action level, organizing both symbolic and practical activities for alternative security policies.

The international environmental movement now sees itself as related to the peace movement, based on the environmental threat of nuclear war. The most recent evidence of this new development is the formation of the Global Greenhouse Network, a coalition of scientists, religious leaders, peace activists and environmentalists. NGOs like the World Council of Indigenous Peoples see superpower wars or a Third World War alike as endangering both their environment and their very existence.

The Structure of the International NGO System

The important things to remember about international NGOs is that they are organized by national sections, and national sections are organized by local branches, so NGO networks reach directly from individual households to world forums. No other type of diplomatic activity has this capability. To give an example of what this means in terms of local coverage, in the United States 5,700 grassroots peace groups, many with national and international linkages, were identified in a recent Directory.[14]

At present international NGOs are for the most part small in terms of organizational membership and budgets, and weak and isolated from one another in terms of the magnitude of the concerns they address. However, this is changing. Increasingly NGOs with common concerns are forming ongoing liaison groups with their own secretariats. This is true for disarmament, the environment and development, and other issues as well. Each major UN conference, beginning with the Stockholm Conference on the Environment and continuing with the Rome World Hunger Conference, the three International Women's Decade Conferences in Mexico City, Copenhagen, and Nairobi, and the UN special sessions on disarmament, have been the occasion for the development of new international NGO liaison groups that have continued working together.[15]

In addition, there is growing momentum to establish a Second Assembly at the UN to be composed of international NGOs, to introduce the vitality and inventiveness of NGOs more directly into the UN system. (Many NGOs already have accredited status at the UN and may contribute commentary, but only on a case-by-case basis.) Devising a workable formula for an additional Assembly that does not simply reenforce the power of nation-states with the strongest international NGOs will take time, but it will come. One version of this proposal is Marc Nerfin's suggestion for three UN chambers for "the Prince, the Merchant and the Citizen."[16] A good formula to involve direct NGO participation at the UN will release more of the diplomatic capability of NGOs into the international system. It would at the same time strengthen diplomatic capabilities in member states because of the national-section organizational format of international NGOs. Since countries vary in the extent to which their citizenry participate in NGOs, some countries have more of this type of people-resource than others. It happens that the top eight countries in the ranking of states by numbers of international NGO sections (a way of measuring people-resource) are all West European, and do not include the superpowers.

We have already examined something of the relationship between investment in military security as measured by percent of GNP devoted to military expenditures, and diplomatic capacity as measured by treaty obligations, IGO memberships, and international NGO sections present in a country. (See in Table 9.1 and 9.2) When international NGOs are active in their respective national societies, what kinds of activities take place? Let us look at some examples of the changing ecology of the international system generated by NGOs.

THE NEW ECOLOGY AND THE CHANGING DIPLOMATIC/MILITARY BALANCE

Civilian-based defense, zones of peace, citizen's diplomacy, and peace education have been chosen as examples of the way new nongovernmental initiatives intersect with governmental initiatives in building peace. The examples given are by no means intended to be a comprehensive listing of nongovernmental inputs to peace building, only illustrations of what the interface possibilities are in the new ecology of the international order.

Civilian-Based Defense

"Transarmament," a term first used by Gene Sharp, means "the process of changing over from a military system to a civilian-based defense system."[17] It includes what Sharp calls the "instrumentally effective action to defend" a people's way of life, institutions, and opportunities for future development. The concept came out of observations by Sharp of how the Norwegians successfully conducted a civilian-based defense of their country during its wartime occupation by Germany, when the normal structures of the Norwegian state were inoperative. Civilian-based defense (CBD) was thus historically a civilian initiative undertaken in aid of a government temporarily without power. The altered nature of state-people relations under these conditions is highly suggestive of a new political ecology.

The concept of non-offensive defense[18] (NOD) covers a broader range of transition strategies in a transarmament process. NOD includes a variety of alternatives to current NATO doctrine, ranging from simple territorial defense, through gradualistic approaches to defense reform, to civilian social defense relying on behavioral techniques of nonviolence.

Nonviolent community action to deal with conflict is found on all continents. The International Peace Brigade and Witness for Peace are examples of civilian-based defense NGOs functioning in combat zones. The Shanti Sena, the Indian nonviolent civilian brigades separating warring groups in India's border conflicts were the original models for later civilian defense projects. Gandhian theory and practice have played an important role in developing this type of people's action. Many CBD strategies do not depend on government initiative, but all involve some degree of cooperation with existing or to-be-transformed governments.

Zones of Peace

The zone-of-peace concept, going back to ancient customs of asylum, sanctuary, and safe-passage corridors through hostile territories, has become an important tool of the people's Nuclear Free Zone movement (NFZ). NFZ strategy calls for local citizens' groups to persuade a city, a province, and sometimes a whole country to declare itself a Nuclear Free Zone. Governmental interest in NFZ as a defense measure is based on the fact that such zones are free of threat and are unlikely to become bombing targets. These zones become social spaces in which peaceful futures can be negotiated.

The nearly five thousand Nuclear Free Zones around the world declared by local governments[19] are a suggestive indication of the effect of NGO activity on governments, although many of the governmental units declaring NFZs do not in fact have the jurisdictional authority or sovereign power to do so.

Citizens' Diplomacy and Conflict Resolution

Former diplomat and political scientist John Burton has developed an international facilitation process involving nongovernmental as well as governmental participants, which enables adversaries with serious objective conflicts to arrive at a settlement that allows for each side's values, interests, and needs. This method has been used in Asia, the Middle East and Soviet–U.S. conflicts. It is sometimes referred to as Second-Track Diplomacy to emphasize citizen involvement.[20] The Harvard Negotiation Project has developed a related but somewhat different approach to negotiated settlements.[21]

The evolution of the Conference on Conflict Resolution and Peacemaking into a federation of groups working at dispute settlement at every level from the family to inter-state disputes has given new visibility to conflict-resolution-oriented NGOs. A new government/NGO partnership has evolved with the establishment of government-funded peace institutes and university peace chairs (Stockholm

International Peace Research Institute, Canadian Institute for International Peace and Security, U.S. National Institute of Peace, Australian National University Peace Institute, and Netherlands government-funded peace professorships). The general mandate for these new institutions is to assess existing defense policies in the light of possible security alternatives being developed in academic and community settings.

Imagining Alternative Futures

There is a general feeling permeating social movements and the NGO world that the end of the twentieth century is a transitional era. Some groups anticipate social restructuring, others anticipate social transformation. All have intuitions of the new social ecology, the changed relations between international NGO and IGO structures. Techniques for imagining totally "other" futures in a mental mode combining fantasy, social imagination, and analysis have arisen from several sources. One important source for social scientists has been the work of the recently deceased Dutch sociologist Fred Polak, expounded in his *Image of the Future* (1955/72).[22] One particular workshop format based on Polak's work has been used by scholars, policy makers, and activists.[23] This format has allowed for analysis of best-case scenarios for a future social order (in contrast to the worst-case scenarios featured by security analysts), thus expanding social understanding of the range of possible futures.

Peace Education

Some of the most far-reaching conceptualizations of the new social ecology have been undertaken by NGOs concerned with peace education from kindergarten to university. The Peace Education Commission of the International Peace Research Association and related groups in various countries have provided leadership in redefining national security in terms of the interrelationships of peace, development and human rights.[24] Their educational innovations have included linking formal and nonformal education, the teacher's world and the learner's world, and learning itself to the settings in which learning takes place. These pioneering educators have explored the pedagogy of liberation and the meaning of dialogic education. Their dialogues have encompassed both East-West and North-South interactions. Their very diverse transnational membership has made it possible to explore the economic, political, and social dynamics, including those of gender, of the continued reproduction of the war system in most societies. Because teachers have a special relationship to the state and to society as transmitters of knowledge and culture to the next generation, there has been a tense but continuing dialogue between teachers and their governments in many countries, about what a school curriculum should include about the roles of the citizen, and the nature and demands of national security and national defense.

• • •

This overview of the changing ecology of the international system has focused on the role of the nation-state, the UN, and international NGOs in increasing the world diplomatic capability in the context of a world diplomatic/military balance. Considering, first, the treaty involvements of countries with high and low military expenditures, we explored the way in which UN and international NGO structures enhanced diplomatic capabilities. We saw that nations varied widely in the extent to which they had NGO resources. After examining the special properties of NGOs as international actors and different types of NGO activity, we looked at examples of how NGOs interacted with governments in (1) civilian-based defense, which actively involves a nation's citizenry in a range of social defense behaviors; (2) zones of peace, which by citizen action provides territories free of weaponry for the development through negotiation of enduring peaceful relations with adversary nations; (3) citizens' diplomacy, with a focus on developing people-to-government and people-to-people process skills for all conflict levels; and (4) peace education, the efforts of teachers to develop a pedagogy that will produce individuals empowered to work with existing institutions to reshape the world.

All these activities involve interaction between nongovernmental or people's associations and the institutions of governance. They also involve the social imagination of scholar and citizen applied to the problem of war and the generation of alternatives to war.

Ultimately, social imagination is the key to shifting the balance between military and diplomatic initiatives toward a more humane international order. The new order is a new ecosystem based on this process. It is social imagination that will enable people's associations and NGOs to discover, legitimate, and implement strategies of peaceful change through the continuous creation of crucial points of contact between them and intergovernmental and UN institutions. No one set of institutions can create the new order alone.

NOTES

1. Note the following: H. T. Odum, "Self-Organization, Transformity, and Information," *Science 242* (1988): 1132–1139; the five world order values first articulated by Saul Mendlovitz, *On the Creation of a Just World Order* (New York: Free Press, 1975) are: peace, economic well-being, social justice, ecological balance, and positive personal identity.

2. Peter H. Rohn, *World Treaty Index,* 2nd ed. 5 vols. (Oxford: ABC-Clio Press, 1984).

3. This is 1974 data. Since many more countries have joined Non-Aligned Movement (NAM) since 1974, it is highly likely that the number of countries having diplomatic relations with both superpowers has increased.

4. K. Venkata Raman, *The Ways of the Peacemaker: A Study of UN Intermediary Assistance in the Peaceful Settlement of Disputes* (New York: 1975).

5. Vratislav Pechota, *The Quiet Approach: A Study of the Good Offices Exercised by the United Nations Secretary-General in the Cause of Peace* (New York: UNITAR, 1972).

6. Davidson Nicol, ed., *Paths to Peace: The UN Security Council and Its Presidency* (New York: Pergamon Press, 1981).

7. United Nations, *Everyone's United Nations: A Handbook on the Work of the United Nations,* UN Publication no. Ed.85.1.24 (New York: UN World Bank, 1986); and Indar Rikhye, Michael Harbottle and Byron Egge, *The Thin Blue Line—International Peacekeeping and Its Future* (New Haven, CT: Yale University Press, 1974).

8. Shabtai Rosenne, *The Law and Practice of the International Court,* vol. 2 (Leiden: Sijthoff, 1965).

9. K. Venkata Raman, *The Ways of the Peacemaker: A Study of the UN Intermediary Assistance in the Peaceful Settlement of Disputes* (New York: 1975).

10. Sean MacBride, *Many Voices, One World* (Paris, UNESCO, 1980).

11. United Nations, *Everyone's United Nations: A Handbook on the Work of the United Nations,* UN Publication no. Ed.85.1.24 (New York: UN World Bank, 1986).

12. Elise Boulding, "Image and Action in Peace-Building," *Journal of Social Issues 44,* no. 2 (1988): 17–37.

13. Birgit Brock-Utne, *Educating for Peace, a Feminist Perspective* (Oxford: Pergamon Press, 1985); and Betty Reardon, *Sexism and the War System* (New York: Teachers College Press, Columbia University, 1985).

14. Elizabeth Bernstein, Robert Elias, Randall Forsberg, Mathew Goodman, Debra Mapes and Peter Steven, *Peace Resource Book* (Cambridge, MA: Ballinger, 1986).

15. Examples of INGO liaison groups are: NGO Liaison Committee on Disarmament, with groups at both Geneva and the UN in New York; Environmental Liaison Centre, Nairobi; International Coalition for Development Action, Brussels; International Women's Tribune, New York; and regional groups such as the new Nordic Alternative Campaign, a coalition of one hundred Nordic organizations around the issues of environment, human rights, local autonomy, and alternative defense policies.

16. Marc Nerfin, "An Introduction to the Third System," IFDA working paper (Nyon, Switzerland: International Federation of Development Alternatives, 1985).

17. Gene Sharp, *Making Europe Unconquerable: The Potential of Civilian-Based Deterrence and Defense* (Cambridge, MA: Ballinger, 1985).

18. Bjorn Moller, "Criteria of a Rational Defense," working paper (Copenhagen: University of Copenhagen Centre of Peace and Conflict Research, 1985).

19. New Abolitionist, March 1990, p. 91.

20. John Burton, *Dear Survivors* (London: Frances Pinter, 1982); and *Global Conflict* (London: Wheatsheaf Books, 1984).

21. Roger Fisher and William Urey, *Getting to Yes: How to Negotiate Without Giving in* (Boston: Houghton Mifflin, 1981).

22. Fred Polak, *The Image of the Future,* tr. E. Boulding (San Francisco: Jossey-Bass/Elsevier, 1972, original pub. 1955).

23. Elise Boulding, *Building a Global Civic Culture: Education for an Independent World* (New York: Teachers College Press, 1988).

24. Elise Boulding, "Peace Education as Peace Development," *Transnational Associations,* 1987, no. 6, pp. 321–325.

Part III

THEORIZING

10

World Order and the Reconstitution of Political Life

R. B. J. WALKER

Modern political analysis is heir to two distinct accounts of what it means to engage in political life. On the one hand, the dominant traditions of political thought are preoccupied with the conditions under which political communities may be established and nurtured within the relatively secure confines of sovereign states. On the other, theorists of international relations examine the relative disorder that seems to characterize relations between these states. This division of labor expresses an understanding established in early-modern Europe both of what politics is about and where it can occur. It is reproduced through theoretical assumptions and disciplinary codes that affirm the claims of state sovereignty as the satisfactory and even natural horizon of permissible thought and action.

In order to understand the significance and characteristic problems of the literature on "world order" that has emerged over the past two decades, it will be suggested in this chapter that it is necessary to understand what is involved in challenging the early-modern distinction between statist politics and interstate relations. Contrary to persistent claims that the distinctive feature of this literature is its concern with the global or planetary dimensions of human existence, I will suggest that this literature is best understood as an expression of the difficulty and importance of rethinking both the character and location of political life under conditions of profound spatio-temporal dislocation.[1]

SPATIO-TEMPORAL HORIZONS

Intimations of profound historical transformation are an intrinsic feature of contemporary socio-political thought and practice. Claims about urgent practical and ethical imperatives for change have characterized Western conceptions of political life since at least the eighteenth century. Such claims are generally articulated within historically specific understandings of time and history. They resonate, most insistently, with the hopes of the European Enlightenment. "Modernity" has even been defined as an attitude of temporal expectation. The possibility of the radically new, of revolutionary emancipation from the present, is already blessed and encouraged by the most conventional discourses about where we have come from, who we are, and where we might be going to. To speak now about the transformative character of the modern era is to invoke themes that were already familiar to Adam Smith, August Comte, John Stuart Mill, and Karl Marx. To take the dynamics, dangers, and opportunities of contemporary historical transformation as the starting point for scholarly analysis and normative ambition is to be caught within accounts of temporal possibility that are already routine. An openness to the future is readily susceptible to nostalgia. Whether as generalized platitudes about progress, as theories about the efficient mechanisms of economic development, or as speculative visions of a postindustrial convergence and the end of ideology, universalizing teleologies and linear projections have inspired some of the most tenacious clichés of modern political life. They inform epistemologies and ideologies; they underwrite moral codes, diplomatic postures, and commercial promises; they shape influential accounts of what is to be done. Some analysts explain the details and causations by technological innovation. Some try to make sense of the dynamics of an internationalizing political economy. Some simply fall back on an intrinsic spirit of progressive reason and liberal/socialist virtue. The variations diverge, but the theme builds on automatic memories.

The theme is easily remembered, but not always joyously celebrated. Once intimations of historical transformation are interpreted as an extrapolation of linear progress and development, both tradition generally and specific traditions are likely to be declared obsolete. Hence come laments for *l'ancien régime* or classical *virtù* as well as complaints about the arrogance of universalizing cultures. Hence also, in a more ambivalent and even tragic rendition, the acknowledgement that progress and development are also a loss. Disenchantment is simply the price of modern instrumentalities and achievements. The conservative, the romantic, the nationalist, the dour Weberian pessimist, all make their familiar repudiations of Enlightenment. In any case, those who remain skeptical about the promises of Enlightenment reason do not have to look very far for supporting evidence. Exterminations and repressions, marginalizations and the survival of the richest—these remain all too characteristic of a world acutely aware of temporal accelerations that are barely understood, let alone under effective control.

These familiar excursions organized by modern philosophies of history inevitably invoke their own spatial horizons. No matter how temporal trajectories are plotted, they are, in principle, subject to the autonomous authority of spatially differentiated political communities. Against those who prophesy, celebrate, or lament the temporal dynamism of the contemporary era comes the counterinsistence on the continuity, even permanence, of the fragmentation of particular human communities within states. Intimations of historical transformation may be caught up within post-Enlightenment accounts of history and time, but they are even more sharply circumscribed by the spatial principle of state sovereignty that was initially articulated in early-modern Europe.

The apparent contradiction between transformative potentials suggested by so much recent experience and the persistent spatial articulations of statist politics has not always seemed so intractable. For disciples of Adam Smith and Karl Marx alike, the forces of capitalist expansion implied the eventual demise of autonomous states. Similar predictions have emerged from some recent commentaries on the development of international institutions, multinational corporations, and patterns of functional and regional integration. Yet evidence of the declining significance of states is, at best, unconvincing. For many analysts—especially those who combine, under the dark mantle of political realism, a skepticism about Enlightenment reason with an ahistorical understanding of what states are—all claims to historical transformation must remain unconvincing precisely because temporal possibilities are still circumscribed by spatial or structural necessities.

It is with the modern theory of international relations that hopes for emancipation through historical transformation have found their most intransigent limits. Where, for post-Enlightenment sociopolitical thought in general, the possibility of historical progress has become the necessary precondition for emancipation over time—the condition permitting struggles for justice, freedom, and democracy—theories of international relations have found temporal possibility to be inherently problematic. Conventional theories of historical transformation are brought up sharply at the spatial boundaries of the territorial state, where they are made to seem most implausible, most speculative and utopian.

This divergence between a pervasive but imprecise sense of historical accelerations and the spatial categories of international relations theory has stimulated a discursive arena that appears to be right at the margins of contemporary scholarly debate. Participants in this arena reflect different experiences and intellectual traditions. Many are preoccupied with immediate dangers and frame their concerns in relation to specific goals: peace, justice, development, ecological sensitivity, human rights, democracy. But all are caught between a conviction that profound historical transformation is underway and an acute awareness that this conviction is at odds with established forms of political life. The literature that has emerged under the rubric of "world order studies" is perhaps the most sustained attempt within the modern theory of international relations to come to terms with the implications of this dilemma. When framed within the prevailing categories of political realism or empirical social science, this literature has clearly played a marginal role in contemporary social and political analysis. From other perspectives, however, this conception of which perspective is central and which marginal is much less clear-cut.

The literature that has been produced in this arena has seemed marginal not only because it expresses dissatisfaction with the more intransigent reminders of the realities of geopolitical fragmentation but also because it seems to challenge many of the established conventions of progressive politics. The great ideals of Enlightenment that have informed the dominant doctrines of recent history depend upon its aspirations for universality. But these aspirations have found their most persuasive expression in the ambitions of particular communities. To seek power, to ask what is to be done, is to covet the state. To extend speculation about historical transformation into questions about world order (or "planetary politics," "world politics," "global civilization," or similar attempts to place a name on processes that elude conventional categories) is to attempt what, according to those who retain their faith in those conventional categories, cannot be done. It is to force claims about history and time beyond the limits of established geopolitical space.

Those who nevertheless sense the need to speculate beyond the limits of the conventional categories find that they are inevitably caught up in a powerful discursive politics. They participate especially in a discourse in which the established horizons of geopolitical space are translated into rhetorical strategies constraining our capacity to say what it now means to speculate about historical transformation. In this discursive politics, two primary themes that have characterized so much of the world order literature—the need to grapple with questions about ethics, values, ideals and so on, and claims about the fate of the state—take on a special significance. The rhetorical strategies set in motion by references to "the normative" and by claims about the state are frequently deployed to demonstrate the implausibility of any aspirations for world order, let alone a world order that can be described as somehow just and peaceful. These strategies thus become the conditions constraining the very possibility of speaking about world order at all.

Indeed, the world order studies literature cannot be adequately understood in the context of claims about the possibility of "peace," the term that already suggests how this literature may be fixed in relation to the discursive rituals of realism/utopianism and the necessities of war. Rather, the most important questions posed by this literature concern the character of political life under conditions of both temporal and spatial transformation, questions that suggest the entrenched assumptions about peace, war, necessity, and future possibility must be placed in considerable doubt.

CRITIQUE AND CO-OPTATION

The literature that has emerged under the rubric of "world order studies" is reasonably heterogeneous. International legal theory, peace research, economic dependence theory, critiques of militarization and maldevelopment, theories of political culture, dilemmas of Third World liberation, the politics of social movements, ecology, human rights, supranational institutions; all have their place in a shifting conversation among sharply contrasting modes of enquiry. And yet this literature has been represented in the codes of modern social and political analysis in a consistently monolithic fashion. Perhaps the most striking feature of world order studies, in fact, is not what they are, or what scholars working in their context have tried to achieve, but what they have been taken to be. The reduction of a heterogeneous dialogue to an apparent monologue affects the interpretation of particular writers and texts, and places sharp constraints on the manner in which categories and assumptions available for thinking about contemporary political life can be challenged.

In relation to temporal trajectories, world order studies have been situated most persistently under the sign of the normative, and thus firmly at the intersection of ethics and international relations. Moreover, references to the normative have come to have two quite different meanings, both delineated in relation to distinctly modernist claims: to the scientific, on the one hand, and to the instrumental or utilitarian, on the other.

In North America, at least, the broad context in which socio-political analysis has been structured in the second half of the twentieth century is dominated by the claims of empirical social science. These claims have remained hegemonic even as their philosophical legitimacy has become more obviously threadbare. Other forms of enquiry, especially those rooted in historical explanation, hermeneutic interpretation, or a critical interest in the relation between theory and practice—forms of enquiry that predominate in the world order studies literature—have been effectively marginalized. Even disciplinary boundaries have been effected. The distinction between political science and political theory, between the objectively scientific and the normatively historical, has become paradigmatic in this respect.

As participants in a newly institutionalized discipline, students of international relations have been especially enamoured of empirical social science. Recalcitrant scholars have been consigned to a variety of sites that parallel the marginalized location of contemporary political theory. International law is an obvious case, although its more philosophical inclinations are redeemed by a professional and policy-making capacity largely unavailable to political theory. More historically and philosophically informed British and European traditions have sometimes been treated in this way. World order studies fit conveniently into this strategy. In a discursive universe defined by the epistemological claims of social science, to be assigned to the normative is already to be cast into a netherworld of frivolity, or at least of theory and philosophy.

Nevertheless, the distinction between the scientific and the normative is exceptionally tenuous. While questions about the nature of scientific knowledge remain contentious, the old positivist dichotomies of objectivity and subjectivity, facts and values, are no longer taken as the obvious starting point for discussion. In any case, those who have been strongest in their claims for the methods of social science have also been the least shy about advancing models, analogies, ideologies, and philosophical assumptions incorporating powerful accounts of how the world should be, and doing so under the guise of empirical theory formation.

Perhaps the boldest in this respect are those who invoke the other principal meaning now associated with the normative, that is, the instrumental act of deploying appropriate means in order to reach a given end. This is the meaning popular in liberal economic theory, a discourse with the convenient advantage of being able to take its assumptions about the character and meaning of human existence more or less for granted precisely because these assumptions have become so influential and even hegemonic in the modern world. To invoke Weberian language, the normative is thereby associated with a formal or instrumental rationality of means, not with the substantive rationality of intrinsic ends. Weber himself saw these two forms of rationality, or alternative meanings of the normative, as inherently in tension, as colliding in a manner that is constitutive of modernity as both progress and disenchantment. Influential sectors of modern social science have simply taken instrumental efficiency alone to be the *raison d'être* of human action.

With either meaning, the normative is rendered unproblematic. On the one hand, the normative is distinguished from the objective and scientific, and put in its appropriate place among subjectivities, the humanities, and philosophy. On the other side, modernity is conceived of as having already achieved the supreme insight that human beings are precisely what liberal economists have always known them to be: efficient, utilitarian bourgeois individuals able to choose rationally under conditions of scarcity. That this is itself a severely contested ideological and ethical stance—one predicated on a convenient forgetting of the historical circumstances and metaphysical assumptions through which this particular accounting for human beings' choices and actions has been constructed—is of little consequence. Questions about ideology, or ethics, or metaphysics are already rendered out of bounds.

Thus, whether deferred to the margin or compared to the achievements of liberal economic theory and its influential analogical corollaries in the theories of conflictual cooperation and international regime formation, world order studies are readily susceptible to rhetorical strategies made possible by a specifically modernist reading of the achievements of modernity. In attempting to preserve a space for "values," or "ethics," or the "visionary," world order studies have, like many forms of political theory, often reenforced the very intellectual strategies that have rendered it marginal. In fact, the problem is not to save the normative from the instrumental and empirical (despite Weber's insight that this may be a necessary condition for a meaningful life under conditions of modernity). It is, rather, the need to resist the rhetorical strategies through which a modernist reading of epistemology, coupled with a liberal utilitarian reading of human affairs, has managed to take the place of a critical assessment of what it means to engage in social and political enquiry at all. The old positivist distinction between the empirical and the normative still needs to be challenged, not reproduced. To engage with the normative in this context must be understood less as a concern with applying established ethical imperatives than of challenging the conditions under which it has been deemed possible to speak of ethics at all.

World order studies may be situated in relation to modernist accounts of temporality, but it is even more easily fixed in relation to discursive strategies that appeal to the spatial claims of the sovereign state as the locus of all authentic political life. Here the labels are likely to read "utopian" or "idealistic"; and the point of comparison to be the achievement of political community within the bounded territoriality of the state. Instead of the opposition between the scientific and the normative, rhetorical strategies build on the opposition between statist community and international anarchy. Relations between states are understood to be precisely what political life within states is not. In this way, discussions of world politics, or world order, or global politics, are subject to a general prohibition against the extrapolation of assumptions, practices, and hopes from the realm of political community within states to the noncommunity between states.

"Utopianism" and "idealism" thus take on a specific meaning with respect to the claims of state sovereignty. What is at issue is not the general validity of utopian aspirations or speculative ideals. These may be ruled out on other grounds, usually having more to do with judgments about modernity than about problems of world order as such. What is ruled out is the domestic analogy, usually in its temporal form: the claim that we ought to be moving towards a global political community modelled after the political life familiar from the modern state. What is ruled in, therefore, is a pervasive double standard. Within states, it has been possible to appeal to universal truths, either as an achievement (reason) or as a temporal possibility (history). Between states, however, it is necessary to recognize that whatever their universalistic pretensions, states are in fact merely self-righteous and are forced to coexist in a universe of competing sources of self-righteousness.

This double standard is open to a variety of interpretations. It is possible to assume that relations between states and political life within states are radically different, and amenable to understanding only through quite distinct traditions of enquiry. It is also possible to specify certain limits on what is understood as "normal political life." The conflict between "democracy" and "national security" or "national interest" is paradigmatic in this respect. Most crucially, this double standard comes to define the limits of political possibility. Universalistic aspirations for justice, democracy, progress, historical transformation, all are presumed to be possible at least in principle, but only within the territorial confines of established political communities; any attempt to extend them beyond these bounds of possibility must be either naive, or subversive of the sovereign authority of the state, or both.

It is easy enough to see why world order studies have become caught up in the discursive strategies made possible by this delineation of limits. It has been regularly located in precisely that discursive space made available for all attempts to resist the principle of state sovereignty as the answer to all questions about what political life can be. That discursive space is already produced by the principle of state sovereignty. It postulates a vision of the new as a reproduction of the old, although on a larger scale. The possibility of historical transformation is interpreted as the possibility of moving from the fragmentation of states to some kind of global society understood through an imagery of the state writ large. Because no such world state seems imminent, because any prohibition against the domestic analogy has been ignored, because the hope for greater universality violates the need for diversity as both a fact of life and as a general principle, the vision of historical transformation must be futile. Therefore, political "realism" demands only a vigilant, if tragic, accommodation with statist fragmentation, and not the stimulation of utopian hopes for a universalizing global community.

However, there are two difficulties with the interpretations constructed through these discursive strategies. One involves the reduction of a complex dialogue to a conveniently single-minded monologue. The literature on world order studies has indeed been concerned with the possibility of constructing more effective international institutions, with establishing more centralized forms of global authority, and with encouraging a more cosmopolitan awareness of global processes and dangers. But these themes have by no means monopolized or even dominated discussion. On the contrary, the literature of world order studies has often been thoroughly statist in orientation, although admittedly reflecting nationalist, Kantian, or even Marxist understandings of the state, rather than the Weberian or utilitarian accounts that dominate the conventional literature of international relations theory. Much of the literature on world order also explicitly challenges both statist politics and alternatives that stress the emergence of global institutions and authorities, whether by focussing on ecological and cultural accounts of political community or on the practices of social movements. In this sense, world order studies reflect much of the diversity of contemporary political debate in general, and are not usefully understood in terms of the convenient stereotypes rendered by terms like "utopianism" and "idealism."

Second and more significantly, even to the extent that the literature on world order studies has been concerned with global processes and more universalistic forms of political authority, it is not clear that the principle of state sovereignty and the domestic analogy offer much help in clarifying these concerns. There is no doubt that global processes and institutions play a crucial role in contemporary political life. In this sense, the world order literature responds as much to historical achievements as to future possibilities. The difficulty, however, lies in knowing how these processes and institutions are to be interpreted, and what kinds of political practices they encourage and resist. To be skeptical of both realist reifications of the state and images of future possibility generated by the principle of state sovereignty is to be aware of the extent to which the categories and assumptions of contemporary political analysis are being stretched to their limits by contemporary historical trends and structural transformations. In reacting against conventional categories, the literature on world order studies has in part become a captive of the categories being challenged, but has also been able to show more clearly what is at stake in demanding more appropriate responses to new historical conditions.

THE TEMPTATIONS OF UNIVERSALITY

Although the conversation recorded in the world order studies literature is much more varied and complex than the conventional stereotype suggests, the call for greater global awareness and even for new forms of global authority has been a dominant theme. In this call can be heard echoes of many intellectual traditions that have refused to accept the principle of state sovereignty as an adequate response to the most fundamental questions about political life. Where state sovereignty privileges claims of citizenship in particular communities over claims of people as such, many have urged precisely the reverse. Where state sovereignty expresses a logic of exclusion, a claim to universality made on behalf of particular peoples, many have urged that political life be reconstructed so as to express a logic of inclusion, of participation in some common community of humankind.

The crucial difficulty, one affirmed by the principle of state sovereignty, is that we do not know what it means to speak of "people in general" or "humankind" as such in any politically meaningful way. Or rather, to the extent that it is possible to draw upon existing accounts of a universalistically conceived humanity, we find that they enter into political discourse in three different—and quite inadequate—forms. They may be explicitly apolitical, speaking of some kind of naturalistically conceived humanity existing prior to political community and having characteristics and rights that are essentially ahistorical, and thus prepolitical. Religious and natural law traditions have been especially important in this approach and account in large measure for the apolitical or even anti-political character of much contemporary writing about peace. Or they may be expressed through the spatial resolutions of state sovereignty, and thus through the paradoxical claim that universality may be possible but only through the particularistic communities of autonomous states. Or they may be expressed through the temporal resolutions offered by an account of modernity as the achievement of a universalizing history in which differences in both time and space (tradition and traditions) may be erased in favor of a common or global way of life.

The problem posed by the world order studies literature is not adequately expressed as just the need for greater global awareness or new forms of global authority. The claim to universality as such is neither novel nor radical. Only in the context of a universalistically conceived account of reason, justice, and community within states does it make sense to claim that a properly political community is impossible between states. This explains how political realism has been constituted historically as a tradition by a set of negations: the negation of Christian eternity in the fallen condition of humans' life on earth; the negation of Enlightenment from despair at human irrationality; the negation of Progress under conditions of contingency, nihilism, and power politics; and the negation of political theory as a narrative about an absent community, a dispersal of authority, a fragmentation of power. In fact, the principle of state sovereignty must be read as an expression of claims to universality before it can be understood as an expression of fragmentation. The elegance of the principle of state sovereignty is that it allows for—indeed, insists upon—both of these options simultaneously: It permits the familiar rhetoric of presence and absence, community and anarchy, obstinacy and obsolescence, realism and idealism. It allows universalistic claims to be incorporated into the claims of particular states ("God," "Reason," or "History" "is on our side") just as easily as it permits universalistic claims to be overridden by statist appeals to autonomy and self-determination.

The appeal to modernity as such permits a correlative resolution. It is possible, for example, to point to the historical achievement of certain universalistic principles. The field of human rights has been especially important in this respect. It is also possible to celebrate the principle of state sovereignty as the condition under which modernist autonomies might be properly realized. Instead of state sovereignty being understood as an expression of universalizing but particularistic communities situated in an anarchical realm of violence and power politics, it becomes an expression of precisely the reverse: of the participation of particular communities in a broader field of explicitly modernist values. Sovereignty comes to be revalorized as a precondition for inter-state cooperation and détente rather than as a guarantee of conflict and insecurity. The dismal images attributed to Machiavelli, Hobbes, Rousseau, Hegel, and Weber begin to give way to the more guarded optimism associated with Kant.

Therefore calls for greater global awareness and new forms of global authority are likely to evoke universalistic claims already constitutive of the way the world is now, whether in relation to modernity in general or the principle of state sovereignty in particular. Consequently, it cannot be enough to understand the world order studies literature as a demand that existing fragmentation be overcome through an appeal to universality as such. The desire to move from particularity (the state) to the universal (global community, world politics) is already an effect of the specific resolution of the relation between universality and particularity affirmed by the principle of state sovereignty. But the historically specific resolution of universality and particularity making this desire possible is problematic, and not just the immediate problem of fragmentation.

To challenge this resolution is not necessarily to either affirm or deny the continuing significance of the state in human affairs. As economic, cultural, and institutional, as well as legal and territorial, entities, states are more complex phenomena than the principle of state sovereignty would suggest. They have been able to adapt to often drastic transformations in spatio-temporal relations generated by the expansion of capitalist economic relations and by technological innovation. It is in part because states have been able to change and adapt over time, to become more powerful and threatening than anything envisaged even by, say, Thomas Hobbes, that state sovereignty is widely regarded as a less than helpful founding principle for contemporary political life. But it does not necessarily follow that calls for greater global awareness or even new forms of global authority imply that the state is passé. They do suggest that claims to an absolute monopoly on power and authority—always more absolute in principle than in practice—will need to be rearticulated.

Nor is such a challenge necessarily a denial that fragmentation and diversity will remain a primary feature of political life in the future: in fact, precisely the reverse. The inevitability of diversity, like the continuing power of the state, is often advanced as a necessary limit to the articulation of global awareness and authority. But it is only a limit given the assumption that greater universality must entail a denial of diversity. Such is, of course, the prejudice of a very influential metaphysics, one enshrined in the principle of state sovereignty, which postulates the resolution of diversity into unity as a guarantee of truth, beauty, and goodness. Yet it must be remembered that state sovereignty itself permits only a very restricted degree of diversity: It does not begin to accommodate the variety of even nationalist identities struggling for expression in the modern world. In any case, a metaphysics that gives priority to unity over diversity is not the only context in which it is possible to speculate about what universality, or global awareness, or global authority must entail. Nor does a claim about global awareness and authority necessarily suggest a process of homogenization, an erasure of difference and diversity in the name of global community, common security, planetary ecology, or human identity.

If neither the persistence of states nor the erasure of diversity is necessarily implied by calls for greater global awareness and new forms of global authority, what exactly is the nature of the challenge being posed by the world order studies literature? It is the need to reopen those questions for which the principle of state sovereignty has provided a persuasive answer for so long. These questions are quite familiar, having an air both of banality and pretentiousness: questions about who "we" are, about what it is that constitutes a political community, and about how such communities can be established and sustained in space and time. They are banal in that these are questions rehearsed over and over again in the standard texts of the history of political thought. The received answers can be, and usually are, reiterated without the questions themselves being taken very seriously. We are individuals; we are members of the universal class; we are citizens of states. But once the questions come to seem more difficult, they also become pretentious—too speculative and philosophical, too open to the grandiose gesture, too far removed from precise and meaningful specification. The most serious difficulties posed by the world order studies literature do not arise from the repetition of what are considered to be inappropriate affirmations of the normative or the utopian. They arise because it insists that we no longer really know what political life can be about. If the state can no longer successfully claim to resolve all contradictions, the claim that it should exercise a monopoly on power, authority, and identity becomes tendentious. Accounts of political life as the competitive struggle to achieve and maintain state power became increasingly anachronistic.

In this context several alternative options can seem very tempting. It is possible to revert to some ahistorical and prepolitical account of humanity as such, in which case claims to universality may be deployed merely to shout truth to power, and not to attempt to reshape the configurations of power and authority through which more effective political practice can be constituted. It is also possible to succumb to the domestic analogy or to a modernist teleology in which the central metaphysical conceits of state sovereignty are reproduced as an image of future possibility. But these options are too easy. They involve a refusal to take seriously enough the political character of claims about historical transformation and the need for greater global awareness and new forms of global authority.

POLITICAL LIFE AND GLOBAL AUTHORITY

To situate questions about world order in this way may seem excessively abstract. After all, while the world order literature is characterized by frequent references to the normative, to state sovereignty and to historical transformations, the cutting edge of most of this literature has been the theme of emergency, danger, and crisis. We confront concrete problems that demand practical proposals. To ask questions about what is to be done about the global predicament is to expect "policy relevance," and to expect it in the short run. To refer to the problematic character of aspirations for universality or to the politics of discourse is to court dismissal in the name of metaphysics and theory. The difficulty here, however, is that such dismissals already presuppose very dubious distinctions between theory and practice, idea and matter, knower and known, distinctions which are part of the problem to be overcome, not a ground from which the global predicament can be unproblematically addressed. The demand for short-term options cannot be divorced from the need to place our understanding of policy within a broader account of what politics can now be.

While undoubtedly abstract in some senses, the foregoing discussion does suggest three sets of conclusions about what it means to respond to the global predicament by demanding concrete policies and authorities at the global level. One set of conclusions is essentially negative, and involves claims about what the demand for greater global awareness and new forms of global authority cannot be. One set is more positive and involves an emerging dialectic between two different understandings of political life. A final set concerns the relation between politics and policy, between the practices through which political life may be reconstituted and the claim that new historical conditions require new institutional and even constitutional forms.

The demand for world order cannot usefully be articulated within a discursive politics constituted through the principle of state sovereignty. To claim that the only alternative to state sovereignty is some kind of supranational authority is to engage in the fallacy of the domestic analogy. To this extent, the supposedly realist critics of utopianism are correct; but this critique needs to be taken further to show how the critique itself already presupposes the kind of universalist aspirations that have made the domestic analogy possible.

Realism and utopianism in the theory of international relations are mutually constitutive. They both derive from the historically specific resolution of the claims of universality and particularity as these are reified in the principle of state sovereignty. To challenge the principle of state sovereignty is to be caught within, and thus also to seek to evade, a discursive politics in which the principle of state sovereignty defines the alternatives that are to be taken seriously.

Once this discursive politics is avoided, the two contrasting understandings of political life are opened up. One of them is readily familiar, and one is not. The familiar understanding is one that takes states as an historically constituted form of political practice, not as the reified abstraction presented by the principle of state sovereignty. To take states seriously is to be concerned with their historical and spatial variety, and with the developing patterns of inter-state cooperation. Contrary to the metaphysical claims of so many political realists, relations between states do not constitute anarchy. Although they may not resemble the kind of society that has become familiar from the interaction of individuals within states, yet they do have coherence as a consequence of both structural patterns of interaction—not to say hegemony—and the development of certain rules of the game. The claim to state sovereignty already presupposes a collective universe in which claims to autonomy can be intelligible. The principles elucidated by, say, the Treaties of Westphalia (1648) and Utrecht (1714), or the Congress of Vienna (1814–15), or the Charter of the United Nations (1945), all build upon an account of the essential coherence of a system of states. The precise nature of this coherence can be clarified by attention to the development of international law, adherence to a common diplomatic culture, participation in a global system of economic production, distribution, and exchange, and so on.

The possibility of new global authorities and institutions is also easy to interpret in these terms, for this possibility is already a constitutive part of the state system as an historical ensemble of political practices. The character of the institutions of interstate cooperation has changed over time. Theories of incremental bureaucracy, functional integration, utilitarian public choice, and so on have been deployed to explain these changes. But they are, in principle, not especially novel. What is more interesting, and perhaps more novel, is the extent to which patterns of inter-state cooperation have once again begun to transform the character of the modern state, reshaping both the character of state apparatuses and also their degree of relative autonomy—autonomy from other states, but also from global economic processes and from their own citizens and civil society.

Thus to the extent that contemporary policy makers are increasingly driven to ask about possible new forms of cooperation, they continue an old tradition. And to the extent that the world order studies literature is concerned with what kind of new institutional arrangements ought to be devised, it also is well within a conventional understanding of international institutions as a product of inter-state cooperation. The difficulty is to know at what point terms like "international cooperation" or "international order" start to become misleading or to take on meanings usually held by terms like "global" or "world politics." The autonomy of states may become so dependent on processes of cooperation that it becomes especially unclear what autonomy can mean. The experience of the European Economic Community, the coordinating mechanisms of the Group of Seven industrialized states, the internationalization of production (especially in aerospace, automotive and micro-electronic technologies), these are all areas in which the development of mechanisms of inter-state cooperation have generated institutional forms that make it difficult to think of states in the image of state sovereignty. Once we move to questions about, say, security—to recognize that notions of national security now depend upon a clearer understanding of collective or common security—then it becomes more and more obvious that we, whether policy makers or theorists, do not know what we are talking about.

Consequently, while it is possible to understand the demand for new sources of global authority as a continuation of established forms of inter-state cooperation, it is also possible to see certain limits to this tradition of understanding. It is here that the domestic analogy becomes especially tempting, becomes a way of responding to the unknown through the comfortable image of the state writ large. But, I have tried to suggest, questions about the emerging character of inter-state and/or global authority are too interesting and too difficult to be resolved in this manner.

Moreover, it is not only our understanding of inter-state cooperation that needs to be freed from the exclusionary logic of state sovereignty. States do not in fact exercise a complete monopoly on political power, authority, or identity. Even less does the principle of state sovereignty offer a completely persuasive account of what political power, authority, or identity are. An insistence on the continuing significance of states is not incompatible with an insistence that the questions once answered by the principle of state sovereignty are being pushed with renewed urgency to the center of the political agenda.

Nor is it just the state or the principle of state sovereignty that has come to seem inadequate as an answer to these questions. The categories through which states and state sovereignty are understood are quite fragile. Contemporary spatio-temporal trajectories seem to be quite different from those that made possible states' claims to resolve all contradictions. It may be misleading to interpret new technologies, the generation of global relations of production, and so on as implying the demise of the state. But it seems perfectly plausible to interpret them as part of a significant rearticulation of spatio-temporal relations to which all states are now being forced to respond and adapt. Similarly, the categories through which we seek to understand contemporary spatio-temporal strategies are distinctly at odds with the metaphysical assumptions that have permitted the principle of state sovereignty to enclose histories within the spatial boundaries of territorial politics.

Thus, rather than understanding the possibility of new forms of global authority only in relation to established practices on inter-state cooperation, it must also be understood in relation to a renewed engagement with the most basic questions about the nature and location of political life. This renewed engagement is occurring in an era in which familiar spatio-temporal relations are being reconstructed in ways that largely elude our categories of analysis. In a world of potential nuclear spasm and of the nearly instantaneous circulation of capital and information, familiar distinctions—between here and there, them and us, present and future—begin to dissolve.

What this articulation of spatio-temporal relations (or the decentering of intellectual categories which seems to accompany it) will mean in the long run is not at all clear. Yet again, while the state remains crucial to the reproduction of global capitalist relations, as well as to the ambitions of those who seek to engage with the primary foci of power and authority, neither the transformation of the contemporary world economy nor the practices of contemporary social movements can be understood just in terms of the centered image of the sovereign state. To act in the modern world—as Marx argued over a century ago and as many social movements have begun to appreciate more clearly—is to work within relations of power that are simultaneously global and local. The precise resolution of this simultaneousness varies. It is clear that the state and state sovereignty are merely one possible resolution. The relation between capital and labor has often been understood as another resolution. Ecologists, feminists, and other critical social movements have begun to explore other possible resolutions. But neither the spatial distinction between inside and outside, nor the temporal resolution of difference into unity now hold any convincing monopoly on the location of political community, the teleology of emancipation, or the categories through which people are able to establish their political identities and obligations in relation to others.

This suggests that the precise meaning of global awareness or global authority remains to be established in practice. It also suggests that this meaning will have to be established not in relation to states but in relation to the capacity of people to generate new patterns of interaction between global and local practices, between identities of exclusion and those of inclusion. In this sense, global authorities not only are something that may now be constituted and given a constitution, but may themselves also become constitutive of, may generate, new forms of political community and practice.

For this reason, finally, it is necessary to distinguish the possibility of new forms of global authority from received images of government and policy. Those images depend upon forms of political community—states—that are well established. Whatever it may eventually mean to speak of human identity, global awareness, or world politics, it cannot imply an image of political community as the state writ large, because that image depends on a specifically spatial and exclusivist resolution of the relation between universality and particularity. To speak of global authority and so on must imply a reconstruction of this relation.

Global awareness, global authority, world politics, human identity, world order, all imply the need to see the development of international institutions and constitutions as part of a process of reconstructing the spatio-temporal horizons of political community. This suggests the need to take the possible development of global institutions very seriously indeed, without giving in to the temptations of the domestic analogy. To the extent that questions once answered by the principle of state sovereignty are being pushed with renewed urgency to the center of the political agenda, it is unlikely that they will find a persuasive resolution just through an institutionalized centralization of authority at the global level. Yet global institutions are likely to become more and more important, and to develop in ways that are not helpfully analysed through analogies with the governments of states.

To attempt to speak of new forms of global authority as a response to contemporary processes of historical transformation is thus to work with three sets of images. One, I have argued, is less than helpful. It is not the state that has to be rejected, but the confusion of the state as a complex historical practice with the principle of state sovereignty as an ahistorical reification of a historically specific account of spatio-temporal relations. To be critical of this principle is also necessarily to be critical of the account of the alternatives to the state that are also generated by this principle. A second image looks to the historical emergence of a society of states, and the dependence of that society on institutional arrangements that are inadequately grasped as either inter-state or global politics. It is primarily in relation to this image that the search for more effective forms of international/global institutions will be pursued. The third image is much more inchoate. It draws on analyses of the rearticulation of spatio-structural relations generated by structural transformation in the world economy. It also draws on attempts to create new forms of political practice that respond to new spatio-temporal processes without fetishizing the historically contingent claims of state power.

With both the second and third images it is not the continuing presence or imminent absence of the state that is in question. It is the meaning of political community (and thus all those questions about "who we are" that have been presumed to have their answer in the principle of state sovereignty) that is radically problematic. Understood in relation to these questions, the world order studies literature cannot be read just as a contribution to "international relations" (the negation of statist politics) nor as a contribution to "peace" (the negation of international relations but understood in universalist terms). It should be read first and foremost as an engagement with the conditions under which it is now possible to speak about political life at all, and what it means—ethically and practically—to do so.

NOTES

1. The underlying argument of this paper is drawn from a more extensive critique of modern theories of international relations in my *Inside/Outside: International Relations as Political Theory* (Cambridge: Cambridge University Press, 1992).

11

Constitutional Thought versus Value-Based Thought in World Order Studies

FRIEDRICH KRATOCHWIL

Since the international system, and for that matter any type of social order, is not "natural" but one of artifice, its creation, reproduction, and transformation present the researcher with a variety of puzzles. Why do certain institutions emerge and maintain themselves, adapt to changed circumstances, and/or fall by the wayside? Whatever the explanatory power of certain functional arguments might be, probably everybody agrees that norms, constitutive of certain practices, as well as the value considerations of the actors, matter in this context.

Two aspects of the process of reproducing a social order seem particularly salient. There are, on the one hand, certain practices constituted by legal norms (whether customary or positive) that provide, together with their stable interconnections, for the emergence of structures. Controversies arising out of those practices can usually be settled with reference to seemingly "factual" questions, such as, "Was there a contract in existence between the parties concerned?" or "Was this foreign government recognized or not?" Thus via a special "jural ontology" we can easily move between the realm of the "is" to the "ought" and back again. Claims made in accordance with those practices constituted by institutional rules lose their idiosyncratic character and can command assent because they provide backing by intersubjectively valid reasons.

The other aspect of this process of reproduction is characterized by an ongoing contest over the "oughts" and "musts" that follow from the existing institutional frameworks. This contest calls into question the very institutional arrangements upon which the duties and obligations of the actors are based. If arguments are not to degenerate into simple indications of personal preferences, they must adduce some type of intersubjective backing that can serve as justifying reasons for the establishment, modification, or abolition of practices and jural ontologies.

The present paper will examine more closely these two types of arguments, which roughly coincide with legal (or constitutional) and political ways of arguing. While I do not deny that in both cases preferences of some sort are involved, it is not the preferences per se that are at stake in our legal and political debates, but rather the weight and persuasiveness of the validity claims we make while arguing.

Such an investigation serves at least three purposes. First, it corrects the commonly held belief that normative and value-based arguments are both of the same character since they are located on the "ought" side of the Humean fork. Second, it demonstrates the invalidity of the argument that normative and value questions are beyond reasoned debate, even though it is true that the inference patterns in either case do not exhibit the steps familiar from either deductive or inductive reasoning. Third, it reclaims for politics and law the peculiar form of a practical rationality that goes beyond the goals-means nexus of instrumental reason and even beyond the criteria of strategic rationality. To that extent, this investigation provides some support for the proposition that the criteria of rationality, familiar from the rational-choice approach for explaining the emergence of norms and institutions, is seriously misleading since it misconstrues the very nature of legal and political communication.

In order to elaborate these points more fully my argument takes the following steps. The second section examines the nature of normative arguments, taking legal arguments as the paradigm. The third section takes up the issue of value-based arguments, before addressing in Section Four the issue of ideology. I distinguish the technical usage of the value-laden terms, from "ideological" thinking, as institutionalized in particular discourses. An "ideological" style of argument is typically characterized by a reduction of the complexities associated with gaining assent to value arguments. This reduction can be seen in the utilization of discursive gambits in which issues of rational assent are either eliminated by appeals to emotions, or are presented as merely or solely problems of instrumental or systemic reasoning. Section Five elaborates on some of the implications of these arguments for discourse on international politics, international law, and world order.

LEGAL (NORMATIVE) AND VALUE-BASED ARGUMENTS

Learning to think like a lawyer, Christopher Stone reminds us, is to learn to view the world through particular glasses. In this world,

> People not only walk and punch, they "trespass" and "commit battery." . . . The legal language answers the fundamental question of jural ontology. Who, for example, will populate the juridical world as its first-class citizens, the bearers of legal rights: men, women, corporations, minorities as groups, fetuses, states, rivers, trees? The language, too, determines what attributes of the world are to be noticed: monetary value and certain mental states have gained a place, as have pain and suffering, and consent. Sincerity's place is not so clear. Terms such as *res ipsa loquitur* and "proximate causes" are not just handy descriptions of what is; they ingrain our worldview with important presumptions of how the world works.[1]

This passage makes several important points: First, the legal ontology is not necessarily derived from "natural facts." Thus, the argument that the rights of states must be derived from those of their citizens, because states do not exist while people do, is obviously legally irrelevant (and of dubious value otherwise).[2]

Second, the legal ontology is nearly always based on interpretations that transcend "observables" (e.g., by including such unobservables, such as mental states). Thus, it consistently intertwines objective and subjective elements (if we follow the conventional Humean distinction between the observer and the observed).

Third, these interpretations are not based on idiosyncratic assessments but are bounded by common understandings of "how the world works," in Stone's phrase. But things are even more complicated than this innocent passage suggests. While it may be true that any incident is susceptible to a wide variety of "fact descriptions," the jural ontology imposes certain limits on the choices for possible "narratives." As is the case in moral discourse (but not necessarily in the rational choice approach, which is also "normative"),[3] no description of actions is acceptable that hides or evades the effects they have on others' interests. It is this consideration that provides a privileged status to some accounts over others. As D'Arcy has noted,

> For instance, "Macbeth stabbed Duncan and as a consequence, killed him" may be redescribed simply as "Macbeth

killed Duncan; but "Macbeth killed Duncan, and as a consequence, succeeded him," may not be redescribed simply as "Macbeth succeeded Duncan."[4]

Given this "jural ontology," two further implications deserve attention. First, it seems clear that in characterizing "the law" and its workings we cannot be satisfied with defining it as a system of rules. After all, what legal arguments are about is to (1) ascertain that certain events occurred, (2) that these events exemplify some legal concept, which is (3) embodied in certain institutional arrangements (e.g., the law of contract, anti-trust, etc.), which (4) entitle a party to a remedy. Only in this framework can a seemingly innocent lunch among business executives, at which they "talk shop," become a "conspiracy in restraint of trade" which entitles a plaintiff to triple damages. Second, it is precisely these links between the facts as established by a jural ontology, and the embeddedness of rules in institutional arrangements which make it possible in legal reasoning to move from apparently simple cognitive statements to normative judgments without invoking values or preferences.

Similarly, when we promise or contract, we easily move from the ascertainment of certain "facts," such as the signing of a paper, or the utterance of "I do" in a marriage ceremony, to the normative conclusion that the person having utilized these signs and other expressions is now under at least a *prima facie* obligation. The conventional aspects of these practices beyond the confines of individual intentionality becomes visible. True, obliging oneself requires the free volition of oneself as agent, but it also requires conformity with certain formulas or signs by which the obligation as such is confirmed. Thus the person who fails to sign a peace of paper on the dotted line or who says "much gusto," instead of "de acuerdo," in Spanish simply does not have a contract and has not entered into a promissory obligation.

VALUE-BASED ARGUMENTS

Having sketched the distinct characteristics of the legal style of reasoning, we can proceed now to examining value-based thought, and ideological thought in the next section. For this purpose, it is useful first to review some of the most important distinctions between values and norms.

The most obvious distinction concerns the specificity of rules and norms, and the generality of values. Norms, especially when formulated in rule form, contain the range of their applicability to a specific set of events. Thus, the prescription that "every male" has to register for the draft after his 18th birthday, or that anyone driving a vehicle "while intoxicated" will have his drivers licence revoked, are typical examples of normative formulations carrying the specification of their range of application.

On the other hand, values such as fairness, justice, generosity, love, dignity, etc., are much more encompassing and serve largely as evaluative standards of a peculiar kind. They are not based on empirical regularities, like the grading standards that enable us to assign eggs or ice-skaters to superior or inferior classes. Values let us rate actions in terms of their goodness or badness, their rightness or wrongness, and hence their desirability or nondesirability. This, after all, is Hume's valuable insight, i.e., the recognition that value statements are not (solely) matters of cognition but that they involve "feelings" of approval and disapproval. However, in saying this I do not want to commit one of the standard liberal fallacies of arguing that something is desirable or good because someone actually prefers or desires it.

Values, although informing our preferences, are not simply preferences. Rather they are "second-order" desires by which we rate our preferences themselves in terms of their conduciveness to a particular way of life. Values have, we might say, a "subject-referring import"[5] that makes it possible for individuals to make qualitative discriminations among their goals and actions, to rate some of them higher and others lower, some as good and others as discreditable or even evil.

As distinguished from mere preferences, value choices have to filter idiosyncratic desires not just through a longer-term perspective of the individual. After all, even our good utilitarians admonish us to maximize "long-term happiness," rather than short-term satisfaction. But the value perspective goes beyond this individual maximizing strategy: It calls attention not only to our own long-term interests and desires but also to those of others who are affected by our choices. It is this circumstance that roots values in inter-subjective understandings and allows us to make claims that go beyond mere indications of personal preferences.

In short, values allow us to draw a "moral map" of ourselves as members of communities, as persons with life plans, embedded in various ongoing concerns and social obligations. Those who "have no values,"—who cannot discriminate between "higher" and "lower" desires and are blind to the qualitative differences between "pushpin or opera," to use Bentham's phrase, whose "happiness" consists only in single-minded satisfaction of their own primary desires to the greatest degree—are not only abstractions, like the *homo oeconomicus,* they are a pathetic caricature of human existence.

The important implication of the argument above is that value-based thinking exhibits a different "style" than normative thinking. As we have seen, it is possible in the legal style of thought to move from largely cognitive statements to "oughts" and "musts." These cognitive statements of jural ontology might be either unproblematic, such as a statement in the U.S. immigration law that a "spouse" of an American citizen is entitled to the "green card," or they might be more complicated, by being part of institutional contexts (e.g. a contract).

Value-based thinking, on the other hand, in its pure form, derives its "oughtness" and action-directive character directly from the value itself without the intercession of a specific ontological trigger. Consider in this context the prophet Amos' exhortation:

> I hate, I despise your feasts, and I take no delight in your solemn assemblies. Even if you offer me your burnt offerings and cereal offerings, I will not accept them. . . . Take away from me the noise of your songs; to the melody of your harps I will not listen. But let justice roll down like waters, and righteousness like an every-flowing stream.[6]

Here an appeal for a change of heart is communicated by the strict opposition of two ways of life. But rather than seeing "value" in strict obedience to the "law," justice is seen here as elementary "inner" force breaking through. Instead of the specific prescriptions of "the law," the "oughtness" is here communicated through a metaphor that catches us in our moral awareness.

Since metaphors make understandable to us the unfamiliar through likening it to the familiar by means of imagery (rather than by logical analogies),[7] communication is likely to be unspecific, but susceptible to elaboration. In our case the "oughtness" implied in the value of "justice" is derived by linking a way of life with the properties of a natural element. Like water, justice will be a force that flows freely and unceasingly like a stream, giving life and dissolving contamination and pollution.

Another way in which the meaning of values can be communicated is through a paradigmatic example. In this case the narrative through a dramatization makes transparent the values and their implications for a way of life. Different from the power of suggestion conjured up by the imagery, as in Amos's example, more cognitive elements become important in narratives, since the "moral" of the story has to be gathered by drawing the appropriate lessons. This style of communication is perhaps best exemplified by fables and by the parables of the New Testament.

But value thinking also encompasses other modes of argument of a less pure kind, i.e., instances where value elements are intrinsically linked to cognitive categories, and the "oughtness" results from the fusion of cognitive and value elements. We shall discuss these next.

CONTESTED CONCEPTS AND THE CASE OF IDEOLOGY

As we have seen, there exists, besides "pure" values and value-based arguments, another class of value concepts that are not "pure." As exemplified by our political language, certain terms firmly link value and cognitive components. Consider in this context the term "progress," which exhibits such a blend. It combines a cognitive assertion about the direction of historical development with a value assertion that such a development is desirable and good.

> If the cognitive component were removed, there would be no concept of "progress" but simply the pure statement of value that some envisaged future would be desirable. If the value component were removed, there would also be no concept of "progress" but simply the value neutral cognitive assertion that there is some sort of directionality in human history. The very meaning of the concept depends upon the combination of cognitive and value elements.[8]

Other concepts of the same type are "democracy," "freedom," "legitimacy," "faction." In short, these are the "essentially contested" concepts of our political discourse. They are essentially contested because cleansing from them their value component would deprive them of their function as means of appraisal in our language, and in doing so we would lose a basis for communication and for action. After all, having one's characterization of an act accepted as an instance of "factionalism," rather than as one of "interest-group politics" is to bring others around to see the phenomenon in the same light, and to commit them to actions congruent with this appraisal.

Even if it were possible—as proponents of the classical dichotomy between descriptive concepts and "values" are fond of pointing out—to effect a rigid separation of the value dimensions by respecifying the criteria of usage, it is difficult to fathom what would be gained by such sterilization of the discourse. After all, the fact that such a separation of denotive (descriptive) and connotive elements is logically possible does not—by the very cannons of positivism itself—establish "that it is also justifiable or reasonable."[9] Obviously, the justification for such a separation rests on several unstated premises. First among them is, a questionable notion of science and of language by which concepts have to correspond to "things" in the outer world. Second is a concept of reason that limits it to "calculation" at the "mercy of passion." Third is the assumption that everything but sense perceptions must be "private" and thus not susceptible to inter-subjective validating procedures.

Whatever the (de)merits of this position might be, it is on all fours with our experience. Not only do we spend an awful lot of time on such "irrational" matters as political or moral arguments, we also do have the experience that coming to agreement is sometimes possible,[10] and our discussion shows why. It is precisely because we share a common language, which has certain values attached to some of its concepts, that we can share the same attitudes toward a set of phenomena, and persuade others by "naming" rather than merely by describing certain events and actions. As in the case of jural ontology already discussed, naming an action is not simply describing but appraising it from a certain point of view. Thus, contestability is the very reason why agreement as well as disagreement is possible.

This dialectic of our communication also shows that political order, although an artifice of human contrivance, is not an artifice in the same way as machines are, which, once established, run from then on according to their inherent logic. Consequently, the language of *techne* and instrumental reason is not rich enough to capture the process of value argumentation and the continuous reconstitution of our social and political order through ongoing debates and interpretations that reaffirm and/or alter our practices. Hayward Alker has argued persuasively against the present attempts to understand politics in terms of instrumental reason alone, as exemplified by the rational choice approach:

> Even though one could conceivably model certain aspects of persuasive communication game-theoretically, anarchy-derived game trees cannot represent the non-strategic communicative aspects of negotiations pragmatically oriented toward consensus seeking—the reaching of agreements. Nor can non-cooperative game theory, or micro-economic models, formally give adequate attention to the sharable and contentious value orientations—including notions of just and unjust conduct in war and peace—which are the infectious stuff of politics.[11]

The flip side of this argument is, of course, that through acceptance of these contestable concepts signified by their embeddedness in discourses, "power" is created and exercised. It has been the merit of Foucault's analysis that his "archeology" demonstrates the historical nature as well as the repressive and power-generating function of discourses.[12] Going beyond Thucydides' masterful account of the revolution in Corcyra where political decay is analyzed in terms of the breakup of common meanings of the political language,[13] Foucault shows that even in "scientific" discourses this constitutive institutionalization occurs, determining what can be said and referred to.[14]

My discussion has tried to establish two things. First, that communication, particularly communication about practical matters, is inherently value-laden and that therefore attempts to eliminate value components are unlikely to enhance our understanding or ability to communicate in a distortion-free way. Second, we deal with issues of validation by accepting particular ontologies—value-laden concepts—that allow us to draw action imperatives from instances of the accepted ontology or of the contestable concept. It is only when these ontologies themselves, or the discourses in which the common understandings are embedded, are no longer assented to that questions of ideology arise. Thus, ideologies have little to do with values per se but rather with the justification of frames of reference; it becomes clear why even "scientific theories" can become "ideological" in this sense. This should come as no surprise, since the meaning of terms is not simply conveyed by their semantic dimension, i.e., how they correspond to events or instances, but rather by their use, i.e., by their pragmatic function.

Such a meaning of "ideology" or "ideological" is not only quite in tune with our common understanding, but it helps us in clarifying the criteria of usage. When we call someone an "ideologue" or his or her arguments as "ideological," we seem to suggest that this person is narrow-minded, not open to other points of view, or lacking in a certain awareness or insight. Instances that call into question this critical position by pointing to at least potentially disconfirming evidence, or to alternative explanations, are either pooh-poohed or swept under the carpet; worse yet, they are even embraced and represented as compatible with the critical argument even when it runs up squarely against their main point.

What distinguishes an ideological argument from a simple lie or plain dishonesty—despite the fact that some of the gambits ideologues use might in effect result in the same distortions—is that we consider the ideologues at least "subjectively" well-intentioned. Also, we do not suggest that they are "incompetent," or that they have made just a "mistake." Rather, we interpret their tenacity as due to strong but "unreasonable" commitments, and/or to the incapacity to reflectcritically, not upon this or that concept or argument, but on the whole frame of reference or discourse within which the issue is embedded.

To that extent, the characterization of ideology as "false consciousness" taps an important dimension. Thus, irrespective of whether we share Marx's point of view as to its origins, "ideology" is a useful concept in distinguishing validity claims on the meta-level from personal idiosyncracies or preferences, or from disagreements that occur among those within the same discourses or frames of reference. In other words, questions and charges of ideology arise when either the consensus-establishing practices have broken down or new formulations have not been successful in establishing a widely shared consensus, in short, when there is no agreement to bracket issues of the validation of claims by at least accepting a common institutionalized world of references.

LEGALISM AND WORLD ORDER THINKING

From the foregoing remarks, the possibility of ideological argument utilizing norm-based arguments becomes visible. This is the problem of "legalism." Its most important antidote can be found in the counter-hegemonic discourses rooted in explicit value-based arguments that explore alternative conceptions of domestic and international politics. In going beyond the existing arrangements, their contestable character comes to the fore. Thus, while international law is truly constitutive of the international game, the success of this conceptualization of politics is hardly separable from the historical record of Europe's domination over other parts of the world and the resistance it engendered. Like economics, "law" is usually quite silent on the establishment of first entitlements (rights) or on certain facts that have, in Kelsen's unrivalled formulation, "the normative force of facticity."

The idea that law is simply there as a system of rules that for all intents and purposes can be abstracted from politics by treating it like a game is characteristic of legalism. Legalism consists in the uncritically held belief that the distinctions made for analytical purposes are also sufficient justifications for claiming that our practices are thereby appropriately characterized by a simple jural ontology. If conflict is recognized as part of social life, it is viewed as a combat according to rules in which the adversaries establish their case by making moves very much like those of players in a game. Thus, the original analytical separation of legal from other type of phenomena is treated as a universal and self-justifying frame of reference for understanding social interactions. Judith Shklar has pointed out these temptations of legalism:

> Unhappily, perhaps, law and legal systems are not games but social institutions, and they do not exist in the social

> vacuum of a game of chess. The behavior of men involved in social conflicts and conditions under which these may or may not be resolved by appeals to rules simply does not resemble games.[15]

Furthermore, legalism becomes ideological when it systematically misinterprets the very activity of arguing with rules and norms, even within a well-specified game of adjudication. Representing law as a system of rules leaves out important aspects of judicial decision making. As I have tried to show,[16] much of the *ars legis* consists in choosing among competing narratives that transform events into "facts" of the legal ontology. In addition, contrary to Kelsen and Hart, questions about the validity of norms are not simply established by tracing the logical connections among various norms and their pedigrees. Rather, the decisions are the result of quite different procedures, of "weighing" competing principles, of evaluating actions or outcomes in terms of prevailing "customary" practices in a society (by introducing explicitly extra-legal considerations into the decision-making process), and of invoking even more straightforward value considerations, such as those embodied in the interpretive principle of *res magis valeat quam pereat.*

In other words, the question of validity is never simply internal to the body of rules such that only the *Grundnorm* has to be justified in other than legal terms. The practice of judging, of validation and justification even within the specialized style of legal reasoning, is systematically distorted when we view it as a simple tracing of normative pedigrees.

Furthermore, legalism stands in a curious relationship to the hegemony of realism as a theory on international politics. Thus, despite their differences, legalism and realism as two hegemonic discourses about international reality feed upon each other. It is no accident that the success of realism came in the aftermath of World War Two after the great disappointments of two failed attempts at basing international relations on a principled legal footing.

Thus legalism, having eliminated—at least on paper—not only coercion but virtually any form of unprincipled agreement, such as bargaining and ad hoc deals, was paralleled by a conceptualization of international politics that took "anarchy" as its defining characteristic. An entirely extravagant image of politics as a state of war not only legitimized realism's preoccupation with power (usually misconceptualized as an assortment of capabilities), but indirectly contributed also to the legitimization and perpetuation of legalism in international relations. It was precisely against the background of politics as a war of all against all that the alternative of legalism made sense. Given the horrors of modern war, it became increasingly the task of international law not only to constitute the arena in which political action could occur, but to replace politics altogether in the international arena. This change was either to take place through the establishment of a world government—i.e., order by the hierarchy and fiat of the world sovereign—or through legal modes of conflict resolution.

Viewed from this perspective, value-based world order thinking shows some important continuities and discontinuities with these hegemonic forms of discourse. In adopting a broader set of values as explicit points of reference, instead of simply accepting the existing structure of formal institutions and practices, the World Order Models Project (WOMP)[17] is not only critical of statism and its agenda, but also abandons that legalist route to change. While the role of law is not eschewed as a strategy for transformation—the emphasis on human rights and those of subnational groups is important in this context—the image of creating world order through international tribunals is replaced by a broader conception of the political process in which right claims are powerful mobilizing factors for *political* action.

The shift in focus away from the extension of existing practices to more fundamental questions concerning the appropriateness and the (d)efficiency of existing arrangements, has important repercussions. It provides for a more creative approach to institution building in the international arena, and it legitimizes critical evaluations of formal organizations and regimes and the purposes they serve. In this context the starkly inegalitarian norms of distributing the world's products and the nexus between the armaments burden and poverty cast doubt on the adequacy of existing practices and the desirability of reproducing these structures by treating them as the givens of international politics.

On the other hand, there are also important continuities between the world order discourse and the more benign liberal visions of politics out of Locke rather than Hobbes. The focus on disarmament, with its abolitionist stance, echoes the liberal hope that people left alone will opt for peaceful competition rather than for martial adventures. Thus much of the argument reproduces the traditional dichotomy between "state" and "society." Not only can the state system be identified as the problem, but the assertion of societal and group rights is not seen as reproducing at least potentially the same anarchy and security dilemma's familiar to us from structural realism. There is a strong belief based on a second-image theory of international relations,[18] that structural uncertainties can be ameliorated by the existence of compatible, democratic domestic orders.

At least some of the experiences with WOMP suggest that imagining relevant utopias of yesteryear or alternative futures is restricted to a relatively small repertoire of concepts with which to argue, make ourselves understood, and rally support for our arguments. Once more the problem of politics and the contestability or key concepts rises its ugly head. It is here that the process of transformation envisaged by WOMP is far too simple and apolitical: apolitical because with the specification of the global problematique, politics is again reduced to a set of technical "how-to" problems and to the setting of appropriate targets and schedules; apolitical also because the endorsement by a heterogenous assortment of movements throughout the world does not augur well for the translation of these guidelines into actual policies.

Social transformations, even the most fundamental ones, do not follow such rationalist paths even if their prophets are accepted and their message is heard. This is why the image of a transformation according to a path of well-defined technical processes is too simple. The acceptance of the Christian message did not lead to the end or the radical transformation of the world but to the formation of a church; the victory of popular sovereignty did not bring the end of wars; the French Revolution did not result in the establishment of the rights of man. Nevertheless, all of these teachings and historical events have fundamentally influenced our social order.

Having criticized the future-oriented prophecies of global modelling as too apolitical and simple, I do not want to suggests that the proper task of a scholar is to wait for the dusk and the flight of the owl of Minerva. Our task remains to rethink once more the links between thought and action, and then to work for the establishment of political order on the basis of shared notions of communicative rationality rather than coercion.

NOTES

1. Christopher Stone, "From a Language Perspective," *Yale Law Journal*, 90 (1981); 1149–1192, at p. 1158.

2. See the controversy between Michael Walzer, Gerald Doppelt, and Charles Beitz a few years ago in *Philosophy and International Affairs*, vols. 8 and 9. The Doppelt-Beitz thesis referred to here seems to suffer from an egregious fallacy of composition and the further mistakes of assigning existential status only on the basis on the crudest empiricism, as well as holding that rights can be attributed only on the basis of natural ascriptivism. None of these positions seem sound.

3. For a further elaboration of these points see ch. 5, "The Discourse of Grievances" in my *Rules, Norms, and Decisions: On the Conditions of Practical and Legal Reasoning in International Relations and Domestic Affairs* (Cambridge: Cambridge University Press, 1989).

4. Eric D'Arcy, *Human Acts.* (Oxford: Clarendon Press, 1970), pp. 18–19.

5. For a further discussion of this point, see Charles Taylor, *Human Agency and Language* (Cambridge: Cambridge University Press, 1985), ch. 1, 2, 4, 9.

6. Amos 21, 23, 24.

7. For a further discussion, see Kenneth Burke, *A Grammar of Motives* (Berkeley and Los Angeles: University of California Press, 1969), Appendix D. See also Lakoff and Mark Johnson, *Metaphors We Live By* (Chicago: University of Chicago Press, 1980).

8. Vernon K. Dibble and Berton Pekowsky, "What Is and What Ought To Be: A Comparison of Certain Characteristics of the Ideological and Legal Styles of Thought," *American Journal of Sociology* 79 (1973); 511–549, at p. 515.

9. William E. Connolly, *The Terms of Political Discourse,* 2nd ed. (Princeton, NJ: Princeton University Press, 1983).

10. For a formal elaboration of the criteria such a discourse must satisfy, see Jürgen Habermas, "What Is Universal Pragmatics?" in Habermas, *Communication and the Evolution of Society,* tr. Thomas McCarthy, (Boston, MA: Beacon Press, 1979), ch. 1; see also a different attempt by Oswald Schwemmer, *Philosopie der Praxis* (Frankfurt: am Main Suhrkamp, 1980).

11. Hayward Alker, "The Presumption of Anarchy," in Alker and Richard Ashley, eds., *Anarchy, Power, and Community* (New York: Columbia University Press, forthcoming), p. 34 of ms.

12. See Michel Foucault, *The Order of Things: An Archeology of the Human Sciences* (New York: Random House, 1970).

13. Thucydides, *The Peloponnesian War,* tr. John Finley (New York: Modern Library, 1951), Book 3, 70–84.

14. See, e.g., his *The Birth of a Clinic: An Archeology of Medical Perception,* tr. A.M. Sheridan Smith (New York: Random House, 1975).

15. Judith Shklar, *Legalism: Law, Morals, and Political Trials* (Cambridge, MA: Harvard University Press, 1986), p. 105.

16. See my *Rules, Norms, and Decisions: On the Conditions of Practical and Legal Reasoning in International Relations and Domestic Affairs* (Cambridge: Cambridge University Press, 1989), ch. 8.

17. Saul Mendlowitz and Richard Falk (among many others) were active in the World Order Models Project. For a brief summary of the

various positions espoused by its adherents, see Richard A. Falk, Samuel S. Kim, and Paul H. Mendlowitz, eds., *Toward a Just World Order* (Boulder, CO: Westview Press, 1982).

18. The term "second image" is derived from Kenneth Waltz's argument about the courses of war. See his *Man, the State and War: A Theoretical Analysis* (New York: Columbia University Press, 1959).

12

A Feminist Perspective on World Constitutional Order

BETTY REARDON

THE MEANING OF AND THE NEED FOR A FEMINIST PERSPECTIVE

This essay invites consideration of why a feminist perspective should be central to all efforts to achieve a just world peace during the last decade of the twentieth century. If this decade is to see any of the viable global constitutional order that world order scholars once foresaw for this time, then what feminists would designate as "authentic globalism," a quality I take to have been a fundamental value of these scholars, must become an operating principle as well as a guiding value of world order scholarship and world peace activism.

An authentic globalism would be fully inclusive of the Earth's human diversity. It would, therefore, of necessity place equal emphasis on the needs, concerns, and perspectives of both men and women. And it would seek to be as fully representative as possible of all human cultures. Sadly, the discourse on the global future, even that conducted by those who are among the challengers of mainstream thinking on world policy issues, sorely lacks the participation of women and of cultural minorities and Third World Societies. It is in most ways still far too exclusive to meet the standards being demanded even by the world's feminist movements, whose voices are at least now heard far more widely than those of cultural minorities. This exclusiveness I believe to be a major obstacle to the resolution of the problem of worldwide militarism, which in turn stands as the major obstacle to a just world peace.

The case for the relationship between militarism and sexism, the indisputable links between patriarchy and war, and even the arguments asserting the necessity of feminist approaches to global problems are by now well documented. There are few who would, at least publicly, deny the desirability and equitability of representing women and women's concerns in all public policy making. This essay will not restate that case nor review the links between war and sexism. It will, however, attempt to extend the arguments for the necessity of feminist approaches to global problems, using as their arena of involvement the planning and implementation of a world constitutional order intended to strengthen the possibilities of achieving and maintaining a just world peace. The extension of the argument will be stated in terms of particular qualitative concepts currently lacking in but essentially necessary to the speculative discourse on transforming the world political system into one constituted so as to manifest a range of humane qualities. Their absence is most evident in the violence, repression, deprivation, and devastation that now blight the natural and social environments of this planet. We shall argue that a feminist perspective on a world constitutional order is essential for introducing these concepts into the world political discourse.

As used here, the term "feminist" is defined as that which validates the equal human and social value of women and men, their experiences and priorities. So defined, it is not limited to gender but also connotes social, economic, and political egalitarianism applied to all human groups. Feminism in this context is as much a rejection of racism, ageism, classism, colonialism, militarism, indeed all forms of discrimination and oppression as it is of sexism alone. In its focus on women's oppression, concerns, values, and visions, it comprehends not only the double oppression of women in the public and private spheres of human affairs, but also the interrelationships of all forms of oppression, and it seeks to transform the patriarchal assumptions, values, practices, and structures that produced and sustain them.

While the practices and structures are currently undergoing some revision, the assumptions and values of patriarchy are still prevalent and creep into even the most radical of proposals for global change. Thus, feminism has a special concern with the conceptualization and construction of a global constitutional order, by which is meant world institutions and structures established for governing the relations and interactions among all the human groups and societies of the planet. The order may or may not comprise a world government or other "central guidance system." However minimally it is constituted, its processes would be regulated by a universally accepted set of world social norms.

It is primarily for this reason that feminists insist on the inclusion of a feminist perspective in all considerations of any and all developments in the world political order, constitutional or other. For it has been the acceptance of patriarchal norms in virtually all cultures of the world which has allowed for both women's oppression and for militarization. Such norms have made it possible for all who are without power in the present system to be dealt with as mere passive objects of policy planning rather than subjects participating actively. Authentic globalism is based on the fundamental value of human dignity which demands that all people be the subjects and deciders of their own destinies. This is the basic norm feminists have sought to establish for women and all of the oppressed.

Feminist peace research brings to the field the insights and knowledge gained from all feminist scholarship. It poses research questions and pursues knowledge from a perspective that assumes the equal human value of men and women and of the powerful and the vulnerable, while asserting the validity of women's ways of knowing within the whole spectrum of human learning capacities. It accords as much significance to women's concerns, that is, problems defined from the point of view of the persons involved, as it does to men's concerns, that is, problems defined from the point of view of the structures or rules in question. Like most feminist approaches to problem definition and resolution and to building knowledge, feminist peace research tends to be holistic and inclusive, and it applies feminine modes of relating to the exploration of issues and the construction of social relationships. Qualities such as complementarity, mutuality, attention, representation, and inclusion are all characteristic of the feminist perspective applied to the questions posed as research problems in world order.

Such a feminist perspective applied here would thus define an authentic globalism as one in which the various constituencies of the human community are full participants in conceptualizing and implementating global policies and ultimately in the design and function of a world constitutional order. It is a perspective in which the interests and needs of all are fully considered and in which those of the vulnerable are given particular attention. Authentic globalism, the most sorely lacking quality of both mainstream and alternative world political discourse, has been a significant principle of the strand of the worldwide feminist movement that has emerged from and within the international peace research community.

AUTHENTIC GLOBALISM: INTERPRETATION, INTEGRATION, IMPLEMENTATION

Authentic globalism requires not only that world order movements and projects include representatives from the various human cultures, ideologies, and other categories by which human beings identify themselves, but also that their representations—the articulation of their concerns, values, and experience—be attended to. Attention in this sense is "feminine" in its connotation, as it implies listening with both concentration and care, qualities that are characteristic of the loving parent, the respectful child or student, the conscientious pastor, or the committed counselor, yet rare in those persons or constituencies who now give and receive political representations, transactions in which the currency is power and pragmatism rather than care and commitment. For the most part this quality of attention is found mainly in personal intimacy, or client or patient professional relationships (and not consistently or universally even in those relationships), sometimes in constructive collegiality or teacher-student relations. It is an element of nurturing which is feminine in that women in particular are socialized to offer it in their care-giving roles.[1]

It is this role more than the biology of reproduction which links women's concerns to those of children and other vulnerable segments of society. It is also the quality seldom introduced into public arenas or economic and political interactions, an omission that some feminist peace researchers assert accounts for the public tolerance of what the peace and world order movements deem to be humanly unacceptable levels of injustice, deprivation, and oppression. Attention also assures authenticity, the quality derived from and reflecting the lived realities of the subjects concerned. Only by sincere, intense attending to them can these realities be thoroughly comprehended. The ten years of research and struggle that went into the drafting of the recently adopted UN Convention on the Rights of the Child is a significant example of such attention and a rare one in the public affairs arena. Thus more varied representations and more expressions of care and concern in assessments of problems and in policy recommendations should become truly constitutive of the global polity, and the constitutional order should be designed so as to interpret, integrate, and implement them.

Interpretation from a feminine mode of attending would translate the respective representations into the global context, determining what its meaning is in human terms not only for particular constituencies but for the global community. It would involve negotiating the meeting of needs and the fulfillment of hopes, insofar as possible preserving and respecting the diversity of the various constituencies while maintaining the health and possibilities of the global whole. It would in this process seek to find modes and mechanisms more just and creative than the quantitative method of vote by population as proposed by federalists or than means which seek to bring into balance little more than the existing components of geopolitical power. Such means are all-equipped to represent the vulnerable and voiceless, such as the children of the poor and of war. Feminists have little confidence in many aspects of supposedly democratic process, as in voting. Decisions by number can be made without the full involvement of all the enfranchised or of their representatives, who often have many points of view and presenting evidence considered "secondary." Since the concerns of women, like those of the vulnerable and the "powerless," have most often been considered secondary in most policy matters, women are inclined to seek more inclusive and thorough methods of decision making. There is little doubt that a federalist, representative constitutional order would reduce violence in conflict resolution and probably increase economic stability. However, even with the inclusion of enforceable human rights and of processes for the remedy of violations and grievances, it is doubtful that they alone would assure authentic globalism.

Many of the elements of cultural identity, the traditional sources of meaning and of structures of social and personal relations, would be in danger of further homogenization in such a structure. Exclusion of such identities would likely continue to be a problem under structures so similar to those historically derived from patriarchy. And while feminists are indeed sensitive to the disadvantages suffered by women in some minority cultures, women who have had to conform for centuries to male standards of identification are not eager to impose exogenous standards on other cultures. Indeed, much of the violence in the world today results from such imposition. A feminist perspective would seek a process of global interpretation of multiple representations to remedy the present homogenization of human cultures from globalizing the dominant representations of Western technocratic male constituencies.

There is, as well, the need to take into account the loss of human cultures which is in our time as prevalent as the loss of living species. As biodiversity is now recognized as essential for preserving the planet's ecosystems, cultural diversity is equally necessary to the survival of a rich and varied human civilization. It most certainly is an essential characteristic of authentic globalism manifest in a just and equitable constitutional order. Just and equitable integration of diversity may be the major challenge of a world constitutional order. Authentic globalism implies a healthy functioning whole, a unity of fully viable component parts. The well-being and integrity of the whole is dependent on the health of its various parts. An imbalance or inequity anywhere in the system will weaken the viability of the entire system. Destruction of the rain forest has demonstrated this distortion in the world's ecological system; and peace research has demonstrated it in regard to the inequities of the global economy. World militarization, a symptom of illness in socio-political systems affecting both the global economy and the ecosystem, serves to illustrate the relationships among these various systems. Healthy wholeness and equitable integration are becoming virtually standard principles in assessing and planning world order.

However, in a world concerned with the crime of genocide and the social sins of racism, sexism, religious and cultural discrimination and oppression, there is, even now, little attention given to assuring cultural integrity and integration as an essential component of the policy sciences and of proposals for world order. Perhaps there is no greater evidence of this than the paucity of women invited to and involved in those committees and councils that deal with these matters (the Brundtland report notwithstanding). For their part, many women, not only feminists, see much of the discourse in these bodies as irrelevant to the fundamental concerns of how people live their daily lives and behave toward one another, to that of which cultures are comprised, to the issues of human welfare, and to the personal and social relationships that take women's primary attention and are the stuff of which most of their public efforts as well as private responsibilities are comprised. If those global reports intended to remedy the major global problems are in fact to have any real impact, they must affect not only governments and politics but the daily lives of ordinary people and the norms by which they live, namely, their cultural values, many of which are transferred, taught, and applied by women. Global policies need to be formulated, interpreted, and implemented in terms relevant to women and the cultures of those outside the dominant Western patriarchal culture, and applicable to their everyday experiences. If a global constitutional order is to be viable, it, too, must meet these same criteria. And it must recognize that such relevance and applicability transcends the distinctions made between public and private, personal and political. While the liberal tendency has been to decry some of the personal disclosures made by and about recent American candidates for elected or appointed public office, these rather clumsy inquiries and badly articulated issues may be a sign of the recognition of the dangers in these distinctions and separations.

For women, there has always been a narrow-to-disappearing dividing line between the realities of the two spheres, and the policy processes that tranform such realities into abstractions are seen as barbed-wire border markers between public accountability and personal responsibility, between individual moral decisions and social ethics. These borders divide the whole and disintegrate the possibilities for humane social policies. It is this resistance to compartmentalizing and fragmenting human endeavors into public and private or personal and professional which most distinguishes the feminist view of policy issues and approaches to world order. It also marks feminine cultures as distinct from the dominant masculine cultures. It is now argued by feminists that women both within and across cultures are culturally different from men, even though they are agents of transmission of that masculine culture to the young. In a sense, every woman is bicultural, although she may speak only one language and live her whole life in one small village. Perhaps this is why women tend to be more culturally sensitive.

These divisions and the damage they cause are not likely to be remedied by the establishment of a "parliament of cultures" (which usually refers to masculine cultures) with a global parliamentary order structured by standards of the same level of abstraction as produced by our present order and that still pervades the search for alternatives. Quantification and conceptual abstractions are not adequate for implementating a world constitutional order of integrity, by which is meant the health and wholeness of all constituent components, nor for the process of integration, a complementary interrelationship among the component parts functioning together for their mutual survival. So conceived, integrity and complementarity are attributes women have traditionally brought to social endeavor. Thus, it is not enough that women be present in equal numbers on the committees and councils that plan and operate a global constitutional order. They must be, as must be the various minorities, fully attended to and fully participant, from the conceptualizing through the daily functioning of the global order, in the halls of the parliament and behind the desks of the bureaucracy.

While the intensity and scope of the challenge of social integration are probably greater at the global level than at any other, and the stakes in the nuclear age are undoubtedly higher than at any previous time, the natures of the challenge and of the component tasks are not unprecedented. What is most unprecedented in the present situation is the breadth and variety of human skills, capacities, talents, and experiences we have to draw on in meeting the challenge and in defining and performing the tasks.

It has become painfully evident that we have so far called on but a few of these skills and experiences. The total pool of human capacities has been drawn upon neither in defining problems nor in forming policy, nor in research and social design. Women and minorities may now be factored into some policy making, and often play important roles in doing the real work of any social enterprise, yet their talents are rarely brought into the most significant stages of design and decision making. Thus, the greatest possible breadth of view and the entire range of alternatives in approaching any task is rarely open to planners, and so the possibilities for success are always more limited than need be. As noted, this problem has come to be noted as a serious obstacle in development planning. It is now being identified, as well, as a major impediment in the formulating of new security policies and to progress in arms control and disarmament.[2] In both cases, the local and global priorities were approached most often in terms of trade-offs, imposing sacrifice on some to achieve benefits for others. This Western masculine mode of thinking which has dominated both levels has been cited as a significant barrier to meaningful achievement in those fields intended to move the world in the direction of justice and peace.

Surely we cannot expect to derive a more equitable, less violent world order from essentially the same sources that have produced our present crises. Neither can we expect to design global institutions that will function to an advantage for local communities equal to that for world society, if most of those who know and live primarily in the local sphere are not involved in determining what such institutions should do, why and how, and in carrying out the how. Nowhere is the need for practical application of the principle of complementarity more necessary than in the design of institutions that can do justice to both global and local needs and priorities. Nowhere is the significance of representations more crucial. Representations authentically articulated and sincerely attended to are a primary necessity for the implementation of a just and viable constitutional order.

IMPLEMENTATION: INCLUSION OF MULTIPLE CULTURES

Representating diverse constituencies within a world constitutional order will involve its performing specific social, economic, political, and cultural tasks in particular local settings, if that order is in fact constructed to attend to the actual concerns and needs of these constituencies. Implementation then, will, require the knowledge and energies of those who live in those localities. It will also require that people in local areas be fully knowledgeable about global realities and needs, and most significantly that there be far freer access to information on all levels. People who are going to live with the actual consequence of structures, policies, and programs are most motivated to fully assess their necessity and desirability and assure their success. People who are directly familiar with the conditions and culture(s) of a local setting are best able to judge the potential efficacy and equity of particular approaches to the tasks of implementing global policies and standards at the grassroots. Indeed, the building of a world constitutional order will require simultaneous and complementary planning and initiation at the global structural and local community levels within an integrated system of local-global cooperation in which universal standards are interpreted and implemented according to local realities. An adequate assessment of local realities requires full knowledge of the culture, customs, and conditions of the locality, a knowledge fully possessed only by those who are a part of the locality. The task of communicating across the cultural barriers that separate the mediators of international (or in this case, transnational or supranational) standards from the locally responsible is one which needs to be addressed in the design of and transition to a world constitutional order. The disasters of the development decades were precipitated in large part by the exclusion of local community people, particularly women, from the planning stages; the ecological tragedy of the Amazon Basin sacrificed the authentic needs and potential of the rain forest to exogenous standards of progress in which the excessive consumption of the industrial North was pitted against the ecological balance of the region and the environmental health of the planet. Both attest to the necessity for local indigenous participation at every stage, from interpretation through implementation.

What is being argued for here is not simply inclusion for the sake of justice and equity. While the ethical is, indeed, paramount to all of us who approach world order issues within a normative context, the argument here is in terms of necessity and efficacy. Even the most refined technology and most precisely structured political systems and the most technological and political minds cannot expect success where there is ignorance of the human and natural environments in which the new structures are to be built and new policies enacted. In planning and bringing into being a world constitutional order there is an essential need as much for knowledge of how the natural world works, and perhaps even more how various groups of people see the world, as for an understanding of social, political, and economic theory. The actual knowledge, beliefs, and experiences of traditional peoples, minorities, and most especially women, indeed all human groups must be factored into conceptualizing, constructing, and operating any global institutions intended to guide and influence the multiple communities, localities, and peoples of the Earth.

Inclusion has been a major theme of women's movements, mostly as a matter of equity, in that explicit exclusion is not only an extremely blatant form of discrimination, it is a very effective mechanism through which the patriarchy limits the holding of power to the male-elect, which on a global scale means mainly Euro-American technocrats. However, such issues as sexist language, often perceived as a carping detail in the entire range of problems related to the oppression of women, have served to demonstrate that the conceptual and epistemological reasons for inclusion are in fact more significant. There is a growing body of evidence that, for whatever reason, women think differently from men.[4] The way we humans think, our styles of conceptualizing and reasoning; the way we view the world, that is, how we think the world works and what we value; our learnings and experiences; all have a profound effect on our approaches to problems and our creative expression. Given the nature and scope of our present global problems, there need be no argument that limiting approaches to their resolution to one particular mode of thinking or cultural perspective is self-defeating.

Humans have long recognized that different cultures produce different ways of thinking, and, unfortunately, have assumed that one culture's way (usually our own) was superior to others'. This assumption is beginning to erode, largely as a result of transnational economic cooperation, as much as from dissemination of the kinds of enlightenment offered by the social sciences. However, the acknowledgment that women have different cultures than men, rather than merely providing a complementary tributary to the mainstream of masculine cultures is still fairly new and limited. Even some feminists have refused to entertain this possibility, mainly because gender differences have been a major basis for the exclusion, discrimination, and oppression women have endured under the patriarchal order. Yet now, within the context of the present order, out of which the world constitutional order must emerge, and in the future, the maintenance of justice and equity in a reconstructed order demands both positive acknowledgement and effective use of human differences, more particularly the difference between men and women, which, like cultural diversity, offers humankind a rich feast of possibilities for social design and policy making.

Women's cultures have produced many of the attributes most required to bring about a global order that limits violence, promotes justice, and respects the environment. Cooperation in the achievement of group goals, whether of the family or of the larger community, is a general characteristic of most women's cultures, as are avoidance of harm and the maximum use of minimum resources. All of these tendencies are vitally necessary to heal and rebuild a human society rent by violent conflict, and to save the life support systems of planet Earth, assaulted nearly unto death by masculine standards of progress and production. Feminist world order and peace researchers would argue, that the kind of policy criteria and ideas for social processes and designs of the structures of interrelationships which women are likely to introduce into the constitutional planning discourse are among the most fundamentally necessary features of the kind of world constitutional order we seek.

They would further argue that such features are in fact constitutive of a just and equitable world constitutional order, that is, make up its very substance. Without attention to the kinds of concerns that women's ways of thinking would bring to the discourse, the fundamental human qualities essential to authentic equity and authentic globalism (i.e., derived from participation, not ordered by authority) are not likely to be explicitly and intentionally built into the process. Authentic globalism proceeds from a process of inclusion, as universalized a participation as possible. What would make for an inclusive order that is authentically global is the intention to universalize participation, to constantly widen the basis of the constitutional process, and to enrich the pool of human capacities and skills from which the process can draw. Inclusiveness, which women have traditionally worked to achieve in groups for which they are responsible—e.g., families, classrooms—from this particular feminist perspective is also constitutive of a desirable global order.

The notion of planning an order from the constituent components of the human and other living elements to be involved, while more feminine in style, is beginning to influence people of both sexes and all cultures who apply what has been called an ecological approach to global issues, raising questions of how to develop a humane human community in harmony with the planet that sustains it. The questions raised by the ecological, or indeed any approach, will reveal the values and purposes that inform the approach. An ecological approach is holistic and process-oriented, and places emphasis on finding a proper balance and life-enhancing accommodation between the human and the natural worlds, to bring to awareness the concept of humanity itself as a part rather than in charge of the natural world. Thus, feminist constitutional planning is organic in its impetus towards a healthy life-enhancing balance among the components of the various Earth systems, and holistic in its inclination toward universal inclusiveness.

It does not, then, stand in opposition to, nor is it intended to contrast with, other modes of constitutional construction or social planning. Rather, it complements, synergizes, and "comprehends" (i.e., integrates into one total process) the other modes.

The complementarity of feminist constitutional planning is reflected in the convergence and synergy between a standard world order approach and a feminist global security approach. While both stand in contrast to present conventional modes of security analysis, each has a somewhat different perspective that broadens the overall view. From a feminist perspective, the major contribution of a world order approach is the explicit identification of a set of social values against which policies and their consequences are to be measured, and for the realization of which global institutions are to be designed and developed. As the world order values of peace, social justice, economic equity, ecological balance, positive identity, and participation (the field has always had a masculine ambivalence about the value of participation) are applied to the task of devising global policies and/or designing a world constitutional order, questions are framed so as to fulfill the purposes of realizing the values on a global scale to be enjoyed by all. It is these questions that set the parameters for the tasks of institution building and policy inquiry.

The questions posed within the context of world order values of how to reduce and eliminate organized violence, how to increase and broaden social justice, how to assure economic equity and ecological balance, and how to enhance participation and positive identity are intended to stimulate speculation as to the most effective institutions and policies for realizing these values. Yet they are primarily questions of "disembodied" institutional design. Both the conceptualization and the articulation tend to be abstract, as is the nature of institution planning so as to facilitate the formulation of the basic principles of design and policy. Equally as necessary as formulating principles, however, are conceptualizing ideas and images of behaviors and relationships, both corporate and individual, putting flesh on the bones of abstract principles. Feminist insistence that the distinctions between the political and the personal, the private and the public are false and dangerous dichotomies is not purely ideological. It is a fundamental principle of feminist epistemology, which in its essential holism transcends all false and unnecessary separations and reductions, insisting on holistic frameworks for both analytic and social purposes. This observation is not intended to contrast the feminist with the world order approach, which is in fact far more holistic than conventional policy approaches and always takes the relationships among problems into consideration. Rather it emphasizes the human and interpersonal approaches with which a feminist perspective complements world order and other peace research approaches to the projection and assessment of global institutions, and argues that the behavioral is as important as the institutional. In fact, the two are interdependent, in any constitutional order, and thus must be included in the planning.

AUTHENTIC SECURITY AS THE PURPOSE OF THE GLOBAL ORDER

Like the world order approach, the feminist approach acknowledges the need for an explicit educational dimension in planning and implementation. Thus the questions it raises serve heuristic as well as analytic purposes. Examples of such questions and how a feminist approach would complement world order in the development of a world constitutional order are raised by the way feminists, indeed many women peace activists and researchers, not all of whom are feminists, conceptualize and assess security matters. The holistic feminist approach, even more starkly than a world order approach, contrasts with conventional security views and policies that reduce virtually all issues to questions of "national security" and "military preparedness." The dysfunctionality of this reductionist view of security is readily evident to all who are concerned with the quality of the life to be made secure. Feminists see in its deleterious effects on women and children how the inordinate priority given to the military erodes authentic security,—global, national, and local. Human security at any level appears in feminist terms to have four dimensions. The questions raised by these dimensions serve to illustrate the relational and behavioral flesh that feminist perspectives might put on the institutional skeleton of a world constitutional order, complementing the inquiry pursued in a world order approach.

While a feminist approach complements the more inclusive approach offered by world order, it is also, in one vitally significant respect, quite different. Most conventional and even world order approaches make a common assumption about the ultimate purpose of security policy, particularly military security or peacekeeping capacities, which is that the purpose of the policies is to reduce and, if possible, eliminate the vulnerability of some parties to the others in the system. Feminists understand that all viable human relationships involve vulnerability. Indeed, the more satisfying and productive the relationship, the more vulnerability exists. This is the essence of interdependence. Thus, feminist security policy would seek not so much to reduce vulnerability as to develop relationships in which vulnerability can exist without necessarily threatening security. The masculine drive for invulnerability has been as damaging to world peace as the drive to dominate nature has been to the environment.

There are four feminist security dimensions best described as expectations, the fulfillment of which makes for human security. These security expectations are expressed as such because each recognizes the element of vulnerability and acknowledges that security erodes when vulnerability is exploited. Sissela Bok has pointed out that peace is to a large degree dependent upon the balance between trust and mistrust in the system of relationships.[4] Similarly, peace requires a balance between vulnerability and security. The dimensions and expectations of a feminist approach to security are based on the assertion that the balance required for peace demands accommodation to rather than exploitation of vulnerability. The expectations arising from the core concerns and qualities characteristic of a feminist perspective might be summarized as follows: that our environment be able to maintain life; that our basic human needs be met; that our persons be sustained and respected by our own society; that we be protected from harm. There is clear and abundant evidence that the first three of these expectations receive inadequate attention from our present patriarchal policy-making systems, else the planet itself would not be in danger of death from the ecological wounds we have inflicted upon her. Millions would not endure dire poverty unto starvation and famine. Racism and sexism would not continue to violate the human rights of the majority of the human family. It is evident that little success has been achieved, despite the inordinate attention and share of resources spent on meeting even the fourth concern, protection from harm. An arms development process and sustained militarism continue in spite of the East/West accommodation, as does the menace of multiple forms of terrorism, against which no one can be protected, and the growth of ethnic and regional armed conflict.

With regard to the first expectation, of environmental security, feminist questions would address the fundamental issues involved in the relationship between human society and the Earth. What kind of institutions and processes could transform the present exploitive, extractive relationship in the dominion of humankind over the Earth into one of mutual nurturance and enhancement? Such environmental policy questions inherent in a world order perspective would be complemented by inquiry into the social norms and individual behaviors, values, and attitudes required to initiate and maintain a relationship of mutuality.

If a proposed constitutional order is to assure the second expectation, the universal fulfillment of basic human needs (which we have reason to believe is technologically possible), questions about human behavior also need to be addressed. For example, how can the needs that traditional people have sought to meet through large families of many children be otherwise fulfilled? Keeping in mind that such needs are not only economic, the responses must deal more with cultural factors than population control, increased food production, child survival, and more equitable distribution systems, important as they are. Consideration must be given to the way in which the needs for meaning, identity, continuity, and respect as well as sustenance have been met through large families. Relational questions on this issue might inquire into how to protect the survival of cultures, how to establish dignified and humanly satisfying relations of mutual interdependence, and how to derive general principles of economic relations that can bring these qualities even to those who continue to be dependent, like children, the aged, and the physically or mentally challenged. No matter what constitutional or structural changes may be made, those who carry the scars of deprivation over generations will still be struggling to catch up, so severe have been the inequities. It is conditions like these that demand accommodation to vulnerability. We need to ask not only how to create structures that prevent the dependency/dominance relationships at the extremes of poverty and affluence, but how to transform the patriarchal relationships, attitudes, and values that make these extremes possible. A feminist approach to all such questions assumes that the primary need is learning, learning not only to look at goals such as economic equity as a security need, but to take a comprehensive enough view to see the cultural and social dimensions that are part of any process for achieving the goal. An intentional educational process, essentially a cultural evolution, is also necessary for achieving a just world peace, the fundamental purpose of any constitutional order.

Education is absolutely essential for meeting the security expectations of social soldarity and personal respect. What kinds of relationships can be structured among and between minority and majority cultures which will permit all to flourish and yet not deprive any within them of respect and sustenance? How can we confront homophobia, ethnocentrism, racism, sexism, and all identity-based forms of oppression so that they will not continue to plague world society even under a new constitutional order? How can we move beyond even the present human rights concepts and standards so as to assure the full and universal enjoyment of dignity and equity as well as prevent the violation of rights? How can we develop not only the political will but the social intention that all should be assured dignity and equity, what has been defined as "cultural solidarity"?[5] What standards of behavior can be institutionalized as the social norm so that we can learn how to live in a society guided by such intentions? As such intentions are so radically different from those which characterize the global patriarchy, this expectation too demands the inclusion of an educational dimension in the development of a restructured global order and a culture of peace.

With regard to protection needs, a feminist perspective would move beyond both the best of conventional policy, limiting the risks of war through minor political accommodation and arms control, and even beyond the system-changing proposals for disarmament, peacekeeping, and the application of law rather than armed conflict to resolve international disputes. It would pose the fundamental question of how we can change the relationships among nations so that they no longer wish to threaten or harm each other and can live with their vulnerability to each other. How can nations behave so as to increase both the actual and perceived security of other nations? And how can we learn these behaviors?

The "we" in such questions in previous constitutional discourse usually referred to society in the abstract or to the policy makers or national or world leaders. While a feminist perspective would include all of these, it would place far more emphasis on people in relationships, on structuring all human relationships, personal and corporate, so as to effect the culture itself. Personal and cultural development are the essential components of effective change in values, norms, and standards, and thereby of lasting social change. Social change in the form of a world constitutional order may be conceptualized on the drawingboards of scholarly research and in political discourse, but it can only be realized, made real, by actual day-to-day human behaviors. Thus, human relationships are crucial to the creation of an ethically acceptable, politically viable constitutional order. This is the essential political realism that a feminist perspective can bring to the discourse. This is the locus in which fundamental learning must take place, and the source of authenticity, of authentic security and authentic globalism upon which any order must rest.

It has always been my perception that such authentic change rooted in the fundamental value of universal equity was the basic purpose of world order studies and, as such, a chief motivator of their generative contributions to peace research and the peace movement. Clearly such an assertion by the designer of a fundamental set of planetary rights for all humankind is one indicator of such an intention.[6] Indeed, that declaration reflects some of the very qualities with which a feminist perspective complements that of world order. Risking the "outrageous" has been a major factor in bringing us to the present stage of discussion. The "truly" outrageous I take to be the inclusion of the real, the stuff of everyday human life. To risk the outrageous, let's dare to be truly real and fully inclusive, for inclusiveness constitutes authentic globalism, and nothing less should be the fundamental purpose of a world constitutional order.

NOTES

1. Nell Noddings, *Caring: A Feminist Approach to Ethics and Moral Education* (Berkeley, and Los Angeles: University of California Press, 1984).

2. Scilla McLean, *Who Decides* (Oxford: Oxford Research Group, 1987).

3. Mary Belenky, B. Clincky, N. Goldberg, and J. Tarule, *Women's Ways of Knowing* (New York: Basic Books, 1986).

4. Sissela Bok, *A Strategy of Peace: Human Values and the Threat of War* (New York: Pantheon Books, 1989).

5. Toh Swee Hin and Virginia Florescu Cawagas, *Peaceful Theory and Practice in Peace Education* (Quezon City: Phoenix, 1990).

6. Saul Mendlovitz, address to World Federalist Conference, Washington, D.C. October, 1989.

13

Toward an Ambiguous World Order

MARY CATHERINE BATESON

There are two families of solutions to the problem of world order, expressing very different premises about how human communities can best be organized. One type of solution is modelled on the state, and proposes a specific and unambiguous locus of power. This might be achieved by the establishment of some form of world government with unquestioned authority, at least in certain areas, with powers of enforcement achieved by a degree of voluntary abdication of sovereignty by participating nation-states. Equally, it might be achieved by the dominance of a single power. This form of organization, depending as it does on the same kind of power as the nation-state, is necessarily seen as inimical to those who identify with existing forms of government. Power is not readily abdicated by those who believe they have it.

The alternative approach suggests that the problem of world order might be solved by the emergence of what has been termed a "global civilization,"[1] a form of organization not analogous in structure to the governments of nation-states, but that represents rather an additional layer of civility and commonality rather than an abdication of sovereignty. Such an emerging pattern of commonality might of course be a predecessor to more formal structures, as seems to be the case in Europe, where a common civilization is gradually leading to economic and political unification. The use of the term "civilization" presents certain problems because it has sometimes been used invidiously. At the same time, it does express the notion of a shared body of ideas transcending political boundaries.

A GLOBAL CIVILIZATION

The concept of an emerging global civilization, as a replacement for the notion of a world government, is intended here to suggest a loosely integrated system that might have the following characteristics: (1)It could develop gradually and is already in the process of development; (2) it would be characterized by ongoing change, indeed by evolution; (3) it could coexist with rich cultural and political diversity; (4) it would not rely on the centralization of power that has characterized the concept of the state. All of these characteristics are related to another, the focus of this paper. (5) it would make a virtue of ambiguity, in the traditional sense of the term, finding in what might be construed as a flaw or weakness a source of strength (*virtù*). Change, fluidity, diversity, diffuse focus, these are all characteristics alien to traditional concepts of political power, as is ambiguity, for since the days of the Medes and the Persians or even earlier, rulers have wanted to know how far their writ will run. But if such a loose, flexible form of organization were to develop, it need not present an obvious threat to existing structures.

Such a development is already under way, for arguably the modern world, with its increasing density of communications, is a gradually self-organizing system. The necessary models for understanding such a emergent order come from ecology rather than from traditional political science.

A global civilization is not achieved by negotiation as we know it, where the process of international negotiation has been pervaded by a search for fixed, verifiable, and unambiguous formulations. Rather it is achieved by a dense web of communication of many different kinds, forms of exchange that percolate into the daily lives and imaginations of ordinary people around the world. What is needed is not unambiguous agreement but rather a homely and familiar sense of relationship, a resilient substructure of global community that will allow more flexibility in tackling the vast and urgent issues that we as a species must face together. Trust and a tolerance for ambiguity within some broader framework are built from the ordinary. At the local level, such a substructure is built up from day-to-day, face-to-face interactions; at the global level, it is likely to develop by listening to the radio and walking in a marketplace that draws on worldwide resources, rather than through legislation and formal educational programs.

Thus, in discussing the kind of integration implied by the idea of a global civilization, it is important to include a discussion of the way's in which a multitude of exchanges and borrowings, each one perhaps trivial, create a structure of familiarity. A viable form of world order must be pieced together from only partially shared systems of meaning, crossing over existing cultural diversity. Such systems of meaning will be very different from the systems developed by diplomats or philosophers, for they will be improvisational and ambiguous, with room for both contention and humor.

ASSUMPTIONS AND MODELS

Models of world government are affected by the existing "commonsense" of ideas carried over from the state system, with its focus on central authority. Beyond this, they gain their appearance of self-evident necessity from the conguence between established conceptualizations in different spheres, such as religion and family life. Yet central control, in the sense of an unambiguous locus of power and of authority as the only possible basis of integration, is by no means universal or necessary. Substantial human communities may be organized acephalously—without central authority. This does not mean they are anarchic, for normative expectations and patterns of influence and authority (not necessarily benign) always emerge in human groups wherever there is direct contact within them, and have been observed consistently in social groups of all primates. The question really is, What, for our species, can serve as direct contact?

The state, as described by Bodin and others, presented central authority as the only solution to the problems of disorder and conflict, to the Hobbesian war of all against all. This was based on a notion that conflict is so embedded in human nature that it can only be resolved from above. Certainly conflict is inescapable, but Hobbes lacked the knowledge of alternative forms of order now available from anthropology. We have many models of communities in which, in the absence of central authority, we do not see all pitted against one another. Indeed, we now know that Hobbes' grim vision is a projection, no more descriptive of human prehistory than the myth of Eden. Total harmony and total anarchy, although the brief illusion of either sometimes appears, are both evanescent. As thought experiments, they are less interesting than the study of limited conflicts and the ways of resolving these, a question of far greater moment in a world where certain familiar expressions of conflict have become unacceptable.

It is of course reasonable to question whether acephalous forms of order can be extended to large areas like nations, much less to the whole planet, because the familiar anthropological examples seem to depend on shared cultural premises and a high level of day-to-day, face-to-face familiarity and communication. The invention of the state provided a solution to a problem that has not disappeared: the problem of coordinating large populations lacking dense links of intercommunication. But it is important to recognize that the populations of France, say, and of Germany, when these states emerged, were far less richly intercommunicating than the entire world is today. The solution, then, to inadequate interaction was the centralization of power. Today, the increase of communication offers an alternative solution to the same problem. The recognition of an emerging world civilization is essentially a recognition of the high density of new forms of communication saturating the ether.

Another kind of solution can be seen in the history of constitutionalism. The United States Constitution was deliberately designed to prevent the concentration of power in any one institution of government. It has demonstrated that deliberate pluralism, permitting substantial conflict, with power at multiple points of the system and strong protection for communication and expression of diverse views, is imperfect but possible. Interestingly enough, it has often been argued that the strength of the U.S. Constitution lies in its ambiguity, its openness to debate and evolving interpretation as times change.

MONOTHEISM

Historically, much of the Western dislike of ambiguity has come from its religions. The idea in Western religion of an unambiguous locus of power seems to have an even more compelling logic than the concept of the state to which it is analogous. But it is not necessary. The ancient Hebrews asserted the presence and power of a single omnipotent deity, and since that time the Western religious tradition has struggled with the belief in one God; any belief in more than one has come to seem absurd. But because so many Western thinkers and scholars today reject all religious forms, they tend to be unaware both of the hints of multiplicity within unity that exist even in monotheistic traditions, and of the subtle difference between their rejection of polytheism and of monotheism, for it is not clear that the superiority of monotheism should be self-evident when theism of any kind is rejected. It is one thing to urge that pluralism requires the mutual tolerance of different religious groups, even when such tolerance is intellectually alien. It is quite another thing to propose an intrinsically pluralistic metaphysic, to deny that the "ground of all being" is necessarily solid underfoot. Yet polytheism was apparently not at all absurd for the ancient Indo-Europeans, including the Greeks and the ancestors of present-day Hindus and most Europeans, and for most other human communities whose sense of the divine has been more ecological, multifaceted, and interdependent.

In fact, it is only habit that makes monotheism, like the idea of the state, so persuasive. The Hebrews found monotheism a difficult belief to sustain, perhaps because it was so dissonant with their tribal social organization, their neighboring peoples' religions, and their dispersal across the notably varied terrain of Palestine. They strayed repeatedly, following multiple deities, perhaps most regularly when central political power was in question. Yet the Hebrew prophets made a fateful analogy, from the invention of monotheism to the unity of belief, for Judaism, Christianity, and Islam in their orthodox forms all assert that not only is deity single, but that religious knowledge is also necessarily single and absolute.

In the Middle Ages, when political power was pluralistic and fragmented, divine absolutism was also ambiguous, multiply delegated to a flock of intercessory beings—angels, saints, and clerics—like a corrupt Byzantine bureaucracy. The Virgin Mary played the supreme intercessory role, and one cannot help but feel that much of her significance lay in her ability sometimes to persuade her son to do something against logic or his better judgment, as appears to have been the case at the wedding at Cana. While not in entire synchrony, the emergence of absolutism as a political form corresponds to the inexorable logic of the Counter-/Reformation, with its assertion of clear lines of authority. The religious preference for a single unchanging and transcendent deity leads to the preference for unambiguous doctrine and to the whole history of creeds, orthodoxy, heterodoxy and the persecution of heretics, and the Inquisition. Once formulated, the idea of the singular *and* omnipotent has survived as central in Christianity and Islam to this day, focusing the imagination of a great part of the world's population, and accompanied, logically, by the immensely costly conviction that doctrine is either true or false.

Can one imagine a return to a world in which polytheism would seem at least as persuasive as monotheism? Or at least one in which respect for the beliefs of others is not a superficial patina on the conviction that beliefs are either right or wrong? Must even post-religious societies model family and political life on religious forms they no longer accept? At the same time, in other areas, alternative models have been developing. Scientific knowledge has come to seem less determinate. In cognitive science, there is the developing body of thinking about autopoiesis, the self-organizing capacity of complex systems. In organizational theory, hierarchy is rapidly going out of fashion as too rigid for creativity, and feminists point out its analogy to patriarchy. The theory of a necessary single locus of power, with its metaphorical extensions, begins to seem less and less useful.

Early theorists of the sovereign state asserted that only with a clearly definable locus of power could the rule of law be assured, guaranteeing domestic peace and tranquility. It is interesting today to find these intellectual arguments echoed in fundamentalist tracts about family life: It is necessary and logical, they assert, that there should be one voice able to make a final decision, and therefore any attempt at equality between men and women is necessarily unworkable, as absurd as the idea of multiple gods managing the universe by a system of consultation and compromise. There is no difficulty with delegation and subsidiarity, providing hierarchy is unambiguously defined; every ship, they assert, must have a captain.

IN PRAISE OF MUDDLE

The preference for a single center of authority is both temperamental and aesthetic. The alternative argument would be that, if only conflict can be contained, a certain amount of muddle is both beautiful and creative, both in society and in the family. There need not be a single locus of authority—not in the family, not in society, not in the cosmos. It is not easy to maintain a sense of commonality based on partial and ambiguous sharing, but that may be the only option for world order. If this is the case, then many kinds of contemporary efforts to move toward unequivocal rules, precise language, and verification are misguided. There is little willingness to rely on unarticulated and partially shared understandings, and yet the search for fixed and explicit understanding may prove to be self-defeating. Certainly the insistence on total explicitness and verifiability has crippled arms limitation negotiations. The United States over the last twenty years has in many areas been engaged in a flurry of specification and regulation, trying to define exact procedures for decision-making to make these processes more determinate, to make the functioning of democracy less ambiguous—to eliminate ambiguity in a society where consensus is in doubt. If ambiguity is an essential lubricant for the system, that effort may be self-destructive.

The very flurry of disambiguation that draws us in one direction is a reaction that derives from the pluralism and ambiguity of the U.S. Constitution, which serves us because of its supreme ambiguity, but does not always satisfy us with definitions of exact rights. The writers of the Constitution built in provisions for conflicting types of authority and for disagreement in the form of the balance of powers and the protections of minorities. Yet a certain fluctuation in levels of ambiguity and a variable level of tolerance for ambiguity within the population may be a necessary characteristic of pluralistic systems.

During recent years, most of us have had enough contact with computers to experience the process of reducing ambiguity from another point of view. Most computers to date, unlike human beings, are incapable of dealing with ambiguity, which makes them, as they are sometimes fondly called in the United Kingdom, TOMs: totally obedient morons. If there is even a trace of unclarity in an instruction given to a computer, it will not comply. The human mind can, however, tolerate high levels of ambiguity, finding in it one of the sources of creativity. Even as the average number of words in drafts of new legislation is increased, and each attracts additional volumes of administrative specification, it must be clear that we are engaged in a *reductio ad absurdum* of the attempt to escape ambiguity.

In an emerging world civilization, the forms in which ideas are shared, whatever their sources, will be variable and continually liable to diverge, floating in a sea of pluralism and ambiguity, and kept together not by orthodoxy but by a continual process of rapid interchange and the steady need to address practical problems.

We may indeed need to consider the *purposeful creation* of ambiguity. Yet this idea runs counter to great many common assumptions. The same kinds of aesthetic preference that wound their way through the development of Western religion may respond with distaste to the compromises of pluralism. Yet any constitution appropriate to such an order would require high degrees of ambiguity.

I do not believe we have at present the capacity to generate a world constitution with a level of fruitful ambiguity comparable to that devised two centuries ago. It is as if the forms of a world order would have be created by biologists and artists rather than by lawyers. But it is possible that patterns of shared understanding might emerge without any single constitutional document. If such a document were to develop, the first requirement would be that it protect the openness of the system to new ideas.

CONCLUSION

A viable form of world order must exist in the context of a partial sharing of systems of meaning, crossing over existing cultural diversity, and such a development is already under way and might be referred to as a "global civilization." It is not clear that such systems of meaning need to be explicit and formally agreed upon. Probably they will be very different from the systems developed by diplomats or philosophers, for they will be partial, piecemeal, and ambiguous. In order to recognize and benefit from emerging forms of global commonality at every level, it will be necessary to rethink the notion of civilization and the kind of integration necessary to it. What we can see today, however, is that the process is itself not a singular one but a convergence of many streams of thought and effort.

Since the dawn of human history, visions have been drawn from the ambiguous, as diviners imagined the future in the forms of clouds and swirling waters. Social change and innovation are always stimulated by the awareness of difference, the understanding that there are no fixed dogmas, no fixed answers to the most fundamental questions. This is a disturbing prospect for many, but the very ambiguity of the emerging world civilization promises a massive liberation of the human imagination.

NOTES

1. This was the term proposed at the conference for which the ideas in this paper were first developed, "The Coming Global Civilization" sponsored by the World Order Models Project and the Soviet Political Science Association, Moscow, October 10–16, 1988, and published as *Contending Sovereignties: Redefining Political Community,* edited by R. B. J. Walker and Saul H. Mendlovitz (Boulder, CO.: Lynne Rienner, 1990). See my paper in that volume, "Beyond Sovereignty: An Emerging Global Civilization" for a further discussion of the use of the term civilization in this context. Portions of this essay are drawn from that earlier publication.

Part IV

LOCALIZATION

14

Protecting Local Autonomy in a Global Constitutional Order

CHADWICK F. ALGER

Many concerned with constitutionalism and world order have tended to focus their attention on what some would call "the world beyond the states." They have proposed new kinds of inter-state institutions that would enhance possibilities for diminishing violence between states and for enabling them to cope with a growing list of global problems. We need more of this kind of creative thinking. But the purpose of this chapter is to argue that a constitutional order for dealing with global problems limited to the realm beyond the state is not enough. Rapid growth in the impact of political, economic, social and military institutions with global reach on towns, cities, and provinces now demands the attention of those concerned about constitutionalism and world order.

Local people now live their lives in a sea of worldwide transactions, as consumers of products and resources from all over the world, as workers for transnational corporations, and as unemployed whose jobs have been taken abroad. Local communities throughout the world are now potential international battlefields. International terrorism can occur in the airports, public buildings, and workplaces of any community, and people in thousands of cities across the world fear that a nuclear war could incinerate their city at any time. It is in the light of these changes in how local communities are linked to the rest of the world that some citizens and local officials believe that the traditional view that international issues should be the exclusive concern of national governments is no longer valid.

Challenges to the traditional view that foreign policy and international issues are beyond the purview of local authorities can be approached from two perspectives. First, local citizens are becoming increasingly aware of the ways in which the foreign policies of national governments—their own and other states'—affect them in their local communities. As a result, there is a growing number of local movements through which local citizens themselves are taking action on international issues, and they are also demanding that local governments take action on these issues. Second, worldwide economic forces—through trade, foreign investment, and local activities of transnational firms—are having a growing impact on the quality of life in local communities and on the policy options available for local authorities. These two aspects of growing global interdependence are making new kinds of demands on local authorities which their education and past experience have not prepared them to meet. On the one hand, they are not prepared to match the growing competence of some of their own local people to cope with "foreign" policy issues, and on the other hand, their more parochial view of "local" business makes them no match for local corporate executives who may be as familiar with New York, Tokyo, London, Manila, and Rio de Janeiro as they are with their own home town.[1]

INNOVATIVE LOCAL PEOPLES' ACTIONS ON FOREIGN POLICY ISSUES

Recent innovative actions by local citizens on foreign policy issues is dramatically different from more traditional international activities of local citizens. In the past these activities have tended to be confined to relief aid for those in need abroad, and to exchange programs and international education. These kinds of local activity operate comfortably within the context of the traditional division of labor, in which the state makes foreign policy and voluntary organizations create favorable background conditions that help the state system run smoothly. But dramatic changes are now taking place in the willingness of local people to become actively involved in "foreign" policy issues. Many now have adopted the slogan "Think Globally, Act Locally." This approach notes that the intrinsic character of a global issue is that it affects all human settlements. This being the case, it ought to be possible to act on the local manifestation of that issue, whether nuclear weapons, military bases, or poverty and violation of human rights in distant cities and towns. An overview of these local movements can be approached through brief descriptions of activities in the context of (1) war prevention and disarmament, (2) poverty, and (3) human rights.

War Prevention and Disarmament

Some exchange programs have evolved into activity pointed at foreign policy issues. An example would be the Citizen Exchange Council, which each year sends hundreds of people from the United States to the Soviet Union and Eastern Europe. The CEC believes that

> the experience sharpens participants' abilities to analyze daily news reports and discern rhetoric from fact. Better understanding of Soviet society passes to participant's neighbors, friends, students, or classmates, helping more Americans make informed judgments about international events.

Other examples of more issue-focused exchanges are the Peace Pilgrimage to the USSR, Peace Study Tour to Russia, the Volga Peace Cruise, and the Iowa Peace Mission to the USSR. Somewhat similar have been numerous programs in which citizens of the United States and Europe visited Central America, particularly Nicaragua. Eighty-seven cities in nine European countries now have "Twin-City alliances" with Nicaraguan cities. This first-hand citizen experience contributed to widespread citizen resistance to United States government efforts to escalate military action against the Sandinista government.

As local citizens have become more knowledgeable about military strategy, arms races, and arms production, they have also become increasingly informed about the ways in which they and others in their local community are personally involved in military production and deployment, and about the conflict between military expenditures and the ability of a society to satisfy human needs. Local plans for conversion from military to civilian production appeal to the self-interests of workers by citing studies such as one by the U.S. government indicating that investment of one million dollars in "defense" production creates 76,000 jobs, whereas the same investment in civilian production would produce over 100,000 jobs.[2] Groups in many cities have developed conversion plans. Perhaps the best-known conversion effort was the corporate plan published by the Lucas Aerospace Workers in England, in 1976.[3]

Another local approach has been prevention of weapons deployment. Perhaps the most reported effort to prevent deployment of weapons has been the efforts of the Greenham Commons Women in the

United Kingdom to blockade a U.S. base. They have even brought an unsuccessful suit into the U.S. courts, charging that cruise missiles are unconstitutional. They argued that the missiles, capable of being quickly and secretly launched, deprive Congress of its right to declare war, threaten to deprive life and liberty without due process—in violation of the Fifth Amendment to the United States Constitution—and violate several canons of international law because of their indiscriminate and long-lasting potential effects. Hundreds of U.S. and British churches, disarmament groups, and labor organizations joined the suit as "friends of the court."[4] Efforts have also been made to block the deployment of MX missiles in Nebraska; to blockade a Bangor, Washington, naval base in a campaign against the Trident submarine—perceived to be a first-strike weapon—and to resist deployment of sea-launched cruise missiles (SLCMs) in eight U.S. cities.[5]

Another local approach to military policy is the application of deterrence by citizens. In the Pledge of Resistance campaign in the United States, people have agreed to engage in either legal vigils or nonviolent civil disobedience in case the United States invades, bombs, sends combat troops to, or significantly elevates its intervention in Central America. By January 1985, some forty-two thousand had signed the Pledge. Local groups have created plans of action for civil disobedience at nearby military facilities, and are already engaged in training for nonviolent action.[6]

Poverty

Over the past couple of decades local voluntary programs to relieve suffering abroad have gradually evolved into programs for overcoming poverty through long-term economic and social development. Participation in Third World development has in turn involved leaders of voluntary programs in a complicated political process as they simultaneously attempt to raise funds from affluent people at home and use these funds to serve the needs of the poor in the Third World. Jorgen Lissner's *The Politics of Altruism* graphically portrays the tension between the expectations of many who donate to aid programs and those administering the programs overseas. As this Danish scholar sees it, donors tend to think of aid in terms of "resource aid" to improve the standard of living by means of various social services (e.g., education, health, agriculture) within the given economic and political structure. On the other hand, people involved in administering programs in the Third World tend to see the need for "structural aid," i.e., transforming the local socio-economic environment by "conscientization through literacy training, establishment of rural credit institutions and rural cooperatives, support of trade unions and liberation movements."[7] Even more difficult to communicate to affluent supporters is the discovery "that many (but not all) of the problems of the low-income countries originate in and are sustained by factors and policies in the high-income nations."

In response to these insights, agencies involved in development programs in the Third World have created development education programs in their home countries. Programs for development education are most highly developed in Europe and Canada, and U.S. programs are patterned after them. Canadian efforts include development education centers in such cities as Toronto, London, and Kitchener-Waterloo. In essence, development education is largely education in global political economy to provide a framework for understanding how people in local communities in both Third World and First World countries are linked to the global economy. This can open the way for specifying local policies in First World countries that are responsive to the needs of local communities in the Third World.

Human Rights

There has been a tendency to view fulfillment of human rights as promulgated in the UN Declaration on Human Rights as a responsibility of states. Nevertheless, the two covenants drafted to fulfill the declaration (one on civil and political rights and the other on economic, social, and cultural rights) both assert in their preambles:

> Realizing that the individual, having duties to other individuals and to the community to which he belongs, is under a responsibility to strive for the promotion and observance of the rights recognized in the present Covenant.

One organization that endeavors to fulfill this responsibility is Amnesty International (AI), particularly its program through which local AI groups work for the release of prisoners of conscience throughout the world. The primary approach of these local AI groups is to bring pressure on foreign governments through publicity, letters, phone calls, and other governments.

The struggle against apartheid in South Africa has also been localized through boycotts of local companies and banks doing business in South Africa and in efforts to change their policies by participation in shareholders' meetings. There were also campaigns on many college campuses attempting to pressure boards of directors of colleges and universities to disinvest in corporations doing business in South Africa. In these cases the investments consisted principally of endowment funds.

Another form of local human rights activity is efforts to provide new homes for refugees from political oppression, war, and economic deprivation in other countries. Normally this means settling legal immigrants in local communities. But the Sanctuary Movement in the United States has offered refuge for refugees from El Salvador whom the U.S. Immigration Service has declared to be illegal aliens. Sanctuary believes that these refugees would suffer punishment or death if they were returned to El Salvador or Guatemala. The movement reports that over two hundred religious congregations have declared themselves Sanctuaries, and that over fifty thousand people are involved. The Sanctuary Movement asserts that it is acting legally under the Refugee Act of 1980, which provides for asylum for those persecuted or having "a well-founded fear of persecution in their own countries." They see themselves as following a U.S. tradition, exemplified by the Underground Railroad before the Civil War. They note that then too those helping the slaves were indicted and imprisoned.

Still another local form of human rights action has been the INFACT Campaign against the Nestlé Corporation for its infant formula marketing practices in the Third World. INFACT action included local boycotts of Nestlé products, disinvestment campaigns, and national and international efforts to set standards for the marketing of infant formula in the Third World. This culminated in the approval of recommended standards by the Assembly of the World Health Organization. There was only one negative vote, cast by the representative of the United States. This led to the acceptance of WHO standards by the Nestlé Corporation.

LOCAL GOVERNMENT ACTION

As citizens have intensified their efforts to cope with local manifestations of international issues, they have increasingly sought support from local governments on issues such as anti-apartheid, the nuclear weapons freeze, nuclear-weapons-free zones, a nuclear test ban, sanctuary for political refugees, and conversion from production of weapons to production of products serving human civilian needs. Janice Love's 1985 study of the anti-apartheid campaigns in Michigan and Massachusetts[8] reported that twenty-two local governments in the United States had withdrawn investments from corporations doing business in South Africa. By 1986 the American Committee on Africa reported that fifty-four cities had divested themselves of such investments.

The nuclear weapons freeze campaign put much of its effort into obtaining pro-nuclear freeze votes by city, town, and county councils and by local referenda. The freeze called for a bilateral U.S.-Soviet stop to the production of nuclear weapons. Based on figures from the Nuclear Weapons Freeze Campaign National Clearinghouse in St. Louis, Hanna Newcombe[9] reported in 1983 that 240 city councils, 466 New England town meetings, and 63 county councils had passed freeze resolutions, for a total of 769. In addition, referenda were passed in over fifty cities and counties. This effort was followed by a comprehensive test ban campaign which had received support from 154 cities by 1987.

Cities have also declared themselves to be zones free of nuclear weapons. A nuclear-weapons-free municipality is generally one that does not permit the stationing of nuclear weapons and also does not permit transport of such weapons across its territory. This may also mean not stationing nor transporting weapons systems associated with nuclear weapons, and refraining from the production of these related weapons systems. A few cities have broadened the nuclear-weapons-free zone into a "nuclear-free zone," which prohibits civilian nuclear power stations, as well. The Campaign for Nuclear Disarmament (CND) started the municipal nuclear-free-zone movement in Great Britain where 224 local councils with over sixty percent of the British population have approved the proposal. Nuclear Free America in Baltimore, Maryland, reported in July 1989 that there were 4,279 nuclear-free-zone communities in 23 countries.[10]

In Europe the Towns and Development movement encourages town councils to create policies for international development cooperation, and to establish "Twinning" relationships with Third World cities. In support of this program, there is a campaign in Belgium to have an Alderman for Development Cooperation appointed in each municipality. In Bruges the Alderman for Development participates on a 15-member Third World Committee composed of all organizations in Bruges involved in development cooperation. This committee advises the Bruges Town Council on matters pertaining to development cooperation, conducts awareness-building activities for the Bruges population and coordinates initiatives of the various local organizations involved in Third World activity. In Leiden the municipality decided in 1979 to make available an annual amount of 10,000 guilders for informing people about Third World developments. In Tilburg in the Netherlands, the Mayor and Aldermen in 1979 examined the possibilities of municipal authorities contributing to local awareness about inequality in the relations between industrial countries and countries of the Third World. This led to the creation in 1980 of an Advisory Board composed of members of the Town Council and representatives of community organizations.

The Sanctuary Movement in the United States involves an unusually strong direct defiance of national authority by local government. In response to the local movements advocating sanctuary for Central American refugees, local governments in twenty-two cities have offered sanctuary to refugees fleeing El Salvador and Guatemala. These actions defy agencies of the federal government which take the position that these people are not refugees fleeing political oppression but people attempting to escape from poor economic conditions.

CHANGE IN THE WORLDWIDE ECONOMIC AND SOCIAL CONTEXT OF CITIES

A second challenge to local authorities is the growing impact of worldwide economic and social forces on local communities and the authorities that govern them. On the one hand, an increasing number of local citizens and authorities are aware of the impact of world markets and production on local employment, such that many cities/provinces have now created development offices that actively seek to attract foreign investment and attempt to market local products abroad. On the other hand, few local citizens or officials really understand the multifaceted ways in which worldwide interdependence now affects daily life in their community. Michael Timberlake believes that scholars have contributed to this lack of understanding because

> urbanization processes have typically been studied by social scientists as if they were isolated in time and explicable only in terms of other processes and structures of rather narrow scope, limited to the boundaries of such areas as nations or regions within nations. However, . . . [more recent] study of large-scale social change . . . [reveals that] processes such as urbanization can be more fully understood by beginning to examine the many ways in which they articulate with the broader currents of the world economy that penetrate spatial barriers, transcend limited time boundaries, and influence social relations at many different levels.[11]

Of particular concern to those analyzing urbanization in the Third World has been "overurbanization" produced by the migration of people from the countryside to Third World cities. "Overurbanization" is a term used to indicate that these cities have far larger populations than can be employed and than the present developed countries had at a similar stage of development. As portrayed by Stanislaw Wellisz, "Overurbanization, in short, stands for a "perverse" stream of migration sapping the economic strength of the hinterland without correspondingly large benefits to urban production. Instead of being a sign of development, overurbanization is a sign of economic illness."[12] In a data-based study, Timberlake and Jeffrey Kentor[13] found support for the proposition that dependence on foreign capital leads to overurbanization.

While world system scholars have tended to focus primarily on the impact of capitalist enterprises on Third World cities and countries, Richard Child Hill notes that the impact of transnational production systems "is as true for [U.S.] Great Lakes or [British] West Midlands governments . . . as it is for development planners in Malaysia or People's China. . . . "[14] Kent Trachte and Robert Ross, attribute the decline of economic life in Detroit to increased mobility of capital and specifically to the transfer of production facilities from Detroit to areas where there are lower wages.[15] In their study of New York, they note how both the transfer of production facilities, and the threat of transferring them, have contributed to high rates of welfare dependency, declining income of workers, and unemployment. The main point of this study is to direct our attention to a paradox, "the contradictions of the existence of such physical concentration of capital and control over it and the condition of the working class resident in such places."[16] Thus, they conclude, "In the global city, one finds jobs, wages, and levels of living reflecting the range of working-class life and work throughout the world, including the world's poor regions."[17]

R. B. Cohen points to a particular consequence of the rise of transnational production, the emergence of a hierarchy of cities, with "global cities" at the pinnacle. At the top of the hierarchy of cities there is

> a series of global cities which serve as international centers for business decision making and corporate strategy formulation.[18] These global cities have not only become centers for international decision making by major firms, but also have become centers for corporate services such as banks, law firms, accounting firms, and management consulting firms who have expanded their international skills and overseas operations to serve the needs of transnational corporations. Even the international activities of firms headquartered outside these cities are increasingly linked to financial institutions and corporate services located within them.

Looking to the future, Cohen expects corporations to become increasingly global, producing a number of contradictions within the world hierarchy of cities. He expects that large multinational corporations and banks will undermine or contravene established government policies, particularly in "contributing to the erosion of the position of certain traditional centers of government policy where corporate head offices or major financial institutions are not present in large numbers."[19] He also expects conflicts between the centers of finance in the new Eurodollar market and the older, more national ones. He predicts particularly strong impact on cities in developing nations, resulting from accelerated creation of foreign subsidiaries of transnational corporations, aided by transnational banks. Drawing on the work of J. Friedmann and F. Sullivan,[20] Cohen expects that the relatively high wage costs and subsidized capital investment in the corporate sector [will] lead to more capital-intensive development, decreasing the labor absorption capacity of this sector." This will create "urban crisis even when a nation's gross national product is expanding because of the inability of manufacturing companies to create enough new jobs, the destruction of jobs in the family enterprise sector, and the accelerating flow of people into the cities."[21]

LOCAL RESPONSES TO WORLDWIDE ECONOMIC AND SOCIAL INTRUSIONS

What recourse do people have who live in local communities that are in the vortex of intertwined processes of overurbanization, transnational production and finance systems, and decisions emanating from headquarters in global cities that may produce Third World conditions even in cities at the apex of the world city hierarchy?

Cities Freed from State Constraints

In a refreshing frontal assault on conventional economic assumptions, Jane Jacobs advocated that cities be freed from the constraints that states place on cities' economic activity, so that they can become more autonomous units in the worldwide economy. In her *Cities and the Wealth of Nations,* she ignored the work of world systems scholars and focused her attention on the limitations that states place on the capacity of cities to pursue their own economic interests in the world economy. Recognizing that "nations" are political and military entities, she observes that "it doesn't necessarily follow from this that they are also the basic, salient entities of economic life." Indeed, "the failure of national governments and blocs to force economic life to do their bidding suggests some sort of essential irrelevance." Nevertheless, says Jacobs, despite the fact that nations are "not discrete economic units, . . . we pretend that they are, and compile statistics about them based on that goofy premise."[22] Significant to Jacobs is the fact that "nations include, among other things in their economic grab bags, differing city economies that need different corrections at given times, and yet all share a currency that gives all of them the same information at a given time."[23]

The way out of the negative impact of national economic policies on cities for Jacobs would be to free cities to maximize their economic advantages by dividing single sovereignties into a family of smaller sovereignties. "A nation behaving like this would substitute for one great life force, sheer survival, that other great life force, reproduction." She sees this as a "theoretical possibility" rather than one that is likely to happen. Meanwhile, she concludes that "things being what they are, we have no choice but to live with our economically deadly predicament as best we can. . . . Societies and civilizations in which the cities stagnate don't develop and flourish further. They deteriorate."[24]

Taking a dramatically different approach, David Harvey would "curb interurban competition and search out more federated structures of interurban cooperation . . . . certainly those forms of interurban competition that end up generating subsidies for the consumption of the rich at the expense of the social wage of the poor deserve instant attack." Although not presenting a concrete strategy for achieving these goals, Harvey emphasizes the importance of severing "the tight connection between self-realization and pure consumerism,"[25] and of distinguishing between money (and the individualism enhanced by money) and capital (and the use of money power to procure privileged access to life chances). He advocates a new kind of urban consciousness based on an alliance of progressive forces, which Harvey admits would be difficult to achieve.

Political Movements

Critics of both urban political economy and world systems research look to political movements as the source of city resistance to the intrusions of global capital. Hill, in an overview of the "emergence, consolidation and development" of urban political economy," makes this parting declaration:

> If, as some scholars imply, the city has become the "weak link" in the world capitalist system, then the most pressing

> urban research issues today center upon investigation of the conditions under which global–local contradictions . . . give rise to political movements and public policies directed toward changing the structure and dynamics of the translocal system.[26]

Craig Murphy makes a similar criticism of world systems research, as in the title of a 1982 paper; "Understanding the World-Economy in Order to Change It: A Plea for Including Studies of Social Mobilization in the World System Research Program." As we have seen, powerful actors in transnational production systems, and in global cities, do understand the world economy and they are changing it. But Murphy has a different kind of concern, noting that "the trouble comes when world systemists are asked to define what dynamic role, if any, Third World cultures have in the transformation of capitalism." But before this can be done Murphy sees the need for "a theory of the role of political consciousness and social mobilization in the dynamics of world capitalism."[27]

Some insight into relevant social mobilization is to be found in studies of grassroots movements in the Third World. Snow and Marshall offer particularly acute observations on the way in which Islamic movements have been provoked by "cultural degredation and desecration" caused by the "market-expanding efforts of Western multinational corporations."[28] Not very encouraging is Alan Gilbert and Peter Ward's study of community action among the poor in Bogota, Mexico City, and Valencia.[29] They found that regimes in each city were successful in deflecting opposition by making concessions, by providing services, and by coopting leaders. The results of their study would tend to confirm the conclusion of Manuel Castells, based on his cross-cultural study of grassroots urban social movements, that "the state has become an overwhelming, centralized, and insulated bureaucracy. . . . Local communities are, in reality, powerless in the context of world empires and computerized bureaucracies."[30]

Basing his analysis on Indian experience, Rajni Kothari is somewhat more encouraging. His starting point is a view similar to that of the world systems analysts, in that he perceives tendencies:

> that seek, on the one hand, to integrate the organized economy into the world market and, on the other hand, remove millions of people from the economy by throwing them in the dustbin of history—impoverished, destitute, drained of their own resources and deprived of minimum requirements of health and nutrition, denied "entitlement" to food and water and shelter—in short, an unwanted and dispensable lot whose fate seems to be "doomed."[31]

In response he sees "grass-roots movements and non-party formations" springing "from a deep stirring of consciousness and an intuitive awareness of a crisis that could conceivably be turned into a catalyst of new opportunities."[32] These new movements are attempting to "open alternative political spaces" outside the traditional arenas of party and government.

Kothari observes that the very content of politics has been redefined. Issues that "were not so far seen as amenable to political action . . . now fall within the purview of political struggle."[33] These include people's health, rights over forests and other community resources, and women's rights. Not limited to economic and political demands, the struggle extends to ecological, cultural, and educational issues. While basing his analysis on Indian experience, Kothari sees these movements as part of a "phenomenon [that] has more general relevance."

New Approaches to Research and Education

There is increasing recognition that research and education traditions prevent people from coping with problems and opportunities presented by the local impact of worldwide production and financial organizations, as well as local "development" strategies of states and international organizations. Basing his reflections on grassroots experience in Bangladesh, Anisur Rahman emphasizes the development of the creativity of the people through their own thinking and action.[34] For him participation consists of investigation, reflection and analysis, decision making, and application of the decisions. Korten and Rudi Klauss reach compatible conclusions in emphasizing the difference between "people-centered development" and production-centered development according to them, the former has three prime characteristics: (1) creation of enabling settings that encourage and support people's efforts to meet their own needs, (2) development of self-organizing structures and processes, and (3) local control of resources.[35]

Emphasis on development based on local initiatives and power has intensified interest in nonformal education. As Rolland Paulston and G. LeRoy put it, "If one seeks to find education that does more than legitimize and reinforce gross inequalities in life chances, then one must look outside formal schools to the educational activities of reformist collective efforts seeking individual and social renewal."[36] This requires nonformal education that is more than just an adjunct of the system of formal schooling. Thomas LaBelle emphasizes the importance of involving people in their own learning, with a maximum of control over their own learning activities. He also stresses is the importance of creating direct links between educational programs and application of learning by people in their daily lives.[37]

Catalin Mamali has succinctly described the connection between research and participation by observing that "the conscious participation of the members of a social community in its evolution [any] process, also depends upon the level and quality of the participation of its members (specialists and laymen) in knowing the reality they live in." Pointing out that each member of a community has a double cognitive status, that of observed and that of observer, he notes that prevalent research practice inhibits "the subjects' natural observer status." Thus he concludes that a "just distribution of social knowledge cannot be reached unless its process of production is democratized."[38]

One limitation on research and education that might empower people to cope with the impact of worldwide economic and political systems on their communities is the absence of theory or even penetrating description of how local communities are linked to the world. In response, some scholars studying grassroots movements in the Third World are attempting to gain insight on what some refer to as the micro–macro dynamic. Perceiving "macro" and "micro" as "only differential expressions of the same process," Kothari calls "for a review of ideological positions that continue to locate "vested interests" in local situations and liberation from them in distant processes—the state, technology, revolutionary vanguards."[39] Out of experience with the Lokayan movement in India, D. L. Sheth writes:

> It is the dialectic between micro-practice and macro-thinking that will actualize a new politics of the future. . . . In brief, a macro-vision is the prime need of these groups and movements, and this can be satisfied only by a growing partnership between activists and intellectuals in the process of social transformation.[40]

Sheth perceives a new mode of politics arising across regional, linguistic, cultural, and national boundaries. It encompasses peace and anti-nuclear movements, environmental movements, women's movements, movements for self-determination of cultural groups, minorities, and tribes, and a movement championing non-Western cultures, techno-sciences, and languages.

This bears a striking similarity to the vision of two Swedish economists, Mats Friberg and Bjorn Hettne, who see a worldwide "Green" movement emerging that offers an alternative to the "Blue" (liberal market capitalist) and the "Red" (state socialist planning). From the Green perspective, they see that "the human being or small communities of human beings are the ultimate actors."[41] Majid Rahnema, too, points to the emergence of informal networks that not only link "together the grass-roots movements of the South but also establish new forms of co-action between those and those of the North."[42]

CONCLUSION

We have focused on two ways in which global interdependence is infringing on local autonomy: (1) the growing local impact of the foreign policies of states and (2) growth in the incorporation of local communities into worldwide economic institutions and systems. In responding to the first challenge, citizens have created a remarkable array of local movements in an effort to develop local response to issues formerly assumed to be the sole responsibility of national governments. These movements are particularly active with respect to war prevention and disarmament, poverty abroad, and human rights. Confronted with the growing impact on local communities of states' foreign policies, local movements are challenging traditions that assume that foreign policy is exclusively in the domain of national governments. Although more often implicitly than explicitly, they seem to believe that the survival of their local community, and its autonomy, require that the sharing of power between national and local governments be extended to include certain aspects of "foreign" policy.

In many respects the intrusion of global economic and social forces into local space presents an even more severe challenge to those desiring a constitutional world order that protects local autonomy than to state foreign policies. Nevertheless, we have presented some creative insights and proposals. Jacobs' espousal of the economic sovereignty of cities creatively challenges assumptions about state economic sovereignty. On the other hand, it is necessary that her city-centered view be broadened to take into account the fate of rural people surrounding the cities. Harvey's notion of "federated structures of interurban cooperation" merits more concrete elaboration. Kothari's emphasis on "alternative political space" outside the traditional arenas of party and government suggests that people in India, at least, are struggling to create a new kind of constitutional order that would preserve local autonomy. Sheth, Friberg, Hettne, and Rahnema discern the significance of transnational and transcultural links among grassroots movements. At the same time, other scholars emphasize the importance of more participatory research and education in creating possibilities for local autonomy; in effect, they challenge scholars to broaden their role within the global constitutional order.

Overall we have uncovered much creative action and thought directed toward the development of strategies for preserving local autonomy against the assault of powerful institutions with global reach. This activity would seem to be responsive, although indirectly, to Robert Dahl and E. R. Tufe's assertion that political theorists should "do what democratic theory has never done well: to offer useful guidance about the appropriate relations among units."[43] Dahl and Tufte ask for a theory of "complex polity:"

> Rather than conceiving of democracy as located in a particular kind of inclusive, sovereign unit, we must learn to conceive of democracy spreading through a set of interrelated political systems. . . . The central theoretical problem is no longer to find suitable rules, like the majority principle, to apply within a sovereign unit, but to find suitable rules to apply among a variety of units, none of which is sovereign.[44]

Unfortunately no theory has been devised which would guide efforts by local people who aspire to protect local communities (both their own and those afar) against annihilation, local emplacement of nuclear weapons, poverty, human rights violations, and ecological disasters. Nevertheless, the approaches that activists in many parts of the world have invented offer challenging possibilities to those who would attempt to develop constitutional principles for a world order protective of local autonomy.

NOTES

1. More extensive analysis of issues raised in this chapter can be found in Chadwick F. Alger, "Perceiving, Analysing, and Coping with the Local-Global Nexus," *International Social Science Journal* 117 (August 1988): 321–340; his "The Challenge of Global Interdependence to Local Autonomy," *Home Rule and Civil Society* (Chuo Gakuin University, Abiko, Japan), 1, no. 1 (1989): 1–17; and his "The World Relations of Cities," *International Studies Quarterly* 34 (1990): 493–518.

2. U.S. Department of Labor, Bureau of Labor Statistics, *Projections of the Post-Vietnam Economy.* Washington, DC: U.S. Government Printing Office, 1972, cited by R. Lindroos in "Disarmament Employment and the Western Trade Union," *Current Research on Peace and Violence,* no. 2 (1980): 85–92.

3. Hilary Wainright and David Elliott. *The Lucas Plan: A New Trade Unionism in the Making* (London: Allison and Busby, 1982), p. 243.

4. *Defense and Disarmament News*, March-April 1985.
5. *Disarmament Campaigns*, May 1985.
6. *COPRED Peace Chronicle*, February/April 1985, p. 5.
7. Jorgen Lissner. *The Politics of Altruism: A Study of the Political Behavior of Voluntary Development Agencies* (Geneva: Lutheran World Federation, 1977), p. 22.
8. Janice Love. *The U.S. Anti-Apartheid Movement* (New York: Praeger, 1985).
9. Hanna Newcombe, "Peace Actions at the Municipal Level," paper presented at the 10th General Conference of the International Peace Research Association, Gyor, Hungary, August 1983.
10. *The New Abolitionist* 7, no. 2 (June/July 1989): 7.
11. Michael Timberlake, "The World-System Perspective and Urbanization," in Michael Timberlake, ed., *Urbanization in the World Economy* (New York: Academic Press, 1985), p. 3.
12. Stanislaw Wellisz, "Economic Development and Urbanization and National Development," in L. Jakobson and V. Prebesh, eds., *Urbanization and National Development* (Beverly Hills, CA: Sage, 1971), pp. 39–55, cited by Michael Timberlake and Jeffrey Kentor, "Economic Dependence, Overurbanization, and Economic Growth: A Study of Less Developed Countries," *The Sociological Quarterly* 24 (Autumn 1983): 489–507, at 493.
13. Timberlake and Kenton.
14. Richard Child Hill, "Comparing Transnational Production Systems: The Automobile Industry in the United States and Japan," paper for the 28th Annual Meeting of the International Studies Association, Washington, DC, April 14–18, 1987, p. 17.
15. Kent Trachte and Robert Ross, "The Crisis of Detroit and the Emergence of Global Capitalism," *International Journal of Urban and Regional Research* 9, no. 2 (1985): 186–217.
16. Robert Ross and Kent Trachte, "Global Cities and Global Classes: The Peripheralization of Labor in New York City," *Review* 6, no. 3 (Winter 1983): 393–394.
17. Ross and Trachte, p. 429.
18. R. B. Cohen, "The New International Division of Labor: Multinational Corporations and Urban Hierarchy," in Michael Dear and Allen J. Scott, eds., *Urbanization and Urban Planning in Capitalist Society* (New York: Methuen, 1981), p. 300.
19. Cohen, p. 308.
20. J. Friedmann and F. Sullivan, "The Absorption of Labor in the Urban Economy: The Case of the Developing Countries," in J. Friedmann and W. Alonso, eds., *Regional Policy: Readings in Theory and Applications* (Cambridge MA: MIT Press, 1975), pp. 475–492.

21. Cohen, p. 309.

22. Jane Jacobs, *Cities and the Wealth of Nations: Principles of Economic Life* (New York: Random House, 1984), pp. 31–32.

23. Jacobs, p. 162.

24. Jacobs, pp. 215, 219, 220, 232.

25. David Harvey, *Consciousness and the Urban Experience: Studies in the History and Theory of Capitalist Urbanization* (Baltimore: John Hopkins Press, 1985), p. 275.

26. Richard Child Hill, "Urban Political Economy: Emergence, Consolidation, and Development" in Peter Smith, ed., *Cities in Transformation: Class, Capital, State* (Beverly Hills: Sage, 1984), p. 135.

27. Craig Murphy, "Understanding the World Economy in Order to Change It: A Plea for Including Studies of Social Mobilization in the World System Research Program," paper presented at the International Studies Association Convention, 1982, p. 1.

28. David A. Snow and Susan E. Marshall, "Cultural Imperialism, Social Movements, and the Islamic Revival," in Louis Kriesberg, ed., *Research in Social Movements, Conflicts and Change: A Research Annual* 7, (Greenwich, CT: JAI Press, 1984), p. 146.

29. Alan Gilbert and Peter Ward, "Community Participation in Upgrading Irregular Settlements: The Community Response," *World Development* 12, no. 9 (1984): 913–922.

30. Manual Castells, *The City and the Grassroots: A Cross-Cultural Theory of Urban Social Movements* (Berkeley and Los Angeles: University of California Press, 1983), p. 329.

31. Rajni Kothari, "Party and State in Our Times: The Rise of Non-Party Political Formations," *Alternatives* 9 (1987): 541–564 at 551.

32. Kothari, pp. 551.

33. Kothari, p. 552.

34. Anisur Rahman, "NGO Work of Organizing the Rural Poor: The Perspective," *IFDA Dossier*, no. 50 (November/December, 1985): 15–20.

35. David Korten and Rudi Klauss, *People-Centered Development: Contributions Toward Theory and Planning Frameworks* (West Hartford, Conn.: Kumarian Press, 1984).

36. Rolland G. Paulston and G. LeRoy, "Folk Colleges and Change from Below," in *Other Dreams, Other Schools: Folk Colleges in Social and Ethnic Movements*, ed. Rolland G. Paulson (Pittsburgh: University of Pittsburgh Press, 1980), p. 20.

37. Thomas J. LaBelle, *Nonformal Education and Social Change in Latin America* (Los Angeles: University of California at Los Angeles, Latin American Center, 1976).

38. Catalin Mamali, "Societal Learning and Democratization of the Social Research Process" (Bucharest: Research Center for Youth Problems, 1979), pp. 13–14.

39. Kothari, pp. 560–561.

40. D. L. Sheth, "Grass-Roots Stirrings and the Future of Politics," *Alternatives* 9 (Summer 1983): 23.

41. Mats Friberg and Bjorn Hettne, "The Greening of the World: Towards a Non-Deterministic Model of Global Processes," photocopy, University of Gothenburg, Sweden, 1982, p. 23.

42. Majid Rahnema, "Under the Banner of Development," *Development* 1/2, (1986) 43.

43. Robert A. Dahl and E. R. Tufte, *Size and Democracy* (Stanford, CA: Stanford University Press, 1973), p. 140.

44. Dahl and Tufte, p. 135.

15

Politics of Social Transformation: Grassroots Movements in India

D. L. SHETH

The scene in which grassroots movements in India occur is varied and complex. The natural temptation is to begin with a discussion of definitional and morphological issues involved in identifying the phenomenon called "grassroots movements." I shall avoid this temptation as far as I can, for such an exercise may end up in drawing abstract conceptual boundaries around a phenomenon that is fluid and growing. Instead, I will directly describe the phenomena that I view as grassroots movements, although a better term could be found for it, no doubt. To be sure, anything that happens at the base of politics and acquires some political salience can be described as a political happening at the grassroots, and if it acquires some durable organizational form, one may even be tempted to describe it as a social movement.

For the present, however, my interest is limited to describing a particular genre of the grassroots movements which became politically visible in the mid-1970s and to examine its potential for transforming Indian politics, an avowed goal of these movements. Whatever may be their self-perceptions, these movements in the view of some observers of the grassroots scene in India have over the last decade or so been growing into the "Fifth Estate" of Indian politics. For others they represent bubbles on the political surface of India, which appear, burst and reappear from time to time without leaving much impact on the ongoing political life of the country. For still others, they represent seeds of change, with a potential to transform the nature of Indian politics.

Before forming a judgment, one way or the other, let me describe the phenomenon. I shall do this first by locating these movements in the political space from which they operate and which they have created for themselves. I shall then describe the issues they have raised in Indian politics, and the organizational forms they have evolved to tackle these issues. Having done this, we hopefully shall be in a better position to judge their potential for transformation of the Indian polity.

THE DECLINE OF INSTITUTIONAL POLITICS

A large number of these movements occupy social spaces created by the decline of the conventional mainstream politics of legislatures, elections, political parties, and trade unions. This decline, although it began earlier, became visible during the Emergency (1975–1977) and has continued since.[1] The result is the retreat of democratic institutions from open, competitive politics where they continually sought to establish their claims for legitimation, into the pure politics of power and maneuvre.[2] In the process, the political parties lost their national character, both in political and geographical terms. Their role in inducting new groups into politics through waging struggles for their legal and political rights was considerably reduced. Their ability to process issues arising in the economy, society, and culture declined greatly.

The parties failed to convert the economic demands of the poor and the deprived into effective political demands. Instead, some parties took the easy course of ethnicizing and communalizing the economic issues for electoral gains. The result was that the political process, which in the 1950s and 1960s worked for inclusion of the middle castes into the mainstream of Indian politics, got halted in the mid-1970s, keeping out large sections of ex-untouchables, the tribal peoples, the occupationally marginalized and economically extremely poor groups from among the ritually low-ranking Hindu castes, and the other poor and landless among the minorities. Of course, they were approached for their votes but only with all kinds of electoral gimmicks—the 1971 elections being the biggest of them all. Being leaderless, their struggles were sporadic and local in character and for that reason their survival and dignity ceased to be issues in mainstream politics. The populations involved in these struggles were dispersed and fragmented on many dimensions besides that of class. For that reason they were written off by the parties, especially those of the left, as unorganizable. In sum, the parties prematurely gave up their "movement" aspect, becoming increasingly just electoral machines operating with make-shift arrangements at the grassroots at election time.

Having lost the capacity to retain the durable social and economic support they had once built, they have sought to forge such support anew at every election since 1971. The elections became more like referenda, and electoral mandates lost their appeal, at least, they ceased to inform the process of government formation and policy for any party elected to power.

The trade unions, which to begin with were like labour wings of the political parties, with little autonomy of their own, became virtually bargaining counters between the people of the same class, supposedly representing different interests. The unions showed a complete incapacity to expand their activities in the growing informal and unorganized sector of the economy. Workers in this unorganized sector had little to offer, either electorally or in membership fees. Whatever ideological incentive was still there for expanding the activities of the trade unions to incorporate the workers outside the big factories and white-collar establishments, got eroded as trade unions' incomes grew ever larger from the frequently raised membership fees and not infrequently from the wheeling and dealing of the leadership. Tired after long years of struggle, the union leadership got used to a cushy lifestyle and to a mentally non-taxing bureaucratic mode of functioning. In all this, their activities assured a sound financial base to the parties to which they belonged. So party leaders had no reason to complain.[3]

The legislatures reflected this change in the wider politics. Gone were the days when a Ram Manohar Lohia could raise and sustain a protracted debate on poverty in the Indian Parliament. The Parliament increasingly became a handmaid of the executive branch, with the ruling party using the brute force of its majority to silence any debate on issues it considered inconvenient and uncomfortable for the Government or its leaders. The net result was, the executive became the most powerful branch of governance and the Judiciary a final arbitrar of all political disputes. The political discourse began to be increasingly informed by narrow constitutionalist positions held by the executive and often endorsed by the law-courts rather than by issues emerging from democratic politics.[4] The Indian Constitution which was held not only as an instrument of governance but also as an agenda for social transformation, became a document sanitized from the flesh and blood of social and political movements which enriched democratic politics.

THE CONTEXT

It is in this context of the decline of institutional politics that the grassroots movements emerged on the Indian political scene. They moved into niches yielded by the retreat of institutional politics. They took up issues and constituencies abandoned by the political parties and the trade unions, and those ill-served by the bureaucracy. In the process, they reformulated the issues and expanded their constituencies in a framework of politics that was nonelectoral; the organizational form that evolved was not of a political party or a pressure group. It was a participative and mobilizational form of politics which sustained struggles on issues articulated by the people themselves and worked for their empowerment. Through these struggles they expanded the meaning of constitutional politics in so far as they sought to justify their struggles in terms of the Directive Principles of State Policy—a chapter in the Constitution provisions of which are not justiciable in courts of law.

Although they share common political arenas and a broadly similar perspective on social transformation, the grassroots movements vary a great deal amongst themselves. The differences are with respect to their political lineage, size, geographical level of operation which may vary from a highly local to the provincial and national levels, the importance they attach to some issues over others, the populations they work for, and the organizational form they adopt. There are sporadic, short-term movements addressing a particular issue, like the liberation of bonded labor. There are also the long-term movements, with a developed organizational form, working for a specific constituency, like the farmers' movements. Then there are a series of single-issue movements active at the national, state, and local levels. These include the human rights organizations, working both in urban and rural areas. The most widespread ones are those that can be described as the "movement groups of social activists". These are groups of committed social activists forming themselves as a nucleus and working self-consciously as "agency" for social and political transformation. Through involving and mobilizing people, to begin with on issues concerning them directly, they seek to harness the social energy so released, to a long-term movement for transforming power relations in the society.

In the decade after 1975, these groups of social activists multiplied into thousands and spread into different parts of the country.[5] They are now led by young men and women, usually from the middle or lower-middle classes, who have left their professional careers and founded or joined these movement groups in the rural areas and the tribal belts of the country. They take up various causes on behalf of the marginalized populations of the *dalits,* the tribal peoples, the landless, and women. They work on a long-term basis in small geographical areas for the goal they describe as "empowerment of the people." Some socially committed professionals and social activists have organized themselves for national-level campaigns for the right to shelter and to work.

Then there are legal aid groups, the groups for better health care for the people, popular culture and people's creativity groups, and popular science movements. There also are the new trade union movements launched by small groups of social activists organizing workers in the informal sector. These include organizations for self-employed women, the *beedi* workers (involved in hand-rolling of Indian cigarettes), workers in construction and public works, and those working in the small industrial and semi-industrial units like the powerloom and handloom factories. Included in this list, which is incomplete, are only those grassroots movements that self-consciously see themselves in the role of creating social transformation by using new means of political action. The traditional philanthropic and welfare organizations, the non-political developmental organizations, various front organizations of political parties and the sect-like organizations of the religious movements have been excluded, although the line dividing some of these organizations and those described above as grassroots movements is often thin.

The central thrust of these grassroots groups and movements is the politics of issues. They have not only raised new issues but have kept alive the old unresolved ones, issues long since given up by the political parties. These include such broad issues as human rights, women's rights, child labor, ecology, and communalism (chauvinism based on caste/religious identities or sentiments). More specific issues are also raised by different movements. These include bonded labor, atrocities perpetrated by the dominant castes on the *dalits* and tribal peoples, and the rights of the populations displaced by the big development projects of the state, private companies, and multinational corporations.

Long-term issues are also addressed by the movement groups at the micro-level but these have yet not acquired political salience at the national level. These issues pertain to the legal rights of the landless to minimum wages and working conditions, the access of the tribal peoples to the forest and forest products, and the poor people's rights to the village commons, such as to village grazing land, to use of the so-called "waste lands", to till dried-up lakes, ponds, and water reservoirs, to fishing rights in common waters, and so on. Social issues are also taken up involving political mobilization around such controversies as dowry deaths (murdering of the wife by the husband and or his kins for inadequate sums of dowry received or for re-marrying another woman for dowry), burning of widows, rapes, and child labor. The list goes on and on.

The important fact is that almost all issues raised by the grassroots movements are ones on which the state is committed to act positively as ordained in the Directive Principles of the State Policy in the Constitution but, being non justiciable, they are not resolvable through recourse to the law-courts. Direct action by the people on these issues becomes, therefore, a preferred means of political action for the movement groups. Today, there is some group or the other working on these issues even in the most remote rural and tribal areas of the country. And yet the reach of the grassroots movements remains limited, both politically and geographically.

The enormity of the problems the grassroots movements have taken upon themselves is so great, that one wonders how long they can withstand the pressures and trials of their efforts, to continue to serve as a buffer between the state's growing coercion and the chaos in Indian society. It is the inability of the state, its bureaucracy, and its institutionalized politics to process these problems into their own arena that has created this overwhelming situation that the grassroots movements feel they are required to tackle. The activists of these movements are constantly on the move, spending most of their time and energy on firefighting; this leaves them little time for reflection or for interaction with those in movements other than their own.[6]

MICRO-MOVEMENTS AND LOCAL POLITICS

While they operate at the base of the Indian polity, the movements are not a part of what is conventionally understood as local politics. Until recently, that is while the one-party dominance of the Congress Party reigned, local politics was vertically even if loosely, coordinated by the macro-institutional structure of politics. The panchayats (village councils whose members are periodically elected through universal adult franchize), the cooperatives, the block development committees were also operated and politically coordinated through holding diverse caste-based factions into the politically accommodative structure of the Congress party. These factional alignments characterized the party system at the local level. But local politics has substantially changed, especially since the 1971 elections. This change, often attributed to the breakdown of one-party dominance is, in my view, rather the result of changes that have been taking place at the base of the society. And these changes have created new political space at the local level, which has been now occupied by the movement groups.

Let me quickly index only a few of such changes. The relations between castes, which often are hereditary occupational groups, were hitherto based on the principle of a barter-like reciprocal system of goods and services (the *jajmani* system). They have now been fully monetized. A much greater proportion of the rural population, over two-thirds, now lives in bigger villages, with populations of over one thousand. At the same time, the bulk of the population in an average village now consists of owner-cultivators and the landless laborers. The other categories such as the priestly, trading, and artisan castes, are either moving out of the villages into the nearby towns or are getting absorbed into the ranks of owner-cultivators or the landless laborers. The Indian village, which was primarily a social system within which economic activities subsisted, is now acquiring the character primarily of an economic organization in which social relationships are getting defined in terms of relations between employers and employees, between wage labor and capital. The so-called "caste conflict" is now mainly between the dominant castes of the owner cultivators and the castes of the landless laborers, with the former having lost their traditional claim on the labor of the latter.

The changes in the village social structure have changed the nature of conventional local politics. The political parties, operating on the old assumptions, have not been able to address themselves to the new issues that have sprung up in rural India. Instead, as we saw earlier, these issues are being taken up by the movement groups operating from outside such institutions of local politics as the panchayats, the cooperatives, and the local units of the parties.

MICRO-MOVEMENTS AND MAINSTREAM POLITICS

From this description of the micro-movements, the political spaces they occupy, the issues they articulate, and the organizations they have spawned, it should be clear that they represent a fairly heterogeneous but vigorous element of political action at the grassroots of Indian politics. But they function as disparate micro-movements, each zealous in guarding its identity, autonomy, and territory. They resent any effort by a macro-organization, even by a non-party political formation, at the national or regional level to coordinate their activities or to federate them into a larger political entity. They do align with some others on issues, join up for common causes, even create joint fronts. But they do all this only around specific issues and for the duration for which the struggle lasts. They refuse to become organizational parts of, or to create for themselves, any larger long-term movement. This, despite the fact that many among them share a common perspective on problems, especially in terms of their critique of the existing political and social order and the model of development. Not only this, in their programmes and activities they manifest a common approach and methodology of struggle. They work on similar issues and for the same types of constituencies, albeit in different geographical areas. There may be cultural explanations for such a strange situation of separation, but they will not be resorted to for the present.

The important fact is that there seems no possibility, in the foreseeable future, of these micro-movements' emerging as a larger nationwide political movement by forging coalitions, alliances, and mergers among themselves. It is for this reason that the activists and intellectuals of the political parties and some observers of the grassroots scene in India do not attach much political significance to the micro-movements. In this view, any movement that does not make a visible impact, either on government policies or electoral politics, has no political future. The activists of the movement, however, do not share the view of conventional revolutionary politics, in which movements are conceived and carried out with the ultimate objective of capturing state power.[7]

For them, the capture of state power is not a precondition for social transformation. There indeed are some differences within the micro-movements on whether they should completely rule out, even from a longer-term theoretical perspective, the goal of acquiring or capturing state power, however remote that possibility might appear today. As we shall see later, this particular issue has become quite important, linked as it is with the issue of the use of violence, and the controversy has resulted in the splitting of some groups and movements. But a large number of the movement groups, including those inheriting the Marxist-Leninist tradition of struggle, prefer to leave this issue dormant, if not to ignore it totally. They believe that a premature and excessive concern about capturing state power suppresses the real issues of politics and social transformation, distorts the priorities in struggle, and gives rise to authoritarian tendencies within the organizations of the movements.

The groups belonging to the Gandhian, *sarvodaya* (a neo-Gandhian movement which emphasized cooperation as against conflict between classes as a means of social transformation), socialist, and even liberal traditions, however, clearly reject capture of state power, even as an ideal. They find the concept overly political and distracting from the long-term struggles for the decentralization of economic and political power. According to them, this can only be achieved through changing the forms of organization and building peoples' own capabilities, rather than through changing the administrative structure with the use of power from the top. Such changes, if achieved in the broader society and culture, may ultimately result in the transformation of the state itself.

Whatever the nuances of their positions on the issue of state power, in practice the micro-movements of all types function away from mainstream politics. Theirs is the politics of issues, of winning rights, and of changing the consciousness of the people. This often brings them into confrontation with the state, the bureaucracy, the law and order machinery, the local power structures, and sometimes even with the political parties and established trade unions. They view such confrontations as an aspect of the larger, long-term struggle for political and social transformation, and not as a means of directly competing with the political parties for the legitimacy claims in the prevalent system. Instead, they emphasize withdrawal of legitimation, by separating themselves from the institutions of mainstream politics and devoting their energies to building the people's own organizations. In the process, they view situations of conflicts as the means of raising people's consciousness and building the awareness of the people, rather than as the means of capturing state power.

This, however, does not mean that they are opposed to the institutional framework of Indian democracy. In fact, they consider institutional democracy as a necessary condition for their functioning, but not a sufficient condition for their long-term goal of political and social transformation.[8] For this goal to be achieved, they believe that the political battleground needs to be shifted away from mainstream politics into the society and culture. In this sense, while they do not view the functioning of institutional democracy as representing forces hostile to their agenda of social transformation, working within and for it is not something high on their agenda. Their political agenda, instead, is further democratization, not only of the political institutions but of the family, the community, the workplace, and the society at large.

MICRO-MOVEMENTS AND THE POLITICS OF TRANSFORMATION

The self-perception of these grassroots movements is, thus, not merely of being pressure groups working for the rights and benefits of specific constituencies. They view themselves as movements for political and social transformation, and their methodology consists in involving the people in redefining the basic issues concerning the relationship between society and politics. Let me illustrate this point briefly with a reference to the three major grassroots movements: the human rights, the ecology, and the feminist movements.[9]

The issue of human rights as viewed by the activists of several human rights groups is not limited to the conventional legal notion of civil liberties; it also extends to situations in which individuals and groups are denied satisfaction of their basic needs. The poorest among the poor have in their view lost out in both respects. Thanks to the model of development adopted by the state, the poor are neither entitled to become full wage-earners in the economy nor full-fledged citizens in the polity. The politics of micro-movements, therefore, lies not merely in fighting particular infringements of legal rights of citizens, but in creating and expanding new political and civic spaces for them by converting the survival and development needs of the poor and the deprived into struggles for their economic, political, and cultural rights and these not only of individuals *qua* individuals but of groups and communities surviving on the margins of the civil society. In the process the activists link rights of access to and benefits from the development process with the issues of ethnic identity and human dignity, and view the satisfaction of material needs as a pursuit not detached from the spiritual and cultural aspects of human existence. Several movement groups that are not single-issue organizations for human rights relate to human rights movements through such a perception of rights.

Similarly, the ecology movements do not view ecology as merely a cost factor in development, as many ecology academics do. Nor are they interested in specifying tolerable levels of ecological destruction necessary for achieving higher levels of economic development as modernizing regimes tend to do.[10] Instead, they view ecology as a basic principle of human existence, which, if reactivated, can yield higher level principles for reorganizing the economy in human terms and refocus development in terms of well being, in which, to use Gandhiji's well-known phrase, "everybody shall have enough for his or her need, but not for his or her greed."

The activists of the women's movements have lately been defining their problem not merely in terms of achieving equal benefits and access for women in the present system. They self-consciously take up such issues mainly for finding entry points to the submerged world of Indian womanhood; but their long-term goal, as they put it, is to change the working of the gender principle itself in the economy and society, such that both society and economy become more just and humane. They find the ecological world view of the movements more aligned with the feminine principle. The fusion of the ecological and gender principles, they argue, is conducive for a humane economic and political organization of the society than that of development which, in their view, is founded on the principle of male-domination over all aspects of human life and nature. Their project, working together with the human rights and ecology movements, is thus to change the forms of organization and consciousness in society.[11]

Guided by this broad perspective, these movements are often able to forge links with each other in fighting for issues at the grassroots. It is not accidental that ecology movements like the Chipko movement have the participation of women, and that the Bodhgaya movement for the rights of the landless in Bihar is viewed by its participants as a movement for total revolution in which women play significant leadership roles. Women are in the forefront of the movements fighting for the rights of the population displaced by development projects, especially in Madhya Pradesh and Maharashtra. Similarly, human rights organizations often team up with womens' organizations on issues of dowry, *sati* (self immolation of a widow by burning herself on her husband's funeral pyre), rape, and equal wages. Similarly, activists in women's groups took on an active role in mobilizing and assisting the victims of the Bhopal chemical disaster. At no time in independent India, in the movements led by the parties and trade unions, was there ever such a high degree and such a sustained level of participation by women as one witnesses today in the non-party political movements at the grassroots.

Even as these movements seek to acquire greater perspective and coherence, they confront situations of division and splits within their own organizations. Currently there is active debate among these groups on five issues which has resulted in spliting some groups and joining together of some others. The issues are over the appropriate attitude the grassroots movements should adopt towards (1) the use of violence, the specific issue being violence as a justifiable means of self-defence for the people versus complete reliance on nonviolent methods of *satyagraha* as a mode of conducting struggles; (2) acquiring/capturing state power, the specific issue being their participation (or lending support to political parties) in the electoral politics versus engaging themselves solely in the non-electoral and non-party politics; (3) the kind of relationship the group/movements should maintain with the political parties in the conduct of their own struggles (4) co-operating with the state in implementing certain development schemes that may provide immediate, short-term benefits and relief for the poor; (5) accepting foreign funds.

These controversies have resulted in some activists leaving the movements and joining political parties; some have formed themselves into apolitical-type NGOs. The issue of violence has, for example, split an old movement in the Bodhgaya but it has also given rise to larger formations of two types of movement groups in Bihar—those who believe in tactical use of violence and those who assert their faith in the *satyagraha* type of non-violent struggle.

This review of the large, almost overwhelming, canvass of the grassroots movements suggests that the grassroots movements in India can best be viewed as stirrings within the civil society which, by acquiring self-conscious organizational forms, expand the frontiers of the civil society to include the vast population on its periphery. Their long-term objective, it seems to me, is to bring the modern state in India, which has hitherto remained away and above the society, under the command of the civil society.

Such stirrings indeed are noticeable in many countries of the world today.[12] The moot question is whether the world constitutional order will emerge and expand through the process of the formation of a civil society at the global level, with concomitant growth of global citizenship, or will it be imposed top-down *a la* the GATT, the G-7, the International Monetary Fund, the World Bank and now the new Eco-regime which may be fabricated in the post-Rio Earth Summit politics of big powers. The grassroots movements in India, as do the "new movements" in other parts of the world, represent a powerful counter-vailing force to the top-down process which has acquired a new clout in the post-Cold War world. If there is still any hope for achieving a just and peaceful order for the world as a whole, the thinking on the constitutional order has to align with the new politics of movements.

NOTES

1. On June 25, 1975 Internal Emergency was imposed in India by the then Prime Minister Mrs. Indira Gandhi as a strategem to continue in power after she was disqualified from her membership of the Indian Parliament on being found guilty of electorate malpractice by a High Court judgement delivered on June 12. During the Emergency, which lasted for two years, the constitutional rights of citizens including some Fundamental Rights were suspended. The Emergency regime was stiffly resisted by several political parties and social activists. For an account of how the constitutional rights were undermined by the emergency regime, written during the Emergency, see, Rajni Kothari, "End of an Era", *Politics and the People: In Search of a Humane India*, (Ajanta Publications, Delhi) 1989, pp 235–250.

2. For an illuminating analysis of the decline of the institutions of democratic governance in India see, Rajni Kothari, "Decline of the Moderate State", *State Against Democracy: In Search of Humane Governance,* (Ajanta Publications, Delhi) 1988 pp. 15–36. An incisive account of the decline of political parties can be found in Kothari's "Decline of Parties and Rise of Grassroots Movements", *State Against Democracy, op cit,* pp. 33–54.

3. The decline of the Trade Union Movement is graphically illustrated by Sandip Pandey. See, his "The Datta Samant Phenomenon", *Economic and Political Weekly,* (Vol. 16, Nos 16–17) April 1981, pp. 1–8.

4. For an account of the erosion of the legislative and judicial institutions in the decade of the 1970s see, Rajni Kothari "Taking Stock of the Seventies", *Politics and the People: In Search of Humane India, op. cit,* pp. 343–353.

5. The political and historical context from which these groups emerged and their typology is provided in my "Grass-roots Stirrings and the Future of Politics", *Alternatives,* Vol. 9, No. 1, March 1983.

6. The problems faced by the activists of grassroots movements are discussed in my "Grass-roots Initiatives in India", *Economic and Political Weekly,* Vol. 19, No. 6, February 1984.

7. For a critical assessment of the role of grassroots movements in the politics of social transformation see, Harsh Sethi, Groups in New Politics of Transformation", *Economic and Political Weekly,* Vol. 14, No. 7, February 18, 1984, pp. 305–316.

8. For a more comprehensive discussion on this point see my, "Alternative Development as Political Practice" *Alternatives,* Vol. 12, No. 2, April 1987.

9. The political thinking and positioning of the movements described in this section is based on my participation in about a hundred dialogues with social activists in different parts of India in early 1980's sponsored and organized by *Lokayan.*

10. For a critical assessment of attitudes and thinking of various ecological movements in India see, Harsh Sethi, "Some considerations on Ecological Struggles in India", *Asian Exchange* Vol. 4, No. 1, pp. 49–74.

11. The leading exponent of this position is Vandena Shiva. See her *Staying Alive: Women, Ecology and Survival in India* (Kali for Women, New Delhi) 1988.

12. For a comprehensive statement on the Global potentials of Social Movements see, Richard Falk, "The Global Promise of Social Movements: Explorations at the Edge of Time" *Alternatives* Vol. 12, No. 2, April 1987.

16

Constitutionalism and Foundational Values: Philippine Constitutional Authoritarianism Revisited

LESTER EDWIN J. RUIZ

INTRODUCTION

The end of the twentieth century may well be an axial moment in the struggle to articulate a new constitutional order of the human community. So-called "globalists" argue that we are moving from a society of states to a global society, and "are groping for . . . the constitutive order of that [global] society;"[1] and that the future of the planet is tied to the quality of this emerging "global society." Critics of this perspective, particularly from the realist tradition of international relations, would undoubtedly dismiss such a claim. The future of human society, they argue, is profoundly linked to the future of the states system; what is necessary for human survival is not the supersession of the states system but its revitalization. The debate is an important one. It raises questions about the process of constituting a human polity adequate to the needs and realities of the twenty-first century.

This chapter is concerned with some of the questions raised by this debate. In particular, I am concerned with the interplay of constitutionalism (the process of articulating the form of a society's polity), its foundational values (those principles or human aspirations that shape both the process and the form of human polity), and the political practices that emerge from them (including institutions, strategies, policies). The chapter examines the contours of this interplay by focusing on Philippine Constitutional Authoritarianism, itself an attempt to articulate a new constitutional order.[2] Not simply a historiographical curiosity, Philippine Constitutional Authoritarianism provides an interesting site for the exploration of this interplay; it provides some clues to the process of creating a new constitutional order as well as underscoring the pitfalls that need to be avoided in the creation of a fundamentally new and better social and political order.

MODERNIZATION AND REVOLUTION: POLITICAL DISORDER AS THE PRIMARY ADVERSARY OF PHILIPPINE CONSTITUTIONAL AUTHORITARIANISM

On September 21, 1972, Ferdinand E. Marcos, then President of the Republic of the Philippines, placed the Philippines under martial law. The immediate reasons for what some liberal democratic thinkers considered a constitutionally questionable measure[3] were meticulously stated in Proclamation No. 1081 "Proclaiming a State of Martial Law in the Philippines." Martial law, this document argued, was a response to a profound crisis in the Philippines.

As early as 1970, theorists of what later came to be known as Philippine Constitutional Authoritarianism already noted that a "revolutionary situation" existed in the country.[4] This revolutionary situation was dramatically portrayed by the "First Quarter Storm," a period of massive and intense confrontation between a broad cross section of civil society, on the one hand, and the Government's military and paramilitary forces on the other. The Marcos government, along with most of its critics, acknowledged this confrontation as an expression of a deeper societal crisis.[5] The confrontation, called by many the "rebellion of the poor," was, in fact, a struggle to achieve fundamental changes in the political, economic, and cultural life of the nation.

The so-called "rebellion of the poor" was recognized by the Marcos government, at least rhetorically, as the most serious challenge to its existence. It was exacerbated by the alleged immediate threat posed to the Republic by a conspiracy of leftist Communist and rightist oligarchic elements, on the one hand, and by a Muslim secessionlist movement supported by foreign groups, on the other hand.[6] The imposition of martial law, in fact, had two interrelated goals. First, it sought to prevent these so-called lawless elements from inciting chaos by destroying the "duly constituted government."[7] Second, it was seen as a tool to address the issues raised by the rebellion of the poor.[8]

This rebellion of the poor was also understood by the Marcos government within the larger historical process of modernization which the Philippines, like many other so-called developing Third World states, was experiencing. Sweeping changes in its political, economic, and cultural life required to meet the imperative of development made the Philippine experience of modernization a "disquieting, at times convulsive [i.e., revolutionary], undertaking." While Marcos agreed with his nationalist and Marxist critics that the Philippines was immersed in a revolutionary situation, he argued further that the Philippine situation was unique in that the process of modernization was converging with the revolutionary situation. Not only did modernization make revolution inevitable, but modernization required revolution.[9]

For Marcos theorists, the convergence of modernization and revolution was not only the historical context of the rebellion of the poor nor simply its consequence; the convergence itself was part of and defined the crisis. In the context of this "swift, violent, often disruptive" change, a choice was being posed between chaos and order, between being the "masters or victims of change," the latter demanding the unilateral assertion of political will by the sovereign not only to preserve political order but to guarantee that change itself would be mastered. Thus, the crucial question for the Marcos Government, as it faced the crisis of 1971, in the words of Samuel Huntington which it cited approvingly, was whether nor not the "processes of political modernization and political development have lagged behind the processes of social and economic change.[10] Here, two fundamental questions needed to be faced: first, Why was modernization necessary? Second, What kind of revolution was necessary?

THE POLITICS OF THE OLD SOCIETY: THE NECESSITY OF MODERNIZATION

Philippine political, economic and cultural life was correctly perceived by the Marcos theorists, themselves schooled in the Western liberal democratic tradition, as primarily oligarchic in character. They recognized that political inequality rested on the existence of social inequality. However, unlike its nationalist and Marxist critics who attributed inequality to maldevelopment and the dynamics of the capitalist-dominated world economy, the Marcos government viewed the problem of political and social inequality as being rooted in the "irresponsible exercise of public and private power." The principal issue was not the existence of an oligarchy but the abuses of that oligarchy.[11]

This oligarchic structure was historically rooted in the Spanish *encomienda* system, which established an aristocracy built on an iniquitous land-ownership structure later modified into a client-patron structure at the turn of the century by the American so-called "experiment in democracy." The modification had two fundamental consequences for contemporary liberal democratic politics. On the one hand, the aristocracy-turned-patron viewed the established liberal democratic institutions and processes as vehicles for maintaining their position of political, economic, and cultural privilege. On the other hand, the "masses" viewed the oligarchy as guarantors of their survival and well-being. Thus, a "culture of patronage" was institutionalized in contemporary Philippine politics, creating a politics of status quo maintenance and of dependence.[12] Liberal democracy was transformed into oligarchic democracy.[13]

Undergirding this oligarchic political-institutional arrangement was a political culture that was populist, personalistic, and individualist. This type of politics, the Marcos theorists maintained, undermined public institutions. Public resources and offices became viewed as spoils for the winners and their supporters, thereby jeopardizing the public and collective goals of the state. Coupled with an absolutist view of private property legitimated by the judicial system, this nepotistic and symbiotic relationship between patron and client corrupted political authority and undermined any kind of innovative change.

Moreover, this view of public institutions as instruments of privilege was accompanied by a minimalist view of the state. In fact, oligarchic democracy preferred a weak state that acted only and primarily to safeguard the elite's privileges and guarantee the conditions that would enhance these privileges. Not surprisingly, architects of post-war Philippine political institutions drew their inspiration from the liberal Lockean philosophy, including its preference for laissez faire capitalism."[14]

Thus the Marcos theorists, at least in rhetoric, repudiated, on the one hand, the old oligarchic politics that "intervened in government to preserve the political privileges of [its] wealth, and to protect [its] right to property";[15] on the other hand, they rejected not only the "weak politics" of Western liberal democracy but especially the political consequences of its economic ideology, which relegated the Philippines to the status of a dependent client-state.[16] Philippine Constitutional Authoritarianism, in fact, was the Marcos answer to oligarchic democracy. Whether the Marcos government successfully carried out its claim to revolution and modernization, however, has now been practically settled. Indeed, the transformation of oligarchic democracy into "crony capitalism," for example, belies Marcos' claim that the repudiation of the old oligarchic politics was done in the name of his new constitutional authoritarian politics.

THE POLITICAL PHILOSOPHY OF PHILIPPINE CONSTITUTIONAL AUTHORITARIANISM: LIBERAL DEMOCRACY'S UNDERSIDE

The Nature of Revolution

Theorists of the Marcos government argued that democracy was the only polity that recognized a people's inherent right to revolution. The people's right to rebel, an idea inspired by Locke, was a basic human right that was inviolable.[17] Not simply the "violent confrontation of two national groups having irreconcilable interests," revolution was the process by which radical changes are sought, where the "total reorientation of the instrumentalities of government and other institutions of society" is effected in order to achieve the goals and aspirations of its people.[18]

This "right to revolution" was grounded in an egalitarian ideal which Marcos theorists understood as a social and political norm that "urges those persons who occupy positions of power and responsibility in government or the private sector to treat equally every individual in society. Located within a broader humanistic credo that affirmed both human creativity and rationality as the driving forces of democratic ideals, this egalitarian ideal was the moral basis for all public and private transactions. When a government's institutions violate this ideal, rebellion against it becomes justified.[19]

This right, however, was balanced with the public "right to suppress rebellion," the right and obligation of the duly constituted political authority to defend itself and preserve the public good.[20] Three decisive premises were implied by this public right. First, rebellions are of two kinds: those that are legitimate challenges posed by the people to the political authority, and those that are illegitimate assaults on it. Second, because it is "duly constituted," the government has the right to protect the people by suppressing those rebellions that are illegitimate. Third, the "right to revolution" is never absolute.

When the consciousness of the political authority coincides with the revolutionary demands of the masses, it was argued, a revolution initiated by the government becomes a matter of necessity.[21] For the Marcos theorists, this necessity arises historically because of the rebellion of the poor by their existence in the midst of an affluent oligarchic minority, the poor challenge the existing polity and its legitimacy, and make revolution necessary.

Revolutions in democratic theory are indeed rooted in the historical aspirations and experience of particular peoples but are carried out by the people themselves. For the Marcos theorists, in contrast, it is the "duly constituted government," the state, that wages this revolution. Presupposing, without having demonstrated, that the revolutionary demands of the people had in fact coincided with the political consciousness of the Marcos Administration, its theorists proclaimed, "It is for the people that we embark on the democratic revolution in order to alter or transform society."[22]

The speciousness of this identification of his administration with the Filipino people was never acknowledged by Marcos. Constitutional Authoritarianism, in fact, rested on an illusion of unity between civil and political society. It took the February, 1986, uprising not only to finally demystify this illusion, but more important, to call into question the viability and desirability of this elite conception of politics.

Democratization of Wealth: The Problem of Economic versus Political Rights

In Marcos' theory, his "democratic revolution" in the Philippines was waged primarily against an oligarchic democracy built on the concentration of economic power in the hands of a few, who, through this power, controlled the political institutions of governance. In practice, however, the Marcos government refused to destroy the politico-economic structure of oligarchic democracy. In fact, Marcos replaced the old oligarchy with his own cronies. Their presence, in and out of government, underscored the rise of a new oligarchy, which came to be popularly known as "crony capitalism."

Nevertheless, at the theoretical level, the democratization of wealth was understood as a problem of the relationship between political and economic rights, the distinction of which became crucial to the political philosophy of Philippine Constitutional Authoritarianism. While arguing for a broad notion of human rights, Marcos theorists argued for the primacy of economic rights, at least as a programmatic strategy for the democratic revolution. In a discussion obviously intended as a polemic against liberal democratic human rights activists, Marcos deplored the unfortunate emphasis on political rights. He argued that,

> It is unfortunate that in the context of our political experience the concern for human rights has always been a concern for "political" rights: the right to free speech, of assembly, and so on . . . [but] is it possible . . . that for the masses of Filipinos themselves, the primordial concern is the economic right to survive with dignity . . . ?[23]

This rhetorical question was rooted less in the concrete observation that the poor were deeply concerned with their economic situation than in the political understanding, ironically shared by liberal democrats, nationalists, and Marxists alike that only within a society where basic needs are met can political rights have any real significance.[24] For this reason, the Marcos theorists rejected the liberal democratic emphasis on political and procedural rights since it failed to acknowledge that these rights presupposed the fulfillment of basic needs. Put differently, formal or political equality had to be undergirded by substantive social and economic equality.

Thus, the question of rights underscored a deeper political-institutional challenge for any government concerned with social change. The obligation of the so-called "democratically elected leadership" was not simply to "achieve and maintain an authentic democratic process which rests on such ideals as freedom of speech, of the press, of assembly," but "to establish first of all, the credibility of government as an institution oriented to working for the welfare of the many and not just the few." The political task, therefore, was to establish a government that was responsive to the basic needs of its people, which in this context required the creation of "the [economic] institutions and the milieu that would make the exercise of political liberties the privilege not only of the few but of all."[25]

This, for Marcos, was the essential meaning of the democratization of wealth. Ironically, this involved the redistribution of wealth, but not the restructuring of the means for creating wealth. And since this redistribution rested on the political goodwill and benevolence of the oligarchy, the necessary structural transformations were seriously compromised, if not rendered altogether impossible.

The Necessity of a Strong State

Marcos argued that the necessary institutional precondition and consequence of the challenge of revolution posed by the rebellion of the poor against an oligarchic democracy was the establishment of a strong government fully committed to the welfare of the majority of its people. Marcos argued that the nature and role of government was as an advocate of its people, and that in order to fulfill this role government had to be an autonomous institution of society.

In the first place, as an advocate for its people, and in response to the cry for social change, the government initiates the "radicalization of existing social arrangements." It does so not only because it is a duly constituted authority, but because it is "the only authority

ity morally bound to act in behalf of the people."[26] A democratic government, by its very nature, "is obliged to make itself the faithful instrument of the people's revolutionary aspirations."[27] This assertion, in fact, was a direct repudiation of the liberal notion of an "umpire state" whose function is limited to the adjudication of competing claims. It was a rejection of the Jeffersonian dictum that the best government is that which governs least, a claim that the increasing complexities of human community, domestically and internationally, necessitated new obligations, and consequently, increased authority for government.[28]

In the second place, arguing against those who viewed the state as merely the instrument of class interests, Marcos theorists proposed the concept of a relatively autonomous state, one able to exert its own will apart from other societal forces, as the political and philosophical centerpiece of constitutional authoritarianism. Unlike the classical Marxist-Leninist theory of the state, which Marcos theorists understood as requiring the revolutionary overthrow of the existing social and political structure and the establishment of a "dictatorship of the proletariat," the relatively autonomous state was viewed as an institution that "will not favor one and injure the other." "Our theory," they argued, "requires a conscientious government that will preside over the interaction between the rich and the poor, or among various sectors of society, in the spirit of fair play."[29] Rather than being the instrument of one class, government became the guardian of policies that seek to equalize opportunities for the people as a whole.

This view sought to affirm, on the one hand, the Marxist-Leninist insight into the necessity of a vanguard of the proletariat, while avoiding what was perceived to be its distorted view of a state captive of the dominant class and, on the other hand, to affirm the liberal Lockean principle of the primacy of the citizen while repudiating its kind of ineffectual umpire state.[30] Both were judged to be inadequate for a modernizing and revolutionary society. What the Marcos theorists failed to acknowledge was the impact of the centralizing logic of a strong autonomous state, which tended not only to identify the so-called "spirit of justice and fair play" with its own interests but which also shifted the center of gravity from civil to political society.

A Different Conception of Liberty, Freedom, and Rights

The Marcos argument for the necessity of a strong state claimed legitimacy by a conception of liberty, freedom, and rights which differed significantly from the Western liberal democratic tradition. In an essay entitled "Liberty and Government in the New Society," Onofre D. Corpuz, a Marcos theorist, posed the dilemma of the contemporary Filipino intellectual as having to chose "between the social and political concepts of the old and those of the new social order" but forward to ground the politics of the New Society.[31] Corpuz argued that the Anglo-American political tradition, essentially paraphrasing the political ideas of Locke, "was concerned primarily with the preservation of individual life, liberty, and property as they are threatened by Government."[32] Its view of liberty, therefore, was largely that of autonomy from government, particularly by the propertied classes. Contrasting this to the more populist understanding of *liberté, egalité, fraternité* of the French Revolution, Corpuz argued that the Lockean tradition not only excluded the vast majority of the people, but also became the most "powerful of respectable justification in Western political thought of the oligarchic domination of society."[33] Thus, the Lockean notion of liberty could not provide the basis for a truly democratic society.

In a different although related context, Marcos argued that if the notion of political liberty was to be adequate to the realities of a modernizing Philippines, it had to be enlarged by a commitment to equality. He agreed with Corpuz that the struggle for equality, not liberty, was at the heart of the rebellion of the poor, and that it was the more powerful driving force in a developing society. Citing Leslie Lipson to expose the inadequacy of the Lockean understanding of liberty, Marcos asserted:

> The interrelationship between liberty and equality is obvious. Differences in status produces differences in liberties. Some individuals are more free than others, and such differences are also inequalities. When equality of opportunity is provided, liberties are equalized. To abolish differences of status is . . . to enlarge the freedoms of those at the bottom.[34]

The emphasis on political liberty, Corpuz further argued, led to an unwarranted, if not erroneous, emphasis on the Bill of Rights as the primary source of liberty, security and welfare. While a necessary dimension of governance is the protection of the citizen from arbitrary acts of government, this Bill of Rights tradition, which emphasize's rights as limitations on government, could not provide the foundations for a broader vision of the national community. Not only was it not possible to establish political community exclusively on negative rights, such a view offered nothing meaningful or substantial to the propertyless class, which in the Philippines is the larger portion of the population.

Marcos theorists therefore sought to establish a government that allowed it to act on behalf of the poor. Indeed, for them, it was important that the government be formally obligated to promote the common welfare and that it be authorized and adequately empowered to promote the well-being of all citizens, which would thus be beyond the capacity of factions and class interests to frustrate.[35] The necessary task, it was argued, was to ensure that government works for the common welfare, and to not limit its powers. This became the fundamental justification for a strong i.e., authoritarian, state.

Contrary to those who understood political liberty as autonomy, and who therefore saw the strong state as implying the contraction of political liberty, Marcos theorists proclaimed that the essence of political liberty was human capacity.[36] Corpuz argued that whatever diminished human capacity had to be repudiated, be it abusive government or social and economic deprivation. The political authority had the "moral obligation to use the community's substance and intelligence to defend the dignity of every citizen."

At its core, however, the notion of liberty as capacity rested on the idea of human freedom. Drawing on the Aristotelian notion of the fully human being as one who has attained excellence of body, mind, and soul, which thereby endows the individual with virtùe as a citizen, Corpuz argued that this excellence "requires that man [sic] be free . . . in the sense that he is free from violation [by] other men . . . that his capability is not destroyed by the afflictions of bodily infirmity, intellectual ignorance, and moral depravity."[37] To be fully human, one must be fully free. Yet freedom must be understood within the structural and material relations that tend either to restrict or promote human liberty. Freedom does not mean pursuit of private desires, which would permit each person to constitute a society of one. Rather, freedom becomes the pursuit of common interests and desires. As a description of social relations, freedom is constituted by participation in a common life[38]— but a common life defined primarily by the government.

This comprised a decisive point for Philippine Constitutional Authoritarianism. Not unlike the Marxist contention that freedom is inextricably related to the material conditions of society, the Marcos theorists rightly understood that the struggle for freedom required "altering and improving upon the structures and institutions that confine or diminish human possibility of fulfillment." The democratic revolution had to be translated into a social and political task. Indeed, for Corpuz, this meant that all human institutions, including government, had to be placed in the service of the political community to "restore, promote, or enhance, human capability." Rather than representing a limitation on human freedom, government must reflect the people's enlightened conscience, assisting rather that hindering the attainment of their full potential. "In other words," Corpuz concluded, "government becomes the community's instrument of liberation and freedom because the government helps men [sic] to become free and human."[39]

In their repudiation of the classical Lockean conception of liberty, freedom, and rights, the Marcos theorists rightly underscored the inadequacy of the liberal democratic tradition for a modernizing and revolutionary Philippines. Indeed, such a truncated view of social and political life tends to eclipse other equally important dimensions of human life. Corpuz has rightly pointed out, for example, that other matters like "sustenance and shelter . . . faith and religion . . . cooperation and conflict . . . revenge and hatred, and the gentle emotions of affection and love" occupy the common *tao* ("common person") more than the matter of political liberty.[40]

It is ironic, therefore, that such a theoretical sensitivity to the need for addressing the larger questions of political and economic life failed to recognize, perhaps deliberately that one of the decisive elements on which the theory of a state-led democratic revolution rests, namely, the unity of civil society with the state, the confluence of the "will of the people" and the "will of the state," was precisely that which theoretically and practically could no longer be sustained. In retrospect, despite the claims of legitimacy and the appeals to its "duly constituted authority," the Marcos government as early as 1969 had already began to lose its legitimacy. By 1971, the rupture between state and civil society in the Philippines was practically irreversible. In the context of this fundamental rupture, the political project of Philippine Constitutional Authoritarianism, particularly its attempt to wrestle with the changing social, political, and economic order and to articulate a new normative constitutional order, quickly gave way to legalism, i.e., a commitment to rules and an obsession with formalism, which capitulated to the seduction of violence.[41]

THE PRIMACY OF ORDER: THE OPERATIVE FOUNDATION OF PHILIPPINE CONSTITUTIONAL AUTHORITARIANISM

The conviction that government is the instrument of liberation and freedom was rooted in even more than the pragmatic recognition that only a strong state can successfully wage a democratic revolution against a deeply entrenched oligarchic minority in a rapidly modernizing world. A more profound underlying philosophical assumption shaped this conviction, which the Marcos theorists shared with the liberal democratic tradition, namely, that order is necessary for political life.

It bears repeating that for the Marcos theorists the imposition of martial law in the Philippines was due largely to the threat posed by lawless elements seeking to destroy the duly constituted government.[42] Drawing on U.S. constitutional law, to which Philippine law is indebted, Marcos theorists argued that martial law entailed "the military merely being utilized to strengthen the civil government in the enforcement of existing law;" that martial law "is not a substitute for the civil law, but is rather an aid to the execution of the civil law."[43] Marcos argued, therefore, that the imposition of martial law was not a surrender of the civilian authority to the military. Rather than being alien to the democratic heritage, martial law was an extraordinary measure provided by democracy to protect itself.[44] Marcos went even further, however, early arguing that martial law in the Philippines was a "creative, if extraordinary measure to break this circle of futility," the inhospitable social and economic conditions of the people.[45]

Implicit in this extraordinary, although not unprecedented, use of martial law, was the value of the primacy of order for the existence of political community. Marcos theorists noted Samuel Huntington's observations of the problems confronting developing countries, that "the primary problem is not liberty but the creation of a legitimate public order [since] men [sic] may have order without liberty, but they cannot have liberty without order."[46] Significantly, Marcos theorists appeared unwilling to define "order" as such. They preferred to argue for its necessity. In fact, this argument for the primacy of order in political and social life turned out to be grounded on a metaphysical assertion that order was a constitutive element of the universe.[47] What is interesting, moreover, is the consequence for politics which Marcos drew from this assertion. "On the plane of human society," he noted,

> this correspondence of order and moral value has a counterpart in government and community. No matter how numerous the individuals . . . and regardless of the variousness of their wants and interests . . . they have a collective interest in the preservation of order . . . , [for] the supreme and eternal good, the highest morality, is the avoidance of self-destruction. To assure itself that this high moral duty is performed, human society has instituted law and fashioned the instrument of government with which to enforce it.[48]

Indeed, this "collective interest in the preservation of order," identified with the human instinct for self-preservation, for Marcos theorists served as the "prime mover of peace and order in society." Like Hobbes, self-preservation comprised the moral justification for the necessity of order in society.[49] Unlike Hobbes, Marcos interpreted order as intrinsic rather than regulative. On the one hand, Marcos argued that society had an implicit order beyond the self-interests of individuals, although he understood it as not being self-regulating or self-enforcing. On the other hand, he recognized that political reality was comprised of the perpetual struggle of individuals and groups committed to the preservation and enlargement of their self-interest. He therefore argued for the necessity of enforcing "law and order" to protect these individuals not only from the ravages of self-interest, but especially from the threat of destruction. "The collective rights of the citizens to protect themselves from destruction," wrote Marcos, "becomes, to a government of laws, an obligation to impose order—as the maxim goes, public welfare is the highest law."[50]

The argument for the primacy of order drew on a particular notion of authority and law. Marcos theorists exposed their liberal democratic affinities in their construal of authority as *legal* authority.[51] The notion of authority as such, however, was an elusive one. Marcos theorists simply presupposed it. They determined that only in its expression as "legitimate public order," to borrow Huntington's phrase, could authority be recognized. The authority, initially proclaimed as rooted in the people's will or the Constitution, in reality was transferred to the structures of public order. Moreover, within these structures, of which law was its underlying principle, and in the instrumentalities of government—the military, police, and bureaucracy, its institutional expressions—authority, echoing Hobbes, became understood as command and coercion.[52]

Convinced by Huntington's grave reservations about the so-called "Lockean American's" indifference to political development, Marcos theorists argued that the fundamental problem that most developing societies like the Philippines face had less to do with elections than with creating organizations that would meet the goals of development. In fact, what is decisive for these countries, so they argued, is the existence of stable public institutions, like the military, which could guarantee the meaningfulness of any electoral process. Sounding the warning that a government administered by persons over persons must first "enable the government to control the governed" before it "obliges it to control itself," Marcos theorists applied to the Philippines Huntington's argument that the primary problem was not liberty but the creation of legitimate public order. As Huntington put it, "Authority has to exist before it can be limited, and it is authority that is in scarce supply in those modernizing countries. . . . "[53]

Politics: The Practice of Creating Public Order

Within this framework, politics, despite the rhetoric that proclaimed it as the practice of freedom,[54] became the practice of creating public order. Authority was no longer understood as an ongoing deliberative relationship between the government and its people in the context of shared values and obligations. Rather, authority was construed as the prerogative of government to command its people. Rather than the law being an expression of authority, it became that which conferred authority. Thus, the Marcos government pursued the creation of structures of governance designed to maintain stability.[55] The increased militarization and bureaucratization of the state, both of which greatly increased its repressive and coercive powers, comprised significant aspects of this process.[56] Somewhat ironically, what originally had been conceived as a way to safeguard the very source of authority on which legitimacy rested, namely, the people, evolved into the primary threat of the destruction of the people. The consequence of politics became its condition: what was regulative became constitutive. In fact, law became an ahistorical, noncontingent principle that disciplined human reality. Severed from history, it became the Archimedeon point from which authority emanated.

The fundamental issue, of course, was not whether legitimate public order was necessary or even desirable; nor whether the adjudication of competing claims was an integral part of a democratic society. Rather, as most critics of the Marcos government noted, the issue was whether its creation included the meaningful participation of those for whom public order had been created.[57] Despite Marcos' insistence that participation had been guaranteed through institutions like the Citizens' Assemblies and the National Assembly, in practice there were no institutional mechanisms for effective and meaningful participation.[58] In reality, the Marcos government had already predetermined the nature and extent of participation: The state acted on behalf of its people by creating the institutions in which the people might participate. Participation devolved into assent.[59] In fact, citizenship was reduced to a legal status making individuals the passive recipients of specific rights, no doubt protected by the law, but with greatly diminished capacities for challenging the law.

In retrospect, this particular conception of participation resulted, at least on the level of electoral politics, in what Ellen Trimberger called the "depoliticization of the masses."[60] With the Marcos government's monopoly of political institutions, most Filipinos developed a fatalistic, if not cynical, attitude not only toward traditional political institutions but to law and the rule of law. The sense of belonging to or identification with the *res publica,* crucial to political community and the vitality of law and public order, was eclipsed. On a deeper, especially clandestine level, however the absence of meaningful and efficacious participation in the governance of the body politic resulted in the creation of a vast network of peoples' organizations committed to fundamental social change: human rights advocates, feminist collectives, ecological groups, in addition to the more traditional workers', peasants', students', and women's groups. In fact, the February, 1986, uprising, which saw the eruption into Philippine politics of peoples' organizations—from the spontaneous although relatively unorganized liberal bourgeois sector, to the more highly organized nationalist and leftist-inspired "cause-oriented" groups—suggests that the depoliticizing of the masses was more apparent than real. Indeed, the fall of the Marcos government may be attributed, in large measure, to the peoples' direct participation in the creation of alternative structures and patterns of governance, both at the open and clandestine levels. Civil society had repudiated the state apparatus.

Moreover, the question of legitimate public order cannot be reduced to the question of adjudication of competing claims. For the question of public order, then as now, is fundamentally a problem of community and identity, that is, what it means to be constituted as a human community. Marcos theorists failed to fully understand that the rejection of "public order" was only a symptom of the larger loss of authority resulting from the disintegration of the structures of relationships that constitute human life. No doubt, this disintegration paved the way for the imposition of order as a compensatory principle for common life. In the absence of this common life brought about by the complex process of modernization and revolution, law and order became the only structure for political life. Because they emphasized the creation of public order as the central task of politics, and focused on exclusive legitimacy as its primary goal, Marcos theorists were unable to address the question of political community. Political community, if it has disintegrated, cannot simply be restored by circumscribing the disintegration with an external system of laws.[61] Nor can formal legitimacy replace substantive legitimacy without undermining the latter's emphasis on consensus and on authority from the ground up.

The Death of Political Dissent

The discussion of dissent under Marcos' constitutional authoritarianism further illustrates the consequences of reducing politics to the creation of "legitimate public order." After affirming the right of political dissent, including the implied repudiation of any claim to absolute political authority, as fundamental to democratic society and the concept of political liberty, Marcos theorists moved quickly to circumscribe political dissent. They enclosed dissent, ironically limited to free expression, within the framework of legitimate public authority, the latter implying the existence of authority, for them residing in duly constituted government.[62]

Procedurally, the right of political dissent was balanced by the right of the government to preserve itself in order that it may continue to preserve the system of law that was assumed to guarantee rights and the public welfare.[63] Any threat to law and order, therefore, became a threat to those rights that were initially valued. Consequently, the former had to be preserved at all cost. In this sense, the right of political dissent required that it be subordinated to the government when by its exercise it threatened what the latter construed as the public welfare. Yet the determination of what constituted not only the public welfare but of political dissent, as well, was left to the Marcos government, particularly the courts and law enforcement agencies. Political life was defined primarily by the government, not by the people. Accountability to the people disappeared into the mandate supposedly given once and for all. Authority devolved into authorization and authoritarianism.

This state-centric construing of political dissent was challenged by liberal democratic, nationalist, and Marxist critics of the Marcos government. In the mid-1970s, for example, liberal democrats questioned the legitimacy of the Marcos government from a juridico-procedural perspective, challenging Marcos for conflating law with state. Unfortunately, because they accepted his premise of the rule of law as the Archimedean point from which politics is understood, this blunted the weapon of their criticism. With the gradual emergence of popular criticism, particularly in the late 1970s and the early 1980s, this formal/procedural challenge was relocated within the context of the substantive opposition to the Marcos government. Thus, Jovito Salonga argued in 1980:

> In the final analysis, our hope is not in any foreign power, nor in a Constitution, nor in any statute or law, nor in any court of justice. Our true hope is our own people, who thanks to current developments, including the so-called lifting of Martial Law, are asserting their right to be free-with increasing boldness and courage.[64]

In short, Salonga was challenging the formal/procedural basis on which the Marcos government had built its argument for the rule of its law. More important, he implied that the proper locus of politics was at the juncture of political and civil society, and that social and political transformation ultimately rested with the people who were struggling for justice and freedom. By underscoring that law and human community were dialectically related rather than dichotomous, he directly challenged the central assumption of Constitutional Authoritarianism, as well as underlining its destructive consequences. Marcos theorists assumed that the state was the *primum movens* of political life. Consequently, the state had to have the capacity to impose its will absolutely. This not only led to depoliticizing the masses, but also to the contraction of political space under the Marcos regime. The state as *locus politicus* meant that those who dissented "outside" the framework of the state were identified as "enemies of law and order," and therefore enemies of the state. They were thus disenfranchised, their claims dismissed out of hand. Where disorder prevailed, coercion became not only the sole prerogative of the state, but justifiable and necessary: Locke surrendered to Hobbes.

Power as Coercion

State coercion, of course, was not limited only to its overt expression as political and military repression. For the most part, the coercive character of Philippine Constitutional Authoritarianism rested on its adherence to what Roberto Unger calls the "legal mentality," that is, construing social life as being mediated primarily by calculable rules and enforced through coercion. By privileging formal equality over equity, and command over participation, it not only undermined differences and pluralism, but it reduced justice to uniformity and gave impetus to the leveling of status in society. Citizenship as an expression of political identity created through one's identification with the *res publica* was reduced to a legal fiction. In the context of a society of rules this meant the subjugation of all individuals to the state. It also meant, and with equal significance, that meanings and informal institutions not congenial with impersonal rules were systematically excluded from the realm of politics—and therefore, from accountability. In fact, the legal mentality was a consciousness of order transformed into the practice of coercion. Needless to say, such a truncated view of political life failed to recognize the plurality of political forms, structures, and practices necessary for a democratic society. Philippine

Constitutional Authoritarianism reduced democracy to a system of rules enforced by a political authority accountable only to itself; the ideology ignored the fact that democracy at its most profound level was a process of consensus building, reciprocal accountability, and dialogue within the context of difference and plurality with the recognition of a set of ethical and political values, standards, if you will, that governed individual behavior.

Social Change as Mastery and Control

Implicit in claiming the necessity of absolute state power for the creation and maintenance of public order is the assumption that social and political change on an institutional level requires a minority within society that initiates and sustains revolutionary activity. Adopting a perspective somewhat similar to the Marxist-Leninist vanguard, although more like Hobbes' sovereign as the Great Definer of political life, Philippine Constitutional Authoritarianism identified this minority with the Marcos government. It affirmed a theory of the relationship of the state to social change that was thoroughly modern, but combined with this the traditionalist values of hierarchy and domination. As Marcos himself asserted, "The power to control and change his [sic] environment is a cardinal belief of modern man [sic], and revolution is the ultimate expression of this outlook—the modernizing outlook. . . ."[65]

These values converged with the statist assumptions of the Marcos government. Conflating the assertion of political will with the monopoly of violence and legitimacy, the Marcos government imposed its authority to govern through all the instrumentalities of the state, with destructive consequences for both people and environment. In constitutional authoritarianism, human agency, understood as the autonomous political subject, was wedded to social change as mastery and control. The outcome of social change is inescapably shaped—even determined—by the historical and institutional practices that are adopted. That is, the political choice of the state to be the sole agency of social change in the Philippines turned out to be that which closed off the very possibility of social change. The political, economic, and cultural legacy that the Marcos government left: the foreign debt, a practically nonexistent domestic infrastructure for production and distribution, a highly politicized and fractious military, to mention only a few, underscores not only its vision of a democratic revolution as nothing but an illusion, but the bankruptcy of the state to carry forward the agenda for change. That which was seen as the bearer of social change, namely, the state, was, in the last analysis, that which devoured not only its children, but its creator.

QUO VADIS CONSTITUTIONALISM?

It is one of the ironies of Philippine history that the Marcos legacy, with its almost obsessive insistence on the rule of law, included the emergence of a generation of Filipinos profoundly skeptical of any contribution that law and constitutionalism might have to the creation of a more just and humane society. Philippine Constitutional Authoritarianism failed to capture the imagination and loyalty of thoughtful Filipinos primarily because, in practice, it did not provide a meaningful alternative to liberal democracy. In fact, any attempt to transcend liberal democracy was doomed to failure from the outset, for Philippine Constitutional Authoritarianism was itself a child of liberal democracy.[66]

As an historical attempt to grapple with the changing social order and as an effort to articulate the foundations for a new one, Philippine Constitutional Authoritarianism was destined to fail. First and foremost, the attempt rested on the mistaken notion that it was possible to uncover and/or articulate the emerging order without the full and effective participation of the peoples of the Philippines. Second, it lay down the notion of order as the ultimate ground of political life, clearing away the pluralistic character of civil and political society. Similarly, it insisted on a narrowly construed understanding of the law, reducing the latter to legalism, and severing it from its historical moorings to the human community. Third, the ideology uncritically identified law with the state, failing to recognize the intensely problematic and contested character of both in the life of the Filipino peoples.

Moreover, for all their arguments about the dismal failure of the old order and their assertions of the creation of a new order, in their phrase a "New Society", Marcos theorists, in fact, failed to appreciate the interplay between constitutionalism, foundational values, and political practice. They assumed that constitutionalism—the process of articulating the form of a society's polity—was the most decisive element of the political process. In addition, they underestimated the importance of the normative order built over time in both creating an alternative constitutive order and undermining the operative order of constitutional authoritarianism. First, the foundational values and political practices of constitutional authoritarianism were so profoundly at odds with its proclaimed values and constitutional form that the latter eventually collapsed from within. Second, the rebellion of the poor, as well as the leftist and secessionist movements, while shaped by the very normative order which the Marcos theorists also affirmed, understood the interplay of constitutionalism and political practice differently. That is, they affirmed the values of justice, liberty, and equity, but from their own understanding of how the new order and political practice was unfolding historically. This alternative view, systematically excluded by the Marcos theorists, eventually frustrated the latter's project. Put differently, in its exercise of its authority, and in the arbitrariness of its political practices, Marcos undermined his own foundations of constitutionalism and the rule of law.

More important, Marcos theorists failed to understand the radically contingent character of contemporary political reality. While proclaiming the necessity for modernization and revolution, they chose to deal with it by retreating into a politics disciplined by a particular metaphysics of order. Machiavelli surrenders to Hobbes; politics capitulates to metaphysics. Thus, differences are erased; political spaces are closed off; democratic practices are compromised.

It is in this sense that while Philippine Constitutional Authoritarianism was in practice a dying regime's strategy to prolong its life, the process of articulating the form of a society's polity continues to be a revolutionary project provided it attends equally to its foundational values and political practices. Indeed, constitutionalism, by historical definition, invites not only the creative human imagination, but the participation of human communities in creating and recreating society in the light of what they understand practically to be good, true, and beautiful. Ironically, it is here where Philippine Constitutional Authoritarianism has made its contribution to this revolutionary project: It has revealed a pathway best avoided, and through its commanding silences and deliberate exclusions, has opened the way for future struggles to articulate a new order for the human community in the Philippines.

NOTES

1. Saul H. Mendlovitz, "Memo to Richard Falk, et al." April 15, 1989.

2. In contrast to some scholars and politicians who held that Philippine Constitutional Authoritarianism was nothing more than a convenient mask for dictatorship, Marcos theorists insisted that it was a serious attempt not only to respond to the crisis of the deteriorating political, economic, and cultural order, but also an exercise in consti-

tutionalism. The perspective taken in this paper is that, indeed, Philippine Constitutional Authoritarianism was an attempt to wrestle with the disintegration of the old order and to articulate a new one.

3. Diosdado Macapagal, *Democracy in the Philippines* (Ruben J. Cusipag, 1976), pp. 28–29; Raul Manglapus, *Philippines: The Silenced Democracy* (New York: Orbis Books, 1976), pp. 12–20; cf. Rolando del Carmen, "Constitutionality and Judicial Politics," in David Rosenbert, ed., *Marcos and Martial Law in the Philippines* (Ithaca, NY: Cornell University Press, 1979), pp. 85–112.

4. Ferdinand E. Marcos, *Today's Revolution: Democracy* (Manila: National Media Production Center, 1971), "Introduction," p. i.

5. Ferdinand E. Marcos, *Revolution from the Center: How the Philippines Is Using Martial Law to Build a New Society* (Hongkong: Raya Books, 1978), pp. 32–35; See also Ferdinand E. Marcos, *Democratic Revolution in the Philippines*, 2nd ed. (Englewood Cliffs, NJ: Prentice-Hall, 1979), pp. 140–150; cf. Amado Guerrero, *Philippine Society and Revolution* (Oakland, CA: International Association of Filipino Patriots, 1979); José Maria Sison, *Struggle for National Democracy* (Manila: Amado Hernandez Memorial Foundation, 1972).

6. Marcos, "Proclamation No. 1081," *Democratic Revolution*, pp. 335–351; see also pp. 111–131. *Ibid.*

7. Marcos, *Democratic Revolution*, p. 14; see also Ferdinand E. Marcos, *Progress and Martial Law* (Manila: National Media Production Center, 1981), pp. 1–20.

8. This was suggested by the Mansfield (Valeo) Report to the U.S. Senate, which read in part: "Beyond the ostensible objective of restoring law and order, martial law had paved the way for a reordering of the basic social structure of the Philippines. President Marcos has been prompt and sure-footed in using the power of presidential decree under martial law for this purpose." Cited in Marcos, *Democratic Revolution*, p. 141; cf. Macapagal, *Democracy*, pp. 18–19.

9. Marcos himself noted in *Democratic Revolution* (p.2): "It can bear repeating that the only immutable object in human life is the principle that everything is susceptible to change . . . we provoke and welcome change to survive the shocks and tensions of man's headlong flight to technology . . . we live in a time of revolution. Mankind is in a ferment of change. . . . in the democracies, change has the special property of volition. . . . " For the substance of this "modernization," see pp. ii–iii (see also Marcos, *Progress*, pp. 38–45.

10. Samuel Huntington, cited in Marcos, *Democratic Revolution*, p. 70.

11. Marcos, *Democratic Revolution*, pp. 93–94.

12. Marcos, *Revolution from the Center*, pp. 19–22.

13. Marcos, *Revolution from the Center,* pp. 22; see also Marcos, *Democratic Revolution,* p. 94.

14. Ferdinand E. Marcos, *In Search of Alternatives: The Third World in a Age of Crisis,* 3rd ed. (Manila: National Media Production Center, 1980), pp. 83–92.

15. Marcos, *Revolution from the Center,* p. 21.

16. Robert Stauffer, "The Political Economy of Refeudalization," in Rosenberg, pp. 180–218.

17. Marcos, *Today's Revolution,* p. 2.

18. Ferdinand E. Marcos, *An Ideology for Filipinos* (Manila: National Media Production Center, 1980), p. 23.

19. Marcos, *Ideology for Filipinos,* p. 13., 17; cf. Marcos, *Today's Revolution,* pp. 1–3.

20. Marcos, *Democratic Revolution,* p. 218.

21. Marcos, *Today's Revolution,* p. 7.

22. Marcos, *Ideology for Filipinos,* pp. 15–16.

23. Marcos, *Ideology for Filipinos,* p. 17.

24. Marcos, *Ideology for Filipinos,* p. 17.

25. Marcos, *Ideology for Filipinos,* p. 19, 21. As theorists of Philippine Constitutional Authoritarianism asserted elsewhere: "Equality is the fundamental demand of the rebellion of the poor: It should be the ideological force behind the New Society." Marcos, *Democratic Revolution,* p. 151.

26. Marcos, *Ideology for Filipinos,* p. 29.

27. Marcos, *Today's Revolution,* p. 12. Thus, Marcos wrote: "Governments are now judged according to their willingness and capacity to act as instruments of social change. The people—the governed—look to their governments for leadership not only in the political order but also in the social and economic orders" (p. 9).

28. Ferdinand E. Marcos, Blas Ople, O. D. Corpuz et al. *Toward the New Society: Essays on Aspects of Philippine Development* (Manila: National Media Production Center, 1974), p. 57.

29. Marcos, *Ideology for Filipinos,* p. 27.

30. The notion of a "relatively autonomous state," particularly in the case of the Marcos government, flies in the face of the actual situation. See Note 7 and William Branigin, "The Phillippines: A Society Adrift," *Washington Post,* August 16, 1984 p.20; cf. Robin Broad, "Behind Philippine Policy-Making" (Ph.D. dissertation, Princeton University, 1983) and Raymond Bonner, *Waltzing with a Dictator: The Marcoses and the Making of American Policy* (New York: Times Books, 1987).

On the theoretical level, the Marcos argument for a "revolutionary" and "autonomous state" may be seen as part of a growing scholarly corpus, both Marxist and non-Marxist, that seeks to evaluate the relationship of civil and political society in terms of the theory and practice of social and political change. See for example, Theda Skocpol, *States and Social Revolution: A Comparative Analysis of France, Russia, and China* (New York: Cambridge University Press, 1979); Ellen Kay Trimberger, *Revolution from Above; Military Bureaucrats and Development in Japan, Turkey, Egypt, and Peru* (New Brunswick, NJ: Transaction Books, 1978); Nicos Poulanzas, *Political Power and Social Classes* (London: NLB, 1973).

More recent discussions, particularly in the neo-Marxist/ Gramscian tradition, while not explicitly dealing with the revolutionary potential of the state and the states system, address the issues implicit in the discourse of the "autonomous state." See, for example, Ernesto Laclau and Chantal Mouffe, *Hegemony and Socialist Strategy: Towards a Radical Democratic Politics,* Winston Moore and Paul Cammack (London: Verso: 1985). Of course, the radical character of these later discussions—for example, the notion of hegemony and the repudiation of the dichotomy between "base and superstructure,"— was never addressed by the theorists of Philippine Constitutional Authoritarianism. The refusal by the theorists of Philippine Constitutional Authoritarianism to deal with these critical issues is significant and indicates their commitment to a rather conventional understanding of politics.

31. Marcos, Ople, Corpus, et al., *Toward the New Society,* p. 46.

32. Marcos, et al., p. 49. The first significant encounter of Filipino intellectuals with modern political thought, e.g., the ideas of national self-determination, popular sovereignty, liberty and political rights, was with the ideas of Voltaire, Rousseau, Paine, and the later European Enlightenment. This was eclipsed at the turn of the century by the Anglo-American political tradition, which has since then shaped the Philippine tradition of jurisprudence.

33. Marcos et al., p. 53.

34. Marcos, *Democratic Revolution,* p. 278. For the most explicit discussion of the meaning of "equality" in the Marcos corpus, see pp. 151–167, "Equality and Politics."

35. Marcos, *Democratic Revolution,* p. 56. Cf. pp. 217ff, "The Constitution and Martial Law."

36. Marcos et al., p. 57.

37. Marcos et al., p. 58.

38. Marcos et al., p. 60. See also Marcos, *Democratic Revolution,* p. 259.

39. Marcos et al., p. 62.

40. Thus, Marcos theorists asserted: "The achievement of equality [and therefore of political liberty], if it is to contribute at all to human freedom and to social good, must not be seen merely in terms

of possession, but more important, in terms of power and potential. The abiding faith is that where men enjoy equal rights and opportunities in the social order, where they are not weighed down by structures that inhibit or discourage their actions, they will be able to create and contribute to their personal welfare and dignity, and to the growth and strength of their community." Marcos, *Democratic Revolution,* p. 279.

41. This insight is Roberto M. Unger's, who noted rather cryptically that "legalism and terrorism . . . are rival brothers, but brothers nonetheless." *Knowledge and Politics* (New York: Free Press, 1975), p. 75.

42. Marcos, *In Search of Alternatives,* p. 140.

43. Burdick, Willis and Willoughby, quoted in Marcos. *In Search of Alternatives.*, pp. 140–142.

44. Thus, Leslie Lipson argued in his book, *The Democratic Civilization:* "As a system of government of existence, democracy has a right to preserve itself. Liberty can be protected against abuses committed in its name. While all liberties depend on maintaining some order, and too many orders mean sacrificing too much liberty, democracy is not required to commit suicide." Quoted in Ferdinand E. Marcos, *The Phillippine Experience: A Perspective on Human Rights and the Rule of Law* (Manila: National Media Production Center, n.d.), p. 37.

45. Marcos, *Philippine Experience,* p. 36.

46. Samuel Huntington, quoted in Marcos, *Philippine Experience,* p. 31.

47. Ferdinand E. Marcos, "Martial Law and Human Rights," *Democratic Revolution,* pp. 1–2.

48. Marcos, *Democratic Revolution,* pp. 1–2. Nowhere in the Marcos corpus more than here is the confluence of positivism and natural rights theory, of "premodern" and "modern" thought, expressed. The argument, as Unger has noted, is that so-called "premodern societies" draw a clear line between what is immutable in the social order and what falls under the discretion of the rulers. In contrast, modern states tend to construe every aspect of social life as subject to political will. See Unger, pp. 305–306. Philippine Constitutional Authoritarianism, in fact, cannot be reduced to either one: It is both. Cf. Henry Maine, Lectures on the Early History of Institutions (London: Murray, 1897), pp. 373–386.

49. Thomas Hobbes, *De Cive* or *The Citizen,* ed. Sterling Lamprecht (New York: Appleton-Century-Crofts, 1949), Part 1, ch. 1, secs. 2–3. The rational principle of "self-preservation" in Hobbes is rooted in the nonrational fear of violent death. The distinction is crucial, attest-

ing to the dichotomy of reason and desire in Hobbes. See the persuasive argument of Unger in *Knowledge and Politics*, pp. 38–54.

50. Marcos, "Martial Law and Human Rights," p. 25.

51. Marcos "Martial Law and Human Rights," pp. 1–24.

52. Compare, for example, Thomas Hobbes, *Leviathan: Or the Matter, Forme and Power of a Common-Wealth Ecclesiastical and Civil*, ed. C. B. Macpherson (New York: Penguin Books, 1968), ch. 26, p. 312; In this context, Philippine Constitutional Authoritarianism shows affinities with the national security state ideology. See for instance José Comblin, *Le pouvoir militaire en Amerique Latine: L'ideologie de la Securité Nationale* (Paris: Jean Pierre de Large, 1977); cf. Augusto Pinochet Ugarte, *Geopolitica* (Santiago de Chile: Andres Bello, 1974); For an explicit discussion of the similarities between Philippine Constitutional Authoritarianism and the national security state system ideology, see my essay "Power, Justice, and the Concept of Human Development," paper presented at the 23rd Annual Convention of the International Studies Association, Cincinnati, Ohio, March 26, 1982; cf. Unger's argument that "the less one's ability to rely on participation in common ends, the greater the importance of force as a bond among individuals. Punishment and fear take the place of community," p. 75.

53. Samuel Huntington, *Political Order in Changing Societies* (New Haven, CT: Yale University Press, 1968), pp. 7–8; cited also, in part, in Marcos, *The Philippine Experience*, p. 31.

54. Marcos, *Ideology for Filipinos*, pp. 13–22, 75–84; Marcos, *Democratic Revolution*, pp. 151–167.

55. Marcos, *Democratic Revolution*, pp. 335–351; Ferdinand E. Marcos, "Optimism Resurgent in Country Today," the President's Report to the Nation During the 5th Anniversary of Martial Law, September 21, 1977, p. 8; Marcos, *Progress and Martial Law*, pp. 49–52.

56. Herbert Feith, "Repressive-Developmentalist Regimes in Asia," *Alternatives* 7, no. 4 (Spring 1982): 491–506; Delia Miller, "Memorandum on U.S. Military Assistance to the Philippines" (Washington, DC: Institute for Policy Studies, 1979); Walden Bello and Severina Rivera, eds., *The Logistics of Repression and Other Essays: The Role of U.S. Assistance in Consolidating the Martial Law Regime in the Philippines* (Washington, DC: Friends of the Filipino People, 1977); Noam Chomsky and Edward S. Herman, *The Washington Connection and Third World Fascism: The Political Economy of Human Rights*, 1 (Boston: South End Press, 1979).

57. Compare, for example, Guerrero, pp. 129–169; Renato Constantino, *The Nationalist Alternative* (Manila: Foundation of Nationalist Studies, 1979), pp. 65–90; United Democratic Organization, "A

Program for a Just Society in a Free and Democratic Philippines," (Malina; United Democratic Opposition, n.d.); National Democratic Front, "Ten-Point Program of the National Democratic Front in the Philippines" (Oakland, CA: Union of the Democratic Filipinos and the International Association of Filipino Patriots, 1978).

58. Macapagal, pp. 30–37. For a fuller understanding of the Philippine situation in relation to the political and philosophical argument for participation as the linchpin of politics, see, L. E. J. Ruiz "Towards a Transformative Politics: A Quest for Authentic Political Subjecthood" (Ph.D. Dissertation, Princeton Theological Seminary, 1985).

59. Ruiz, pp. 37–53.

60. Trimberger, pp. 110–115; cf. Benjamin Barber, *Strong Democracy: Participatory Politics for a New Age* (Berkeley and Los Angeles: University of California Press, 1984).

61. See, for example, the insightful remarks of Unger on the relationship between the disintegration of community and the dominance of the "legal mentality" in *Knowledge and Politics,* pp. 72–76; cf. Marcos, *Democratic Revolution,* pp. 305–306.

62. Marcos, et al., p. 60; cf. Hobbes, *Leviathan,* p. 188.

63. Marcos, et al., pp. 61–62.

64. Jovito R. Salonga, "The Democratic Opposition and Its Vision of the Society Our People Want," speech at the Manila Rotary Club, Manila, October 9, 1980, p. 7.

65. Marcos, *Democratic Revolution,* p. 65.

66. For the philosophical argument for this claim, see Unger's *Knowledge and Politics* above and C. B. Macpherson's *The Theory of Possessive Individualism: Hobbes To Locke* (New York: Oxford University Press, 1962).

Part V

SPECIAL APPLICATIONS

17

The Role of Constitutionalism in the Transformation of Eastern European Societies

RADMILA NAKARADA

Life demonstrates the limits of our knowledge, the relativity of even undeniable values, the play of forces from the past that incomprehensibly undermine the intentions of the present. Just when we convince ourselves that some societies are hopelessly static, and irreversibly petrified, unprecedented changes and radical reforms are initiated. Just when we decide that a more rational direction of development is evolving, an unpredicted regression and involution occurs.

At one moment the character of the political system is the obstacle to change. At another an economic crisis is a grave hindrance to political democratization. We may assume that dramatic economic/political problems are directly and exclusively the result of an existing political system, only to find that after its radical dismantling the same problems are repeated. Some societies seem to be confronted with modernization problems, no matter which political system is in power. In other words, the matrix of social change is to a large extent a mystery of unexpected continuity, unpredictable consequences, disheartening paradoxes that do not fit existing theoretical codes. These ambivalences and paradoxes are reflected in the role constitutionalism played in the transformation of East European societies. Transformations from totalitarian authoritarianism to post-Communist societies reveal the unexpected powers and limitations of constitutionalism. In this paper the complex phenomenon of constitutionalism is primarily understood as the institutionalization of principles of liberty (human rights) and the control of state power by the people, that is, the establishment of the rule of law.

TOTALITARIANISM AND CONSTITUTIONALISM

The emancipatory potential hidden in the ambivalent nature of the constitutional order and its internal contradictions was difficult to perceive in the totalitarian phase. The party state had captured the whole of society, turned it into what appeared a monolithic entity. The rule of the party took the place of the rule of law. Constitutionalism was a voluntaristic force, and an instrument for control and subjugation of the individual in the interest of the party. If human rights were to become a determining constitutional principle, the precondition seemed to be the eradication of the system itself. Any idea of evolutionary change, which would, for instance, breathe life into rhetorical constitutional norms pertaining to human rights, was by and large considered an agonizing illusion.

The conception of these societies as unmoving, monolithic systems, thriving only on a combination of naked and subtle violence, collapse being the only viable form of "social transformation," was in its extreme form an oversimplification but not a complete misreading of reality.[1] The totalitarian description corresponded to a Stalinist phase of social development and some features of social life.[2] But it remained insensitive to evolutionary changes in the social reality of its pluralistic features. The once-dominant totalitarian theory itself proved to be petrified to just one image of these societies.

The discrepancy between the general principles of the Communist constitutions and the principles actually applied was self-evident, as were the internal inconsistencies of these constitutions. For instance, the East European constitutions, by and large, proclaimed some off the universal democratic norms ("all power belongs to the people") and individual rights (freedom of expression, thought, association), but in their elaboration severely limited or even suspended these norms. This was accomplished in accompanying articles of the same constitutions, or in articles of the penal code, in the name of protecting collective rights, defining obligations to the state, building communism. As an illustration, freedom of expression was severely restricted by Article 133 of the Yugoslav Penal Code dealing with hostile propaganda, and Article 190 of the Soviet Penal Code, dealing with slander. Furthermore, these restrictive articles were usually vague, allowing totally arbitrary interpretations. Under Article 62 of the Soviet

Penal Code, dealing with treason and espionage, many citizens have in fact become "prisoners of conscience."

However, one needs to recognize at the same time the evolution in the declining degree of discrepancy between the constitutional order and reality, the rule of law and its arbitrary implementation. The evolution is evident when one distinguishes the phase of total discrepancy, symbolized in the coexistence of universalistic, humanistic norms in the constitution and the Gulag system in reality, from partial discrepancy symbolized in constitutional guarantees of social rights under state tutorship, and severe restrictions of political rights.

Furthermore, the constitutional order, besides its obvious repressive function, contained ingredients later utilized in social transformations that led to the dismantling of the real socialist order. All Eastern European constitutions paid some tribute, albeit rhetorical, to universal, humanistic, libertarian principles of liberty, human rights, and rule of law: (1) the constitutional legitimatizing of the protagonists of democratic change, and (2) the initiating of substantial social changes by demanding the consistent implementation of these articles. Reality thus was to demonstrate the unexpected, theoretically ignored or underestimated, potential of constitutionalism in promoting the principles of conflicts, a certain degree of congruence between demands from above and from below occurred at a decisive moment before the collapse of the state-socialist system. Calls for irreproachable adherence to the constitutional rights and freedoms of citizens (Moscow Trust Group), the constitutional division of power and strict respect for the law (Soviet Communist Party, Polish Workers Party), establishing a truly legal state (Hungarian Socialist Workers Party, East German Peace and Human Rights Initiative) are representative of a chorus of demands coming from above and from below.[3]

Constitutionalism gained in credibility for several reasons: (1) the type of crisis these societies were confronted with; (2) the new type of social actors that surfaced; (3) general conscientization concerning the importance of human rights and the rule of law; (4) international pressure.

The acute economic crisis of the state-socialist societies was pervasive, permeating all spheres of social life. It was not part of the natural economic cycles of prosperity and recession, but threatened the very existence of these societies. The old Soviet formula for development was definitely exhausted. It was unable to secure the conditions for self-reproduction, nor to address the new challenges and imperatives of modern development. The crisis was simply unresolvable on the basis of statism and repressive collectivism. The particularly severe economic crisis endangered the dominant principle of social consensus, the authoritarian social compromise, that is, the satisfaction of some basic existential and social needs in exchange for relinquishing civic rights.

The existing political institutions were also in overt crisis, lacking legitimacy and efficacy. Being institutions of the Party and not the society, they were unable to rationally channel social energies, provide the means for articulating plural interests and creatively resolve social conflicts. The Party's old reformist formula, promoting limited changes only in the economic realm was in this situation obviously insufficient. Political democratization, constitutional reforms, and respect for human rights, all surfaced as unavoidable aspects of reformist attempts.

The second force contributing to the growing credibility of constitutionalism was the reemergence of the civil society. This was the result of a combination of factors. First, under the frozen surface, tradition and historic memory were actively surviving. In political captivity, an immensely transformed social and occupational class structure emerged, accompanied by the pluralization of interests and conflicts. In spite of the Iron Curtain, communication with the world was nevertheless established and nurtured.

Second, new social movements—parties, clubs, groups—appeared, with a persistence and influence (often far surpassing their numbers) that could not be neutralized by repression and media blockage. They promoted an alternative political culture, based on solidarity, individual responsibility, living in truth. As autonomous social forces, they were able to exert some control over the state apparatus, limiting its arbitrary interpretations of the law, breathing life into the unapplied constitutional articles pertaining to human rights, demanding the elimination of existing articles that undermined them, and seeking the introduction of new provisions that enlarged the scope of rights. Directing their efforts for political change to the sphere of law, constitutionalism, the civic initiatives and social movements contributed to the delegitimizing of the existing order, and gained far-reaching social credibility and political legitimacy as actors in nonviolent reform.

However, the novelty on the social scene was not only the new movements, groups, citizen associations, the forces of civil society, but a new type of reformer within the ruling elite. Among the Party reformers, unusual features become noticeable: elements of the self-limiting principle, initiation of political competition, demonopolization, support for democratic institutions, the establishment of control over the police and army, promotion of the rule of law.[4] The reason the Party reformers attached importance to constitutionalism and human rights was that they relied for their continued political existence on democratic revitalization. It was a means of countering and neutralizing the conservative, dogmatic factions within the establishment. By promoting political democratization and the rule of law, the reformist were gaining support from the social movements and a substantial number of intellectuals and workers, support that could not be easily erased by a conservative Party coup. Secondly, the constitutional promotion of human rights was their chance for renewed legitimation. However, the events in most East European countries proved far more radical, surpassing the intentions of the reformist elites, and in most countries removing them from the political scene.

Being universal values, human rights had their own self-propelling force. By this we mean that their renaissance in the East European countries was the result not only of a crisis of material deprivations but of social and cultural achievements. The crisis gave vent to the accumulated resentment against the negation of elemental human rights. But it also gave vent to the accumulated aspirations in this realm, which resulted from the development, refinement, and growth of people's needs more than political and general consciousness. These aspirations were a social pressure in themselves, independent of the crisis. In accordance with this, the struggle for the recognition of human rights was not only focused on the immediate, most acute political deprivations, but also took up the problems all modern nations are facing—ecology, peace, gender, youth.

The growing importance of constitutionalism evolved not only from the character of the internal crisis, the appearance of new actors, accumulated aspirations, but also from the linkage of internal and external problems. Behind the backs of hostile ideological systems, an interdependence had been created, that among other things, allowed for mutual influences and pressures. In the internal recognition of human rights, the international (external) factor gained unprecedented strength in East European societies.[5] Forms of pressure ranged from the political pressure of individual governments and nongovernmental organizations on the basis of the Helsinki accords, to economic pressure from supra-national institutions, like the European Community (EC), and the European Parliament. At one point, the EC cut off economic negotiations with Communist Romania because of the deplorable state of human rights in that country. These pressures had results because improvement in the realm of human rights had become a condition for receiving badly needed economic support and aid. At the same time, these pressures were an additional instrument for combating internally the conservative factions of the establishment.

The international factor was also activated from within, by all those who legitimately demanded the compliance of the national laws with the international human rights agreements, pacts, conventions, charters, that the states had signed.

THE POST-SOCIALIST CONSTITUTIONAL PARADOXES

The wind of change swept, albeit unevenly, through the East European societies. Governments were reformed or unpredictably easily toppled; new actors mounted to the stage of power. Political and economic pluralism exploded, demonstrating both the richness and the complexity of societies.

A feeling of confidence emerged. Radical improvements were finally within reach, once the despised order of lies and repression was eradicated. Coherence between the principles of liberty, the rule of law, and reality was ready to be established. Constitutional changes were initiated to codify the new era of democratization, both political (division of power, erasing the most outrageous articles of the Penal Code, free elections, freedom of the press) and economic (legitimatizing private property, providing for the free inflow of foreign capital). The elimination of lawlessness, arbitrariness, curtailment of political rights in the name of an "insane Utopia," was to be combined with economic efficiency and material prosperity, to ensure social progress. However, a new play of cunning forces speedily reached the scene of hope, the scene of democratization, transforming, dissolving into a multitude of old and new inconsistencies the goal of establishing the rule of law. New divisions between the rhetoric of law, respect for human rights, and reality were created.

In part, these divisions were the consequence of the inconsistent dedication of the principal political actors to the constitution of the democratic system, due to their authoritarian heritage and their overriding interest in gaining power. The rhetoric of human rights, the principles of liberty, the rule of law was, to a large extent, viewed as a short-term political designation, and not as long-term goals.

In part, the split was the result of the explosion of previously subdued regressive, conservative, militant social energies and of violent reactions to the ongoing and deepening economic crisis. The combination of militant nationalism and massive economic pauperization is known to be a poor basis for consolidating democracy and establishing the rule of law.

The relativization of the rule of law, constitutional promotion of human rights, has several forms.

(1) In a number of countries, primarily those with nationalist problems the former Soviet Union, Yugoslavia, Czechoslovakia—the arbitrary suspension of federal laws in particular republics has become a mode of gaining autonomy and expressing self determination, as in the case of the Baltic republics, the Russian Republic, Slovakia, and Slovenia. Concretely, in Slovenia twenty-seven federal laws dealing with vital matters of state regulation were suspended in 1991. The prerogatives of the Federal institutions are suspended, the decisions of the Federal Court are disregarded, the functioning of the Federal Parliament is obstructed, funds for the Federal Army are refused.

In national conflicts between federal units, direct anti-constitutional laws were introduced, resulting in economic war and formation of paramilitary forces. The very appearance of paramilitary forces was a serious anti-democratic symptom, leading to separate national armies and ethnic conflict. It is interesting to note as one of the curious inconsistencies that some of the ex-dissidents previously advocating peace, demilitarization, the right to conscientious objection to military service (CO), having come to power became ardent militarists, refusing to legalize the right to CO, and investing scarce economic resources in their military.

Most of the new rulers are unwilling to promote a broad political coalition, based on the participation of the principled opposition, democratic movements, and autonomous unions, in the search for answers to the deep social crisis. This type of political exclusivity combined with the presence of what J. Linz defines as the "disloyal opposition," opposition that as a rule resorts to the streets, contributes to the weakness of parliamentary institutions and the relativization of the rule of law.

(2) In a number of instances, constitutions were amended in such a way as to restrict the collective rights of minorities. This has been exemplified by restrictions on the public use of the Russian language in the Baltic republics, the language in this case that of a minority, while at the same time equality for their own language was sought on the level of the whole Soviet Union.[6] In Croatia, the new constitution erased the Serbs from the articles that had previously named them as a one of the two constituting nations of the Croat republic. Furthermore, their cultural autonomy, the use of their own alphabet, support for their cultural institutions were also restricted. In Slovenia, the non-Slovenian guest workers from the other Yugoslav republics, are not considered full-fledged Slovenian citizens, and their political rights, the right to take part in elections for instance, are curtailed. The draft of the new law regulating the procedure for acquiring Slovenian citizenship advocated the following preconditions: good health, a job and

residence, fluency in the Slovenian language, loyalty to the present government. All those who did not qualify, even if they have lived in Slovenia for decades, were to be expelled or treated as second-class citizens with limited political rights. In Serbia, the repressive reaction toward Albanian secessionism has resulted in the suspension of the cultural autonomy of the Albanian population. The Yugoslav federal government formed a special body to monitor human rights, stating that while the laws in this sphere had on the whole improved, the practice was again following its own arbitrary course, violating the rights of citizens and minorities.

Besides the national minorities, the social minorities, primarily women, are also under attack by the new "democratic government." As a part of a larger conservative wave, the right to abortion is questioned in almost all East European countries. Under heavy pressure by the Catholic Church, the Polish parliament has come closest to adopting an anti-abortion law.

The discrepancy between reality and proclaimed democratic principles and adherence to the rule of law also comes to light in the sphere of new cadre recruitment. Control of the media is, in spite of the rhetoric of competence, anti-censorship, pluralism of viewpoints, promoted with almost the same homogenizing brutality as in the previous regimes. In countries with intense national conflicts, the mass media is instrumentalized in a manner that is well-illustrated by the Yugoslav case. The Yugoslav Federal Assembly, at the outset of Civil War, according to their analysis, in the "media war" between the federal units, more than thirty international conventions and agreements recognized by Yugoslavia have been violated.

(3) Concerning the implementation of economic reform, and above all the transformation of ownership, i.e. privatization, a new set of violations is appearing, reflecting a corrupt coalition of old and new bureaucrats, with representatives of domestic and foreign capital. For example, East European Green movements have in several cases been able to reveal that a number of contracts with foreign firms have clandestine clauses that are ecologically detrimental. Recently in Belgrade a contract was to be signed with a U.S. pharmaceutical firm that included the obligation to carry out drug experiments in Yugoslavia that were forbidden in the United States itself.

Furthermore, domestic private owners of corporations, and banks willing to financially support the party in power are exempted from various taxes and custom regulations. The transformation of the social and state ownership itself is to a large extent carried out in a corrupt manner. Outrageously cheap price's for such property, simulation of contracts, mock shareholding has enabled a substantial number of ex-directors, ex-aparatchiks to become private owners of profitable firms, large property-holders overnight. Competing with this vicious type of privatization is the opposite trend, of nationalization of social property that is, for instance in Croatia, carried out in a more direct, stronger form than during the previous rule of the Communists.

The concept of human rights in the new regimes is in fact restricted to political rights, since there is a bitter disillusionment with the results of the socialist regimes in the sphere of consumption and economic standards. A passionate apology for the liberal economic model in its harshest version is promoted as the answer to the present catastrophe. Economic social rights are renounced in the name of new, costly promises of future betterment. In spite of the trend in Western Europe toward more social rights, the East Europeans are proceeding in the opposite direction. In a situation where democratization demands moderation in both politics and the economy, and a more even distribution of sacrifices and benefits in order to legitimize and secure authority for the new government, instead extremism, brutal polarization, and vicitimization are propounded. The epitome of this switch is Lech Walensa; the legendary union leader is now forced to promote the IMF principle of harnessing cheap labor.

Furthermore, economic rights, in terms of participation of workers and unions in shaping and carrying out the reforms, are suppressed. Some of the rights that previously had at least a normative legitimacy, even though they were not implemented, are now delegitimized conceptually in the name of efficiency, productivity, etc. What is evolving more and more is in fact a model of transformation that is based on the problematic assumption that political democratization and economic authoritarianism can be successfully combined, to lead in time to the implementation of the principles of liberty and material prosperity. In other words, the initial substantial deficiency in understanding human rights is revealed in the rudimentary, inconsistent democratization that is taking place.

(4) Another form of inconsistency and regression stems from the strong wave of nationalism that is suppressing the individual citizen in the name of an ethnic collectivity. It is again delegitimizing the principle of pluralism in the name of national homogenization, and revitalizing the principle of loyalty as the supreme principle of social life. The principle of political loyalty to the rulers and a consistent respect for citizen rights are inevitably at odds with each other. The change of political label does not alter this, as political purges in Yugoslavia (for example, of Serbs in Croatia) and the Soviet Union (for example, in Georgia) have demonstrated.

(5) A particularly strong contributing factor in relativizating constitutionalism and the rule of law is the new international order. With the end of Cold War, the internal collapse of the Soviet Union and its

divided presence in the international arena, the global hegemonic aspirations of the remaining superpower have openly appeared. Uncontested as a military power, the United States has inaugurated a new era of interventionism. In accordance with its self-appointed role of global policeman, it is making its presence felt in the Eastern European turmoil. This has become, in countries with the most acute crisis, the former Soviet Union and Yugoslavia, an additional factor of disintegration, arbitrariness, and unlawfulness.

Double standards are widely applied in reacting to internal conflicts, disrupting processes of democratization, peaceful resolution of conflicts. False distinctions are made between "democrats" (for example Croat leader) and "communists" (Serb leader) in spite of the fact that both are authoritarian. The authoritarian features of the so called democrat are amnested only because his regime is an obedient *satellite.* Self-determination is recognized as a right for some nations, for others it is contested. Secession is celebrated as national liberation in Eastern Europe while similar tendencies (in Scotland for example) are labeled as vandalism (D. Herd). The violation of the rights of one ethnic group (Serbs in Croatia) are overlooked, while the violation of others (Albanians in Serbia) are overdramatized. Territorial integrity of a country (Yugoslavia) is relativized, while the integrity of one of its federal units (Bosnia) is absolutized in spite of the fact that three ethnic groups live there. Crucial international norms are disregarded to satisfy the dominant political will. The rule of law is substituted for the rule of interest.

It is ironic that in the previous phase the pressure from outside, although it reflected a double standard, did contribute to legitimatizing human rights and the democratization of the repressive political order. But now rhetorical support for democratization and gestures of desintegrative character are by and large counter-productive.

A much-needed condition for democratic consolidation is some degree of economic efficacy, signs of betterment that can prevent the pending social explosions, give credibility and authority to the government. Economic support from the West is lacking, and this contributes to the general disenchantment with the new democratic order, and strengthens nationalist and authoritarian tendencies.

A particular feature that intervenes in the same direction as well, is the inconsistent, irrational, blind attitude of some of the new East European statesmen, in particularly those who were previously dissidents, human rights and peace champions, toward the new international reality. They speak of NATO as an institution of true democracy; they are eager to become part of it; they supported the Gulf War; they articulate old territorial pretensions (for example the

Bulgarian statements concerning Macedonia), they seek regional hegemony, they give new energy to militarization, conflict, imbalance, lack of solidarity. Such a spirit is inconsistent with the long march to democracy that is a common task of these societies.

Within large parts of Eastern Europe an overload of the system has been created by the almost uncorrectable defects from the past, explosions of regressive nationalistic energies, emergence of a desintegrative type of pluralism, incompetent and authoritarian elites, uncontrollable economic crisis, and the intervention of open hegemonic aspirations of the triumphant superpower. This is eroding the constitutional promotion of human rights and the consistent rule of law based on the principles of liberty. Many of the new inconsistencies, actors and principles, unhappily, resemble the old. However, the next act of the drama threatens to increase violence and instability and thus challenges the present strategies of social transition to democratization, as well as the present understanding of human rights.

In rethinking the future role of constitutionalism, one should avoid two illusions: underestimating its role, as well as overestimating its importance. The power of constitutionalism, as the current changes in Eastern Europe demonstrate, is deeply intertwined with the social, economic, and national tissues of society, and with the nature of the decisive political actors, as well as with the process of global democratization. This will in the future demand the reaffirmation of the strategy for global constitutionalism as part of an answer to the present inconsistencies, hegemonic aspirations, and dramatic transitional failures.

NOTES

1. For a developed critique of the totalitarian theory, see S. Cohen, *Rethinking the Soviet Experience* (N.Y.: Oxford University Press, 1980).

2. The classical analyses of the totalitarian order presented by Hannah Arendt no longer describes our situation accurately; it applies only to state institutions themselves. The Polish system consists of [a] totalitarian state coexisting with a society which cannot be controlled through totalitarian methods. The state wants to exercise totalitarian power, but is unable to do so. It is forced to compromise with life. . . .

An interview with Adam Michnik, "Towards a New Democratic Compromise," *East European Reporter,* 3, no. 2 (1988): 27.

3. "Moscow Trust Group News," *Ukrainian Peace News,* 1, no 3/4 (1987): 8; Resolution of the 19th Conference of the CP of SU in

Politika (Belgrade), July 1988, p. 3; the position of PURP is quoted by N. Burzan, "Polish Totalitarian Society Is Becoming a Civil Society," *Borba*, May, 6/7 1989, p. 3; on the Hungarian Socialist Workers Party, see D. Rancic, "Multiparty Pluralism," *Politika*, Feb. 3, 1989, p. 4; "A Way out of Crisis," statement of the Interim Council of the Network of Free Initiative, May 1988, in *Eastern European Reporter*, no. 3 (1988); 55.

4. To illustrate this: PURP has been the first Communist Party in history to voluntarily renounce its power monopoly. The Hungarian party followed.

5. There was of course, a degree of hypocrisy present in Western pressure, that is, the double standard is evident where the oppressive regimes in South Africa, Central America, and Asia are concerned.

6. Another example of inconsistency was the demand of the Baltic republics for economic autonomy with the expectation at the same time that the Soviet Gosplan would secure for them all necessary raw materials.

18

Human Obligation and Global Accountability: From the Impeachment of Warren Hastings to the Legacy of Nurenberg

ALI A. MAZRUI

Two interrelated processes in world history have profoundly affected the fate of human rights and their emergence as a world order issue. One process was Europe's territorial expansion, from Christopher Columbus and Vasco da Gama to the scramble for Africa. The other process was the development of international accountability in upholding human rights. This second process unfolded from the impeachment of the eighteenth-century British imperial administrator, Warren Hastings, to the Nuremberg trials of Nazi leaders after World War II.

These two processes, of territorial expansion and international moral accountability, were interlinked. Europe's territorial appetite and material greed sealed the fate of the Americas as settler colonies. European expansionism also subjugated India, Africa, and much of the rest of the world. Yet that very internationalization helped to shape new rules of conduct, and laid down the principles of wider international accountability.

As human symbols of Europe's territorial expansion we have chosen Christopher Columbus, who helped open the New World, Warren Hastings, who pioneered the British penetration of India, and Otto von Bismarck, the German statesman who hosted the European imperial conference of Berlin in 1884–1885. As symbols of the evolution of international accountability we have the impeachment of Warren Hastings (1788–1795) in the British House of Lords, on the one side, and on the other, the Nuremberg trials (1945–1946) of German Nazis after World War II.

COLUMBUS AND AFRICA: A DIALECTIC

If Christopher Columbus in 1492 helped to open the gates to the colonization of the New World, Otto von Bismarck in 1885 helped to open the way to European control of Africa. The voyages of Columbus in the late fifteenth century put before Europe a whole new world to colonize. The diplomacy of Bismarck in the late nineteenth century helped present to Europe a whole new continent to conquer. Four centuries separated Columbus from Bismarck—but both the European "discovery" of the Americas and the European "scramble" for Africa had enormous consequences for the Black race and for human rights.

One product of the legacy of Columbus is of course the United States of America. Black America is part of that product, with all its significance in the history of suffering. What is not often realized is that the triumph of Columbus was itself partly a product of Africa's impact on maritime history: Africa helped to produce Columbus, and Columbus in turn helped to produce the United States and Black America.

If you asked what urged Christopher Columbus to turn westward in search of a sea-route to Asia, my answer would be "Africa"—that's what compelled him to look to the west in his quest for the Orient. What do I mean?

Africa's earliest impact on world history was simply by being there—a huge land mass with the Atlantic on one side and the Indian Ocean on the other, a vast island which refused to be bypassed or easily circumnavigated. It was a stubborn impediment to Europe's search for a sea-route to India and China. Europe was getting desperate.

Columbus himself had his apprenticeship in the rough waters off North-west Africa. From the Madeira Islands he acquired sailing experience and may have got as far south along Africa's coast as the Portuguese trading post of Mina on the Gold Coast.

Had Africa been easier to circumnavigate, Europe's interest in going west could have been delayed for another hundred and fifty years or more. For one thing, the later the Americas were discovered, the less extensive would have been Spain's and Portugal's share of it. "Latin" America might not have existed at all had the Americas been "discovered" after the decline of Spain and Portugal. By speeding up the discovery of the Americas, Africa may have spared the world an even larger British Empire than in fact emerged. Africa has denied the world an English-speaking Central America.

The Americas as we know them were thus born out of Europe's desperation. Asia was the lure, Africa had been the decisive historical obstacle, and the diverse New World of today accidentally became the prize, culturally more varied than it would have been had it been discovered by an Anglo-Saxon equivalent of Christopher Columbus a century-and-a-half later. On the other hand, a later discovery of the Americas by Europeans could have reduced the scale of genocide perpetrated against the native Americans.

There developed other contradictions in Africa's relations with the New World. While Africa's location had pushed Columbus into "discovering" the Americas, the Americas in turn had their revenge on Africa. The Western Hemisphere developed an enormous appetite for African slaves. Millions were transported from the "Dark Continent" that had originally forced the New World to be "found" in the first place. A major African presence was established in the Americas, but a presence throbbing with pain.

The drama was by no means over yet. Africa had all along been geographically central in the world. It is the only continent cut almost in half by the equator. It is the only continent traversed by both the Tropic of Cancer and the Tropic of Capricorn. At least geographically, Africa is the middle continent.

But the slave trade inaugurated the process of Africa's political marginalization. The continent became almost powerless in global terms, and was easy prey to colonization and further exploitation. This most central of all continents was pushed to the fringes of world affairs.

On the other hand, a reverse process was taking place in the New World. The Americas started off as both geographically on the fringes of Old World contact, and politically peripheral to its development. Today the New World is still distant from the main concentrations of human populations. Some eighty percent of the human race live in Asia, Africa, and Europe—thousands of miles away from the Americas. Geographically and demographically, the New World is still on the fringes. But thanks partly to the Europeans for whom Columbus had blazed the trail, and partly to the African labor that came with slavery, North America by the middle of the twentieth century had become politically central in world affairs.

Africa and the United States had become mirror opposites. Africa was locationally central but politically marginal; the United States was locationally marginal but politically central. In the mirror the left is the right and the right is the left. In the reflection of world power, what is peripheral about Africa is central about America—and vice versa.

That particular disparity in power was worse than ever by the 1980s. The Reagan-Bush years were, by coincidence, a kind of centenary celebration of the years of Bismarck's high diplomacy. The history of the Black experience had become a transition from the imperial politics of 1880s to the hegemonic policies of the North America of Reagan and Bush in the last decades of the twentieth century.

But the impact of the United States on the world was much older than the administrations of its fortieth and forty-first presidents. The American war of independence had reverberations across the globe. When the news reached India in 1778 that General John Burgoyne of Britain had surrendered the previous year in Saratoga, North America, Warren Hastings wrote:

> If it really be true that the British arms and influence have suffered so severe a check in the Western world, it is the more incumbent upon those who are charged with the interest of Great Britain in the East to exert themselves for the retrieval of the national honour.[1]

America's independence helped to seal the fate of India's sovereignty for the worse. In a sense, Calcutta served as Great Britain's historical compensation for the humiliation at Saratoga. And Warren Hastings was part and parcel of the Indian side of this British equation. The expansion of British power in the East was a way of compensating for the decline of British hegemony in the western hemisphere.

THE RAJ IN THE MAKING

Born in 1732 in Oxfordshire, Warren Hastings went to India at the age of 17 as a junior employee of the British East India Company, one of the earliest multinational corporations of the Western world. In 1771, Hastings was put in charge of British East India Company affairs in Bengal as Governor. From 1772 to 1785, Warren Hastings dominated Indian affairs. His was the longest and most eventful governorship of British India. Some would describe Hastings as the virtual co-founder of British India—and perhaps the greatest of the British rulers in India. He brought the Indian government in Bengal directly under British control, with himself first as Governor and then as Governor-General. He got involved in political rivalries within the Company and in British politics, becoming more controversial at home. From 1774 to 1784, he also embarked on a number of expensive wars in India, which interfered with trade. Hastings' reputation in Britain was damaged. He returned to England in 1785. Three years later he faced impeachment, prosecution by the House of Commons before the House of Lords.

What were his offenses? On what issues was Hastings being held accountable? The offenses included extortion, including the requisitioning of the treasures of the mother and grandmother (Begums) of the Vizier of Oudh in India. Hastings was also accused of complicity in judicial murder in Bengal. The seeds of international accountability for violation of human rights were being sown, as Edmund Burke led the prosecution before the House of Lords. An idea was being born, a concept later to mature into the Nuremberg trials some one hundred and fifty years later.

It was in February, 1788, that the seven-year impeachment proceedings against Warren Hastings began. Broadly, three types of rights were involved in the impeachment of Warren Hastings, although they were not framed in precisely these terms. They were:

(a) the juridical rights of states,
(b) the collective rights of groups and races, and
(c) the individual rights of persons.

Hastings was accused of violating the rights of Indian states and principalities. He was accused of violating the rights of such groups as the Afghan Rohillas tribe by hiring out British troops to the Nawab of Oudh. Hastings was also accused of violating the rights of individual Indians by extortion and corruption.

In the fate of Raja Nandakumar (Nuncumar), perhaps all three rights were involved. Nandakumar had accused Hastings of bribery in 1775; Hastings accused him, in turn, of conspiracy. Then Nandakumar was accused of forgery by another Indian. On the issue of forgery, Indian law and custom were more humane and less barbaric than the imported English law, but English law prevailed. He was tried by a Court headed by Sir Elijah Impey, Hastings' contemporary at Westminster. On the charge of forgery, Nandakumar was sentenced to death. Execution for forgery was virtually unknown to Indian society. It was a barbaric punishment imposed by a foreign power. To that extent, it violated the rights of the cultural group to which Nandakumar belonged. And the whole British presence was in turn a violation of the juridical rights of Indian states and principalities. Hastings refused to commute the sentence. Nandakumar was executed. Did Hastings conspire with Sir Elijah Impey to condemn Nandakumar? Or did Hastings simply let his vendetta against the Indian go to the extent of refusing to reprieve him?

The events of the 1770s in India took place against the background of another major convulsion thousands of miles away, the American War of Independence. Today, the United States and India are the two largest democracies once ruled by Britain, and both were destined in the fullness of time to overshadow Britain in world politics.

Warren Hastings saw himself as the redeemer of Britain's national honor. As Britain lost her Western empire, she proceeded to build her Eastern empire. As indicated earlier, North America's independence helped to seal the fate of India's. Hastings did indeed see India as compensation for the humiliation of Saratoga.

After seven long years of impeachment, Hastings was acquitted of all charges. But he could no longer hold public office and was in other ways more dishonored for his great lapses of conduct than rewarded for his great acts of patriotism. Edmund Burke, the great Anglo-Irish thinker, was probably sincere in his outrage. He rejected Hastings' relativist argument that acts judged wrong in Britain could be all right in India. Burke retorted, "This geographical morality we do protest against. . . . "

Burke elaborated as follows:

> [Mr. Hastings] has told your Lordships, in his defence, that actions in Asia do not bear the same moral qualities which the same actions would bear in Europe. . . . These gentlemen have formed a plan of *geographical morality* . . . as if, when you have crossed the equinoctial, all the virtues die, as they say some insects die when they cross the line. . . . We think it necessary, in justification of ourselves, to declare that the laws of morality are the same everywhere, and that there is no action which would pass for an act of extortion, of peculation, of bribery, and of oppression in England, that is not an act of extortion, of peculation, of bribery, and of oppression in Europe, Asia, Africa, and all the world over.[2]

Burke's position was itself somewhat eclectic. He combined moral universalism with cultural relativism. He was enraged by Hastings' apparent insensitivity to the special moral sensibilities of Indians. Yet Hastings himself in turn was a strange mixture.

The man who sometimes violated Indian culture and custom also helped to promote a new legal system based on Hindu law by encouraging special translations from Hindu lawbooks and by encouraging the study of Sanskrit by European scholars. (Hastings himself knew Persian, Bengali, Urdu, and some Arabic.) He encouraged the founding of the Asiatic Society of Bengal in 1784, and founded a college of Arabic studies in 1781.

But Edmund Burke felt that power was a divine trust, and Hastings had abused that power. In many ways, it was the profoundly conservative Edmund Burke who was ahead of his time in the views that emerged in the course of the impeachment. The concept of imperial power as a trust had conditioned both Burke's view about America and his views of India. He defended the American colonies: They had a good case but bad arguments; theirs were not the rights of man but the rights of Englishmen. In India, the rights of the natives were not human rights either—they were the rights of Indians in the light of their own customs and civilizations.

Burke was in many ways a prophet of self-determination guided by a sense of history. "Men will never look forward to prosperity who never look backward to their ancestors," he had once said.[3] He was more sensitive to the collective rights of groups and peoples than to individual rights of persons. He defended Bengalis, Afghans, French Canadians, the Irish, and others. He attacked the French Revolution, but mainly because he thought the French revolutionaries displayed collective amnesia, a loss of memory as to who the French were in history.

The Burkean legacy of power as an imperial trust greatly conditioned the future course of British policies in the colonies. Lord Lugard's doctrine of indirect rule in Africa was in part descended from the impeachment of Warren Hastings: "If you have to rule other societies, try to respect their cultures as far as possible, and rule them through institutions they understand."[4] This was Lugard's guiding principle.

But perhaps the most farsighted aspect of Burke's ideas is only beginning to emerge now. He felt that what we would today call "multinational corporations" should be subject to a code of conduct based on triple accountability:

(a) accountability to the host societies in which they operate;
(b) accountability to the rules laid down by the companies' own country of origin;
(c) accountability to a higher standard of equity, propriety, and justice.

Thus the impeachment of Warren Hastings was in part the trial of a multi-national corporation, the British East India Company.

The quest for triple accountability continues. Perhaps unlike many capitalists today, Edmund Burke realized that human rights could be violated by companies as much as by states, by nongovernmental forces as much as by governments. The United Nations today is still groping for a code of conduct to control transnational corporations. Of Edmund Burke, it may therefore be said, "He was a man of the day before yesterday and a man of the day after tomorrow."

In the years that followed Hastings' impeachment, economic imperialism entered a new phase. And yet the expansion of the British Empire coincided with new levels of British accountability. The campaigns to abolish first the slave trade and later slavery itself were new stages in the history of imperial ethics. Those who were colonized were eventually protected from outright enslavement. The mighty were beginning to be morally answerable.

FROM BISMARCK TO THE THIRD REICH

But while the legacy of the impeachment of Warren Hastings did make Western imperialism more constrained by ethics, this did not leave it more restricted geographically. European domination of other societies was beginning to have rules of self-restraint. But Europe's territorial appetite went still unabated.

This brings us to the German statesman who hosted the Berlin Conference of 1884–1885. The conference was itself designed to help European powers agree on the rules of their own competitive scramble for Africa. The presiding presence was Otto von Bismarck; the venue was the city that was one day to be the headquarters of Nazi Germany. Perhaps the events that would be put on trial in Nuremberg in 1945 had their origins in the imperial conference in Berlin in 1885, which openly conspired to partition Africa among the European powers. In the words of the nineteenth-century novelist, Charles Dickens: "Think for a moment of the long chain of iron or gold, of thorns or flowers which would never have bound you but for the formation of the first link on one memorable day."[5]

Did the long chain of European fascism have its first link in European imperialism? Was the Berlin that was the headquarters of Nazi Germany in the 1940s descended from the Berlin as the host of European colonial regimes in the 1880s? Was Bismarck as a nineteenth-century unifier of Germany a precursor of Hitler as a twentieth-century empire builder?

Prince Otto von Bismarck lived from 1815 to 1898. To his "credit" were three European wars that helped foster German unification, wars with Denmark (1864), Austria (Seven Week's War, 1866), and France (1870). He was made Prince von Bismarck and appointed Chancellor of the German Empire in 1871. He governed the German Empire from then until 1890. Bismarck united the Germans and helped to divide Africa. Bismarck promoted basic human needs for Germans and helped to violate basic human rights for Africans. He was responsible for introducing state insurance in his country: for sickness in 1883, for accident in 1884, and for old age in 1889. He was an innovator in the history of the welfare state and of the satisfaction of at least some basic human requirements. It has been suggested that:

> These measures of state socialism appear now as precursors of the modern welfare state. . . . Despite this policy, Bismarck was opposed to any regulation of working hours or working conditions.

The architect of the welfare state was also the designer of Imperial Germany. In 1889, Bismarck declared, "I am not a colonial man." But he brought Germany closer to a colonial role than any other modern figure, with the exception of Adolf Hitler.

In 1884, Bismarck quarrelled with Britain and within the course of a single year obtained the Cameroons, South-West Africa, East Africa (Tanganyika, Rwanda, and Burundi), and part of New Guinea.

It has been argued that,

> The tragedy of Bismarck's career was that he himself created in united Germany the monarcho-military power which first overthrew him and then in the fateful years of 1914–1918 destroyed his empire.

As Gladstone said of Bismarck: "He made Germany great and Germans small."[6]

In the history of the conflict between human needs and human rights one could do worse than choose the period from Bismarck to Hitler. To some degree, this gives us half a century of Western ambition.

Another reason for linking Bismarck and Hitler is in the dialectic between welfare and warfare. Bismarck was a titled aristocrat, a Junker who had entered statecraft and the arena of politics. Such a background could afford the magnanimity of *noblesse oblige*—readiness to be generous but not necessarily humble. One result was the German welfare state.

Hitler, on the other hand, was not a natural aristocrat. There was little *noblesse oblige* among his supporters. Insensitivity to basic human needs was their hallmark. So, while Bismarck's Germany was decidedly innovative in social welfare, Hitler's Germany became socially retrogressive. Among Hitler's casualties as he constructed a war machine were millions of lives. But his militaristic politics also sacrificed such German achievements as:

meals for school children;
subsidies for urban renewal;

benefits for the blind and disabled;
charity for the poor;
social security for children whose parents had died;
compensation for the unemployed;
subsidies for the non-Nazi arts and humanities;
subsidies for denominational schools;
support for higher education

Bismarck combined the welfare state with the warfare state. His Germany linked social legislation with military discipline. The country provided bread for the poor and arms for the warrior. Hitler's Germany, on the other hand, glorified the warfare state and left the welfare state bleeding. Human rights were violated; basic human needs were increasingly denied. The shadow of the swastika became the shadow of death. Genocide was at hand.

RECKONING AT NUREMBERG

At the end of World War II the principle of international accountability was once again invoked. A tribunal was set up, under the signature of the victorious powers (Britain, the United States, the Soviet Union, and France). The charges were numerous crimes against peace, against humanity, and in violation of conventional rules of war. The accused were specific Nazi personalities and specific Nazi institutions like the Gestapo and the Nazi Secret Police.

The great trial began in that old city of Bismarck and of the Imperial Conference on Africa of 1884–1885. But in 1945 the presiding personality in Berlin was not a Prussian statesman but a Russian general, I. T. Nikitchenko.

In November, 1945, the tribunal moved from Berlin to Nuremberg, and the Presidency passed to the British member of the tribunal, Lord Justice Sir Geoffrey Lawrence. The trial was conducted in four languages—an improvement on the single language of the impeachment of Warren Hastings. But from the global perspective of a world war it was perhaps unfortunate that all the four Nuremberg languages were European—English, French, German, and Russian. From the perspective of crimes against humanity, it would perhaps have been fitting to add either Hebrew or Yiddish as the fifth language at Nuremberg.

From the point of view of world culture, the subsequent trial of Japanese war leaders (1946–1948) was more representative. It is true that the Tokyo trial recognized only two languages instead of the four at Nuremberg. But the fact that the two languages at Tokyo were Japanese as well as English helped to break the mould of Eurocentrism.

Even more significant was the fact that the tribunal of the Tokyo trials included justices from India, China and the Philippines, as well as European and American judges. Judge Delfin Jaranilla of the Philippines filed a separate concurring opinion at the conclusion of the trial. And Judge R. M. Pal of India dissented generally from the majority opinion. The trend towards wider global accountability as a principle took one more step forward at the Tokyo trials.

The nature of accountability at the Tokyo trials made more allowances than at Nuremberg for what might be called "juniority" (as opposed to seniority). Being junior in a chain of command could be a mitigating circumstance by the rules of Tokyo, and to have been obeying orders could mitigate the punishment. Legal minds in the two tribunals of Nuremberg and Tokyo were still grappling with the age-old philosophical problem of the limits of political obligation.

At Nuremberg, three of the individual defendants were acquitted; 12 received the death sentence by hanging, three were to be imprisoned for life, and four got lesser prison sentences. The decision was unanimous, although General Nikitchenko would have preferred the death sentence instead of life imprisonment for Rudolf Hess.

The Soviet member of the tribunal was also more logical than his Western counterparts in defining the boundaries of accountability. General Nikitchenko wanted the Reich cabinet itself to be declared a criminal organization, and not just the Gestapo and Secret Police created by the German Cabinet. The Soviet member was also eager to have the Nazi High Command of the German armed forces declared criminal, but the Western members disagreed. The logic of ultimate responsibility was perhaps on the side of Soviet reasoning.

At the Tokyo trials, seven defendants were sentenced to death by hanging, sixteen to life imprisonment, and two to lesser terms. Two of the defendants died in the course of the trial, and one was declared unfit to plead.

The trials that followed World War II have themselves been on trial on moral grounds from the outset. Were human beings being punished for acts that were not criminal at the time they were committed? Ex-post facto accountability has been of serious ethical concern all along.

Could the vanquished have a fair trial at the hands of the victors? Although the learned judges displayed more fairness than many of their critics had expected, it is still a matter of regret that the Nuremberg trials did not include justices from neutral nations.

Since the victors also committed war crimes, and perhaps even crimes against humanity, the moral credibility of the Nuremberg trials was to some extent compromised by failing to level charges against the victors. Much of the brutal allied bombing of Hiroshima, Nagasaki, Dresden, Hamburg, or even Berlin and Tokyo would have qualified as both war crimes and crimes against humanity had the Allies not been the sole definers of what constituted such "crimes".

But progress was made at Nuremberg and Tokyo toward a world of greater legal as well as ethical accountability. Precedents were set which may contribute towards even higher standards of political and moral conduct. As Justice Robert H. Jackson, the American member of the Nuremberg tribunal, said in his report to President Harry S. Truman:

> One of the chief obstacles to this trial was the lack of a beaten path. A judgment such as has been rendered shifts the power of the precedent to the support of these rules of law.[7]

But the very importance of Justice Jackson at the Nuremberg trials signified a double shift that was taking place in the world. Nazi Germany had not only failed to become the ultimate superpower in the world. It had helped to confirm the United States as the alternative superpower of the post-war years. The United States emerged as the mightiest nation in the world. But Washington also saw itself as a kind of global policeman or sheriff, holding the rest of the human race to a code of accountability.

THE UNITED STATES: SHERIFF ON TRIAL

But the best illustration that there is no room for moral complacency lies in the behaviour of the United States. The self-appointed custodian of the conscience of the world has vindicated Lord Acton's conviction that power does indeed corrupt. The war in Vietnam was the most dramatic illustration of this. Both war crimes and crimes against humanity were perpetrated in the American crusade against communism. The list includes the American use of napalm bombs, the Agent Orange impact on foodcrops, the ruthless bombing of Hanoi and Cambodia, the mining of Haiphong Harbor, the undeclared war on the people of Vietnam as a whole—the entire litany of American violations of the spirit of Nuremberg during the Vietnam War.

And yet American society at home did not take it lying down. The war was the most unpopular in the history of the republic. A new domestic principle evolved during the demonstrations on American campuses and in American streets. Warfare itself was getting democratized as the demonstrators insisted on the principle of "warfare by consent."

However, the moral principle of accountability was still struggling for acceptance, as the legacies of Columbus and Hastings converged in the role of the United States. Geographical expansion and moral accountability continued to be part of the dynamic of Western hegemony.

Can the United States be a credible trustee of Nuremberg and the Rule of Law if in the 1980s Washington could violate international law in instances like the following?:

1. aggressively mine the harbors of Nicaragua;
2. summarily reject the jurisdiction of the International Court of Justice, on the matter of Nicaragua's security;
3. impose a trade embargo on Nicaragua in defiance of a World Court Order;
4. violate a 1958 Treaty of Friendship, Commerce, and Navigation between the United States and Nicaragua;
5. skyjack an Egyptian civilian aircraft in pursuit of Palestinian suspects in the *Achille Lauro* killings;
6. deliberately violate Italy's territorial jurisdiction and airspace on the same issue;
7. bomb the Libyan cities of Tripoli and Benghazi for acts for which it now appears that Libya was not responsible;
8. invade the small island of Grenada;
9. violate United Nations Charter obligations on payment of dues, and seek to expel or close down the mission of the Palestine Liberation Organization to the United Nations in clear violation of international treaties that the United States has ratified;
10. refuse a visa to Yasir Arafat to address the UN General Assembly in violation of the United State's 1947 legal obligations as host country to the UN.

An American international lawyer, Burns Weston, has asked,

> If we say to the Secretary of State, the CIA, and the National Security Council that it's O.K. to bend the law because we don't like another country's ideology, can we rightfully expect that the Attorney General or the FBI will not [also] bend the law a little . . . ? . . . Can we legitimately expect to separate the standards that govern the way our government operates internationally from those that govern it internally?[8] Can the US be a democracy at home and a bandit abroad?

In addition to the Nuremberg trials, the Second World War gave birth to the United Nations system. The United States has gotten less interested in the United Nations precisely as the world body has become more representative of the world community. The United States has pulled out of UNESCO, played havoc by withholding UNESCO and other UN dues, put pressure on other UN agencies, sabotaged Africa's chances of providing a Secretary General of the UN. How can the United States be a leader in democratic accountability when it does not respect majority opinion in the evolving parliamentary institutions of mankind?

In Africa the most basic contribution the United States can make to African democracy is respect for the principle of self-determination. Wasn't making the independence of Namibia dependent on the withdrawal of Cuban troops from Angola a denial of self-determination?

Chester Crocker, U.S. Assistant Secretary of State for African Affairs under Reagan, is on record as having said, "We have no intention of waging economic warfare on South Africa and its people. On the contrary, we firmly believe that economic growth has been—and will continue to be—a principal engine of constructive change in all fields in that country."[9]

If economic warfare is wrong when waged against South Africa, why did the Reagan Administration wage it against Nicaragua and Panama? On the other hand, if it makes sense for the United States to lend direct support to Union for the Total National Liberation and Independence of Angola (whose Portuguese acronym is UNITA) in its fight for control in Angola, why has it *not* made sense for the United States to contribute money to the African National Congress in the fight for democracy in South Africa? How about the role of the world in promoting democracy in the United States? Is there an African role in promoting accountability in the United States?

Could the United States ask Britain to liberate its Black colonies without liberating its own American Blacks? Anti-colonial movements in Africa and the Civil Rights Movement in the United States were part of the same process of democratizing the Western world. Liberated Africa made segregated America increasingly anachronistic. U.S. democracy was still being painfully purged of its historic racist accompaniment as history marked the centenary of the imperial Berlin Conference. And yet the Reagan-Bush years still succeeded in pushing the imperial clock back a little.[10]

When we look at a Black man or Black woman, we are looking at somebody the origins of whose exploitation go back not only to the world before Ronald Reagan but also to the world before Bismarck.

What is the equilibrium between the West and the Black world across the centuries? How accountable is the West?

In terms of basic human needs, Reagan's apparent determination to dismantle the American welfare state had implications for American Blacks as well as for Africans. We were beginning to witness the reduction of unemployment benefits and free lunches for children, the elimination of aspects of Medicaid and Medicare, and curtailment of aspects of social security and old age protection as well as legal services and legal protection for the aged and the poor. Poverty is lack of power.

On the other hand, Reagan's reconstruction of the warfare state meant an enhancement of the war budget (the greatest in peacetime), greater support for such military-oriented regimes as the one in El Salvador, elaboration of ideas like the Rapid Deployment Force, and warfare disguised as welfare in such schemes as: (a) aid to Zaire (least needy); (b) aid to Kenya (median needy); and (c) aid to Somalia (most needy).

Blacks in the United States are caught between warfare and welfare. Zbigniew Brzezinski once talked about encouraging Blacks to enter the armed forces in larger numbers.[11] Was this a case of treating them as cannon fodder? Or was it a case of encouraging Black participation in the military-industrial complex? Eisenhower warned America about the military industrial complex. It is conceivable that Black entry there will be through the military rather than the industrial part of that complex. Black empowerment could be through Black militarization.

But there is also the impact of the American warfare/welfare dilemma upon Africa. Development aid is a child of the ideology of the welfare state, but internationalized. Aid is a modest response to economic accountability within the world system.

Reagan's reduction of foreign aid has hit some African countries hard. But some African countries did receive welfare aid for warfare reasons. Strategically important African countries like Kenya and Zaire did benefit from the security paradigm. In North Africa, Egypt had by far the lion's share of American's largesse for Africa. Aid ceased to be a moral response to economic accountability. It had become merely a strategic expense for the United States.

Ironically, Reagan's policy for Africa and China's African policy emerged as twin sisters—both were so obsessed with relations with the Soviet Union that their African policies became mere derivatives of their Soviet policies. Responding to moral accountability was at best subsidiary.

A CENTURY OF EXPLOITATION

But the puzzle persists: Why should we pronounce Prince Otto von Bismarck in the same breath as Ronald Reagan? Our argument is once again summarized:

First, in the juxtaposition a hundred years of Africa's relations with the West are consummated. The Conference of Berlin of the 1880s sought to establish the rules for the colonization of Africa. The end of Reagan's eight years in office became a dubious centenary celebration of the scramble for Africa in the 1980s.

Second, the 1880s witnessed the colonization of Namibia under Bismarck. The 1980s have witnessed the struggle for the liberation of Namibia partly under the ambiguous auspices of Reagan and Crocker for "constructive engagement."

Third, Reagan emasculated the welfare state for the warfare state. Bismarck had invented the welfare state without relinquishing the warfare imperative.

In the early 1880s, this Prussian prince exercised power over the German nation. In the early 1980s, a Californian film star exercised power over the American nation. One was a case of *noblesse oblige.* The other was a case of *nouveau richesse.* In between was the Black predicament, caught between the white aristocracy of Bismarck and the white bourgeoisie of Reagan. Human rights and basic human needs were at stake.

Bismarck helped to set the stage of the West's penetration of Africa. The Conference of Berlin helped to define the rules of annexation. The United States was similarly ambivalent. Germany and the United States lived to become peripheral to colonialism, but central to capitalism. The two countries built relatively small territorial empires, but against the background of considerable domestic development. Both countries touched the destiny of the Black world. The United States was a major factor in the history of slavery. Germany was a major factor in paving the way for the imperial scramble for Africa.

It just so happens that the last remaining colony in Africa was, in a sense, Bismarck's colony—Namibia, South West Africa. A German colony following the Conference of Berlin, it became a Mandate of the League of Nations after World War I, and was administered by South Africa for more than sixty years. South Africa refused to be morally accountable for decades.

South Africa was very reluctant to grant Namibia independence, least of all under the prospective rule of the South West African Peoples' Organization (SWAPO). Ronald Reagan's election raised South Africa's hopes. Pretoria found an excuse for dragging its feet on the issue of Namibia's independence, waiting for Reagan to order his Western allies to leave the issue alone.

Did Reagan disappoint South Africa in the end and lend his weight to independence for Namibia, if only to facilitate a Cuban withdrawal from neighboring and beleaguered Angola? If Reagan does in retrospect become one of the architects of Namibia's independence, history will have indulged her ironic sense of humor again. The last European colony on the African continent in this century was among the first of Bismarck's colonies in the last century. In retrospect, Reagan will have been cast by destiny to liberate Bismarck's last surviving Black dependency.

As for the interplay between the warfare and welfare state, the United States has never been in love with the welfare state. At best she has occasionally flirted with the idea. But the Reagan Administration showed every sign of turning its back on major areas of welfare, while emphasizing the warfare aspects of the federal machine.

The Black people in America are caught in a paradox. When times are tough, many Black people are laid off. It is a strange fate for them and for that old labor imperative which had brought Black people to America in the first place. America needed Black labor so much that it braved the oceans and tropical hazards to bring back Black slaves. And now America values Black labor so little that Blacks are the first to be forced to join the lines for welfare.

If the Bush Administration now cuts welfare, more Blacks may join the lines for warfare. A volunteer army already draws what is regarded as a disproportionate Black contribution. Opportunities for Blacks in the economy are more restricted than for whites. When the civilian economy lays off Blacks, there are two alternative havens of refuge for unemployed Blacks—the welfare route or the warfare route.

Reagan sought to narrow the welfare solution to the Black predicament. Will the Bush administration expand the warfare option for unemployed Blacks? Both human rights and basic human needs are once again at stake. And accountability—both moral and economic—is at the center.

CONCLUSION

The United States has been a major factor in the history of the slave trade, an even bigger factor in the history of capitalism, but a relatively minor factor in the history of colonizing the rest of the world. This last role was played more extensively by European powers—facilitated in the 1880s by a German statesman called Otto von Bismarck. Historically

Bismarck was crucial in the unification of Germany—but he was also instrumental in the division of Africa.

But while Africa was being colonized, Blacks all over the Americas were being emancipated from slavery. The legacy of Bismarck was creating colonial chains for Africa—while the shackles of the legacy of Columbus were being loosened in the New World.

The final act of the drama includes the future role of Black Americans. They constitute one of the largest Black nations in the world. Black Americans are lodged in the most powerful country in the world, the United States. Will Black Americans one day become as effective and influential in shaping American policy towards Africa as Jewish Americans are in shaping American policy towards the Middle East, or Irish Americans, toward Ireland? There are twice as many Black Americans as there are Jews in the whole world added together. One day the gap in influence between these two groups of Americans will surely narrow—hopefully to the advantage of human rights and equal human worth.

What may then happen could be the final act of a momentous piece of historical theatre. The slave trade had initiated the process of Africa's political marginalization in world power. Descendants of African slaves may begin the process of moving Africa back towards the center of the global scheme of things. The story of Africa's influence on Columbus, and Columbus's influence on the Americas, may one day be synthesized in a momentous dialectic in the history of racism and human rights.

Behind this racial dialectic have been two wider processes—the imperial expansion of the West and the internationalizing of accountability in the world system. We have sought to demonstrate that two milestones in the history of global accountability are the impeachment of Warren Hastings (1788–1795) and the Nuremberg trials of the Nazi leaders (1945–1946). In the ringing words of Edmund Burke at the impeachment of Hastings, "Law and arbitrary power are in eternal enmity."

But just as those who award the Nobel Prize for Peace are entirely Scandinavian, so in the proceedings against Hastings, the Nazis, and the Japanese, the judges were mostly Western. The principle of global accountability has made progress since the British East India Company was let loose on Bengal and the rest of India. But who decides what is a "war crime"? Who determines what is a "crime against humanity"? Accountability is getting globalized, but the rules are still overwhelmingly Eurocentric.

Edmund Burke's prosecution of Hastings implied the accountability of a multinational corporation—the British East India Company.

The Nuremberg trials took the case of institutional accountability a stage further with its case against the Gestapo and other state agencies and officials. It was only a matter of time before the Third World would begin to make the state itself accountable, for example, the offending state of South Africa as the architect of apartheid. The process is still incomplete. The debates are still raging. But out of the humiliations of the Bengalese and the concentration camps of the Nazis, out of the burnt bodies of Vietnam and the brutalities of apartheid, out of the legacy of Bismarck and the regressive tendencies of the Reagan years, the human race has nevertheless taken one more step forward in its search for restraint and global accountability.

NOTES

1. Penderel Moon, *Warren Hastings and British India* (New York: Macmillan, 1949) and Keith Feiling, *Warren Hastings* (Hamden, CT: Archon Books, 1967).

2. Edmund Burke, "The Speeches of the Right Honourable Edmund Burke On The Impeachment of Warren Hastings," (February 16, 1788) *Works,* (London: World's Classic Edition, 1907) Vol. IV, pp. 446–59.

3. Edmund Burke, "Reflections On The Revolution in France," (1970) *Works* (London: World's Classic Edition, 1907) Vol IV, p. 109.

4. This is a paraphrased summary of Lord Lugard's approach to colonial policy. For a comprehensive treatment of his imperial philosophy consult Frederick J. D. Lugard (Baron Lugard) *The Dual Mandate in British Tropical Africa* (Edinburgh and London: W. Blackwell, 1922).

5. Charles Dickens, *Great Expectations* (London and New York: Oxford University Press, 1978 ed.).

6. "Bismarck", *Encyclopaedia Britannica,* 15th edition (1974).

7. See *Report of Robert H. Jackson, United States Representation to the International Conference on Military Trials* (Washington D.C.: US Government Printer, 1949).

8. Burns H. Weston, "The Reagan Administration vs International Law," *Journal of International Law* 19, 3, (Summer 1987), p. 300.

9. *Ibid.*.

10. Michael Clough, *Critical Issues Beyond Sanctions: Reorienting US Policy on Southern Africa* (New York: Council on Foreign Relations, 1988).

11. This view was confirmed by Zbigniew Brzezinski himself in a conversation with Ali A. Mazrui at Villa Serbelloni, Bellagio, Italy in September, 1970.

19

In Quest of World Peace: Law and Alternative Security

BURNS H. WESTON

On December 23, 1991, when the Soviet Union dissolved into the Commonwealth of Independent States (CIS), at least four new nuclear-armed states came into being. "At least four," that is, because, for years, Soviet officials boasted of having tactical nuclear weapons in all or nearly all the former Union's republics. Furthermore, while some appear to have been withdrawn from the Baltic states and from Armenia and Azerbaijan, later admissions of nuclear weapons stored in volatile Armenia and Azerbaijan make clear that many have not been withdrawn. Added to which, there exists not a little uncertainty as to precisely where in Armenia, Azerbaijan, and elsewhere these easily concealed weapons are located and precisely who controls them.*

Will the separate emergence of nuclear-tipped Belarus, Kasakhstan, Russia, Ukraine, and possibly others prove fateful for the CIS and world? Public assurances by Russian President Yeltsin and others are of course encouraging. But with the collapse of central authority and discipline, military demoralization, harsh economic reforms, and ethnic unrest everywhere, the potential for a "Yugoslavia with nukes," as U.S. Secretary of State James Baker put it,[1] is, I think, apparent. History demonstrates little support for the proposition that collapsing empires fade quietly.

---

*This essay is based in part on a lecture presented as the Annual Quentin-Baxter Memorial Lecture at Victoria University of Wellington, New Zealand, on March 25, 1992.

Equally if not more important is the question of whether the separate emergence of Belarus, Kasakhstan, Russia, Ukraine, and possibly other former Soviet republics armed with nuclear weapons will encourage states not now nuclear to go nuclear—whether, that is, it will encourage nuclear proliferation. Again, the answer is far from reassuring. The centrifugal forces unleashed at Alma-Ata in December, 1991, and the economic hard times prevalent ever since (due in part to what I believe are excessive IMF and World Bank conditionality policies), make highly probable, I think, the transnational diversion of fissile materials, weapons components, finished weapons, and scientific know-how to states thirsting for the prestige and influence that comes with membership in the nuclear club. Consider, for example, that of an estimated 27,000–32,000 nuclear warheads in the former Soviet arsenal (the exact number is difficult to determine), some 17,000 (or 63%) are components of tactical weapons which traditionally were linked with individual military units and therefore never subject to the same tight controls that typified the Soviet Union's strategic weapons. In an increasingly decentralized political and military arena, made uncomfortably obvious by the recent tensions between Russia and Ukraine, it remains unclear precisely how actual physical safeguards will be instituted and maintained and who will maintain them.

There are some encouraging signs. Russia and the United States are undertaking significant cutbacks in their strategic (long-range) nuclear arms, down to under 3,500 each.[2] Belarus, Kasakhstan, Russia, and Ukraine have pledged that all strategic and tactical nuclear weapons outside Russia will be disabled within three years and eliminated within seven.[3] Each have ordered the "de-targeting" of their former NATO enemies and indicated their readiness to adhere to the 1968 Nuclear Non-Proliferation Treaty (NPT).[4] Russia, with help from the United States, has agreed to establish storage facilities for radioactive uranium and plutonium from dismantled nuclear weapons. And Germany, Russia, and the United States have announced plans for a science and technology institute to employ an estimated 2,000–3,000 nuclear scientists from the former Soviet Union so as to deter them from selling their highly sophisticated services to countries eager for nuclear clout.

One must bear in mind, however, that none of these developments, most of them still in the talking stage, are guaranteed, and that the dangers of nuclearism will loom large even if they are assured. Remaining strategic warheads, each with the minimum firepower of eighty Hiroshimas, will spell overkills of awesome proportion even under the best of presently projected negotiating circumstances.

Time—an increasingly scarce commodity and an ally of those who are intent upon diverting nuclear weapons and materials—is needed to secure the money and technology required to destroy nuclear weapons. Tactical nuclear weapons, as well as fissionable materials and other weapons components, are easily concealed and transported. The NPT is a loose text, full of loopholes. And the employment of two to three thousand scientists with advanced nuclear knowledge precludes neither leaks from among them nor the seduction of any number of the estimated 7,000–12,000 remaining scientists with classified nuclear knowledge or of the hundreds of thousands of admittedly less skilled but still knowledgeable military officials and civilians previously employed in the Soviet military-industrial complex.[5]

And to all of this must be added, clearly, the refusal of the United States to include airborne weapons and the majority of its existing submarine-launched cruise missiles (SLCMs) among its proposed cutbacks, its insistence upon storing rather than destroying many of the weapons it proposes to withdraw, and its reluctance to submit to the same kinds of inspections and verifications that it claims are needed to prevent proliferation and that, therefore, it asks of others. Policies and positions such as these, which manifestly are inconsistent with the spirit if not also the letter of the NPT, can scarcely be said to encourage adherence to the non-proliferation regime—or, indeed, to reduce the risks of nuclear war, nor does Washington's annual weapons procurement wish-list, or its only somewhat diminished love affair with Star Wars research, or its long-standing refusal to confront Israel's and South Africa's ostensibly secret nuclear weapons programs, or its continuing opposition to a "no-first-use" policy. Britain, China, and France are not much help either. Who, then, can really fault non-nuclear nations for wanting to go nuclear if they can?

And so, despite the ending of the Cold War, ours remains, alas, an intensely nuclear world order. Worse, except as between Russia and the United States perhaps, it is quite possibly more out of control and therefore more dangerous today than it was before the Soviet Union's disintegration, popular wisdom to the contrary notwithstanding. The turning back of the nuclear clock by the editors of *The Bulletin of the Atomic Scientists,* reflecting mainly the easing of East-West but not North-South or South-South tensions, does not change this reality. Indeed, with the possible exception of ozone depletion, global warming, and related environmental concerns, nothing menaces our planet more than the potential hemmorhaging of nuclear technology and weaponry across national frontiers and the threat to use that technology and those weapons if and when sufficiently provoked. As the accelerating Middle East arms race alone makes clear, the need for a nuclear-free world never has been more compelling, never more mandatory.

And what are the nuclear powers doing about it? Unquestionably not enough. Sizable arms reductions and weapons production cutbacks, nuclear "de-targeting" (by Russia at least), and a mounting interest in scientific and military cooperation and information exchange—long sought goals of the peace movement—are of course welcome. But while all this is going on, most of the nuclear powers, East and West, refuse to renounce nuclear weapons as instruments of foreign policy; and they leap at the chance, even while their economies are in extreme distress, to reorient the scientifically discredited and astronomically expensive U.S. Strategic Defense Initiative (or "Star Wars" Program) so as to make use of the sophisticated technologies developed in the former Soviet Union's defense complex (failing to disclose, parenthetically, that this proposed militarization of outer space would result in putting potential Challengers and Chernobyls in the sky). In other words, still operating according to military doctrines that were developed during and for the Cold War, spurred by political hubris and economic greed, and therefore refusing to concede that a space-based missile defense system or some equivalent technological fix would not be necessary were nuclear weapons and other weapons of mass destruction eliminated altogether, they cling to the notion that "arms control" and "minimum sufficiencies" are somehow more "realistic" options than broadbased disarmament and development. They cling to the phantasmagorical idea that it is somehow better to live with the bomb than to try to live without it, citing Islamic fundamentalism where once they cited communist and bourgeois evils, hastily and cynically brushing aside widespread responsible opinion (voiced perhaps most often by retired generals and diplomats) that the only real way to escape the dangers of nuclear and other weapons of mass destruction is to commit to complete nuclear disarmament and, beyond that, to general and complete disarmament linked to some form of "common" or "comprehensive" security.[6] Thus do the post-Cold War Pentagon strategists, in their Defense Planning Guidance for fiscal years 1994–99, brazenly recommend spending $1.2 trillion on the military over the next five years.[7]

To put it all another way, the world community is suffering from a heavy dose of "crackpot realism" and is at grave risk of losing an opportunity of truly historic proportion. For the first time in almost half a century, serious interest in progressive procedural and structural change on the global plane has revived, and with it the possibility of a world largely free of nuclear weapons and the threat of nuclear war, something few of us believed remotely feasible only a few short years ago. But unless our political leaders desist from their big bucks/big brother daydreams and repeal the parochial, piecemeal, and timorous policies that have allowed ours to become a seriously endangered planet, that opportunity will be lost—perhaps forever, and with dire consequences for our children, our children's children, and beyond. It is of course our responsibility, as professionals and citizens, to see to it that they do repeal these policies. We must convince them—and, indeed, ourselves—that "reality" is never fixed, that the magnitude of the struggle is not beyond human capacity, that there *are* realistic alternatives to the horrible undertaking in which they daily participate. We must convince them that it is not so much for lack of ideas than for lack of political vision and will that we fail to move toward them rapidly.

Of course, it is one thing to laud nuclear disarmament and, beyond that, general and complete disarmament linked to some form of "common" or "comprehensive" security; it is quite another to persuade governments and citizens that such policies are feasible even if admitted to be desirable. With conflict likely to be violently expressed in the world system for years to come, people are not going to be easily dissuaded from a nuclear deterrence system that *seems* to have protected them against such conflict for better than four decades now. It is not enough to point out that nuclear deterrence does not guarantee against human perfidy or error, that it does not ward off technological malfunction or mechanical breakdown, that it does not prevent paramilitary terrorism or even relatively large-scale conventional wars affecting perceived vital interests. To persuade people to escape the mind-boggling risks of a nuclear bristled and proliferated world—to persuade them that genuine and lasting world peace actually is feasible and not merely some utopian fantasy—a truly effective alternative or set of alternatives to nuclear deterrence must be established. Nuclear weapons, people understand, are weapons of military decisiveness, so that any substitute for them must be more or less decisive also. Otherwise there will be no getting rid of the nuclear habit; and without letting go of the nuclear habit the world never will be free of the possibility of radioactive annihilation, never capable of real progress toward a just and lasting peace.

All of which is to say, obviously, that world peace requires far, far more than the kinds of "deep cuts" that recently Russia and the United States have been negotiating. Even heightened adherence to the already existing norms of restraint upon the transnational use of force that are part of both conventional and customary international law falls short of the full measure of legal and policy criteria that is required to bring a peaceful world into being. The same may be said of the strengthening, where needed, of already existing arms control agreements and arrangements.[8] Necessary as these and like initiatives are, what is needed, and what peace activists (public and private) must now demand, is an entire complex of policy initiatives—legal, political, economic, military, and otherwise—that jointly can protect against international violence in such a way as will make it unnecessary for states to rely on nuclear and other weapons of mass destruction to safeguard their security.

Elsewhere I have helped to identify some of the mix of "alternative security" policy initiatives that can work to this end.[9] Here, as befits my professional credentials, I review some of the *legal* policy initiatives—normative, institutional, and procedural—that may be counted among them.[10] I do so because, having established more or less the illegality and criminality of nuclear weapons and warfare,[11] it now is time for lawyers—and peace activists in general—to move the antinuclear and more comprehensive antiwar struggle to a new level of concern, toward a broad consensus on the design and construction of a global security system that can ensure the sanctity and stability of life without dependency on the nuclear threat or the threat of other weapons of mass destruction.

NORMATIVE POLICY INITIATIVES

Four normative regimes come immediately to mind as capable of assisting a world free of nuclear and other weapons of mass destruction and toward which all of us, public official and private citizen alike, should strive.

A Comprehensive Nuclear Weapons Ban[12]

The enforcement of existing legal norms that interdict virtually all currently planned uses of nuclear weapons is seriously encumbered by a tradition of political leadership—Machiavellian in character—that typically indulges self-serving interpretations of the legal status of controversial uses of force. A pervasive subjectivity in world politics makes it exceedingly hazardous to tie restraint *vis-à-vis* nuclear weapons to characterizations of warfare either as "defensive" or "aggressive," these labels commonly masking politically congenial and politically hostile uses of force. Thus, a comprehensive anti-nuclear-weapons ban is needed.

Such a ban would embrace at least the following:

a. an absolute prohibition on the development, production, stockpiling, use and threat of use of all nuclear weapons and weapons systems—land-based, sea-based, and air-launched—without exception save for the limited possibility of a less comprehensive but absolute ban on all first-strike nuclear weapons and weapons systems during transition to complete nuclear disarmament (because such weapons and weapons systems increase the pressure to launch on warning and thereby increase the possibility of nuclear war by accident or miscalculation);
b. a presumption that *any* use of nuclear weapons, particularly a first use of such weapons during transition to complete nuclear disarmament (even in a defensive mode) and including a second or retaliatory "countervalue" use against cities and other civilian targets, violates the international law of war and constitutes a "crime against humanity";
c. a declaration that all nuclear weapons research and development (R&D), war plans, strategic doctrines, and strategic threats, especially those having first-strike characteristics, are illegal *per se,* and that all persons knowingly associated with them are deemed engaged in a continuing criminal enterprise;
d. an unequivocal obligation on the part of all states to pursue nuclear disarmament and otherwise minimize the role of nuclear weapons in inter-state conflict (consistent with Article VI of the NPT[13]) by way of, *inter alia,* (i) a renunciation of the policy of first use and the war-fighting doctrines and capabilities that accompany it, (ii) a comprehensive nuclear test ban, and (iii) strengthened nuclear non-proliferation regimes;
e. a commitment to a multilateralized Anti-Ballistic Missile (ABM) Treaty[14] (because pursuit of anti-ballistic missile defense systems stimulates competition in offensive weapons) together with a ban on all space weapons and space-based missile defense systems (because such systems, especially if not preceded by deep cuts in offensive ballistic missiles, are likely to encourage a proliferation of the most destabilizing weapons and weapons systems); and
f. a clear mandate for all citizens to take whatever steps may be available to them, including acts of nonviolent civil

resistance, to expose the illegality of the use of nuclear weapons and to otherwise insist upon the lawful conduct of the foreign policies of their own governments.

A comprehensive nuclear weapons ban such as this, it should be understood, would cause even the "minimum deterrence" strategies currently popular to be legally, if not also morally, suspect.

A Comprehensive Ban on Non-Nuclear Weapons of Mass Destruction

The same arguments that warrant a comprehensive ban on nuclear weapons compel also a comprehensive ban on non-nuclear weapons of mass destruction, *especially chemical and biological weapons.* Indeed, the two are fundamentally interdependent. A comprehensive ban on nuclear weapons makes less likely resort to chemical and biological weapons, and a ban on such weapons lessens the prospect that a belligerent state, especially a beleaguered one threatened by such weapons, might establish or renew dependence upon nuclear weapons. Mirroring the "Comprehensive Nuclear Weapons Ban" outlined above, a comprehensive ban on non-nuclear weapons of mass destruction would include at least the following:

a. an absolute prohibition on the development, production, stockpiling, and use of conventional mass destruction weapons and weapons systems, including chemical and biological weapons of mass destruction, with
   (i) a strengthened Geneva Gas Protocol,[15] prohibiting the possession as well as the use of the gas and bacteriological methods of warfare covered by the Protocol, and
   (ii) a strengthened Biological Weapons Convention,[16] providing for effective on-site inspections and enforcement mechanisms capable of responding to scientific advances and new biological technologies;
b. a presumption that any use of non-nuclear weapons of mass destruction, particularly a first use of such weapons during transition to general and complete disarmament (even in a defensive mode), but also a second or retaliatory "countervalue" use against cities and other civilian targets, violates the international law of war and constitutes a "crime against humanity";
c. a declaration that all R&D, war plans, strategic doctrines, and strategic threats having non-nuclear mass destructive

characteristics are illegal *per se*, and that all persons knowingly associated with them are deemed engaged in a continuing criminal enterprise;

d. an unequivocal obligation on the part of all states to eliminate all non-nuclear weapons of mass destruction from their arsenals, including chemical and biological weapons of mass destruction, and otherwise to minimize the role of such weapons in inter-state conflict; and
e. a clear mandate for all citizens to take whatever steps may be available to them, including acts of nonviolent civil resistance, to expose the illegality of the use of non-nuclear weapons of mass destruction and otherwise to insist upon the lawful conduct of the foreign policies of their own governments.

The point of these limitations, it should be understood, is to restrict all military strategy to a non-offensive/non-provocative defense posture exclusively. Only such an arrangement will permit States to resist the temptation to resort to nuclear weapons.

A Conventional Weapons Non-Proliferation Regime

Just as there has been a proliferation of nuclear weapons since 1945, so has there been a proliferation in the manufacture and export of conventional weapons, particularly to the Third World. This fact is well known. Yet, notwithstanding that this traffic in conventional arms increases not only the destructiveness of conflict but also the likelihood of bloody conflict erupting, the world community stands by and does essentially nothing.

The world community is negligent, however, at great peril to itself. Just as conventional arms are trip wires to conventional wars, so are conventional wars—and their arms—trip wires to nuclear conflict, capable of engaging nuclear powers and thereby risking escalation to nuclear war. Absent a ban on the manufacture, sale, and transfer of conventional weapons, a nuclear weapons-free world is similarly endangered. To the extent that, in such a world, conventional wars could seriously jeopardize the real and perceived interests of nuclear-prone states, so too could they serve as catalysts to the "reinvention" and subsequent actual use of nuclear weapons to safeguard those interests.

Thus, a conventional weapons non-proliferation regime, greatly limiting if not altogether prohibiting conventional arms sales and traffic, would seem as much a necessity to a post-Soviet, post-nuclear global security system as a nuclear non-proliferation regime is essential to the present-day nuclear deterrence system. It seems particularly a necessity relative to such large and potentially provocative weapons and weapons systems as tanks, armored cars, warships, long-range "attack" aircraft, missiles, and other components of "forward defense." In addition to being the most easily regulated because they are the most easily detected, these large weapons and weapons systems are, among conventional weapons systems, the most capable of contributing to mass destruction. At the very least, such a regime should ensure an effective surveillance and record-keeping system, capable minimally of alerting responsible elites to the presence of dangerous world practices and trends.

A Worldwide Nonintervention Regime

It is clear that the current nuclear deterrence system operating among the nuclear powers is in reality a system of extended deterrence, meant to guard against far more than strategic or theater-level attacks (and that it is of necessity nuclear because, as is now being made increasingly manifest, few economies can afford, without major domestic sacrifice, a conventional one). Despite the ending of the Cold War, nuclear powers continue to seek to maintain hegemonic interests, particularly the United States.

Thus, because the strong economic and political interests of nuclear powers simply will not go away (and, indeed, may become even more "vital" to them as they ever more discover that they are unable to control people and events as they once did), a post-Soviet, post-nuclear global security system must include as one of its cornerstones a worldwide compact to refrain from unilateral military intervention under all circumstances save possibly for when the circumstance is defined by a gross and systematic violation of human rights and the simultaneous absence of effective multilateral sanctioning machinery on the global or regional planes. A promise of interventionary self-restraint on the part of all governments, one that would supplement and strengthen U.N. Charter Article 2(4) by ensuring the territorial integrity and political independence of Third World countries especially, would go a long way toward guaranteeing the viability of a post-nuclear global security system. For those occasions when force may be needed to prevent or minimize deprivations of fundamental human rights and freedoms, recourse to improved global and regional intergovernmental organizations that are designed to police such matters should be pursued, in accordance with right process and on a genuinely multilateral basis.[17]

INSTITUTIONAL POLICY INITIATIVES

At least six institutional initiatives recommend themselves to a post-nuclear security system, some operating perhaps within the framework of the United Nations, some perhaps outside that framework.[18] They of course do not exhaust the institutional policy options that might be recommended.

1. *Establish an international arms control and disarmament verification agency* which, through "open skies" satellite observation, seismic and atmospheric surveillance, and on-site inspection, could supplement national means of verification and be capable of transnational monitoring of world military capabilities and movements.[19] Such an agency, with a membership comprising non-nuclear as well as nuclear weapons states, would (a) oversee the implementation of arms control and arms reduction agreements; (b) provide an impartial means of detecting and guarding against the secret testing and production of nuclear weapons and other weapons of mass destruction, including chemical and biological weapons; (c) discourage provocative military buildups and maneuvers; and (d) otherwise acquire the vital experience and reliability needed if arms reductions are ever to proceed very far. As a means of achieving genuine effectiveness, it also would be expected to establish regional oversight boards with authority to conduct on-site inspections of any and all weapons-capable facilities at the request of any state party or qualified nongovernmental organization.
2. *Create an international defense technology development agency*, at least during the transition to general and complete disarmament, to foster joint research, by multilateral teams of scientists, of cost-effective and genuinely defensive technologies, *e.g.*, surveillance satellites, seismological verification, radar systems, submarine-tracking systems, and even sophisticated defensive weapons as remotely piloted vehicles (RPVs) and precision-guided munitions (PGMs)—*i.e.*, accurate, target-seeking weapons

launched from ground-based artillery systems or aircraft—that, when integrated into intelligent defensive schemes, can make conventional invasion difficult or impossible, not to mention far less expensive than the armored vehicles, aircraft and surface ships they are designed to destroy.[20] An agency of this kind would provide former nuclear and other powers, especially Third World countries, with the opportunity to facilitate and share defense research and technology on a more or less equal footing without imperiling such instruments as the ABM Treaty [21] or otherwise exacerbating the arms race. Also, it could reduce inclinations to surprise perceived foes with new and threatening weapons developments and thereby help build confidence among potentially explosive inter-state relationships.

3. *Create risk-reduction opportunities and capabilities* by establishing, for example: (a) a joint inter-state consultation commission with a permanent staff composed of the nationals of disputing parties (among others) capable of handling actual and potential conflicts by way of routine review rather than the usual procedure of consulting only in extraordinary circumstances; (b) a joint inter-state negotiating commission composed of nationals from each side of a conflict, working together to find a solution acceptable to all concerned; (c) regional mediation, conciliation, and arbitration panels composed of persons of recognized competence and fair-mindedness, with authority to investigate and seek the resolution of conflicts and disputes otherwise capable of culminating in hostilities. Where these "local remedies" do not succeed, then appeal should be had to the International Court of Justice or some other permanently constituted tribunal for final and binding resolution of the disputes in question. In any event, the common primary purpose of these risk-reduction remedies would be to facilitate communication between contending parties to avert the possibility of war through miscalculation or misperception.
4. *Create an international "weapons into plowshares" agency* through which the conversion of national arms industries to socially redemptive production could be facilitated and a concrete connection between those who spend resources on armaments and those in economic and technological need could be fruitfully established—

clearly an initiative of great importance to depressed and beleaguered economies worldwide. The overriding purpose of such an agency, which among other things could help bring labor unions and industrial management together in common enterprise, would be to encourage a comprehensive process of reconstruction and renewal conducive to the establishment of a genuinely productive and equitable world economy. This, in turn, would greatly reduce the likelihood that nations would do military battle with one another.

5. *Create permanent global or regional police forces* consisting of persons recruited individually instead of from national military contingents (as in past U.N. peacekeeping experience), each with loyalty to world or regional rather than national authorities. Such forces would be relatively unencumbered by divided loyalties and by the possibility of sudden, unanticipated recall or withdrawal by national governments (as has happened with *ad hoc* U.N. forces in the Middle East, for example). As a consequence, they would be more readily available, more subject to efficient coordination, and thus more effective overall. As such, better positioned to establish useful precedents over time, they would constitute a further significant step in assuring a successful security system not dependent on nuclear weapons. Of course, appropriate precautions would have to be taken to guard the guardians.
6. *Create a permanent international criminal court* with compulsory jurisdiction specifically over war crimes, crimes against the peace, and crimes against humanity, accessible by multilateral intergovernmental organizations, non-governmental entities, and qualified individuals, as well as by states.[22]

In addition to these six institutional initiatives one should mention, of course, the need for United Nations reform, particularly in relation to the antiquated, anachronistic composition of the Security Council, which has primary responsibility for the maintenance of international peace and security. The failure so far to ensure more equitable Third World representation among the Council's permanent members (say, Brazil, Egypt, India, Indonesia, or Nigeria), plus the absence among the permanent members of economically powerful Germany and Japan, raise fundamental questions about the determination and orchestration, not to mention the moral premise and juridical legitimacy, of the U.N.'s peace and security operations. Given the current climate of increased respect for and support of the United Nations, the issue seems ripe for serious and responsible attention.

PROCEDURAL POLICY INITIATIVES

A global security system that forswears reliance upon nuclear weapons can provide no security at all without clearly established and respected procedures for both peacekeeping and peacemaking. If interstate disputes can be kept from degenerating into armed hostilities or settled by peaceful means, they are unlikely to escalate into threats to the peace or acts of aggression and war. It is true that efforts to keep the peace under the aegis of the United Nations and to achieve dispute settlement through international tribunals, arbitration, and similar peaceful means have not always been encouraging, arguably not during the 1990–1991 Persian Gulf crisis (in which, in my view, a pattern of barely polite tolerance for the United Nations and its legal requirements was manifest[23]) and certainly not during the internecine conflict that has raged in the post-Cold War Balkans. But established and respected procedures for multilateral peacekeeping and for the mediation, conciliation, arbitration, and adjudication of international disputes, preferably within the framework of the United Nations but desirably also at the regional level, would seem nevertheless necessary even if not sufficient for the maintenance of world peace and security, as surely the disintegration of Yugoslavia, the ethnic rivalries in Nagorno-Karabakh, and a genocidal civil war in Cambodia make evident. Without active participation in peaceful efforts at mutual accommodation, there is little likelihood of achieving the stability and harmony that a world free of nuclear and other weapons of mass destruction would require.

Thus, the following modest procedural initiatives would seem necessary and useful (perhaps especially at the early stages of international accommodation and nuclear disarmament).

Improvement of U.N. Peacekeeping Opportunities and Capabilities

United Nations peacekeeping opportunities and capabilities can be improved by:[24]

a. *guaranteeing military units* (land, sea, and air) on a more or less permanent standby basis (as envisaged in U.N. Charter Article 43), trained for peacekeeping by the member states in the course of their militaries' basic training and on the basis of expertise and additional training provided by an appropriate U.N. agency;

b. *regularly stockpiling military equipment and supplies* needed to enhance the U.N.'s capacity to undertake peacekeeping operations on short notice;
c. *facilitating automatic peacekeeping action* on the basis of predetermined levels of crisis or thresholds of conflict, thus avoiding the obstructions posed by the exercise of the Security Council veto;
d. *assuring peacekeeping finances* on an automatic basis, thus again avoiding the obstructions posed by the exercise of the Security Council veto;
e. *ensuring access to conflict areas* without requiring the initial or continuing permission of the conflicting parties; and
f. *tying U.N. peacekeeping to peacemaking* (*i.e.*, pacific settlement) to ensure that the merits of any given dispute will receive the attention that is needed to achieve long-term stability in the troubled area.

Improvement of U.N. and Other Peacemaking Opportunities and Capabilities

United Nations peacemaking opportunities and capabilities can be improved by:[25]

a. *enhancing and making greater use of U.N. dispute settlement mechanisms,* including the good offices of the Secretary General, most of which have been rarely if ever used;
b. *encouraging increased consent to mediation, conciliation, arbitration, and adjudication* through
   (i) guarantees limiting the scope of the third-party judgment to the determination of the doctrines, principles, and rules that could guide the parties in approaching settlement, and
   (ii) greater use of technically non-binding advisory opinions;
c. *increasing reliance on private persons and nongovernmental organizations (NGOs) as neutral intermediaries* (thereby helping to avoid escalating arguments into full-scale

inter-state disputes) in pre-dispute consultations, in post-dispute negotiated settlements, and before international tribunals for the purpose of clarifying a customary law norm or a clause in an international agreement;

d. *convening periodic regional conferences on security and cooperation* similar to the one launched in Helsinki for Europe in 1975 to reflect the priorities and circumstances of the separate regions and, with help from the U.N. Secretariat, to serve the essential decision function of appraisal and recommendation not only on matters relating directly to international security but on economic, social, and cultural matters upon which international security commonly depends; and
e. *adopting a code of international peacemaking procedures* (drawn from a variety of existing instruments) that would allow governmental officials to develop confidence in available procedures and that states could accept as binding upon them in whole or in part.

Improvement of Opportunities and Capabilities for Legal Challenges to Coercive Foreign Policies

Opportunities and capabilities for legal challenges to coercive foreign policies can be improved by:

a. *enhancing the role of the International Court of Justice* relative to threats to the peace, breaches of the peace, and acts of aggression, through, for example,
   (i) expanded acceptance of the Court's compulsory jurisdiction and greater use of its advisory jurisdiction relative to actual or potential hostilities between states;
   (ii) broadened standing to petition the Court to permit access by qualified nongovernmental organizations; and
   (iii) increased appeal to the Court's specialized "chamber procedure" in respect of inter-state conflicts unresolved by more local remedies;
b. *facilitating application of the international law of peace in domestic courts* through, for example, the reduction of barriers to "legal standing" on the part of private litigants especially and the narrowing of doctrines of nonjusticiability (*e.g.*, the "political question," "act of state," and "sovereign immunity" doctrines) to encourage public accountability in the statist conduct of foreign policy.

Of course, all of these and similar procedural initiatives have their share of difficulties: winning the confidence of contentious sovereign powers; achieving genuine neutrality in disputes; maintaining effective communication; overcoming legal and political isolationism; and so forth. Nevertheless, all are worthwhile initiatives to pursue because the alternatives are worse and they enhance at least the prospects for international peace and security.

• • •

Thus, it is evident that there exist a number of possible *legal* initiatives that could contribute effectively to a nuclear-weapons-free global security system. But only, as previously indicated, as part of an integrated plan that consists of political, economic, military, and technological as well as legal elements, holistically conceived and interdependently implemented.

In this latter connection, by the way, it bears emphasis that all of the above recommendations are the logical outgrowth of a lexicology that defines non-nuclear security—personal, national, and international—almost exclusively in terms of the absence of war or the threat of war. As a consequence, they bespeak the norms, institutions, and procedures that facilitate the prevention or elimination of *military* confrontation and conflict. And yet, as became increasingly clear from the worldwide economic and environmental pressures of the 1970s and 1980s, a definition of security informed preeminently by concern for military risks and encounters is not adequately responsive to the full range of threats to our personal, national, and international security that we now encounter and are likely to encounter in the 1990s and the years after 2000 as well.

In other words, achieving true global security will require not only a drastic circumscription of nuclear and, more generally, militarist tendencies, but also the progressive development of those norms, institutions, and procedures that can assist the promotion and protection of social justice, economic well-being, and ecological sustainability on a worldwide scale. It is social injustice, economic malaise, and environmental decline that lead, independently and interdependently, to frustration, conflict, and oftentimes violence. The evidence is all around us. Therefore, a non-nuclear global security system is unlikely to succeed if it is not marked also by a broad and deep commitment to the widespread realization of fundamental human rights and freedoms, to the wholesale eradication of grinding poverty and economic dependency, and to the unwavering stewardship of our earth-space environment as a total living organism, meant to be cherished rather than squandered.

But how do we get from here to there? Knowing our destination and knowing how to get there are not the same thing.

Happily, one can be brief. The process by which we achieve a nuclear-free world or, better yet, general and complete disarmament linked to some form of "common" or "comprehensive" security, has been indicated to us already.

I have in mind the Joint Statement of Agreed Principles for Disarmament Negotiations submitted to the United Nations General Assembly on September 25, 1961 by John J. McCloy, on behalf of the United States, and Valerian A. Zorin, on behalf of the Soviet Union.[26] Popularly known as "the McCloy-Zorin Agreement," it called for an internationally acceptable program of general and complete disarmament that would lead to the eventual dissolution of national armed forces beyond what is necessary to maintain internal order, the creation of a standing U.N. peacekeeping force, and the establishment of effective and reliable mechanisms for the peaceful settlement of international disputes in accordance with the Charter of the United Nations. Adopted unanimously by the General Assembly, it also called for multilateral negotiations, the implementation of the negotiated disarmament program in an agreed sequence of stages, procedures that would prevent any state or group of states from gaining a military advantage, and guarantees of strict and effective international control to ensure, in the words of Principle 6, "firm assurance that all parties are honouring their obligations."

Today, some thirty years later, the McCloy-Zorin Agreement seems no less apt. By proclaiming the goal of general and complete disarmament, including the elimination of all weapons of mass destruction, it rejects outright the strategy of nuclear deterrence (minimum or otherwise). By calling for staged and balanced negotiations secured by effective means of multilateral inspection and verification, it dismisses the harebrained proposition that a "minimum deterrence" regime, possibly necessary as a policy of transition, requires vast expenditures in the name of some illusory technological defense. And by embracing measures to strengthen international institutions aimed at preventing war and promoting peace, it endorses the truism that a truly peaceful and just world order depends in the end on the conscious and conscientious building of cooperative norms, institutions, and procedures alternative to the threats and counter-threats that underlie the Cold War doctrine of nuclear deterrence, not to mention the "global cop" schemes that depend on it.

Except to identify more precisely the content and to update the timetable of the McCloy-Zorin program for general and complete disarmament, does really much more need to be said? Is it not clear already that if we are serious about world peace we must sooner or later and at the very least: (1) stop the production of all nuclear, chemical, bacteriological, and other weapons of mass destruction; (2) regulate missile technology to prevent the delivery of mass destruction weapons; (3) disband armed forces and other military institutions beyond what is necessary to maintain internal order; and (4) commit to a worldwide program of economic conversion that will guarantee jobs on the way to general and complete disarmament? Of course, it is common sense that we assess the merits and demerits of the principle arms control and arms reduction measures we have instituted since 1961 and that still are relevant as stabilizing and transitional arrangements in the quest for peace in the 1990s;[27] likewise such initiatives as were recommended by former President Gorbachev on October 5, 1991 in response to President Bush's Oval Office address of September 27: proposals for deep cuts in strategic forces; the withdrawal of airborne tactical weapons along with ground-based and sea-based weapons; a moratorium on nuclear testing that would simultaneously conform to solemn commitments already made and facilitate a permanent comprehensive test ban; an end to the production of fissionable materials; and a global commitment to at least a no-first-use policy.[28] And it is appropriate, too, that we negotiate a 10-to-15 year timetable for these and kindred proposals that proceeds in stages rather than all at once—for example, a demonstration of solemn legal commitment on the part of all states to the rejection of all nuclear testing (maybe even the use or threat of use of nuclear weapons and other weapons of mass destruction) by, say, 1995, the fiftieth anniversary of Hiroshima-Nagasaki; and the abolition of all nuclear, chemical, bacteriological, and other weapons of mass destruction, as well as the abolition of the production of all fissile material, by the year 2000.

But surely it is unnecessary to delay taking the first critical steps on the grounds that we have yet to identify the process by which they may be realized. The McCloy-Zorin Agreement surely has signaled the principled way for us already: multilateral negotiations, an agreed sequence of programmatic stages, equal treatment, and effective interim coordinating and verification controls. We do not require yet another conference to determine the size and shape of the negotiating table. What we need is to reject politics as usual and to join with Bertrand Russell and Albert Einstein, remembering our humanity and forgetting the rest.[29]

Thus, contrary to Gertrude Stein, there is a there there; and, thanks to McCloy-Zorin, there is a way to get from here to there. And to these ends, of course, there is vast room for law and lawyering, both domestic and international.

It is essential to bear in mind, however, that, on final analysis, it is not treaties and charters prescribing specific norms, institutions, and procedures that will guarantee an enduring condition of peace among nations. It is, rather, the ingrained assumptions and habits of men and women everywhere, above all men and women in government and other arenas of social responsibility, that ultimately will be determinative in this regard. And if an international security system that consciously abjures reliance upon nuclear weapons is to succeed, then these assumptions and habits will have to move beyond the present, singular focus on *national* security to the wider notion of *global* security, now made mandatory by economic and environmental strains that increasingly are transcending national frontiers and eroding the sacred boundaries of national sovereignty. The entire human race—not one territorial constituent of it—must become the conscious beneficiary of all alternative security initiatives. A sense of species solidarity and a concern for all peoples, not just the ruling elites, must underwrite all proposals for alternative security as we proceed, in the words of Jesuit philosopher Pierre Teilhard de Chardin, in "the planetization of Mankind."[30]

Have we the acumen and the political will to seize the day before it is too late? That is the real issue in these and all related discussions at the present time. If so, then a new international security is a serious possibility. If not—well, I leave that to your imagination. Bear in mind, however, as William Butler Yeats warned at an earlier critical time of world order challenge, that "there is no long a virtuous nation, and [that] the best of us live by candlelight."[31]

NOTES

1. As quoted in Thomas L. Friedman, "Soviet Disarray: Noting Uncertainty in New Union, Washington Takes Cautious Path," *New York Times*, December 10, 1991, p. A1, col. 4.

2. The recently signed Strategic Arms Reduction Treaty (START) was to bring both sides down to below 9,000 strategic warheads.

3. According to news accounts, a total of 104 SS-18 and SS-24 ballistic missiles carrying 1,040 nuclear warheads were deployed in Kazakhstan as of February 1992, and 248 SS-24, SS-25, and SS-19 such missiles with 1,312 strategic warheads were deployed in Belarus and Ukraine as of that time. See, e.g., R. Jeffrey Smith, "Russia To Be Sole Nuclear Republic; Other Ex-Soviet States Agree to Destruction of Strategic Missiles," *Washington Post*, February 6, 1992, §1, p. A1.

4. Treaty on the Non-Proliferation of Nuclear Weapons, July 1, 1968, 21 U.S.T. 483, T.I.A.S. No. 6839, 729 U.N.T.S. 161, reprinted in *International Legal Materials* 7 (1968): 811.

5. The number of military and civilian personnel employed in the former Soviet military-industrial complex is subject to wide estimation. According to Viktor N. Mikhailov, Director of the nuclear military program of the former Soviet Union, roughly 100,000 persons were thus employed. See Thomas L. Friedman, "U.S. to Offer Plan to Keep Scientists at Work in Russia," *New York Times,* February 8, 1992, §1, p. 1, col. 6. According to Robert M. Gates, Director of the U.S. Central Intelligence Agency, the number is closer to 900,000. See Elaine Sciolino, "Soviet Brain Drain Poses Atomic Risk, U.S. Report Warns," *New York Times,* January 1, 1992, at §1, p. 1, col. 4.

6. Thus was President Yeltsin's proposal for a "zero alert" and a revival of the 1946 Baruch Plan dismissed as "not too much of a stretch" to the wholesale removal of the world's nuclear arsenals. As quoted in Michael Parks, "Russia Urges End of Nuclear Arms Alerts," *Los Angeles Times,* February 13, 1992, p. A10, col. 1. The 1946 Baruch Plan, named after its proponent, American financier and Presidential advisor Bernard Baruch, called for a United Nations body with a monopoly on atomic weapons and nuclear power, a call that was then rejected by the Soviet Union.

7. See Patrick E. Tyler, "U.S. Strategy Plan Calls for Insuring No Rivals Develop," *New York Times,* March 8, 1992, p. A1, col. 6; "Excerpts from Pentagon's Plan: 'Prevent Re-Emergence of a New Rival,' " ibid., p. A4, cols. 1–5. My point is not that the money (equal to US$1,650,437.37 for every day of every year since the birth of Jesus Christ) actually will be appropriated. It is, rather, that it takes a twisted mindset to dream up such schemes.

8. For a list of these agreements and arrangements, see note 27.

9. See Burns H. Weston (ed.), *Alternative Security: Living Without Nuclear Deterrence* (Boulder, CO: Westview, 1990): 78 [hereinafter *Alternative Security*].

10. See Burns H. Weston, "Law and Alternative Security: Toward a Just World Peace," in *Alternative Security:* 78. The ensuing discussion is abridged and revised from this essay. Readers wishing greater detail should consult the original essay and the larger collection from which it is derived. Such consultation is desirable because it will underscore the fact that there is no such thing as a strictly *legal* alternative or set of alternatives to nuclear deterrence. Legal initiatives are important, surely, but only as part of a larger integrated plan.

11. It is true, of course, that not all legal scholars agree with this finding. See, e.g., Harry H. Almond, Jr., "Deterrence and A Policy-Oriented Perspective on the Legality of Nuclear Weapons," in Arthur S. Miller and Martin Feinrider (eds.), *Nuclear Weapons and Law* (Westport, CT and London: Greenwood Press, 1984): 75; John Norton Moore, "Nuclear Weapons and the Law: Enhancing Strategic

Stability," ibid., p. 51; W. Michael Reisman, "Deterrence and International Law," ibid., p. 129. See also Raymond E. Lisle, "Remarks: Nuclear Weapons—A Conservative Approach to Treaty Interpretation," *Brooklyn Journal of International Law* 9 (1983): 275; Eugene V. Rostow, "Is There a Legal Basis for Nuclear Deterrence Theory and Policy?," in Maxwell Cohen and Margaret E. Gouin (eds.), *Lawyers and the Nuclear Debate—Proceedings of the Canadian Conference on Nuclear Weapons and the Law* (Ottawa: University of Ottawa Press, 1988): 175. However, the preponderance of scholarly opinion on the use and threat of use of nuclear weapons clearly favors this view. See, e.g., Burns H. Weston, "Nuclear Weapons Versus International Law: A Contextual Reassessment," *McGill Law Journal* 28 (1983): 542. See also Carl H. Builder and Morlie H. Graubard, *The International Law of Armed Conflict: Implications for the Concept of Assured Destruction* (Santa Monica, CA: Rand Publication Series R-28044-FF, 1982); Frits Kalshoven, *Constraints on the Waging of War* (Geneva: International Committee of the Red Cross, 1987; Dordrecht: The Netherlands: Nijhoff, 1987); Elliott L. Meyrowitz, *Prohibition of Nuclear Weapons: The Relevance of International Law* (Dobbs Ferry, NY: Transnational Publishers, 1990); Istvan Pogany, *Weapons and International Law* (New York: St. Martin's Press, 1987); Bert Röling, *The Impact of Nuclear Weapons on International Relations and International Law* (Polemological Institute of the University of Groningen 1982); Georg Schwarzenberger, *The Legality of Nuclear Weapons* (London: Stevens, 1958); Nagendra Singh, *Nuclear Weapons and International Law* (London: Stevens, 1959); James M. Spaight, *The Atomic Problem* (London: Barron, 1948); C. Weeramantry, *Nuclear Weapons and Scientific Responsibility* (Wolfeboro, NH: Longwood Academic, 1987); Daniel Arbess, "The International Law of Armed Conflict in Light of Contemporary Deterrence Strategies: Empty Promises or Meaningful Restraint?," 30 *McGill Law Journal* 30 (1984): 89; Francis A. Boyle, "The Relevance of International Law to the 'Paradox' of Nuclear Deterrence," *Northwestern University Law Review* 80 (1986): 1407; Ian Brownlie, "Some Legal Aspects of the Use of Nuclear Weapons," International and Comparative Law Quarterly 14 (1965): 437; Erik Castrén, "The Illegality of Nuclear Weapons," *University of Toledo Law Review* 3 (1971): 89; David M. Corwin, "The Legality of Nuclear Arms Under International Law," *Dickinson Journal of International Law* 5 (1987): 271; Richard A. Falk, Lee Meyrowitz and Jack Sanderson, "Nuclear Weapons and International Law," *Indian Journal of International Law* 20 (1980): 541; John H. E. Fried, "International Law Prohibiting the First Use of Nuclear Weapons: Existing Prohibitions in International Law," *Bulletin of Peace Proposals* 12 (1981): 21; ———, "The Nuclear Collision Course: Can International Law be of Help?," *Denver*

Journal of International Law and Policy 14 (1985): 97; Hisakazu Fujita, "First Use of Nuclear Weapons: Nuclear Strategy vs. International Law," *Kansai University Review of Law and Policy* 3 (1982): 57; , "The Pre-Atomic Law of War and its Applicability to Nuclear Warfare," ibid. 6 (1985): 7; ———, "Status of Nuclear Weapons in International Law," ibid. 7 (1986): 1; Kevin C. Kennedy, "A Critique of United States Nuclear Deterrence Theory," *Brooklyn Journal of International Law* 9 (1983): 35; Matthew Lippman, "Nuclear Weapons and International Law: Towards a Declaration on the Prevention and Punishment of the Crime of Nuclear Humanicide," *Loyala Law of Los Angeles International and Comparative Law Annual* 8 (1986): 183; Mary Eileen E. McGrath, "Nuclear Weapons: The Crisis of Conscience," *Military Law Review* 107 (1985): 191; Henri Meyrowitz, "Les juristes devant l'arme nucléaire," *Revue Général de Droit International Public* 67 (1963): 820; Ved P. Nanda, "Nuclear Weapons and the Right to Peace Under International Law: A Fundamental Challenge," *Brooklyn Journal of International Law* 9 (1982): 283; Beth M. Polebaum, "National Self-Defense in International Law: An Emerging Standard for a Nuclear Age," *New York University Law Review* 59 (1984): 187; Peter A. Ragone, "The Applicability of Military Necessity in the Nuclear Age," *New York University Journal of International Law and Policy* 16 (1984): 701; Allan Rosas, "Negative Security and Non-Use of Nuclear Weapons," *German Yearbook of International Law/* 25 (1982): 199; Alfred P. Rubin, "Nuclear Weapons and International Law," *Fletcher Forum* 8 (1984): 45. For a useful overview, see Elliott L. Meyrowitz, "The Opinions of Legal Scholars on the Legal Status of Nuclear Weapons," *Stanford Journal of International Law* 24 (1987): 111.

12. Many of the ideas enumerated here are derived from Richard A. Falk, "Toward a Legal Regime for Nuclear Weapons," *McGill Law Journal* 28 (1983): 519, 537–38.

13. See note 4.

14. Treaty Between the United States of America and the Union of Soviet Socialist Republics on the Limitation of Anti-Ballistic Missile Systems, May 26, 1972, 23 U.S.T. 3435, T.I.A.S. No.7503, 944 U.N.T.S. 13, reprinted in *International Legal Materials* 11 (1972): 784.

15. Protocol for the Prohibition of the Use in War of Asphyxiating, Poisonous or Other Gases, and of Bacteriological Methods and Warfare, February 8, 1928, 26 U.S.T. 571, T.I.A.S. No. 8061, 94 L.N.T.S. 65.

16. Convention on the Prohibition of the Development, Production and Stockpiling of Bacteriological (Biological) and Toxin Weapons and Their Destruction, April 10, 1972, 26 U.S.T. 583, T.I.A.S. No. 8062.

17. The US use of the United Nations during the Persian Gulf crisis of 1990–1991 reflected in my view a perversion of right process and not genuinely multilateral. See Burns H. Weston, "Security Council

Resolution 678 and Persian Gulf Decision-Making: Precarious Legitimacy," *American Journal of International Law* 85 (1991): 516.

18. For the first two proposals enumerated here I am indebted in part to Daniel Arbess and William Epstein, "Disarmament Role for the United Nations?," *Bulletin of the Atomic Scientists* 41 (May 1985): 26, 28.

19. Such an agency—an international satellite monitoring agency (ISMA)—was proposed by a special United Nations commission in 1982 to monitor arms control agreements and perform related other functions. While the plan was ultimately blocked by the superpowers, interest in variations on it have grown ever since.

20. Several plans of this type were at one time suggested for the conventional defense of Western Europe.

21. See note 14.

22. The need for an international judicial body to try violations of international criminal law, either as a chamber of the International Court of Justice or as an independent entity, has been recognized for years. See, e.g., the Draft Statute for an International Criminal Court prepared under the auspices of the U.N. Commission on International Criminal Jurisdiction in 1953, U.N. GAOR, 9th Sess., Supp. No. 12, at Annex p. 23, UN Doc. A/2645 (1954).

23. See my essay cited in note 17.

24. See my essay cited in note 17.

25. The ideas enumerated here are derived in part from Louis B. Sohn, "Peaceful Settlement of Disputes and International Security," a "preliminary draft" of an unpublished manuscript submitted to the Independent Commission on World Security Alternatives.

26. "Joint Statement of Agreed Principles for Disarmament Negotiations," *U.S.-U.S.S.R. Report to the General Assembly,* U.N. Doc. A/4879, reprinted in *Department of State Bulletin* 45 (October 9, 1961): 589–90.

27. See, e.g., the Antarctic Treaty, December 1, 1959, 12 U.S.T. 794, T.I.A.S. No. 4780, 402 U.N.T.S. 71; the Memorandum of Understanding Between the United States and the Union of Soviet Socialist Republics Regarding the Establishment of a Direct Communication Link ("the Hot Line Agreement"), June 20, 1963, 14 U.S.T. 825, T.I.A.S. No. 5362, 472 U.N.T.S. 163; the Treaty Banning Nuclear Weapon Tests in the Atmosphere, in Outer Space and Under Water ("the Partial Test Ban Treaty"), August 5, 1963, 14 U.S.T. 1313, T.I.A.S. No. 5433, 480 UNTS 43; reprinted in *International Legal Materials* 2 (1963): 889; the Treaty on Principles Governing the Activities of States in the Exploration and Use of Outer Space, Including the Moon and Other Celestial Bodies ("the Outer Space Treaty"), January 27, 1967, 18 U.S.T.

2410, T.I.A.S. No. 6347, 610 U.N.T.S. 205, reprinted in *International Legal Materials* 6 (1967): 386; the Treaty for the Prohibition of Nuclear Weapons in Latin America ("the Treaty of Tlatelolco"), February 14, 1967, 634 U.N.T.S. 281, reprinted in *International Legal Materials* 6 (1967): 561; the Treaty on the Non-Proliferation of Nuclear Weapons ("the NPT"), note 4; the Treaty on the Prohibition of the Emplacement of Nuclear Weapons and Other Weapons of Mass Destruction on the Seabed and the Ocean Floor and in the Subsoil Thereof ("the Seabed Arms Control Treaty"), February 11, 1971, 23 U.S.T. 701, T.I.A.S. No. 7337, 955 U.N.T.S. 115, reprinted in *International Legal Materials* 10 (1971):146; the Agreement on Measures to Reduce the Risk of Outbreak of Nuclear War Between the United States and the Union of Soviet Socialist Republics ("the Accident Measures Agreement"), September 30, 1971, 22 U.S.T. 1590, T.I.A.S. No. 7186, 807 U.N.T.S. 57, reprinted in *International Legal Materials* 10 (1971): 1173; the Agreement Between the United States of American and the Union of Soviet Socialist Republics on Measures to Improve the USA-USSR Direct Communications Link ("the Hot Line Modernization Agreement"), September 30, 1971, 22 U.S.T. 1598, T.I.A.S. No. 7187, 806 U.N.T.S. 402, reprinted in *International Legal Materials* 10 (1971): 1174; the Convention on the Prohibition of the Development, Production and Stockpiling of Bacteriological (Biological) and Toxin Weapons and on Their Destruction, April 10, 1972, 26 U.S.T. 583, T.I.A.S. No. 8062, 1015 U.N.T.S. 163, reprinted in *International Legal Materials* 11 (1972): 310; the Treaty Between the United States of America and the Union of Soviet Socialist Republics on the Limitation of Anti-Ballistic Missile Systems ("the ABM Treaty"), note 14; the Interim Agreement Between the United States of America and the Union of Soviet Socialist Republics on Certain Measures with Respect to the Limitation of Strategic Offensive Arms, May 26, 1972, 23 U.S.T. 3462, T.I.A.S. No. 7504, 94 U.N.T.S. 3, reprinted in *International Legal Materials* 11 (1972): 791; the Declaration of Basic Principles of Relations Between the United States of America and the Union of Soviet Socialist Republics, May 29, 1972, *Department of State Bulletin* 66 (1972): 898; the Treaty Between the United States of America and the Union of Soviet Socialist Republics on the Limitation of Underground Nuclear Weapon Tests, July 12, 1974, *Department of State Bulletin* 71 (1974): 217; the Limitations on Anti-Ballistic Missile Systems Treaty Protocol, July 3, 1974, 27 U.S.T. 1645, T.I.A.S. No. 8276; the Joint Statement on the Limitation of Strategic Offensive Arms ("the Vladivostok Agreement"), April 29, 1974, *Department of State Bulletin* 70 (1974): 677; the Final Act of the Conference on Security and Cooperation in Europe ("the Helsinki Accords"), August 1, 1975, *Department of State*

Publication No. 8826 (Gen. Foreign Pol'y Ser. 298), reprinted in *International Legal Materials* 14 (1975): 1292; and the Treaty Between the United States of America and the Union of Soviet Socialist Republics on the Limitation of Strategic Offensive Arms and Protocol Thereto ("the SALT II Treaty), June 18, 1979, S. Exec. Doc. Y, 96th Cong., 1st Sess. 37 (1979); Agreement Governing the Activities of States on the Moon and Other Celestial Bodies ("the Moon Treaty"), December 5, 1979, U.N.G.A. Res. 34/68 (XXXIV), 34 U.N. GAOR, Supp. (No. 46) 77, U.N. Doc. A/34/664 Annexes (1979), reprinted in *International Legal Materials* 18 (1979): 1434; Treaty Between the United States of America and the Union of Soviet Socialist Republics on the Elimination of Their Intermediate-Range and Shorter-Range Missiles ("INF Treaty"), December 8, 1987, *Department of State Pub. No 9555* (December 1987), reprinted in *International Legal Materials* 27 (1988): 90. All of the foregoing agreements are reprinted in whole or in part in Burns H. Weston (ed.), *International Law and World Order: Desk Set of Basicv Documents* (forthcoming from United Nations Publications in 1993); also in Burns H. Weston, Richard A. Falk, and Anthony D'Amato (eds.), *Basic Documents in International Law and World Order* (St. Paul, MN: West Publishing, 2nd ed. 1990).

28. See Serge Schmemann, "Gorbachev Matches U.S. on Nuclear Cuts and Goes Further on Strategic Warheads," *New York Times*, October 6, 1991, §1, pt. 1, p. 1, col. 6.

29. The reference is to the Russell-Einstein Manifesto that appeared in the *New York Times* on July 10, 1955. It was reprinted in leaflet form in the United States by the War Resisters' League and may also be found in O. Nathan and H. Norden (eds.), *Einstein On Peace* 632 (1968). Declared Russell and Einstein:

> There lies before us, if we choose, continual progress in happiness, knowledge and wisdom. Shall we, instead, choose death, because we cannot forget our quarrels? We appeal, as human beings: Remember your humanity and forget the rest. If you can do so, the way lies open to a new paradise; if you cannot, there lies before you the risk of universal death.

30. P. Teilhard de Chardin, *The Future of Man* 115 (New York: Harper & Row, Norman Denny transl. 1964).

31. A. Wade (ed.), *The Letters of W. B. Yeats* 691 (London: R. Fart-Davis, 1954).

Index